COLONIZATION AND SUBALTERNITY IN CLASSICAL GREECE

In this book, Gabriel Zuchtriegel explores the unwritten history of Classical Greece – the experience of nonelite colonial populations. Using postcolonial critical methods to analyze Greek settlements and their hinterlands of the fifth and fourth centuries BC, he reconstructs the social and economic structures in which exploitation, violence, and subjugation were implicit. He mines literary sources and inscriptions, as well as archaeological data from excavations and field surveys, much of it published here for the first time, that offer new insights into the lives and status of nonelite populations in Greek colonies. Zuchtriegel demonstrates that Greece's colonial experience has far-reaching implications beyond the study of archaeology and ancient history. As reflected in foundational texts such as Plato's "Laws" and Aristotle's "Politics," the ideology that sustained Greek colonialism is still felt in many Western societies.

Gabriel Zuchtriegel holds a PhD degree in Classical Archaeology from University of Bonn. He has been fellow of Studienstiftung des Deutschen Volkes, the German Archaeological Institute and the Alexander von Humboldt-Foundation and has conducted fieldwork in southern Italy and Sicily. He has taught courses at University of Bonn (Germany) and at University of Basilicata (Italy). He has worked for the Soprintendenza di Pompeii and is currently in charge of the Museum and Archaeological site of Paestum. Published works include a monograph on ancient Gabii (Latium), edited volumes, journal papers, and articles in newspapers and popular science magazines.

T0371201

COLONIZATION AND SUBALTERNITY IN CLASSICAL GREECE

EXPERIENCE OF THE NONELITE POPULATION

GABRIEL ZUCHTRIEGEL

Paestum Excavations, Italy

CAMBRIDGE
UNIVERSITY PRESS

CAMBRIDGE
UNIVERSITY PRESS

University Printing House, Cambridge CB2 8BS, United Kingdom

One Liberty Plaza, 20th Floor, New York, NY 10006, USA

477 Williamstown Road, Port Melbourne, VIC 3207, Australia

314-321, 3rd Floor, Plot 3, Splendor Forum, Jasola District Centre, New Delhi - 110025, India

79 Anson Road, #06-04/06, Singapore 079906

Cambridge University Press is part of the University of Cambridge.

It furthers the University's mission by disseminating knowledge in the pursuit of education, learning and research at the highest international levels of excellence.

www.cambridge.org
Information on this title: www.cambridge.org/9781108409223
DOI : 10.1017/9781108292849

First published 2018
First paperback edition 2020

A catalogue record for this publication is available from the British Library

ISBN 978-1-108-41903-1 Hardback
ISBN 978-1-108-40922-3 Paperback

CONTENTS

List of Illustrations	*page*	vi
List of Tables		ix
Preface		xi

1 PLACES OF DARKNESS: COLONIAL SETTLEMENTS
AND THE HISTORY OF CLASSICAL GREECE   I

2 HUTS AND HOUSES: A QUESTION OF IDEOLOGY?   46

3 TOMBS: VISIBILITY AND INVISIBILITY IN COLONIAL
SOCIETIES   75

4 FIELDS: COLONIAL DEFINITIONS OF EQUALITY   105

5 FARMS: THE END OF EQUALITY?   141

6 MOUNTAINS: THE LIMITS OF GREEKNESS
AND CITIZENSHIP   164

7 WORKSHOPS: *BANAUSOI* IN THE COLONY   197

8 CLASSICAL GREECE FROM A COLONIAL PERSPECTIVE   216

Bibliography   237

Index   263

ILLUSTRATIONS

1.1 Greek colonization 480–330 BC.   *page* 14
1.2 The Ionian Coast in the fifth century BC.   20
1.3 Thurii: Reconstruction of the urban center on the basis of
    archaeological data and literary sources (Mertens 2006: fig. 643).   21
2.1 Heraclea in Lucania: Urban center.   48
2.2 Heraclea, Area A, from northwest. (Courtesy of F. Giulietti &
    M. Turci: Laboratorio di Meccanica del Volo, Università di Bologna.) 49
2.3 Heraclea, Area A: Hypothetical house plots.   50
2.4 Heraclea, Area A: Hypothetical house plots.   51
2.5 Heraclea (modern Policoro): Aerial photo, 1964. (Courtesy of
    *Archivio fotografico della Soprintendenza Archeologia, Belle Arti e
    Paesaggio della Basilicata.*)   52
2.6 Heraclea, Area A ("*Scavi baracche*"): Classical street flanked
    by rubble walls (fifth century BC).   52
2.7 Heraclea, Area A: House types, early walls in black.   53
2.8 Heraclea, Area A: Obliterated wall of the early type.   54
2.9 Heraclea, Area A: Obliterated walls.   55
2.10 Heraclea, Area B: House types; early walls in black.   56
2.11 Late fifth-century pottery from Heraclea (Giardino 2012: fig. 6).   58
2.12 Amphipolis: Map of the site (drawing by R. Marino,
     Parco Archaeologico di Paestum, based on Lazaridis 1997).   60
2.13 Heraclea, Area A: Aboveground sewers in a Hellenistic habitation.   68
2.14 Heraclea, sanctuary of Demeter: *Manumissio* inscription (?) and iron
     chains (Gertl 2012: fig. 10).   71
2.15 Conca d'Oro: Demeter and Artemis Bendis figurines
     (Osanna, Prandi, Siciliano 2008: fig. 42).   73
2.16 Road from Heraclea to Conca d'Oro with votive deposit HE25.   74
3.1 Heraclea, South Necropolis: Cremation burial with red-figure
    amphora (tomb 53 in via Avellino) (Pianu 1990: pl. VI 1–2).   77
3.2 Heraclea, South Necropolis: Crouched burial without grave goods
    (Lanza 2015: fig. 12).   78
3.3 Inhumation burial from Tarentum, fifth century BC (Dell'Aglio
    2015: fig. 7). (Courtesy of *Archivio fotografico della Soprintendenza
    Archeologia, Belle Arti e Paesaggio delle Province di Brindisi, Lecce e Taranto.*) 79
3.4 Heraclea: Vases from the Tomb of the Policoro Painter
    (elaboration G. Gramegna, based on Degrassi 1967).   80

3.5 Heraclea, Tomb of the Policoro Painter: Reconstruction
drawing (Degrassi 1967: fig. 57). 81
3.6 Heraclea: Tomb of the Policoro Painter (T1) and neighboring
tombs (Degrassi 1967: fig. 46). 83
3.7 Tomb of the Policoro Painter: Vase no. 11, side A (Degrassi 1967: pl. 66). 84
3.8 Tomb of the Policoro Painter: Vase no. 11, side B (Degrassi 1967: pl. 67). 85
3.9 Paestum: Underground chamber in the agora. (Courtesy of *Parco
Archeologico di Paestum*.) 86
3.10 Paestum, underground chamber in the agora: Bronze hydriai and
black-figure amphora. (Photo F. Valletta/G. Grippo, courtesy of
Parco Archeologico di Paestum.) 87
3.11 Heraclea, South Necropolis: Tomb clusters. (Drawing based on
Lanza 2012; 2015.) 98
3.12 Heraclea, South Necropolis: Tomb clusters in via Umbria
(Lanza 2012: fig. 5). 99
3.13 Heraclea, South Necropolis: Tomb cluster in via Salerno
(Crupi, Pasquino 2015: fig. 3 & 4). 100
3.14 Heraclea, South Necropolis: Tomb 52 in via Umbria
(Lanza 2012: fig. 8). 102
4.1 Surveyed areas, 2012–2014. 106
4.2 Heraclea, field survey 2012–2014: Pottery fragments of the
Classical period. 107
4.3 The territory of Heraclea in the early fourth century BC. 109
4.4 Density of rural sites at Heraclea and Metapontum, 450–300 BC. 110
4.5 Piano Sollazzo: Terracotta pinakes (Crupi, Pasquino 2012: fig. 4). 111
4.6 Walking distances from Heraclea, c. 375 BC. 121
4.7 Kamarina (Mertens 2006: fig. 625). 125
4.8 Schematic illustration of the Classical land division around
Chersonesus. (Courtesy of J.C. Carter.) 126
4.9 Pharos: Land division and watch towers (Chapman, J.C., Bintliff,
J., Gaffney, V., Slapšak, B. (eds.). *Recent Developments in Yugoslav
Archaeology*, fig. 9.3 & 10.3. Oxford: BAR). 127
4.10 Walking distances from Metapontum and sites around Policoro,
c. 500 BC. 135
5.1 The territory of Heraclea, c. 325 BC. 143
5.2 Find distribution on early Hellenistic habitation sites in a portion
of the surveyed area, 2012–2013. 144
5.3 Oil press from site HE3. 145
5.4 Pottery assemblages from site HE7. 146
5.5 Excavated farmsteads in the territory of Heraclea. 147
5.6 Hypothetical reconstruction of the *schoinos* mentioned
in the Heraclea Tablets. 149
5.7 Hypothetic location of the lands of Athena and Dionysus mentioned
in the Heraclea Tablets. 152
5.8 Walking distances from Heraclea, c. 325 BC. 156
5.9 *Case coloniche* in the area of Policoro (ancient Heraclea), around 1960.
(Courtesy of Comune di Policoro.) 158

6.1   Lucania during the fourth century BC.   167
6.2   Bronze belt and helmet from tomb 1188 at Policoro
       (Bottini, Lecce 2015: fig. 8).   171
6.3   Fortification wall of Serra di Vaglio. (Courtesy of *Archivio fotografico
       della Soprintendenza Archeologia, Belle Arti e Paesaggio della Basilicata*.)   173
6.4   Viewshed from Mt. Coppolo with Early Hellenistic settlement sites.   178
6.5   Mt. Coppolo: Tower on the southern side of the city wall (partly
       reconstructed).   179
6.6   The Early Hellenistic countryside around Mt. Coppolo.   180
6.7   Timpa della Bufaliera: Late Classical/Early Hellenistic fortress
       (Quilici 1967: fig. 169).   182
6.8   Roof types at Early Hellenistic sites around Heraclea
       and Mt. Coppolo.   185
6.9   Heraclea, Area B: Loom weight types (Meo 2015: fig. 2).   186
6.10   Early Hellenistic habitation sites in the hinterland of Heraclea.   188
6.11   Loom weight types at Early Hellenistic habitation sites around
       Heraclea and Mt. Coppolo.   189
6.12   Sant'Arcangelo: Female burials Cicchelli T. 33 (a) and Mastrosimone
       T. 63 (b) (Mandić, Vita 2015; pl. 7).   191
6.13   The Valley of the River Sinni with Piano Sollazzo (center) and Mt.
       Coppolo (right) in the background, from northeast (site HE86 near
       Anglona).   196
7.1   Heraclea: Pottery workshops, second half of the fourth century/third
       century BC.   200
7.2   Heraclea, Castello Hill, Area A: Pottery workshop in insula 4,
       rooms 6 and 7. (Courtesy of *Archivio fotografico della Soprintendenza
       Archeologia, Belle Arti e Paesaggio della Basilicata*.)   201
7.3   Heraclea, Castello Hill, Area A: Late Hellenistic mint in insula
       I (excavations 2014).   207
7.4   Heraclea: City wall on the southern side of the Castello Hill,
       excavations around 1965 (Neutsch 1967: pl. 8.1).   208
7.5   Heraclea, Castello Hill: Stone marks on blocks from the fortification
       wall (Neutsch 1967: fig. 9).   209
7.6   Tarentum, city walls: Stone marks (Lo Porto 1992: pl. IX).   210

TABLES

1.1	Greek colonies and cleruchies 480–330 BC	*page* 34
3.1	The Tomb of the Policoro Painter	82
4.1	Walking distances and carrying capacity at Heraclea	122
4.2	Urban and rural spaces and demography at Chersonesus	129
5.1	Heraclea Tablets: plot sizes, rents, and yields	150
6.1	Heraclea Tablets: vineyards and yields in the lands of Athena	192

PREFACE

The painted stone slab on the cover is one of hundreds of examples from "Lucanian" tombs from Paestum in southern Italy. It dates to the second quarter of the fourth century BC. From the second half of the fifth century, new burial customs were introduced to Paestum, and in the fourth century official documents at Paestum were written in Oscan, an Italic language. At first glance, the slab may not seem ideally suited to illustrating the cover of a book dealing with "Classical Greece." Yet Greek-speaking people continued to live in Paestum, as graffiti and inscriptions demonstrate. We have no idea whether the person buried in the tomb on the cover identified herself/himself as "Greek" or "Lucanian," and what this really meant in this period. Similarly, the identity and origin of the artists are also unknown.

However, the way in which the figures on the slab are portrayed can be viewed as a product of Greek colonial practices and ideologies. While the rider corresponds to the ideal of the victorious youth as known from Athenian and Tarantine grave monuments, the two prisoners shown behind him, especially the one on the left, are clearly presented as non-Greeks or "barbarians." And while the woman who is greeting the rider has a distinctive headdress that might be of a local type, the vessels she is holding belong to the Greek tradition.

The tomb painting clearly depicts "Greek culture" from a specific standpoint, just as this book attempts to look at Classical Greece from an alternative perspective. By looking at social and economic structures, exploitation, violence, and subjugation in the colonies, it aims to paint a different picture of Classical Greece. Greek settlements of the fifth and fourth centuries BC and their hinterland are analyzed using approaches from the fields of postcolonial criticism and subaltern studies. Archaeological data from excavations and field surveys, part of which is published for the first time here, is combined with literary sources and inscriptions to shed more light on the lives and status of nonelite populations in the colonies.

My original project was far less wide-ranging. When I started fieldwork at Heraclea Lucaniae in southern Italy in 2012, I had no idea of the direction this book would take, nor, I suppose, did those who helped me along the way. I am aware that not everyone will be persuaded by my arguments, but I hope that my work will at least help stimulate further discussion.

I am deeply grateful to all those who supported me over the last few years, particularly to Massimo Osanna who invited me for a three-year stay at the University of Basilicata in Matera (southern Italy) where I had the privilege and honor to work as a Feodor-Lynen research fellow of the Alexander von Humboldt Foundation. My faculty colleagues at Matera were extremely generous and helpful in a variety of matters, from organizing the field campaigns to finding a school for our kids: besides Massimo, whose humanity and expertise were fundamental, special thanks go to Dimitris Roubis, Barbara Serio, Francesca Sogliani, Valentino Vitale, and Mariasilvia Vullo. Further, I would like to thank all the students who participated in the fieldwork campaigns, in particular Luisa Aino, Gabriella Gramegna, and Antonia Miola.

Warm thanks also go to the *Soprintendenza* of Basilicata for granting permits and technical support, to the former *Soprintendente* Antonio De Siena, and the former director of the *Museo Archeologico Nazionale della Siritide* at Policoro, Salvatore Bianco, as well as to the entire staff, especially Pino Battafarano, Alessandro Cirigliano, Pino Galotto, Filippo Guida, and Mara Romaniello. The Italian Space Agency provided satellite data, for which I am also very grateful.

Rossella Pace, Francesca Silvestrelli, and Stéphane Verger, with whom I had the privilege to conduct excavation work in Policoro, were always ready to discuss new ideas and problems with me, and I owe much to their expertise and generosity. The city of Policoro, thanks to the mayor Rocco Luigi Leone and his team, provided logistical support for our fieldwork campaigns.

Maria Luisa Catoni read the manuscript and provided helpful feedback. I also would like to thank two anonymous referees of Cambridge University Press who commented on the text and contributed significantly to improving the final draft.

Furthermore, I would like to thank the following persons for stimulating discussions and feedback on single aspects at various stages of the project: Jon Albers, Roberta Belli, Martin Bentz, Johannes Bergemann, Irene Berlingò, Gert-Jan Burgers, Joe Carter, Antonietta Dell'Aglio, Peter van Dommelen, Gianclaudio Ferreri, Wolfgang Filser, Lin Foxhall, Jonathan Hall, Liliana Giardino, Franziska Lang, Enzo Lippolis, Katharina Meinecke, Francesco Meo, Dieter Mertens, Lisa Mignone, Jacky Murray, Eleftheria Pappa, Stephan G. Schmid, Günther Schörner, Alexander Schütze, Fritz Speckhardt, and Mario Torelli. It was great to be able to count on the language skills and professionalism of Colum Fordham and Judith Edge at various stages of the draft. All mistakes are solely the responsibility of the author.

Finally, I wish to thank Beatrice Rehl and her colleagues from Cambridge University Press for their professionalism, energy, and kindness.

ONE

PLACES OF DARKNESS: COLONIAL SETTLEMENTS AND THE HISTORY OF CLASSICAL GREECE

Oh you, who have founded so illustrious a city in the air,

you know not in what esteem men hold you

and how many there are who burn with desire to dwell in it.

(Aristophanes, *Birds* 1278–9, transl. E. O'Neill, 1938)

It had ceased to be a blank space of delightful mystery – a white

patch for a boy to dream gloriously over. It had become a place of darkness.

(Joseph Conrad, *Heart of Darkness*)

This book aims to paint a different picture of Classical Greece by looking at the experience of the nonelite population in colonial settlements and their hinterland. From a traditional point of view, such an agenda may not seem particularly significant. When we think of Classical Greece, we are used to thinking of Athens, Sparta, the sanctuaries of Olympia and Delphi, Sophocles, or Plato. We are maybe less used to thinking of colonial settlements, let alone nonelite groups living in these settlements and their rural hinterland. Yet I believe that the experience and perception of these groups is crucial to our understanding of Classical Greek culture.

The history of the colonized and the marginalized is never absent; it always emerges in one way or another. It may be nothing more than the history of the "Other," the margins that define the center, as Edward W. Said has argued in *Orientalism* (1978). This is more or less what happened in the history of Greece in the fifth and fourth centuries BC. In Classical scholarship, colonization has never been a central issue, let alone the experience of nonelite groups in the colonies. There are, of course, exceptions that will be discussed later in this book, but on a general level, subaltern and colonized groups have not played a major role in the creation of what could be referred to as the "master narrative" of Classical Greece during the fifth and fourth centuries BC.[1] They were more akin to an obscure backdrop – invisible, though necessary for the performance of the play.

Nowadays, this situation appears more problematic and anachronistic than ever. Authors working in the fields of postcolonial studies and literary criticism have contributed to a radical change in our perception of colonial histories and spaces – not only because they have changed the way in which the histories of certain regions and groups are represented in scholarship, literature, and art but also because they have undermined the hierarchies of center and periphery, colonizer and colonized, civilizer and civilized. The works of Edward W. Said (1978), Gayatri Chakravorty Spivak (1988; 1999), Homi Bhabha (1994), and Jean and John Comaroff (2009) do not, or at least not exclusively, concern a specific region and period, although they all have a very sound historical footing. Beginning from a local, and apparently "marginal," perspective, they address much larger fields, such as the notion of culture, the role of the sciences and art, gender, economy, and religion. In this book, I would like to apply a similar approach to the history and archaeology of Classical Greece. The following chapters address a series of questions regarding the experience of nonelite groups in colonial settlements: To what extent can we speak of colonized, marginalized, and/or subaltern groups in Greek colonies of the Classical period? What role did they play in colonial economies, politics, and ideologies? Can we reconstruct their experience of the Classical world, albeit only in a very fragmentary way? And finally: How does the general picture of Classical Greece change if we focus not on urban elites in Athens and elsewhere in mainland Greece, but on the experience of subaltern groups in the colonies and their hinterland?

While these questions have received little attention in Classical Greek and South Italian archaeology, some groundbreaking research has been carried out by scholars working in other fields. In *The Archaeology of the Colonized*, Michael Given (2004) looks at sites such as "farmsteads, illicit whiskey stands and labour camps," which he finds "far more interesting and instructive than palaces, villas and temples." Robert Witcher (2006) has emphasized the potential of landscape archaeology and field surveys to go beyond text-driven and "processual" research interests and to understand issues such as "identity, power and social

[1] As in Given 2004, "colonized" is meant here in the broader sense of exploited or subaltern groups.

organization." New approaches to the production, distribution, and consumption of pottery and metal objects in Southern France have questioned traditional assumptions on the relations between indigenous, Greek, and Etruscan groups from the Iron Age to the Roman period.[2] Peter van Dommelen and Carlos Gómez Bellard (2008) have analyzed material remains from rural sites on Ibiza and in other regions of the Western Mediterranean in order to reassess the role of agriculture in Punic colonization. These are just a few, though significant, examples of innovative archaeological research that adopts the ideas of postcolonial criticism with the aim of developing new perspectives on the Ancient Mediterranean, though it has had little impact on the history and archaeology of Classical Greece and Classical Greek colonies so far.

The cited studies abandon text-driven and top-down perspectives and start from close readings of local contexts. These might consist in pottery assemblages from rural sites on Ibiza or in cooking wares from Massalia – in both cases the reassessment of colonial histories is based on the analysis of types of evidence that long have been considered 'marginal' or 'less important' (e.g., cooking wares as compared to fine wares).

Similar approaches may be applied to the Classical Greek world. The archaeology of Classical settlements is notoriously based on top-down and text-driven approaches. Hippodamus, Herodotus, and Plato have shaped the image of these settlements to an infinitely higher degree than cooking wares or pottery assemblages from rural sites. This is particularly obvious in one of the most influential contributions to this field, Wolfram Hoepfner and Ernst-Ludwig Schwandner's *Stadt und Haus im Klassischen Griechenland* (1986, 2nd edition 1994). The authors attempt to reconstruct the Classical polis (as an idea) by looking at Classical settlements (as physical structures) at the moment of their foundation.[3] Case studies on newly founded or enlarged cities such as Piraeus, Olynthus, and Rhodos culminate in admittedly beautiful reconstructions that are in large part hypothetical, as critics have stressed. On these grounds, the authors argue that egalitarian and democratic models were successfully implemented in Classical city-foundations and that this involved the construction of standardized or type houses *(Typenhäuser).*[4] Subaltern groups do not feature much in the book.[5] A discussion of rural settlements and the role of peasantry is lacking.[6] Hence, the question of how the owners of the 'type houses' subsisted and how far this involved the labor of subaltern groups remains an

---

[2] Dietler 2005; 2010; Verger, Pernet 2013; Roure 2015.

[3] Cf. Hoepfner Schwandner 1994: xi.

[4] As hypothesized already by David Asheri (1966: 14) for the Classical period ("uniformità delle case").

[5] Two and a half pages refer to *"oikos,* kitchen and women's rooms" as well as "metics, slaves, economy and artisanry": Hoepfner, Schwandner 1994: 328–330.

[6] One reason might be that landscape archaeology had scarcely developed at the time of the first edition; cf. Lauter 1980; Osborne 1985 (both on Attica).

open one. Instead, the authors paint a positive, indeed encomiastic, picture of the Classical polis. They consider Classical city-foundations to be the work of architects commissioned by the people's assembly[7] with the objective of creating "equal living conditions for all" and a notion of "common destiny" within the polis.[8] They also argue that democratic city planning entailed "progress for almost everybody" and a "high level of civilization."[9] "Almost everybody" is one of the euphemisms that reveals a major problem with this approach: What about women, slaves, peasants, artisans, mercenaries, etc.?

To my eyes, this is a very clear example of how the way in which we look at the archaeological evidence shapes our perception of an entire period. Approaches based on abstract topographical and urbanistic visions of colonial spaces – arguably a product of colonialism themselves – produce a colonialist and sexist image of Classical Greece. On the other hand, we may be able to provide a very different picture of these settlements if we adopt a "bottom-up" approach, by starting from the places of daily life and work on the ground. This is what I shall attempt to do here. The chapters in this book are organized around specific places, such as houses, tombs, fields, farms, and so on – places that are often obscured by abstract and ideal views of colonial space. By looking closely at these places, I aim to find out more about the living conditions of a large group of people who lived in the "Classical world": the nonelite population.

The starting point for my study is a research project of the University of Basilicata on Heraclea Lucana, founded in 433/2 BC on the Ionian Coast of southern Italy.[10] Other Classical settlements of the fifth and fourth centuries BC are analyzed on the basis of published data. I am aware that many more sites and regions could have been included in this study. However, I shall focus here on settlements that were newly established in the Classical period, as the characteristics of Classical colonization are likely to emerge more clearly there than elsewhere.

WAS THERE SUCH A THING AS "CLASSICAL COLONIZATION"?

Was the Classical period characterized by colonization in the first place? There are scholars who probably would question this, and they would do so for

---

[7] Hoepfner, Schwandner 1994: 314. The city as a work of art based on an idea or master plan has closer parallels in fourth-century political philosophy than in ancient political practice, as Hannah Arendt (1958: 281–283) has pointed out. The foundation decree of Brea, cited by the authors in support of the role of architects in urban planning, does not mention any architects though (see pp. 16–17 below).

[8] Hoepfner and Schwandner 1994: xi *(Schicksalsgemeinschaft)*. On the term *Schicksalsgemeinschaft*, see Schmitz-Berning 1988: 654; Neubauer 2011: 408–410.

[9] Hoepfner, Schwandner 1994: xiii.

[10] See Osanna, Zuchtriegel 2012; Zuchtriegel 2012b; Meo, Zuchtriegel 2015.

two reasons. The first is chronological. Greek colonization is often seen as a phenomenon typical of, or even restricted to, the Archaic period (eighth to sixth centuries BC, the period of the so-called *Grande Colonizzazione*). We shall see that the evidence does not support such a view. However, the way in which Greek colonization is represented in modern scholarship and popular science tends to associate colonization with early periods and archaism, whereas Classical Greece is not regularly associated with colonization. It is as though European colonialism were considered primarily a matter of the history of the sixteenth and seventeenth centuries. At the same time, a period that many scholars consider virtually overstudied – the fifth and fourth centuries BC – is actually full of blank spaces: the colonies and their hinterland. This is all the more surprising if we consider that the relevant written sources on Greek colonization date almost exclusively from the Classical period onward.[11] Therefore, the archaeology of Classical colonization is fundamental for the understanding of ancient texts and the way in which they have shaped our impression of Greek colonization in general. For example, the word *apoikia*, usually translated as "colony," appears in many Classical sources, whereas it is scarcely attested in the Archaic period. In order to assess whether or not an *apoikia* is comparable to our idea of a colony, we need to engage with the archaeology of Classical settlements.

However, the problem with "Classical colonization" not only concerns the concept of what is meant by the term "Classical" but also, and arguably to an even higher degree, by the concept of "colonization." For if we reflect on colonization, not only are we used to focusing on Archaic rather than on Classical settlements, but we may also feel uneasy about the term "colonization." Is it appropriate to use this term at all? Nowadays, many scholars reject it. They argue that ancient Greek colonization was radically different from the modern colonialism, and that any analogy should be avoided.[12]

This is understandable as a reaction to traditional approaches to Greek colonization, which tended to equate (and legitimize) modern colonialism and ancient Greek colonization. The ancient Greeks were seen as the "masters of colonization" (Curtius 1883) and the modern European colonizers as their successors. Attempts since the 1960s to "decolonize" the past have led to radically different views.[13] Analogies between modern and ancient colonization began to appear out of place.[14] While this has undoubtedly led to a better understanding of Greek migration and interaction with local groups (not least

---

[11] Cf. Graham 1964; Dougherty 1993; Miller, T. 1997.
[12] Hurst, Owen 2005; Malkin 2008; Greco, Lombardo 2010.
[13] Cf. van Dommelen 1996/97; 1998; 2002; 2005; 2006; Malkin 2004; van Dommelen, Terrenato 2007; Pappa 2013.
[14] Hurst, Owen 2005; Bradley, Wilson 2006; Pappa 2013. A different viewpoint is held by E. Greco and M. Lombardo (2010: 38) who reject the usefulness of postcolonial approaches in Classical Archaeology ("In quella sede [that is ten years ago] abbiamo ribadito, una volta

because it permitted leaving simplifying and binary approaches behind), it also entailed certain shortcomings. Scholarship has focused mainly on questioning Greek hegemony and on emphasizing the role of indigenous agency. Some scholars have even hypothesized peaceful and equal relations between Greek and non-Greek groups in so-called mixed settlements on the basis of material evidence.[15] The possibility of peaceful and equal relations should not, of course, be ruled out. However, what I find questionable about this approach is that it is often accompanied by a forgetfulness of phenomena that do have parallels in modern colonialism, such as the subjugation and exploitation of individuals and groups in the colonies and their hinterland. In the nineteenth century, these phenomena were misrepresented in order to prove the superiority of "the Greeks"; today they risk being screened out because they do not fit into the picture of a decolonized past. The question of whether ancient Greek colonization and migration involved inequality, violence, and oppression is rarely asked today.[16] Just as the Greeks as colonizers were once seen as a model for European colonialism, the "decolonized" version of Greek history risks reiterating our own forgetfulness of the colonized in a neocolonial world, for example textile workers in Third World countries from whose workforce Western economies profit but whose living conditions are hardly known in the West.

Exponents of postcolonial criticism have stressed that postcolonialism does not mean that colonialism and imperialism are obsolete and "placed securely in the past."[17] The term "postcolonial" is actually misleading insofar as it implies the beginning of a new era that leaves colonialism and imperialism behind.[18] But this is illusory given that the economic exploitation of former colonies continues in many cases. Thus, it may be open to doubt whether archaeology has reached a "postcolonial" phase yet and whether archaeological research is completely independent from modern forms of colonialism and

per tutte penso, la nostra posizione nella quale auspichiamo ci si possa riconoscere, almeno noi che non abbiamo avuto imperi coloniali vasti e duraturi e tali da rappresentare un passato ingombrante con cui misurarsi: non c'è niente di nuovo, nessuno confonde le colonie degli antichi con quelle dei moderni! Quindi, quando parliamo della colonizzazione greca non pensiamo ad imperi centrali.")

[15] Cf. for example Burgers, Crielaard 2011: 157. See also J. Massenet de La Gerniere, in *Atti del 37° Convegno di Studi sulla Magna Grecia*, 518. Taranto: Istituto per la Storia e l'Archeologia della Magna Grecia. On the basis of terracotta finds, the author concludes: "Indéfendable en bordure de mer, le sanctuaire de Cirò, de lecture difficile parce qu'à la fois grec et non grec, illustre par sa seule existence le climat pacifique qui régnait entre Neto et Nica, au pied des petits cités de Philoctète, aux VIIe et VIe siècles av. J.-C." In the case of Policoro, peaceful coexistence of Greek and non-Greek groups has been hypothesized by Adamesteanu 1972 on the basis of the evidence from the necropolis.

[16] Osanna 1992: 92; Kindberg Jacobsen, Handberg 2010: 711 (with regard to habitation nuclei at Francavilla Marittima, the authors refer to "a rare case of identifiable social differentiation between Greek and indigenous communities within the same settlement"). See also Attema 2008; Esposito, Pollini 2013.

[17] Spivak 1999: 1. Cf. Stockhammer 2012; 2013; Pappa 2013.

[18] McClintock 1992.

imperialism.[19] I also doubt that we should pretend this by banning terms like "colonization." As Michael Dietler (2005: 53) has argued, "the idea of linguistic reform – of inventing and imposing upon the reader a new analytic vocabulary to deal with ancient cases that avoids all Greco-Roman terms already incorporated into modern discourse – seems a cumbersome and quixotic endeavor at best: the intellectual equivalent of spitting into the wind."

If seen like this, "postcolonial" archaeology should not simply consist in abandoning the notion of colonization, exploitation, and subjugation, nor should "decolonizing the past" mean overlooking the colonized and painting a picture of the colonies as equal and irenic communities that have nothing to do with more recent forms of colonization. We should not be too quick in drawing a distinct line between ancient and modern colonizations. For archaeology and history always operate in a contemporary context that shapes our way of asking questions and doing research, which is why we ought to try to make this process explicit and the subject of serious debate. On the other hand, modern colonization is in itself strongly biased by the tradition of Greco-Roman colonial ideology and terminology.[20] This does not, of course, mean that we should simply equate modern colonialism with ancient colonization, nor should we reduce the comparison to a simple yes/no question. However, comparison may help shed light on what colonization really meant in Greek antiquity. To my mind, comparative approaches pose a challenge to look for continuities and differences between ancient and modern colonizations and represent an opportunity to shed new light on the question of why we are interested nowadays in Ancient Greek colonization in the first place.[21]

THE 'VOICELESSNESS' OF THE COLONIZED

The subject of this study – the experience of the nonelite population in Classical colonies – lays hidden beneath three layers of silence: the voicelessness of the colonized, the silence of ancient authors, and the silence of modern scholars. By voicelessness I mean the lack of visibility of subaltern groups in the archaeological record and in the literary sources.[22] Colonized and marginalized groups have left virtually no texts or images of themselves. Consequently, studies on colonial identities (whether Greek, indigenous, female, male, or the like) based on texts and iconographic evidence tend to exclude those who

[19] Nicholas, Hollowell 2007: 60; Hamilakis 2012.
[20] Dietler 2005.
[21] Cf. Ferro 1997; Osborne 2009; Lane 2014: 3–11.
[22] On attempts to use archaeological evidence for the reconstruction of subaltern histories, see McGuire, Paynter 1991; Lomas 1996; Given 2004; Liebmann, Rizvi 2008; Ferris, Harrison, Wilcox 2014.

could or would not express themselves, who "have no voice."[23] In fact, most studies dealing with Classical settlements have looked mainly or exclusively at the living conditions and cultural expressions of the elite.

The lack of visibility of subaltern groups in the evidence – their voicelessness – is of course no coincidence. As the Italian Marxist Antonio Gramsci argued, the lack of visibility of subaltern groups may be explained by their systematic exclusion from certain forms of communication. In his famous "Prison Notebooks," written during the years 1926–1935, Gramsci argues that the southern Italian peasantry represented a subaltern class insofar as they were excluded from the "hegemonic culture" and idiom. In Gramsci's analysis, the cultural hegemony of southern Italy was dominated by wealthy landowners who exploited the peasants, and mediated by a middle class of doctors, schoolteachers, and public employees.[24] The various social groups formed a "bloc" bound together by elite culture. Thus, subalternity inevitably implies voicelessness: the subaltern reside within the bloc, but they have no access to the idiom that structures it.

Elaborating on Gramsci's concept of subalternity, a group of South Asian historians and literary critics (the so-called Subaltern Studies Group) started research in the 1980s on the living conditions and access to social mobility of rural dwellers in India and other countries of the region. They asked if and how subaltern groups could express themselves within or outside the hegemonic discourse and, consequently, from what material or literary traces historians and archaeologists might recognize them. In her seminal paper *Can the Subaltern Speak?*, Gayatri Chakravorty Spivak disputed any possibility of the subaltern being able to express their perception of the world: even the most drastic forms of expression – Spivak discusses the case of a woman who commits suicide to prove her innocence – are misunderstood and reshaped according to the hegemonic discourse.[25]

What, then, of the subaltern and the colonized in ancient Greece? Can we hope to find any authentic evidence of their history? If one looks only at literary and iconographic sources, the answer is probably no.[26] It has been shown, for example, that Athenian vase painting was heavily influenced by the cultural choices of a narrow elite even under democracy, whereas the living conditions

[23] Cf. Ste Croix 1981: 285–289; Morris 1998; Caliò 2012: 204. See also Morris, Papadopoulos (2005), where rural towers in mainland Greece are interpreted as *ergastula* for slaves. In a recent paper, A. Esposito and A. Pollini (2013) try to use funeral evidence to trace subaltern groups in southern Italy during the Archaic period. Garland 2014 presents written sources, scarce as they are, concerning the daily experience of "wandering Greeks," including colonists.

[24] Gramsci [2007].

[25] Spivak 1988; 1999: 198–311. Cf. Medovoi Raman, Robinson 1990 on certain political implications of that notion.

[26] Morris 1998; Osborne 2000.

of the artisans who produced the vases, though occasionally alluded to, remain hidden behind stereotypes and ironic representations.[27] Likewise, representations of slave girls on Athenian grave stelae are far more revealing about certain ideas among the Athenian elite who commissioned the stelae than about the living conditions of real slaves.[28]

When looking for evidence of subaltern histories in ancient written sources and art, what emerges is layers of speech and silence that overlie and obscure the voicelessness of the colonized: the hegemonic discourse of Greek authors who talk about colonial space from a different perspective. Many Classical authors regarded the colonies as a manifestation of Greek civilization and as an ideal space for the development of the (free, male, adult) individual. For example, Xenophon (*Anabasis* V 6,15) speaks of the foundation of a new settlement as a means of "enlarging the outward power/influence *(dynamis)* and the territory *(chora)* of Hellas." Plato (*Laws* 708d) states that "legislation and the foundation of cities are the best for the virtue of men" (νομοθεσία καὶ πόλεων οἰκισμοὶ πάντων τελεώτατον πρὸς ἀρετὴν ἀνδρῶν).

On various occasions, Classical authors refer to matters of political philosophy by putting themselves in the position of someone establishing a colony (e.g., Plato's *Laws* or Aristotle's best state in the *Politics*). These texts draw up ideal settlements from a top-down perspective; their focus lies on the group of free citizens, whereas other groups are defined only with regard to the male citizen, whose autonomy, subsistence, and reproduction has to be ensured. The texts tend to abstain from a number of aspects that are seen as less relevant, among others the living conditions and economic role of artisans, women, merchants, slaves, and peasants. Thus, the voicelessness of the colonized becomes the backdrop on which Classical writers paint their picture of colonial space and history.

Interestingly, there were also critical voices. Some kind of criticism of glorifying and abstract visions of colonial space can be found in *The Birds* by Aristophanes, staged in 414 BC. The play can be read as a satire on fifth-century theories about the ideal polis or colony as cherished by people like Hippodamus of Miletus, Phaleas of Chalcedon, Socrates, and Athenian colonizers and city-founders of the period. Although they sought to escape from depths, lawsuits, sycophants, and the de facto aristocratic government by establishing a "city in the air," the two protagonists end up erecting a regime that is as despotic and unjust as the one they fled from.[29] Aristophanes contrasts the ideal of the Classical polis with the negative, destructive, and exploitative character of colonial ventures. In pointing out this ambiguity of colonial discourse,

[27] Filser, W. forthcoming. *Die athenische Elite im Spiegel der attischen Luxuskeramik*, Berlin.
[28] Himmelmann 1971; Räuchle 2014.
[29] On the *Birds* see Katz 1976; Amati 2010.

he anticipates modern criticism of colonialism. If the play enjoyed some success (it won the second prize in the Dionysia that year), it probably did so because many Athenians in the audience sensed the conflict between utopia and colonial reality.

The Birds shows us that the abstract nature and illusiveness of colonial ideologies was perceived as early as the fifth century BC, and that it was possible to express criticism. However, given that the quoted passage is an isolated case as far as is known, it ultimately confirms the predominance of abstract top-down perspectives in Classical Greece.

The same top-down perspective that has shaped ancient texts can easily be recognized in modern scholarship on ancient colonization. Once again, the relationship between ancient and modern colonization turns out to be extremely intricate. I have already mentioned the study by Hoepfner and Schwandner (1994). Willingly or unwillingly, they belong to a longstanding tradition of viewing colonial space from a particular perspective. The colony is portrayed as a better place, as an opportunity, as a place for development and growth, as an outpost of civilization, and as a new beginning. Of course, this works only if the focus lies on privileged groups within a new settlement. The New World was not new to the Native Americans, whose livelihood and traditions were destroyed by the arrival of Europeans. With regard to glorifying and abstract visions of colonial space, the perspective of the colonized is an element of disturbance; as a result, they receive little attention or are completely ignored. What we have here is another layer of voices that join in the chorus of the Classical tradition and drown out the voicelessness of the colonized.

METHODOLOGY

Is it therefore possible to write the history of the nonelite population, of those who have no voice? As outlined above, what I would like to suggest here is a shift away from abstract spaces toward concrete places and their archaeological analysis. By describing the places of daily life and work, we may be able to restore the fragments of the history of those who inhabited them. In the history of colonial criticism, such a strategy has repeatedly been reenacted. Shifting the focus from ideal representations toward physical spaces is a discursive strategy that goes back at least to the time of Joseph Conrad. In his novel *Heart of Darkness*, glorifying and idealizing visions of colonial space fall apart when the narrator, during his trip up the river to the "inner station," discovers the barbarism of European civilization. "Blank spaces of delightful mystery" turn into "places of darkness;" the idea of colonization as a civilizing mission melts away in the face of the social realities that are encountered. The places that the narrator visits are places of darkness because they are overshadowed by an abstract image, but also because they conceal an unheard reality. In my reading, the move from abstract spaces towards real places in the novel entails a critique of colonial discourse.[30]

In the last fifteen years or so, archaeologists have begun to experiment with similar strategies. I have already mentioned the works of Given (2004), van Dommelen and Gómez Bellard (2008), Dietler (2005; 2010), and others. In a recent paper dealing with the historical subject in archaeology, Reinhard Bernbeck (2010) proposes leaving behind traditional approaches that lead to depersonalized, abstract narratives, and adopting the narrative form of the *nouveau roman* of the 1950s with its postmodern elements. In the *nouveau roman*, the subject is present only as a fragmented reflection in the minute, quasi-archaeological description of places, objects, and landscapes. Bernbeck suggests that the archaeological description of objects and places in the style of the *nouveau roman* might lead to new insight into the formation and structure of social groups of whom we have little or no other evidence, though only in an equally fragmentary and indirect manner. At the end of his paper, he gives the example of the eastern Syrian Tell Umm Aqrubba, "inhabited by people of whom we can assume that as deportees of the Assyrians they had a hard life."[31] The paper ends with a question: Can we describe the site of Umm Aqrubba in a manner that somehow reflects the experience of these people? Sandra R. Joshel and Lauren Hackworth Peterson ask similar questions in *The Material Life of Roman Slaves* (2014), where they explore the "dichotomy between visibility and invisibility" of Roman slaves by looking at physical spaces such as houses, workshops, and villas.[32]

The following chapters on houses, fields, farms, mountain settlements, and workshops are based on a similar approach. I will try to focus on the archaeological contexts where power and subalternity were enforced and experienced, because I think this might be a way to challenge the pervasiveness of the hegemonic discourse in texts and iconographic sources. My working hypothesis is that the study of such places can help to put into perspective any reconstructions that depend entirely on what could be referred to as the master narrative of Classical Greece.[33]

Much of the work simply consists of applying traditional methods such as stratigraphy, distribution analysis, iconography, analysis of epigraphic, and literary evidence to objects that have received less attention. The same accuracy

---

[30] In this reading, 'darkness' is not identified with Africa, although I am aware of the fact that Conrad's novel can be read as a racist description of Africa as the 'dark continent', as pointed out by Achebe 1977. See also Monod *et al.* 2007.

[31] Bernbeck 2010: 82.

[32] Joshel, Hackworth Peterson 2014: 3.

[33] On the link between space, material culture and identity see Ault, Nevett 1999; Goldberg 1999; Cahill 2002; Given 2004; Trümper 2011; Caliò 2012: 199–230; Bintliff 2014; van Dommelen 2014.

and the same methods used to study temples and palaces could be applied to the study of workshops, huts, and farmsteads.

Another important tool is landscape archaeology, which opens entirely new perspectives on Classical colonization. If we look at the situation in the 1980s and early 1990s, Greek landscapes really were "blank spaces of mystery." As extremely little was known about rural settlement and land use, an integral part of the Greek polis remained obscure. In the last few years, intensive field surveys and excavations of rural sites have shed new light on areas hitherto scarcely known.[34] At the same time, many non-Greek areas in the ancient Mediterranean and the Black Sea region have become much better known than they were twenty years ago thanks to excavations and archaeological field surveys. Such areas, which have long been overshadowed by the topography of the Greek world, are fundamental to the understanding of Greek colonization. The objective of this study is therefore not only to move from abstract to concrete places, but also to expand our perception of Classical settlements toward rural spaces and habitation sites.[35] In this context, we need to take into consideration ethnographic research and ethno-archaeological approaches that until now have rarely been applied to Greek colonization. Studies from other fields demonstrate the usefulness of such approaches, in particular when it comes to reconstructing the economy and living conditions of subaltern and rural populations.[36]

CLASSICAL COLONIZATION: HISTORY AND ARCHAEOLOGY

Compared to Archaic colonies, Classical colonies have received surprisingly little attention from modern scholarship. Indeed, Thomas Figueira's article *Classical Colonization* (2008) appears to be the first (!) comprehensive treatment of the subject.[37] Many manuals and dictionaries simply ignore or play down Classical colonization, implying that after the Archaic period it was only in the Hellenistic period that the foundation of new cities revived, though under completely different circumstances.[38] Other publications exclude the Classical

[34] Bintliff, Gaffney 1988; Foxhall 1993; Alcock, Cherry, Davis 1994; Alcock, Cherry 2004; Kolb 2004; Witcher 2006; Bintliff, Howard, Snodgrass 2007; de Haas 2012.

[35] With regard to southern Italy, the emergence of new approaches and methods can be traced in the proceedings of the *Convegni di Studi sulla Magna Grecia* at Taranto; see, in particular, the years 1961 *(Greci e Italici in Magna Grecia)*, 1971 *(Le genti non greche della Magna Grecia)*, 1997 *(Confini e frontiera della grecità d'Occidente)*, 2000 *(Problemi della chora coloniale dall'Occidenta al Mar Nero)*, 2002 *(Ambiente e paesaggio in Magna Grecia)*. The meeting of the year 2014 concentrated on *Ibridazione ed integrazione in Magna Grecia – forme, modelli e dinamiche.*

[36] Forbes 1976; 2013; Foxhall 1990; 1999; 2003.

[37] Figueira 2008.

[38] For example: *Lexikon der Alten Welt*, s.v. 'Kolonisation.'

period from the discussion of Greek colonization as a historical phenomenon. Historical maps and articles on Greek colonization are often limited more or less explicitly to the eighth to sixth centuries BC. At the same time, studies on Classical settlements, e.g., Hoepfner, Schwandner 1994 and Cahill 2002, tend to focus on *synoikismoi* and resettlements in mainland Greece rather than on colonies and cleruchies. In Paul Cartledge's *Ancient Greek Political Thought in Practice* (2009), Classical colonies do not feature at all.

Yet we know quite a number of Classical settlements: Classical colonization was not restricted to a few Athenian cleruchies, as is sometimes suggested, nor was it generally characterized by a shift from the exploration of distant regions to the urbanization of areas where Greeks were already present (Figure 1.1). Actually, such a shift can be observed as early as the sixth century BC. On the other hand, fourth-century-BC colonies in the Adriatic were no less pioneering than, say, most seventh-century-BC colonies in Sicily. It is therefore not surprising that, unlike modern scholarship, Classical authors do not make any substantial distinction between Archaic and Classical colonies. Thucydides's account of the (aborted) recolonization of Epidamnos by Corinth and its allies in the 430s BC (I 27–28) shows that the religious procedure accompanying the foundation of a polis remained unchanged. Alongside a series of profound social and political transformations, there seem to be some elements of continuity in Greek colonization from the eighth to the fourth, and even to the third centuries BC.[39]

Ancient texts leave little doubt that colonization in the Classical period regularly included violence, subjugation, and genocide. This may have been different in the Archaic period; especially in the early periods, Greek colonization was probably much more spontaneous and less aggressive.[40] In the fifth and fourth centuries BC, colonization was accompanied by expropriation, enslavement, and bloodshed. Entire communities were deported, or instrumentalized for imperialist interests by large city-states such as Athens and Sparta.

The following outline of the history of Classical colonization reflects the current state of research within a field that primarily relies on literary sources and sporadic archaeological data. However, even when using traditional types of evidence, the impact of imperialism, exploitation and subjugation can be detected. The subsequent chapters will deal with the archaeological sources that help integrate, and partly modify, the picture.

[39] On Hellenistic settlements, see Brugsch, Erman 1894; Tscherikower 1927; Briant 1978; Kirsten, Opelt 1989; Cohen 1995; 2006; Mueller 2006; Daubner 2010.

[40] Osborne 1998; Malkin 2013.

1.1 Greek colonization 480–330 BC.

- colony
- mother-city

300 km

Kalos
Limen
Chersonesos
Herakleia Pontike
Astakos
Anchialos
Apollonia
Adramyttion
Samos
Sestos
Lesbos
Kabyle
Krenides
Paros
Naxos
Thasos
Philippopolis
Torone
Melos
Skyros
Delos
Heraclea
Sintike
Amphipolis
Eion
Histiaia
Athens
Poteidaia
Eretria
Skione
Aigina
Heraclea
Trachinia
Heraclea
Lynkestis
Sparta
Lissos
Korkyra Melaina
Heraclea
Pharos
Thurii
Issa
Messina
Rhegium
Tarentum
Tauromenion
Ankona
Aitna
Syracuse
Pyxous
Tyndaris
Kamarina
Atria
Himera
Nikaia
Massalia
Antipolis
Olbia
Agathe
Rhode
Emporion

14

Sicily and Rhegium in the Fifth Century BC

In 476 BC or shortly before, many inhabitants of Himera were killed in a civil war. Theron, the tyrant of Akragas, who together with Gelon had defeated the Carthaginians in the battle of Himera in 480 BC, captured the city and sent new settlers, "both Dorians and others who so wished" (according to Diodorus, who speaks as usual of 10,000 colonists).[41] After Theron's death in 472 BC, his son Trasydaeus became the tyrant of Himera, but was deposed in the same year. In 408 BC, the city was razed to the ground by the Carthaginians and never rebuilt.

In the same year when Theron recolonized Himera, Hieron of Syracuse resettled Aitna (ancient Katane) and Naxos (Diodorus XI 49):

> Hieron removed the people of Naxos and Katane from their cities and sent there settlers of his own choosing, having gathered five thousand from the Peloponnesus and added an equal number of others from Syracuse; and the name of Katane he changed to Aitna, and not only the territory of Katane but also much neighboring land which he added to it he portioned out in allotments, up to the full sum of ten thousand settlers.
>
> (transl. C.H. Oldfather, 1989)

Reconstruction work in Aitna and Naxos might have been necessary after an eruption of Mount Etna, which Diodorus fails to mention, perhaps in order to emphasize the arbitrary nature of Hieron's intervention.[42] Where the former inhabitants went remains a mystery. Pindar (Pyth. I 21) and Aeschylus (Aetn.) celebrate Hieron as the founder-hero of Aitna.[43] After his death (467 BC), Syracuse and many of the formerly subjected and recolonized cities became democracies. They now faced the problem of dealing with the populations that had been displaced under Hieron and other tyrants. In the years 466–461 BC, Hieron's colonists in Aitna/Katane, Naxos, and other settlements were expelled and the original inhabitants were allowed to return (Diod. XI 76,4). The mercenaries of Hieron who had occupied many of the subdued cities were offered the chance to settle in Messina. The former inhabitants of Kamarina, who had been deported in 484 BC by Gelon, returned in 461/60 with help from Gela and the land was redistributed (Diodorus XI 76,5).[44]

The colony of Pyxous in southern Italy was established in 471/70 BC under Mikythos, governor of Rhegium, since the sons of the late tyrant of the city, Anaxilaos, were still children (Diod. XI 59). Nothing is known about why the colony was established, how many settlers went there, and what part Mikythos

---

[41] Diod. XI 49,3 (in Diodorus, 'ten-thousand' seems to refer to 'a large number': Schaefer 1961).
[42] Mertens 2006: 351.
[43] Luraghi 1994: 340–41.
[44] On the constitution of Kamarina, see Cordano 2014 who argues that in 461 the city had a 'republican' regime that was transformed into a 'democratic' one only around 424 BC.

played, but it seems likely that Rhegium had a strategic interest in the region. According to Strabo (VI 1,1), the settlers struggled for survival, and many of them abandoned the colony after a short time. Findings dating to the fourth and third centuries BC demonstrate that the city recovered and flourished in the Late Classical period. The territory of Pyxous must have been quite small, given that the important Lucanian settlement center of Roccagloriosa lies only 10 kilometers inland.

Athenian Colonization in the Fifth Century BC

In the seventh and sixth centuries BC, Athenian colonization had been limited to the Troas and the Thracian Chersonesus. Men like Phrynon, victor in the Olympic Games in 636 BC, and Miltiades the Elder conducted military campaigns against local groups and occupied strategic sites such as Sigeion.[45] Miltiades ruled almost like a tyrant over Chersonesus, where both Athenians and allied or subjugated Thracians lived. In the sixth century, colonization enabled Peisistratus to get rid of potential rivals by sending them off as commanders to the overseas settlements.[46] Another side effect (or one of the principal goals) was gaining control of the shipping routes to the Black Sea.[47]

During the fifth century BC, Athens started establishing cleruchies, apparently a new type of colony, although the foundation of traditional colonies (apoikiai) continued. Around 445 BC the Athenian assembly approved the foundation of a colony in Thrace named Brea. The site has not been located so far, but the stele with the foundation decree that was set up in Athens is partly preserved (IG I³ 46, 1):

> – vacat – The colony leaders shall provide the wherewithal for offering auspicious sacrifices on behalf of the colony, as much as they deem appropriate. Ten men shall be chosen as assigners of land (geonomoi), one per tribe, and these shall assign the land. Demokleides shall have full power to establish the colony according to the best of his ability. The sacred precincts already proclaimed shall remain as they are, and no others shall be consecrated. They shall contribute an ox and a panoply for the Great Panathenaia and a phallus for the Dionysia. If anyone marches against the land of the colonists, the cities (of the region) shall come to their aid as speedily as possible in accordance with the covenants concerning the cities in Thrace executed when ... was secretary (of the council). These provisions shall be inscribed on a stele and placed on the Acropolis, and the colonists shall provide the stele at their own expense. If anyone takes a vote contrary to (the decree on) the stele or any orator urges or supports

---

[45] Figueira 2008: 429–434.
[46] Figueira 2008: 430–431.
[47] Moreno 2007: 165.

a proposal to rescind or annul any of its provisions, he and the children born of him shall be disfranchised, and his property shall be confiscated, a tithe going to the goddess; but the colonists themselves may petition (for changes). Those of the soldiers who, when they return to Athens, enroll to be colonists, shall be at Brea to settle there within thirty days. The colony shall be led forth within thirty days, and Aischines shall accompany and pay the money.

Phantokles moved – In addition to Demokleides' motion concerning the colony at Brea, the (next?) prytany of (the tribe) Erechtheis shall present Phantokles before the council at the first session; and the colonists going to Brea shall be from the (classes of) *thetes* and *zeugitai*. – *vacat*

(transl. G. Forsythe)

The way in which the decree expresses power relations and hegemony through religion is surprising. Again, this points to continuity between Archaic and Classical colonization rather than to radical change. The colony was ritually bound to the mother-city, which meant that if it defected the Athenians could justify military intervention and harsh punishment on religious grounds. Furthermore, the colonists were supposed to respect and maintain the "sacred precincts" that existed in the area, as Irad Malkin has argued.[48] Malkin cites a passage in Thucydides (IV 98) to support this interpretation:

According to Hellenic practice, they who were masters of the land, whether much or little, invariably had possession of the temples, to which they were bound to show the customary reverence, but in such ways only as were possible.

(transl. B. Jowett, 1881)

In terms of religion and ritual, becoming "masters of the land" was apparently not a question of establishing new sanctuaries based on the same "rational and functional categories" that determined the spatial organization of public spaces, harbors, street grid, and so on.[49] Instead, hegemony and power were expressed by incorporating and redesigning preexisting cult sites.

The archaeological data from Classical colonies seems to confirm this. The Demeter Sanctuary in Amphipolis existed from as early as 450 BC and continued to be in use throughout the Classical period, although the colony was officially founded only in 437/6 BC.[50] The integration of preexisting sanctuaries can also be hypothesized in the case of the Late Archaic colonization of Lemnos. With the arrival of the Athenians, new burial customs were introduced; the material culture changed completely, and the urban center of Hephaistia was remodeled. However, the cult topography remained basically

---

[48] Malkin 1984.
[49] Malkin 1987: 137.
[50] Malkin 1984: 47.

unchanged, although there is some evidence for changes in ritual activities.[51] Another striking parallel is Heraclea of Lucania, where almost all the Classical sanctuaries have Archaic precursors.[52]

The question of what distinguished Athenian cleruchies from colonies/ *apoikiai* such as Brea and what part they played in Athenian politics is still the subject of debate.[53] Evidence of fifth-century cleruchies such as Histiaia, Eretria, and Karystos – i.e., cleruchies established before the dissolution of the First League at the end of the Peloponnesian War (404 BC) – is extremely scarce. There is some more evidence of Athenian recolonization during the Second League (Imbros, Lemnos, Skyros). An inscription from Samos (IG XII 6,1, 262) shows that political institutions in the cleruchies resembled those in Athens and other democratic city-states.[54]

A major difference between cleruchies and colonies has been seen in the fact that the *klerouchoi* (colonists in cleruchies) maintained Athenian citizenship whereas *apoikoi* (colonists in *apoikiai*) did not, although Thomas Figueira has shown that the latter could also repatriate on certain occasions.[55] On the other hand, *apoikiai* did not always possess full autonomy. Colonies and cleruchies may have differed less in terms of political structure than might initially be thought. However, cleruchs were less tied to the land they received than *apoikoi*. An *apoikos* is literally someone who "goes to live away from home," while a *klerouchos* is someone who possesses a land-lot (from Greek *kleros*, land-lot, and *echein*, to have, to hold). The role of cleruchs was sometimes limited to their being landowners. A striking example is the cleruchy on Lesbos, established in 427 BC (Thuc. III 50). While the former owners continued to farm the land-lots that were assigned to the cleruchs, the latter received an annual allowance of two minae. In this case, the cleruchs were rather like pensioners who might well have lived outside Lesbos.

Most Athenian cleruchies and colonies are characterized by scarce visibility in the archaeological record. Settlement remains dating to the second half of the fifth century have been excavated on the islands of Lemnos and Imbros, but if we had no literary sources and inscriptions, we would never have known that for a certain period these sites were Athenian cleruchies.[56] The same holds for the Athenian settlements of Skyros (476/5 BC), Thracian Chersonesus (448–446, 353 and 346 BC), Histiaia/Oreos (c. 445 BC), Poteidaia (430/ 29 BC), and Melos (415 BC). The physical structure of these sites remained

---

[51] Greco, Ficuciello 2012: 168.
[52] Cf. Mertens-Horn 1992: 64–68; Osanna, Prandi, Siciliano 2008: 35–38; 41–47; Crupi, Pasquino 2012; Gertl 2012; Giardino 2012.
[53] Cf. Miller, T. 1997: 70–84.
[54] Hallof, Habicht 1995; Hallof 2003.
[55] Figueira 2008: 448–449.
[56] Greco, Ficuciello 2012; Ruhl 2012.

largely unchanged, and if there were changes, as in Histiaia, the evidence for this comes from the written sources rather than from archaeology. Histiaia, for example, was founded on the site of a small village called Oreos (Theopompus/ Strabo X 1,3), which has been identified at modern Kastro but has yielded only scarce archaeological evidence.[57] Although Histiaia/Oreos was an official *apoikia* with a *boule* and a *dikasterion* (IG I³ 41), it did not issue coinage.[58] In 415 BC, Histiaia contributed to the Sicilian expedition (Thuc. VII 57,2), but defected from Athens in 411 BC. The relatively detailed picture that emerges from the literary sources contrasts with the paucity of archaeological data. One reason might be that Athenian settlers were either mere pensioners or took over houses, furnishings, and even the clothing of conquered or deported populations, as Thucydides suggests in a passage on the surrender of Poteidaia in 430/29 BC (women were allowed to take two pieces and men one piece of clothing with them: Thuc. II 70; cf. Diod. XII 46,7).

In many Athenian settlements of the Classical period, evidence of large temples and infrastructure is lacking. Tellingly, the most famous monument of a cleruchy stood in Athens: the statue of Athena Lemnia by Phidias known through Roman copies and ancient literary sources.[59] The archaeological "poverty" of Athenian settlements is perhaps due to the fact that the lot-holders did not necessarily share a collective identity. They did share economic interests, but were maybe less interested in expressing collective identity through public and religious monuments.[60]

On the other hand, settlements with a heterogeneous population such as Thurii and Amphipolis, besides being archaeologically "richer" (see Chapter 3), were characterized by inner conflicts regarding economic, political, and cultural issues that could lead to violence and civil war.

Thurii was officially a Panhellenic settlement, although Athens played a leading role in its foundation (Figure 1.2). The interest of Athens in the region around Thurii dates back to the time of Themistocles who claimed that Siris (modern Policoro, north of Thurii) "has been ours since ancient times, and the prophecies say we must found a colony there" (Hdt. VIII 62,2).[61]

---

[57] "ArchDelt" 29, 1973/74: 487–490.

[58] Thuc. VII 57,2. Cf. Figueira 1991: 223.

[59] Steinhart 2000.

[60] Cf. Figueira 2008: 435–440.

[61] According to later sources, Themistocles had a daughter named Sybaris, and another one named Italia: Plut., *Themistocles* 32,2. Some scholars argue that Herodotus, who lived in Thurii, invented the whole story to legitimize Athenian colonization in the area, and that in reality the occupation of Siris would have been unthinkable in the early 5th century (Blösel 2004: 198–200; Raviola 2007; Prieto, Polleichtner 2007: 184–191). At any rate, Herodotus's story demonstrates that by the 430s BC, the establishment of a colony on the Ionian Gulf was seen as a matter of political strategy.

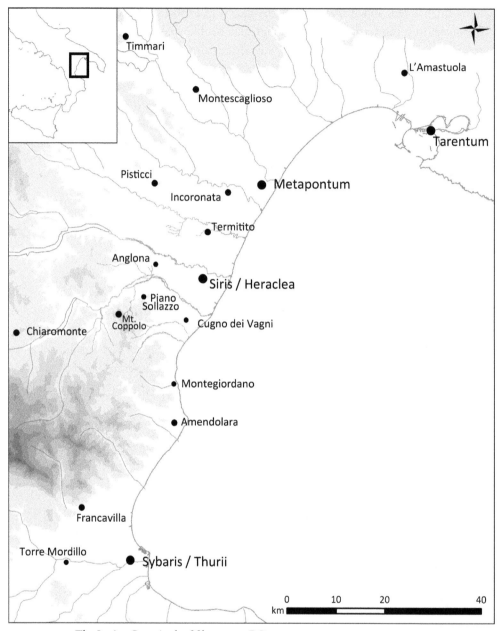

1.2 The Ionian Coast in the fifth century BC.

Thurii lies on the site of ancient Sybaris, which had been destroyed in 510 BC by Croton. A group of survivors had attempted to return with their families (shortly before 476/5 BC, and again in 453 BC), but each time the people of Croton defeated them. In 446/5 BC, the Sybarites called on Athens and Sparta for help, and in 444/3 BC the colony of Thurii was officially established.[62] Diodorus (XII 10,7) describes the layout of the settlement as follows:

[62] On the history of the foundation of Thurii, see Bugno 1999: 112–125; Nafissi 2007.

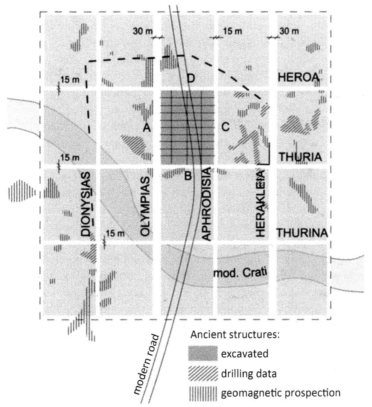

1.3 Thurii: Reconstruction of the urban center on the basis of archaeological data and literary sources (Mertens 2006: fig. 643).

They divided the city lengthwise by four streets, the first of which they named Heracleia, the second Aphrodisia, the third Olympias, and the fourth Dionysias, and breadthwise they divided it by three streets, of which the first was named Heroa, the second Thuria, and the last Thurina. And since the quarters formed by these streets were filled with dwellings, the construction of the city appeared to be good.

(trans. C.H. Oldfather 1989)

Excavations have yielded scattered remains of Classical structures beneath later buildings and alluvial layers that enable the reconstruction of the urban grid and allow comparisons with Diodorus's description which turns out to be fairly reliable (Figure 1.3).[63] Still, how and when the living quarters were filled remains unknown; as excavation data is extremely scarce, the nature and extension of the Classical settlement is open to debate.

In the period immediately after the foundation, a civil war broke out, as Diodorus reports (XII 11,1–4):

[63] Greco 2008; Mertens 2006: 364.

For a short time only did the Thurians live together in peace, and then they fell into serious civil strife, not without reason. The former Sybarites, it appears, were assigning the most important offices to themselves and the lower ones to the citizens who had been enrolled later; their wives they also thought should enjoy precedence among the citizenesses in the offering of sacrifices to the gods, and the wives of the later citizens should take second place to them; furthermore, the land lying near the city they were portioning out in allotments among themselves, and the more distant land to the newcomers. And when a division arose for the causes we have mentioned, the citizens who had been added to the rolls after the others, being more numerous and more powerful, put to death practically all of the original Sybarites and took upon themselves the colonization of the city. Since the countryside was extensive and rich, they sent for colonists in large numbers from Greece, and to these they assigned parts of the city and gave them equal shares of the land. (…) Establishing a democratic form of government, they divided the citizens into ten tribes, to each of which they assigned a name based on the nationality of those who constituted it: three tribes composed of peoples gathered from the Peloponnesus they named the Arcadian, the Achaean, and the Eleian; the same number, gathered from related peoples living outside the Peloponnesus, they named the Boeotian, Amphictyonian, and Dorian; and the remaining four, constituted from other peoples, the Ionian, the Athenian, the Euboean, and the Islander.

(transl. C.H. Oldfather, 1989)

It seems that only about 10 percent of the colonists came from Attica, although two Athenians, Lampon and Xenokritos, were the official leaders. When the Athenians sailed to Sicily in 415 BC, Thurii actually refused to support them (Thuc. VI 44,2 & 61,6–7). In 413 BC, the Athenians were treated as allies again, as shortly before "the party opposed to the Athenians had been driven out by a revolution" (Thuc. VII 33).[64] Aristotle (Pol. 1307a–b) and Diodorus (XII 35) mention a series of revolutions (*staseis*) in the colony, which struggled with political and ethnic factions for several decades after its foundation.

In 390 BC, the city suffered a catastrophic defeat by the Lucanians (Diod. XIV 101). In the following period, Lucanians and Brettioi repeatedly attacked Thurii, although Diodorus's account of a Lucanian conquest should be treated with caution (XVI 15).

Like Thurii, Amphipolis had a mixed population, and besides a few Athenians, there were many settlers from Chalchidike, although the city was officially an Athenian colony founded under the leadership of Hagnon, son of Nikias (337/6 BC).[65] The site lies on a hilltop about five kilometers from the Thracian

[64]   Frisone 2007: 238.
[65]   On the history of Amphipolis cf. Hdt. VII 114; Thuc. IV 102–108; Diod. XII 32; XII 68.

coast on the East bank of the river Strymon, which flows around the city on three sides (hence the name).[66]

Before 437 BC, there existed a small village known as Enneahodoi ("Nine Ways").[67] To the East of Amphipolis lie the Pangaion Mountains with their rich silver deposits. Thracians and Thasians had fought about possession of the region. The Thasians managed to establish a number of settlements along the coast, but Enneahodoi was not among them.

In 476 BC, the Athenian general Cimon captured Eion on the mouth of the river Strymon, an ancient Eretrian settlement that had been the last Persian stronghold in Europe after the retreat of Xerxes in 479 BC. The Athenians aimed to exploit the silver mines of Mount Pangaion and cut timber for their fleet (Thuc. IV 108); they attempted to occupy Enneahodoi in 475 BC and again in 465/4 BC under Leagros and Sophanes, who led a huge army (ten thousand soldiers, according to Diod. XI 70,5) up the Strymon, but they were defeated by local Thracian tribes (the battle took place near Drabeskos; see Thuc. I 100). The Athenians abandoned the plan and only resumed their attempt about thirty years later with Hagnon, who succeeded in capturing the site.

In 424/3 BC, Amphipolis surrendered to the Spartans under Brasidas, who had many followers among the settlers of non-Athenian origin.[68] The Athenians had always been a minority, and some people from other places openly favored Brasidas. Athens attempted to recapture the city under Cleon in 422 BC but failed. Brasidas, who died from a wound after the battle of 422 BC, was honored as the founder-hero of Amphipolis, his grave being situated "on the place where now is the agora" (Thuc. V 11,1).[69] In 357 BC, Philip of Macedonia took the city.

Athenian colonization involved large numbers of people, both colonists and colonized. In 415 BC the Athenians occupied the island of Melos, killed or enslaved the inhabitants (so-called *andrapodismos*), and sent five hundred Athenian colonists there to establish a new city-state based on Athenian "democratic" principles.[70] In the same year, the Athenians sent out an expedition to Sicily with the objective of bringing the island under their control. In the years between about 435 and 415 BC, more than 2,100 Athenians moved to places that were reenforced with Athenian settlers (e.g., Sinope) or captured and recolonized (Poteidaia, Melos).[71] Additionally, 2,700 Athenians

[66] Cf. Asheri 1967; Chatzopoulos 1991; Lorber 1990; Koukouli-Chrysanthaki 2002; Mari 2010.
[67] According to Diodorus XII 68 the site was named Amphipolis as early as 497 BC, when Aristagoras of Miletus attempted to colonize it.
[68] Thuc. IV 102–106.
[69] Mari 2010.
[70] Thuc. V 116; IG XII,3, 1187.
[71] Plut., Pericles XX 1–2 (600 to Sinope); Thuc. II 27 (unknown number of settlers to Aigina); Thuc. II 70 & Diod. XII 46,7 (1,000 *epoikoi* to Potideia); Thuc. V 116 (500 settlers to Melos).

received land-lots on Lesbos.[72] Thus, within less than a generation, about 5,000 Athenian citizens received land outside Attica. Assuming that Athens had no more than 30,000 citizens, nearly 20% of them were directly involved in colonization.[73]

Most of them were probably members of the lower classes. An addendum at the end of the Brea decree states that the colonists shall be *thetes* and *zeugitai*, i.e., members of the two lower tax classes. Members of the class of *thetes*, in particular, could hope to improve their economic and social standing. They were under economic stress in their homeland and thus were ready to face difficulties in becoming part of the ruling class in a new community.[74]

Non-Athenian Colonization in the Second Half of the Fifth Century BC

Athenian colonization and imperialism contributed to a general "race" to establish strategic settlement sites on the part of other city-states such as Sparta and Tarentum. This is evident in the case of Heraclea Trachis, a Spartan colony established during the Peloponnesian War near Thermopylae. The role of Athens is less evident in the case of Heraclea in Lucania, although it does emerge from a careful reading of the sources.

Heraclea Lucana was founded 433/2 BC on the site of the Archaic colony Siris/Polieion (present-day Policoro).[75] Around 560 BC, the Achaean cities of Metapontum, Sybaris, and Croton, who wanted to "chase the Ionians out of Italy" (Iust. X 2,3–4), had destroyed Siris. However, the site continued to be inhabited. Siris probably became part of the empire of Sybaris. When Sybaris too was destroyed (510 BC), Metapontum gained control of the area.[76] After the middle of the fifth century, the site of Policoro seems to have been abandoned for about two decades until Heraclea was founded in 433/2 BC by Tarentum. The foundation of Heraclea was preceded by a war between Tarentum and Thurii over possession of the territory of ancient Siris/Polieion (roughly between 444 and 433 BC). Eventually the two cities ended the war and established a joint colony, which they called Siris as it lay on the river of the same name (not localized); it later became the port of Heraclea.[77]

Heraclea was founded when Tarentum suddenly intervened and "moved the settlement, adding settlers of its own" (Diodorus XII 36,4). From that moment on, Heraclea appears as an *apoikia* of Tarentum only, and there were

[72] Thuc. III 50.
[73] On Athenian demography see Moreno 2007: 28–31.
[74] Cf. Moreno 2007: 143; Figueira 2008: 428–429.
[75] On Siris/Polieion see Osanna 2012a; Verger 2015; contra Bianco, Giardino 2010; Giardino 2010.
[76] Zuchtriegel, forthcoming.
[77] Cf. Prandi 2008.

close relations between the two cities far into the Hellenistic period as findings from Heraclea prove.[78]

The motive for Tarentum's sudden intervention is still the subject of debate. Tarentum had no immediate need to expand its territory, which consisted of about 850 square kilometers.[79] Such a large territory could feed approximately 35,000–45,000 people, a huge number for a Classical polis.[80] Moreover, Tarentum exported many goods, which means that even if it had reached a population of more than 40,000, it might have imported staple foods in return for exported goods.[81]

I therefore believe that Tarentum acted not out of necessity, but from a strategic perspective. During the Peloponnesian War, Thurii and Tarentum were on opposite sides,[82] and hostility between the two was probably still latent in the 430s, in spite of the establishment of a joint colony. Tarentum's intervention has to be seen against this backdrop. It has been argued that it was an internal conflict (*stasis*) in Thurii in 434/3 BC (Diodorus XII 35) that triggered the foundation of Heraclea: according to this view, Tarentum exploited a momentary weakness of Thurii.[83] Yet to my mind, it seems more likely that it was not the presumed weakness of Thurii (before long the conflict had been settled peacefully) but rather the opposite, namely the readiness of Athens and her allies to intervene in Italy that urged Tarentum to act. Between 434 and summer 433 BC, Athens formed an alliance with Corcyra.[84] Thucydides (I 44) explains the motives of the Athenians:

> For they knew that in any case the war with Peloponnesus was inevitable, and they had no mind to let Corcyra and her navy fall into the hands of the Corinthians. Their plan was to embroil them more and more with one another, and then, when the war came, the Corinthians and the other naval powers would be weaker. They also considered that Corcyra was conveniently situated for the coast voyage to Italy and Sicily.
>
> (transl. B. Jowett, 1881)

The last phrase shows that even before the outbreak of the war Athens had concrete plans concerning Italy. The alliance between Athens and Corcyra must have been alarming for Tarentum, especially since the Athenians formed it with clear intentions of embarking on future intervention in southern Italy.

---

[78] Rescigno 2012a (still in the third century BC, *pietra tenera* was imported from Tarentum for a public building at Heraclea; the stonemason came from Tarentum or had worked there before).

[79] Osanna 1992: 13–21; Finocchietti 2009.

[80] Cf. Zuchtriegel 2011a.

[81] Lippolis 1996: 15.

[82] Cf. Diod. XIII 3,4; Thuc. VII 35.

[83] Cataldi 1990: 46; Lombardo 1996: 23; 2009: 136–138; Prandi 2008: 11.

[84] On the date of the treaty see Bengtson 1975, 80–81; Cataldi 1990: 12 (July 433 BC?).

Moreover, the Athenians were also on friendly terms with the Messapian ruler Artas.[85] Against this backdrop, the foundation of Heraclea can be viewed as Tarentum's response to Athenian politics in the West. This would mean that the very establishment of Heraclea was determined by imperialist interests and counter-interests. Tarentum wanted the colonists of Heraclea to occupy the territory of Siris before Thurii and/or Athens could intervene; the colonists did not represent an autonomous self-dependent community, but were subordinated to the geopolitical interests of the mother-city.[86]

The same holds for the colonists of Heraclea Trachinia, founded by the Spartans in 426 BC on the site of ancient Trachis, a Malian settlement mentioned by Homer in the catalog of ships (Il. II 682), seven kilometers from Thermopylae.[87] Trachis had been suffering attacks from neighboring mountain populations and asked Sparta for help. The Spartans intended to make Heraclea a stronghold from where they could control Thermopylae and the channel of Chalkis.

According to Thucydides, the colonists were Spartan citizens, *perioikoi* (inhabitants of Laconia without citizenship), and other Greeks who wanted to take part except for Ionians, Achaeans, and "some other peoples" (Thuc. III 92,5). They were led by three Spartans (Leon, Alkidas, and Damagon). The city was ruled by Spartan governors, until it was captured by the Boiotians and Argives during the Corinthian War (395–386 BC). Soon after the foundation, the Thessalians began to attack the city repeatedly, causing considerable loss of life amongst the population. However, there were also internal problems, as Thucydides reports:

> The Lacedaemonians themselves, in the persons of their governors *(archontes)*, did their full share towards ruining its prosperity and reducing its population, as they frightened away the greater part of the inhabitants by governing harshly and in some cases not fairly, and thus made it easier for their neighbors to prevail against them.
>
> (transl. J.M. Dent, 1910)

The colony apparently had a hierarchic, nondemocratic organization. In 371 BC, Jason of Pherai seized the city, dismantled the fortification walls, and returned the place to the local population.

Deportation and military occupation in Greece contributed to migration and colonization on the borders of the Greek world, as for example in

---

[85] Cf. Thuc. VII 33. Cf. Braccesi 1973/4; M. Lombardo, in Atti del 31° Convegno di Studi sulla Magna Grecia, 97–8. Taranto: Istituto per la Storia e l'Archeologia della Magna Grecia; Cataldi 1990: 78–85. See also IG XIV 672, which seems to testify to an alliance between Thurii and Brindisi in the second half of the 5th century BC. Some critical remarks in Lippolis 1997; Maddoli 2007.

[86] Cf. Figueira 2008: 507.

[87] The main sources are Thuc. III 92–93; Strab. IX 3,13; Diod. XII, 59; Paus. X 22,1.

Adramyttion in Asia Minor and in Tauric Chersonesus, a colony founded during the Peloponnesian War in Crimea. According to Ps.-Skymnos 822–830, the settlers came from Heraclea Pontike and Delos. Thucydides (V 1) reports that the Athenians expelled the inhabitants of Delos in 422 BC, and that some of them settled in Adramyttion, while others went to different places in Asia Minor.[88] Adramyttion in the southern Troas was an ancient town with an important harbor. The Persian Satrap of Daskyleion, Pharnakes, settled some Delian refugees there. The arrival of the Delians (as well as of other possible newcomers) might have contributed to the Hellenization of the site, which later sources refer to as a "Greek city." Another place that received Delian refugees may have been Heraclea Pontica, where they might have participated in an expedition to Chersonesus. In 421 BC, the Athenians allowed the Delians to return (Thuc. V 32,1), although we do not know how many actually did so. If Delians were involved in the colonization of Chersonesus, the most likely date for such a venture is 422/1 BC.[89]

The site was frequented as early as the Late Archaic period, as suggested by finds of pottery fragments, some of which bear Greek inscriptions; however, their dating is still the subject of debate.[90] Archaeological data corroborates the foundation date based on Ps.-Skymnos and Thucydides.[91] From the late fifth century BC onwards, there is evidence for a stable settlement. Chersonesus struck silver and bronze coinage from the early fourth century onwards. Joseph Carter believes that the colony originated in a mixed settlement of Greek and local groups:

> The first substantial evidence of an organized, sizable settlement, in contrast to a polis, dates to the late fifth century BC. It consists of juxtaposed burials of two distinct types in the northern necropolis – a fact that could indicate a mixed settlement of Greeks and natives, though some scholars vigorously deny this possibility. Bodies in the supine position (typical of Greeks) are interspersed with those in a contracted position (found in the Iron Age Kizil-Koba burials), strongly suggesting that natives with their customs intact coexisted and probably cohabited with the Greeks.
> (Carter 2003: 22; the excavation data is unpublished)

Archaeological and epigraphic evidence becomes more abundant only from the mid-fourth century BC onwards.[92] The "Oath of Chersonesus," an inscription dating to the early third century BC (IOSPE I² 401), shows that Chersonesus had a democratic constitution by that time. It remains unclear whether this was the result of a revolution or whether the city was democratic from the outset.[93]

---

[88] Müller 2010: 58–60.
[89] Schneiderwirth 1897.
[90] Posamentir 2005: 105.
[91] Contra Hind 1998: 145, who proposes 377 BC as the foundation date.
[92] Belov 1950; 1981; Posamentir 2007.
[93] Stolba 2005b: 298.

In the fourth century BC, Chersonesus expanded its territory to the area of Kerkinitis, an Archaic Ionian colony north of Chersonesus, and Kalos Limen, a newly established settlement.[94] During the third century BC, local groups repeatedly attacked the city and its territory, and by the end of the second century, Kalos Limen, Kerkinitis, and Teiche (literally "walls" – probably the name of one or more fortified sites) were in the hands of Scythian groups.[95] The city itself had by then become part of the Bosporanian kingdom.

Colonization in Sicily and the Adriatic in the Fourth Century BC

With the return to tyranny in 406 BC, Syracusean colonization revived. In 396 BC, Dionysius the Elder founded Tyndaris and settled six hundred Messenians there, mostly mercenaries.[96] The establishment of the colony on a promontory on the northern coast of Sicily may also have had strategic reasons. Diodorus reports that the indigenous town of Abakainon had to give part of its territory to Tyndaris. The Messenians had initially been sent to Messina, together with people from Locri and Medma, but the Spartans would not tolerate them inhabiting such an important place.

Diodorus sustains that "due to good government" Tyndaris soon reached a population of over five thousand inhabitants. However, the archaeological evidence from the early phases is extremely scarce, and some scholars have even doubted the actual existence of the settlement during the first half of the fourth century BC.[97]

In the following years, Dionysius established new colonies in the Adriatic Sea (Issa, Lissos?, Ancona, Atria: see Figure 1.1).[98] Diodorus (XV 13,1) writes that:

> [H]is idea in doing this was to get control of the Ionian Sea, in order that he might make the route to Epirus safe and have there his own cities which could give haven to ships. For it was his intent to descend unexpectedly with great armaments upon the regions about Epirus and to sack the temple at Delphi, which was filled with great wealth.
>
> (transl. C.H. Oldfather, 1989)

Literary sources on Adriatic colonization are extremely scarce, and some scholars are very skeptical about Syracusean intervention in the Adriatic.[99] The only case where there is some more information is Pharos, a colony of Paros on the

---

[94] Müller 2010: 60–66.
[95] Cf. IOSPE I² 352.
[96] Diod. XV 5,6.
[97] La Torre 2004; Spigo 2005.
[98] Cf. Woodhead 1970.
[99] Cabanes 2008: 176–178.

island of Hvar (Croatia), which the Parians established with aid from Syracuse. Once again our only source is Diodorus (XV 13,4–14,2):

> The Parians, in accordance with an oracle, sent out a colony to the Adriatic, founding it on the island of Pharos, as it is called, with the co-operation of the tyrant Dionysius. He had already dispatched a colony to the Adriatic not many years previously and had founded the city known as Lissus. (…) This year [385 BC] the Parians, who had settled Pharos, allowed the previous barbarian inhabitants to remain unharmed in an exceedingly well fortified place, while they themselves founded a city by the sea and built a wall about it. Later, however, the old barbarian inhabitants of the island took offense at the presence of the Greeks and called in the Illyrians of the opposite mainland. These, to the number of more than ten thousand, crossed over to Pharos in many small boats, wrought havoc, and slew many of the Greeks. But the governor of Lissos appointed by Dionysius sailed with a good number of triremes against the light craft of the Illyrians, sinking some and capturing others, and slew more than five thousand of the barbarians, while taking some two thousand captive.
>
> (transl. C.H. Oldfather, 1989)

Given that Lissos lies more than 200 kilometers from Pharos, Diodorus or his source probably confused it with Issa, which lies less than 50 kilometers away.[100] If this is correct, by the time Pharos was established (385 BC), Issa must have existed already. This was the period immediately after the King's Peace of 387/6 BC, when Pharos's mother-city Paros had become an oligarchy and was under Spartan control. Around the same time, the Spartans aided the Molossians in a war against the Illyrians (Diod. XV 13,3). The foundation of Pharos might have been part of a broader strategy on the part of Sparta and her allies in the region. The island (297 square kilometers) is mountainous, but had a good natural harbor. An indigenous settlement that existed on the site was destroyed by the Greek colonists, as finds of pottery, metal objects, and carbonized wood suggest.[101]

Like Pharos, Issa on the island of Vis had an excellent natural harbor. Vis is the outermost island south of the Promontorium Diomedis and was therefore of strategic importance. A fragment of a *kouros* statue from the middle of the sixth century BC has been found there, but there is no evidence of a stable Greek settlement in the Archaic period.[102] Archaeological data corroborates the hypothesis according to which the colony was established in the first third of the fourth century BC.[103] Issa had an *ekklesia* (assembly) and a *boule* (council) of fifty citizens, as inscriptions demonstrate. The inscriptions also mention

[100] Figueira 2008: 501.
[101] *Pharos* 1995: 51–55.
[102] Milićević Bradač 2007: fig. 34.
[103] Milićević Bradač 2007: 47–48; Cabanes 2008: 177; Figueira 2008: 501. On the question of the mother-city, cf. Ps.-Skymnus 413–414 (Issa *apoikia* of Syracuse).

various magistrates, namely *strategoi*, priests *(hieromnamones)*, *logistoi*, and *grammateis*. In the late fourth or third century BC, Issa established a series of sub-colonies: Tragurion (Trogir) and Epetion (modern Strobeč, south of Split) on the continent, and Korkyra Melaina on the island Korčula,[104] which had a similar political structure.[105]

Assuming that Diodorus's account of the battle of Pharos refers to Issa and not to Lissos, there remain no written sources on the foundation of Lissos (Diodorus would have been the only one). Archaeological evidence is not of much help, as there is almost no material from the Late Classical period. In the Hellenistic period, the settlement consisted of a lower town and a harbor, situated on the River Drin, and an acropolis (Akrolissos) rising up to 413 meters above sea level. The city walls date to the late fourth century BC. As Pierre Cabanes has observed, the fortifications "faced the low valley of the Drin towards the sea – as if its builders had wanted to defend themselves against possible invaders from the sea."[106] This suggests that the walls were not built by Syracusean colonists, but rather by locals who tried to protect themselves against attacks from the sea.

We know of other Greek settlements in the Adriatic, although we are unable to localize them. Finds of bronze coins bearing the head of Herakles and the letters HERAKL show that a colony with the name Heraclea existed in the fourth century BC somewhere in the Adriatic, but we have no idea where it was situated exactly, when it was founded, and where the settlers came from.[107]

Southern France and Spain

According to Strabo (IV 1,5), Greek settlements on the coast of France and Spain such as Rhode, Agathe, and Antipolis were founded by Massalia as "fortresses" and "ramparts against the barbarians." However, the situation was probably more complex, although written sources on Greek settlements in southern France and Spain are extremely scarce, and stories of early foundations belong in the realm of myth.[108] Rhode, for example, was thought to be a Rhodian foundation dating back to before the Olympic games (776 BC: Strabo XIV 2,10). Rhode, Emporion, Agathe, and Antipolis have yielded archaeological evidence from the sixth century onwards. Initially, these sites probably were indigenous settlements or emporia with a mixed population. This is quite evident in the case of Emporion, which originally consisted of

---

[104] Vgl. Polybius XXXII 18; Strabo VII 5,5.
[105] Milićević Bradač 2007: 52–54.
[106] Cabanes 2008: 176–177; cf. Hoxha, Oettel 2011.
[107] Milićević Bradač 2007: 46.
[108] Domínguez 2013.

two separate communities of Greeks and local inhabitants – a *dipolis* (double-city) as Strabo (III 4,8) calls it:

> In former times the Emporitæ dwelt on a small island opposite, now called the old city, but at the present day they inhabit the mainland. The city is double, being divided by a wall, for in past times some of the Indiceti dwelt close by, who, although they had a separate polity to themselves, desired, for the sake of safety, to be shut in by a common enclosure with the Grecians; but at the same time that this enclosure should be two-fold, being divided through its middle by a wall. In time, however, they came to have but one government, a mixture of Barbarian and Grecian laws; a result which has taken place in many other [states].
>
> (transl. G. Bell, 1903)

The unification of the two communities into one political entity may have taken place around 375 BC, when a new city wall was built on the remains of an earlier village, which might have been that of the local community.[109] Around the same period, the site of Rhode was colonized (by Massalia and/or Emporion?), and Agathe had been restructured in the late fifth century BC.[110] Antipolis, which in 155/4 BC belonged to Massalia (Polyb. XXXIII 8,1), might have been colonized in the fourth century BC.

The leading role of Massalia, which continued into the Roman period, might date back to the fifth and fourth centuries BC, when the Massaliotes re-colonized and reinforced a series of existing communities (Greek and indigenous) which Strabo later considered Massaliote fortresses.[111] Massalia had a relatively small territory (about 70 square kilometers), which was well suited to olive and vine cultivation but less so to grain production (Strabo IV 1,5).[112] Yet the city grew constantly from the moment of its foundation around 600 BC. Thus, population pressure may have been one of the reasons for the establishment or occupation of settlements along the coast. On the other hand, some of these settlements were rather small (for example, Emporion 5 hectares, Agathe 4.25 hectares, Olbia 2.7 hectares), which means that while they may have been important military bases, they may not have been very significant demographically.

Philip II and Greek Colonization in the Second Half of the Fourth Century BC

Traditional Greek colonization continued way into the Early Hellenistic period. For example, during the fourth/third century BC, Issa founded several subcolonies (Korkyra Melaina, Epetion, Tragurion), and Athens planned to establish a

---

[109] Sanmartí 1993: 88–89.
[110] Bats 1990; Puig Griessenberger 2010; 2015.
[111] Bats 1992; A.J. Domíngues in Hansen, Nielsen 2004: 162–163.
[112] Arcelin 1986.

colony somewhere in the Adriatic, although the plan was never carried out. Around 300 BC, Greeks settled in Tanais on the Azov Sea. Probably from a relatively early date, maybe from the very beginning, Tanais consisted of two communities that lived together on the same site: the Greeks led by a *hellenarches*, and the local *Tanaitai*, who had their own *archon*.[113] Later, Tanais developed into one of the most important slave markets of the ancient world.[114] This shows that the establishment of indigenous and Greek mixed settlements did not preclude exploitation and enslavement of local populations in the hinterland. In Tanais, Scythians sold other Scythians to Greek slave traders, but it was Greek overseas trade and military force that triggered the boom in the North Pontic slave trade.

On the other hand, under Philip II of Macedonia, colonization started to develop towards new, Hellenistic forms. Philip was the first to name a colony after himself (Philippi), and – more importantly – the first to establish colonies far away from the coast. Philip's inland settlements in modern Bulgaria, Northern Greece, and Albania (Figure 1.1) marked a totally different phenomenon from earlier Greek settlements that were usually situated no further than 5 kilometers from the coast. Macedonian inland settlements in Bulgaria served as strongholds after Philip's victory over the Thracians under Kersebleptes in 342/1 BC. There is another peculiarity about these settlements, namely that Philippopolis and Kabyle were settled by "criminals." According to Theopompus (FgrHist 100 F27), Philip relocated 2,000 perjurers, criminals, and sycophants from Macedonia to Philippopolis. Strabo (VII 6,2) recounts that Kabyle was settled by *ponerotátoi* (literally "villains" or "wicked people").[115] Figueira (2008: 488) suggests that the settlers of Philippopolis and Kabyle were not necessarily criminals, but probably socially and/or politically suspect Macedonians or locals. Since Philippopolis and Kabyle have not yielded any significant evidence of early settlement phases, we have no idea how these settlements were actually structured. However, the idea of combining imperialist expansion with punishment and reeducation is noteworthy as such, especially as it is attested as early as the late fourth century BC, i.e., the time in which Theopompus lived and wrote. Whether or not Philip actually deported criminals to newly founded colonies, the idea of carrying out such a plan was in the air.

Subalternity in the Colonies

However, Macedonian penal colonies may be less innovative than they initially appear. Greek colonies had always been a means of getting rid of certain groups, for example in the case of the colonists of Tarentum, the so-called

---

[113] Ivantchik 2008.
[114] Strabo XI 2,2.
[115] Archibald 1998: 235–9.

partheniai, who were degraded or second-class citizens in Sparta.[116] Often it was socially marginalized or subaltern groups who were forced to leave. The colonists of Cyrene wanted to return to Thera but when arriving were shot at and told to set out again, which they did under constraint (Hdt. IV 156,3). Emigrating to an *apoikia* was never an easy decision. In all periods settlers were under pressure, be it economic, political, or cultural. Xenophon's attempt to found a polis on the south coast of the Black Sea (Anabasis V 6,15–19) failed not because of local resistance, but because his Greek companions preferred to return to their native places. Landless Athenians who went to Brea did so because they wanted to become landowners, while at the same time the ruling class needed valuable, self-sustaining defenders of Athenian interests in the northern Aegean. Of course, neither the colonists of Cyrene nor those of Brea were criminals, but they might well have been "socially and politically suspect." In the majority of cases, the settlers were under some sort of stress: They did not really want to go, but rather had to; often they had no idea of where exactly they were going (cf. Hdt. IV 150 on the foundation of Cyrene: "… they did not know where Libya was, and were afraid to send a colony out to an uncertain destination"); if things went badly they died in battles (Dorieus in western Sicily around 510 BC, Enneahodoi 456 BC, Epidamnos 435 BC, Thurii 390 BC), or had to give up after a while because they were starving or facing other difficulties (Pyxous). Colonization was a dirty and dangerous business. The colony as a community of free and equal men, and as a new beginning, remained an ideal. The written sources show that Greek colonists were instrumentalized for political and military purposes and had to struggle for survival. Nonetheless, we are still talking here about the elite in the colonies. Truly subaltern groups do not even feature in the sources, except for some very rare instances. Their situation must have been even more precarious and dangerous than that of citizen-colonists. To find out more about these groups, we need to engage with archaeology, although our knowledge of Classical settlements is very fragmentary. The field survey and the recent excavations in Heraclea in Lucania are extremely helpful: Heraclea is now one of the best known examples of a Classical colony, and one of the few where there is considerable data both for the urban center and the hinterland. However, a survey of other Classical colonies shows that we have more data than might be suspected. As there are no archaeological overviews or handbooks on Classical colonization, I include here a list of Classical colonies with some brief remarks on the available evidence (Table 1.1).[117]

---

[116] Ephorus ap. Strabo VI 3,3 (=FGrHist 70 F216): "… they [the Spartans] would not honor the Partheniai with civic rights like the rest, on the ground that they had been born out of wedlock."

[117] Based on Figueira 2008. Regional overviews: Mertens 2006 (Western Greece in the eighth to 5th centuries BC); for the Black Sea region see Tsetskhladze 1998; 2008; on the archaeology of Athenian colonies and cleruchies see Moreno 2007; Culasso Gastaldi, Marchiandi 2012.

TABLE 1.1 *Greek colonies and cleruchies 480–330 BC*

Name (year)	Settlement	Colonizer	References	Archaeological data
Himera (476/5 BC)	Original population expelled; Doric colonists	Theron of Akragas	Diod. XI 48,6–8; 49, 3–4	Excavations of living quarters in the upper city, but chronology has been questioned (Allegro 2008); necropolis (largely unpublished); survey in the hinterland (Belvedere *et al.* 2002).
Aitna & Naxos (476/5 BC)	Original population expelled; 5,000 colonists from Syracuse; 5,000 from the Peloponnese	Hieron of Syracuse	Diod. XI 49,1–2; Pind. fr. 105a	Scarcely known; it is still debated whether Aitna lay on the same site as Katane (excavations on the alleged acropolis have yielded pottery fragments from the late fifth century BC but no structures: Frasca 2000: 121); coinage starts only around 461 BC when the former inhabitants of Katane, who had been expelled by Hieron, returned (Boehringer 2008); in Naxos a Classical to Hellenistic living quarter has been excavated (*insula C4*); the houses have rubble-work foundation walls that are not very well preserved, and it is difficult to identify older phases (Lentini 1998); probable reorganization of the town during the first half of the fifth century BC: the urban area was divided into blocks of 39 x 156 to 168 meters (120 x 480 Doric feet), which suggests that the grid was laid out in the years of the Doric colonization under Hieron in the years 476–470 BC (Pelagatti 1976/7: 541; Lentini, Garraffo 1995: 5; Mertens 2006: 343–348).
Pyxous (471/70 BC)	Greek colonists	Mikythos of Rhegion	Diod. XI 59,4; Strabo VI 1,1	Scarcely known; because medieval and early modern settlement (modern Policastro), very little is known of the Classical period; some more materials from the fourth and third centuries BC; the medieval city walls rest on older polygonal walls, which were ascribed to the foundation period, but might actually be much later (Bencivenga Trillmich 1988; Johannowsky 1992).

Eion (476/5 BC)	Natives dislodged?	Athens	Plut., Cim.VII 1–3;VIII 2	Not identified.
Skyros (476/5 BC)	Native Dolopians dislodged? Athenian settlers	Athens	Thuc. I 98,2; Diod. XI 60,2; Plut. Cim.VIII 3–7	Athenian settlement not identified.
Kamarina (461/60 BC)	Returnees that were exiled under Hieron	Helped by Gela and Syracuse	Diod. XI 76,4–5	Extensive excavations in the urban center (cf. Pace 1927; Mertens 2006: 351–354; Bonanno Aravantinos, Pisani 2014); city walls and a tower at the harbor (*Torre A*) date to the fifth century BC; so-called West Stoa on the *agora* was built soon after 461 BC, so-called North Stoa added during the second half of the fifth century; the living quarters consist of regular blocks measuring 34.50 x 134 meters, each one containing two rows of house plots; houses date to the fourth century or later (Mertens 2006: 351–54); south of the city, a Classical necropolis with 5,000 tombs has been excavated starting in 1904 (Lanza 1990; Salibra 2014; Sulosky Weaver 2015); on the site of the Archaic necropolis of Rifiscolaro east of the city, rubble walls and streets form rectangular parcels; in the same area, three Classical farmsteads were excavated (Di Stefano 1996: 26; 2012; 2014); parcels and buildings are oriented in the same way as the urban blocks and are therefore thought to date back to 461 BC or shortly after; the land plots measure about 210 x 270 meters (270 meters equals twice the length of the urban blocks: Di Stefano 1996: 26–28) and contained parallel water drains (mentioned by Pind., Olymp.V 12–15?).
Andros, Eretria, Karystos? Naxos (453–448 BC)	Cleruchies, contingents of 250–500 *klerouchoi*	Athens	Plut. Per. XI 5; Diod. XI 88,3	Colonial settlement not visible in the archaeological record.

(continued)

TABLE 1.1 (*continued*)

Name (year)	Settlement	Colonizer	References	Archaeological data
Chersonese (448–446 BC)	Reorganization of the Archaic colonies, arrival of 1,000 *epoikoi*	Athens	Plut. Per. XI 5; XIX 1; Diod. XI 88,3	Archaeologically scarcely known; location and structure of the urban centers of Paktye, Agora/Chersonesus and Krithotè unknown (cf. Gallotta 2010).
Brea (446/5? BC)	Natives dislodged, contingent of 1,000 colonists	Athens	IG I³ 46	Not located (somewhere in Thrace).
Thurii (446/5–444/3 BC)	Native Greeks integrated, later dislodged/killed; settlers from all over Greece	Panhellenic under Athenian leadership	Diod. XII 9,1; Strabo VI 1,13	Excavations in the urban center difficult (alluvial deposits), some tombs (tumuli) and rural sites have been excavated in the *chora* (Coscia 2012); extensive survey in the 1960s (Quilici, Pala, De Rossi 1968/69), recently intensive surveys in parts of the territory (Attema, Burgers, van Leusen 2010; Carafa, Luppino 2011). Not a single house of the Classical period has been excavated. A Classical farmstead was excavated north of Thurii (loc. Stombi); it is said to date to around 400 BC, but the finds have not yet been published.
Histiaia/Oreos (c. 445 BC)	Natives expelled (to Macedonia); 1,000 or 2,000 colonists/cleruchs?	Athens	Thuc. I 114,3; VII 57,2	Scarcely known.
Amphipolis (437/6 BC)	Natives defeated; dislodged or killed; 10,000 colonists from Athens and other areas	Athens	Thuc. IV 102,3; Diod. XII 32	Archaeological excavations (1919–1926 and 1956 until present) have revealed impressive remains of the Byzantine settlement that was much smaller than the Hellenistic and Imperial city. Large parts of the ancient city walls are still visible (dating unclear: Classical or Hellenistic?). Inside the walls, excavations brought to light the sanctuaries of Clio and Atis as well as the gymnasium (Hellenistic), outside the northern city walls

the Thesmophorion of Demeter. The main sanctuary of Amphipolis was probably that of Artemis Tauropolos, which has not been located so far; maybe it lay on the acropolis (Koukouli-Chrysanthaki 2002: 57). Remains of dwellings dating to between the fourth century BC and the Imperial period on various sites within the walled area (Peristeri, Zographou, Darakis 2006). North of the city extremely well preserved wooden bridge of the Classical period (Lazaridis 1997: 32–36). In 1983, discovery of a necropolis of the late fifth and fourth centuries BC east of the city (114 tombs, largely unpublished: Lazaridis 1983; 1984; 1997: 72–73). New excavations have led to the discovery of other tombs of the Classical period. The extension of the territory of Amphipolis and the rural settlement are unknown.

[Epidamnos] (435 BC)	Abortive colonization; colonists perish	Corinth	Thuc. I 25,1–26; II 27,1	—
Astakos (435/4 BC)	Colony on the site of an older settlement?	Athens	Diod. XII 34; cf. Moreno 2007: 143; 337	Colonial settlement not visible in the archaeological record.
Sinope (430s BC)	Local population reinforced, 600 Athenian settlers dividing up the houses and lands which the tyrant and his followers had formerly occupied	Athens	Plut, Per. XX 1–2	Colonial settlement not visible in the archaeological record.
Siris (430s BC)	Joint colony	Tarentum & Thurii	see above	Not identified.

(continued)

37

TABLE 1.1 *(continued)*

Name (year)	Settlement	Colonizer	References	Archaeological data
Heraclea Lucania (433/2 BC)	Name and place of the settlement changed; settlers from Tarentum added	Taras	see above	Excavations in the urban center in three zones: Castello Hill (c. 28 hectares), the Varatizzo Valley, and South Plateau (c. 60 hectares). Sanctuaries of Demeter, Aphrodite (?), Dionysus and Apollo/Artemis (?) in the Varatizzo Valley; Athena (?) on the Castello Hill (Osanna 2008); Castello Hill fortified (first half fourth century BC?: Neutsch 1967: 110–118), later also South Plateau (Tagliente 1986a: second quarter fourth century?). Living quarters with regular house blocks on the Castello Hill (Area A and Area B, excavated structures mostly Hellenistic) and South Plateau (aerial photography: Schmiedt, Chevallier 1959; Giardino 1998; Ditaranto 2010); three suburban necropoleis known: the East Necropolis (unpublished), the South Necropolis with more than one thousand burials (partially published: Pianu 1990; Lanza 2012; 2015), and the West necropolis located next to the Archaic necropolis at the foot of the Castello Hill (Madonnelle, Schirone: Archaic burials have been partially published: Berlingò 1986; 1993; 2005; 2010); rescue excavations in the *chora* have led to the discovery of a number of farmsteads and sanctuaries (De Siena, Giardino 1994; 2001; Bianco 2000); two bronze tablets found on the banks of the Agri River (IG XIV, 645) deal with the lease of sacred land (fourth/third century BC: Uguzzoni, Ghinatti 1968); extensive field survey in the years 1961–1963 (Quilici 1967); since 2012 intensive field survey around S. Maria Anglona and urban center (Zuchtriegel 2012b; 2015).

Place (date)	Description	Power	Sources	Comment
Aigina (431 BC)	Natives expelled (some of them were settled in Thyrea on the Peloponnese by the Spartans); Athenian *epoikoi*	Athens	Thuc. II 27,1; Diod. XII 44,1	Colonial settlement not visible in the archaeological record.
Poteidaia (430/29 BC)	Natives expelled; 1,000 *epoikoi*	Athens	Thuc. II 70,4; Diod. XII 46,7; IG I³ 514	Colonial settlement not visible in the archaeological record.
Lesbos (427 BC)	Cleruchy; natives expropriated, land divided into 2,700 lots for Athenian *klerouchoi* and 300 *kleroi* for the sanctuaries	Athens	Thuc. III 50,2; IG I³ 66–7	No immediate change visible in the archaeological record.
Heraclea Trachinia (426 BC)	Spartan colonists, reinforced by *perioikoi* and allies	Sparta	Thuc. III 92,1–3; 93,2; Diod. XII 59,3–5	Site has been identified, but is scarcely known apart from the city walls, which are difficult to date; inhabited until Late Antiquity; restoration of city walls under Justinian (Béquignon 1937: 251–260; Malkin 1994a: 219–235).
Adramyttion (422 BC)	Exiled Delians added to local population, many of the new-comers later ambushed by Persians	Pharnakes (Satrap of Daskyleion)	Thuc. V,1; 32,1; VIII 108,4	No change visible in the (scarce) archaeological record.

(continued)

TABLE 1.1 (continued)

Name (year)	Settlement	Colonizer	References	Archaeological data
Chersonesus Taurike (422? BC)	Colonists from Heraclea Pontike and Delos	Heraclea Pontike	Ps.-Skymnos 822–830 (851–856 in Dittrich's edition)	Excavations in the urban center (city-walls, harbor) and in the necropolis (numerous stelae); excavations and survey in the *chora*; ancient Greek land division through streets and rubble walls still visible in the landscape (Carter 2003; 2008: 180–186); state of preservation unique. During a systematic field survey in the *chora* numerous sites were identified, most of them isolated farmsteads; several of them were also excavated (Carter 2003).
Torone (422 BC)	Enslavement/ capture of local population; garrison/ resettlement?	Athens	Thuc. V 3,2–4; Diod. XII 73,3	Colonial settlement not visible in the archaeological record.
Skione (421 BC)	*andrapodismos*; settled by Plateans	Athens	Thuc. V 32,1	Colonial settlement not visible in the archaeological record.
Melos (416/15 BC)	*andropodismos*; 500 Athenian colonists	Athens	Thuc. V 116; IG I³ 1505	Colonial settlement not visible in the archaeological record.
Anchialos (5th century BC?)	Stronghold of Apollonia?	Apollonia Pontike		Scarcely known.
Agathe (late 5th century BC?)	Recolonization or reinforcement of existing community?	Massalia?	Ps-Skymnos 202–8; Strabo IV 1,5–6	The site was probably an indigenous or mixed community (remains of mudbrick buildings; new building technique (stone foundations) and an urban grid might date back to Massaliote colonization in the late fifth century BC (Nickels 1995; Ugolini 2012); in the territory (about 200 square kilometers?), the existence of at least 1,500 regular plots has been hypothesized (Clavel-Lévêque 1982; Guy 1995).

Messina (c. 396 BC)	1,000 colonists from Locri; 4,000 from Medma; 600 Messenians (later removed to Tyndaris)	Dionysius I of Syracuse	Diod. XIV 78,4–5	Scarcely known, no traces of recolonization visible in the archaeological record.
Tyndaris (c. 396 BC)	600 Messenians from Zakynthos and Naupaktos	Dionysius I of Syracuse	Diod. XIV 78,5	Early fourth century BC scarcely attested (Consolo Langher 1977; Spigo 2005).
[Kallatis] (394/3? BC)	Colony	Heraclea Pontike	Ps.-Skymnos 761–762	According to Ps.-Skymnos foundation in the time of Amyntas of Macedonia, but which one? Archaeological evidence points to settlement in the sixth century BC.
Lissos (c. 385 BC?)	?	Dionysius I of Syracuse?	Diod. XV 13,1–3	Early fourth century BC scarcely attested; Hellenistic fortifications.
Issa (c. 385 BC?)	Colony	Dionysius I of Syracuse	Ps.-Skymnos 413–414	Excavations in the urban center (c. 16 hectares) have brought to light parts of the fortifications, remains of houses and numerous tombs east and west of the city (largely unpublished), dating to the late fourth century onwards; grave goods consisted primarily of Gnathia style vases produced on the site. During the third and second centuries BC, local workshops produced painted grave stelae (Milićević Bradač 2007: 51); intensive field survey begun in 1992: relatively dense rural settlement during the Imperial period, but only three 'Greek' sites, all of which are Hellenistic (Gaffney, Kirigin 2006); the city coined money in bronze and silver from the fourth century BC; coins of Issa found in many places in the region, for example in Pharos and in the area of Salona as well as in Novalja on the island of Pag and in Plavno, north of Knin, more than 50 kilometers inland (Visonà 1995; Milićević

(continued)

TABLE 1.1 (*continued*)

Name (year)	Settlement	Colonizer	References	Archaeological data
				Bradač 2007: 48–49): shipwreck at Cape Krava, at the entrance to the port of Issa, with numerous Italiote amphorae of the third/second century BC (Miličević Bradač 2007: 50; see also Zaninović 2004); on economy and money circulation see Visona 1995; Bonačić Mandinić, Visona 2002.
Pharos (385 BC)	Colony	Paros, aided by Dionysius I	Diod. XV 13,4	Urban center (fortification, houses) partly known through excavations (Gaffney *et al.* 1997; Kirigin 2006); remains of a Greek fortification wall proved to be Late Imperial though; corner of a wall with 3 meters thickness in the southeastern part of the site is Late Classical/Hellenistic; wall in the northern part ("Trench III"), approximately 0.4 meters thick, dated on the basis of pottery finds to the early fourth century BC – in both cases the stratigraphy has not yet been published (Kirigin 2006: 48–60); remains of houses in various parts of the city; unclear whether there was a regular urban grid (*Pharos* 1995: 112; Kirigin 2006: 58–61); urban necropolis virtually unknown; extremely well preserved ancient land division that is still visible in the landscape: the major division lines form rectangles of c. 181 x 902 meters (16.3 hectares), corresponding to 1 x 5 *stadia* (Stančič, Slapšak 1988); two watch towers (localities Maslinovik and Tor) datable to the fourth century BC (Kirigin, B., Popović, P. 1988). In 1987, an intensive field survey was begun in the hinterland of Pharos; few Greek sites compared to the number of sites dating to the Imperial period, although the total number of pottery fragments of the Hellenistic period supersedes that of the Imperial period (Bintliff, Gaffney 1988; Kirigin 2006).

Adria?, Ancona (late 380s BC?)	Colony, Ancona settled by refugees from Syracuse	Dionysius I of Syracuse	Strabo V 4,2; Pliny Nat. hist. III 12,111	Ancona: fourth century scarcely attested.
Emporion (c. 400–375 BC?)	Recolonization or reinforcement	Massalia	Ps-Skymnos 204; Strabo III 4,8	Reorganization in the early fourth century BC archaeologically attested (houses, city walls: Sanmartí 1993; Oller Guzmán 2013; Castanyer, Santos, Tremoleda 2015), possibly as a result of Massaliote recolonization or reinforcement of the settlement that existed from around 600 BC; traces of a land division, maybe of the fourth century BC, in the countryside (Plana 1994).
Rhode (c. 375 BC?)	Colony	Massalia? (and Emporion?)	Ps-Skymnos 205–6; Strabo II 4,8; XIV 2,10	The site is overbuilt by the modern settlement of Cuitadella de Roses; frequented from the late sixth century BC onward; fourth century: remains of house foundations consisting of large stones and pottery finds; the layout of the settlement is unclear; the site was completely restructured in the third century BC: regular grid and fortification walls (Puig Griessenberger 2010; 2015).
Krenides (360/59 BC)	Colonists from Thasos and other places in Greece	Thasos	Diod. XVI 3,7; Isoc. VIII 24	Not visible in the archaeological record (see Philippi).
Philippi (356/5 BC)	= Krenides, renamed and reinforced with Macedonian settlers	Philip II of Macedonia	Diod. XVI 3,7; Isoc. VIII 24	Fourth century scarcely attested (largely overbuilt in the Imperial period).

(continued)

TABLE 1.1 (continued)

Name (year)	Settlement	Colonizer	References	Archaeological data
Samos (366/5–352/1 BC)	Reinforcement of the population with Athenian *klerouchoi*; later expulsions	Athens	See discussion in Figueira 2008	Colonial settlement not visible in the archaeological record.
Tauromenion (358/7 BC)	Settlement of refuges from Naxos (destroyed by Dionysius)	Andromachos of Tauromenion	Diod. XVI 7,1	Fourth century scarcely attested.
Heraclea Lynkestis (c. 352 BC?)	Illyrian and Macedonian settlers	Philip II of Macedonia	Steph. Byz. s.v. Heraclea; Diod. XVI 8,1	Fourth century scarcely attested/overbuilt in the Imperial period.
Kalos Limen (fourth century BC)	Colony	Chersonesus Taurike?		Excavations and survey in the hinterland.
Sestos (c. 346 BC)	*andrapodismos*; klerouchoi sent to Sestos and other places on the Chersonese	Athens	Diod. XVI 34,3–4	Not traceable.
Philippoupolis, Astraia, Doberos, Heraclea Sintike (after 346/5 BC)	Macedonian and Greek settlers, many of them mercenaries	Philip II of Macedonia	Strabo VII fr. 36	Not identified, except for Heraclea which is located approximately in northern Greece, south of the modern village of Rupite (Bulgaria).

Place	Population	Founder	Sources	Notes
Philippopolis, Kablye (c. 342 BC)	Both places are said to have been settled by politically or socially suspect Macedonians	Philip II of Macedonia	Pliny Nat. hist. IV 11,41; Plut. Mor. 520b; FgrHist 115 F110 (Theopompus) (Philippopolis); Strabo VII 6,2 ("Kalybe"); Diod. XVI 71,1–2	Excavations at Philippopolis (city-walls, Imperial necropolis) and Kabyle; fourth century in both cases, scarcely known.
Alexandropolis	Mixed population	Alexander of Macedonia	Plut. Alex. IX 1	Not localized.
Antipolis (fourth century BC?)	Colony	Massalia	Ps-Skymnos 216; Strabo IV 1,5	Site lies under modern Antibes; Archaic and Classical materials and inscriptions found in the area might belong to an indigenous settlement or emporion that was occupied by Massalia in the Classical or Early Hellenistic period (Bats 1990; Gras 2003).
Olbia (340/30 BC?)	Colony?	Massalia	Ps-Skymnos 216; Strabo IV 1,5	City wall and regular grid on a rectangle of 165 x 165 meters attested from the third quarter of the fourth century BC (Bats et al. 1995); the territory (only 305 hectares?) divided into regular lots (Benoit 1985).
Unknown in the Adriatic (325/4 BC)	?	Athens	GHI 200	Not localized (maybe the plan was never carried out).
Korkyra Melaina (fourth/third century BC)	Several hundred colonists	Issa	Syll.³ 141	Island known (Korčula), asty not localized. On numismatic evidence see Visona 2005.

TWO

HUTS AND HOUSES: A QUESTION OF IDEOLOGY?

Living spaces clearly play a crucial role in defining and enforcing social hierarchies.[1] Architecture is the expression of power, and power entails the possibility of dominance and subjugation. The question is what this meant for colonial settlements where houses and workshops had to be built up from scratch. Was the structure of dwellings a matter of urban planning and political debate on the part of the colonists? Or was it simply a question of survival where ideological issues were secondary, or even irrelevant? To what extent were social hierarchies enforced through domestic architecture?

In *The Human Condition* (1958), Hannah Arendt argues that for the ancient Greeks, political interaction had to be spatially and functionally separated from the necessities of daily life, which were confined to the household sphere. While the household sphere was characterized by command and obedience, social freedom and equality could be experienced in the political sphere outside the house – of course only by free men.[2] The fundamental opposition between private houses and public space, as implied by Arendt, contrasts with the viewpoint of Hoepfner and Schwandner, according to whom the layout and structure of Classical dwelling houses was a matter of political deliberation and democratic city planning. Hoepfner and Schwandner (1994) argue that the settlers determined the construction of standardized houses at the moment of

[1] Trümper 2011; Bintliff 2014.
[2] Arendt 1958: 22–37.

46

the foundation of a city, and that they commissioned an architect to ensure the uniform and efficient construction of the houses. They further argue that the structure of the houses reflected the social roles and identities of the household members. According to this hypothesis, "type houses" of the Classical period contained rooms for slaves (separated by sex), women's rooms (*gynaikonitis*) in the upper floor, and *androes* or men's rooms for symposia.[3] In this interpretation, the standardization of houses leads to the standardization of social roles and hierarchies: type houses codify the position of slaves and women within the household. Slaves have a shelter, but they can also be locked up; women have to stay in the house (at least in theory),[4] but they are also in charge of important rituals in the central *oikos* room around the hearth.

However, the idea that social relations had an impact on, and can be reconstructed from, house designs is highly questionable.[5] Furthermore, archaeological evidence suggests that house designs were standardized long after the foundation of a colony, if at all. As I argue in this chapter, it is likely that the division of residential quarters into standardized plots took place shortly after the foundation, but the buildings as such do not give the impression of fixed types, especially in the early phases.

CHRONOLOGY AND DEVELOPMENT

Almost all the house remains excavated on the Castello hill at Heraclea belong to the Hellenistic and Imperial periods (Figures 2.1 and 2.2). Yet in several cases, the house blocks, or *insulae*, are divided into regular plots, as would be expected in the foundation period. The house plots measured about 17.9 x 11.4 to 13.4 meters or 55 x 35 to 40 Doric feet, i.e., about 220 square meters (Figure 2.3).[6] At some point, parts of the blocks were reorganized to form larger plots of 17.9 x 17.9 meters (320 square meters), which usually lie on the eastern side of the *insulae*, perhaps because it was considered the better area (Figure 2.4). However, the excavations date back to the 1960s, and there is not much documentation on the stratigraphy.

New excavations in one of the blocks partly explored in the 1960s *(insula* I) demonstrate that large parts of the Castello hill were leveled during the early third century BC, with the result that many Classical layers and structures were destroyed.[7] Two foundation walls along the street between *insulae* IV and V southwest of Area A are the only remains of domestic architecture that survive from the late fifth century BC in the entire area excavated so far.[8] They

[3]   Hoepfner, Schwandner 1994: 327–330.
[4]   Katz 1995.
[5]   Shipley 2005; Trümper 2011.
[6]   Giardino 1998.
[7]   Osanna *et al.* 2015.
[8]   Adamesteanu, Dilthey 1978: 521.

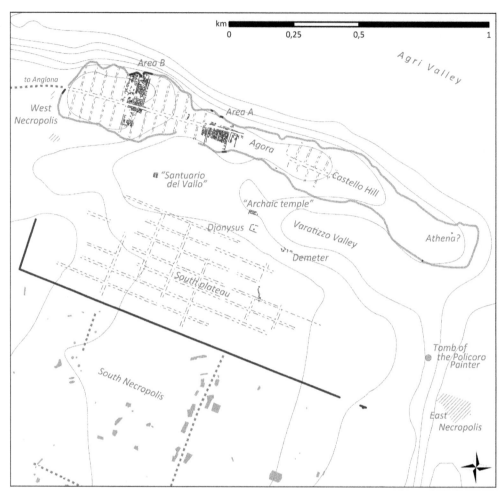

2.1 Heraclea in Lucania: Urban center.

stand on a layer of yellow clay that covers the remains of archaic structures. If the dating of the walls is correct (as I believe it is), this would mean that the grid plan of streets throughout the Castello hill goes back to the early years of the colony.

The southern quarters of the city were also divided into regular blocks, which measure 110 x 55 meters, or 336 x 168 Doric feet, and are visible from aerial photographs (Figures 2.1 and 2.5).[9] The existence of a regular grid plan in this part of the city has been confirmed by recent excavations near the hospital of Policoro.[10] The excavations brought to light one of the streets running east-west. It is c. 6.0 meters or 18.3 feet wide. Hence, the width of the blocks must have been 150 feet. Their internal structure remains unknown, as does

9   Schmiedt, Chevallier 1959.
10   Bianco 2012; Giardino, Calvaruso 2015.

2.2 Heraclea, Area A, from northwest. (Courtesy of F. Giulietti & M. Turci: Laboratorio di Meccanica del Volo, Università di Bologna.)

their precise dating. It is likely that the settlement was initially concentrated on the Castello plateau and that the south plateau was only added during the first half of the fourth century, when it was also fortified.

Although considerable parts of Area A on the Castello hill were leveled and many buildings were completely restructured in the Hellenistic period, excavations in this area shed new light on Classical colonization and urban planning. Surprisingly, centuries after the foundation of the colony, a number of houses were built on standardized house plots. Moreover, they follow specific patterns in their layout. Such features are often seen as typical of the foundation period of a colony; here they are found in a much later period. What is even more surprising is that remains of earlier building phases, though extremely scarce and not well datable, appear to be less standardized than the Hellenistic house blocks.

The old excavations reveal a very complex situation and are not well documented; however, analysis of building techniques makes it possible to distinguish between older and more recent structures, although no absolute chronology can be established on these grounds. As Dinu Adamesteanu has observed, the foundation walls of the early phases, including those of the late fifth century BC, were made only of pebbles, while later structures are made of pebbles, fragments of roof tiles, and pottery fragments (Figure 2.6).

2.3 Heraclea, Area A: Hypothetical house plots.

Very few walls were made of reused blocks of Carparo stone. The upper
parts of the walls were probably made of mud bricks.

Figure 2.7 shows walls without tiles and pottery fragments in Area A, i.e.,
walls that are of a relatively early date. They suggest that a series of houses in
Area A had a roughly standardized layout: a row of shops, sometimes with separate entrances; a courtyard; and another row of rooms, probably comprising
the *oikos*, i.e., the central room that housed the hearth of the house. *Andro(nes)* or
men's rooms for symposia are not attested in any of the houses. It is not possible to identify one fixed type, as the layout and dimensions vary from house to
house, especially with regard to the courtyard and the *oikos*-complex.

At the same time, other houses in Area A were built according to a different
scheme and on larger plots. These houses usually have a peristyle courtyard.
The peristyle houses do not seem to be random modifications of older buildings, since they regularly occupy standardized lots of c. 17.9 x 17.9 meters. In
addition, they usually lie on the eastern side of the *insulae* (Figure 2.4).

What does this mean? Were there at some point two plot sizes and two different house types? Or are there chronological differences that we fail to see

0   25   50   100
m

2.4 Heraclea, Area A: Hypothetical house plots.

in the archaeological record? Were new parcels added as new settlers arrived during the fourth and third centuries BC? An inscription from 340–330 BC, in which Nikomachos asks the oracle of Zeus in Dodona whether he should "enroll (*apographesthai*) in Tarentum instead of Heraclea," suggests that settlers continued to arrive throughout the fourth century BC. The name Heraclea appears on two more inscriptions from Dodona, though one of them probably refers to Heraclea in the Adriatic, as the Adriatic colony P(h)aros is mentioned on the reverse.[11] Perhaps colonization was much more processual and gradual than we are used to thinking. Rather than a single event (the "foundation"), colonization could be conceptualized as a gradual process that involved "colonial" phenomena such as the creation of regular house plots, even long after the arrival of the first settlers.

Hellenistic houses in Area A show that standardization is by no means limited to one fixed house type and that new types could be introduced many generations after the foundation of a colony. In other words, the standardization of

---

[11] Vokotopoulou 1991: 81–83.

2.5 Heraclea (modern Policoro): Aerial photo, 1964. (Courtesy of *Archivio fotografico della Soprintendenza Archeologia, Belle Arti e Paesaggio della Basilicata*.)

2.6 Heraclea, Area A ("*Scavi baracche*"): Classical street flanked by rubble walls (fifth century BC).

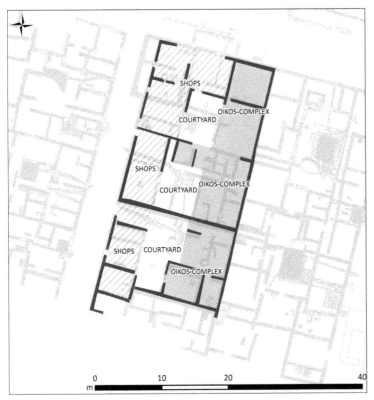

2.7 Heraclea, Area A: House types, early walls in black.

house layouts is not necessarily linked to the foundation of a city, as Hoepfner and Schwandner have argued.

Area A has yielded some scattered remains of older building phases that were obliterated by the structures described above (Figures 2.8 and 2.9).[12] Again, the absolute chronology is unclear. Maybe the oldest visible building phases belong to the second half of the fourth century BC, or to an earlier period. At any rate, the older building phases do not give the impression of standardized layouts. Indeed, they appear less regular than the later structures.

Area B offers a similar picture. As Liliana Giardino has observed, two houses in the southern part of Area B have the same dimensions and a similar layout. They can be dated to around 300 BC, but they are built on older, partly obliterated structures.[13] Again, we find a row of shops toward the street, a central courtyard and an *oikos*-complex (Figure 2.10).

The two houses in question were completely rebuilt together with the neighboring houses during the Early Hellenistic period, as common outer walls of the more recent type (with tile fragments) show. At ground level,

[12] On the excavations, see Giardino 1998; Osanna *et al.* 2015.
[13] Giardino 1998: 179–180, 182.

2.8 Heraclea, Area A: Obliterated wall of the early type.

the remains of older building phases are still visible. While the Hellenistic houses follow some sort of pattern, these older building phases do not give the impression of any standardized model or pattern. As in Area A, the impression is not that of standardized type houses built during the foundation period and modified subsequently, but rather the opposite. If there is a trend, it goes from irregular to standardized ground plans.

The evidence from Heraclea positively contradicts the hypothesis according to which the great innovation of Classical city-planning, which some attribute to Hippodamus of Miletus, was the regular *dihairesis* (division), not only of urban spaces, but also of private houses.[14] We do not know how the earliest dwellings in Heraclea looked, but it seems as if the further we go back in time, the less regular the houses are.

This also holds, at least in part, for other Classical settlements. In Olynthus, entire house blocks were built jointly, but at the same time the houses differed from each other in important ways from the very beginning.[15] While the houses of Olynthus are roughly equal in size and layout, some were more sumptuous than others, and some had specific production or storage facilities that were absent in others.[16] Such differences can be traced from the earliest phases. Furthermore, the inhabitants of the central-place lived in relatively large houses (c. 270 square meters), while other population groups who did not participate in the *synoikismos* and continued to live in rural settlements such as Mekyberna, the harbor of Olynthus at a distance of about 4 kilometers away, received much smaller house plots than their compatriots in Olynthus

[14] M.H. Hansen, in Schuller, Hoepfner, Schwandner 1989: 66 (discussion). M.Y. Goldberg (1999) has pointed out that houses in Athens might also be less standardized than previously assumed. *Androns* and women's rooms may change their position over time, and were not necessarily fixed at the level of architecture.

[15] Kiderlen 1995: 165–166; Cahill 2002: 75–84.

[16] *Ibid.*

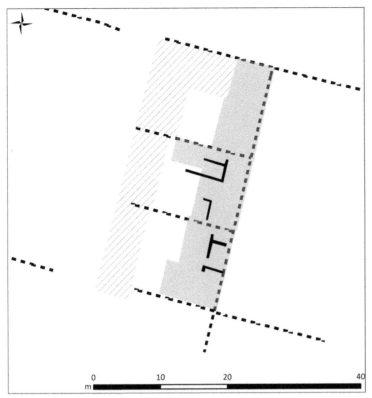

2.9 Heraclea, Area A: Obliterated walls.

(c. 90 square meters).[17] The interiors of the houses in Mekyberna were rather modest compared to the houses of Olynthus. As in Heraclea, various house types and sizes coexisted.

If two or more house types were in use over a long period (Heraclea's court and peristyle houses) and/or in different areas belonging to the same political entity (Olynthus and Mekyberna), this shows that architectural standardization was not necessarily a direct result of the foundation of a colony, let alone democratic urban planning.[18]

As we have seen, it is extremely difficult to reconstruct the original appearance of the settlements in their earliest stages. Not a single house in Heraclea can be securely dated to before 300 BC, even though considerable parts of the city were unearthed during the 1960s and 1970s. To the present day, two foundation walls along the street that separates *insula* IV from *insula* V are the only building remains dating to the late fifth century BC. How can we explain the lack of structures from the early phases of the colony? In general, the

[17] Mylonas 1943; Kiderlen 1995: 170–171.
[18] Olynthus probably had an oligarchic constitution: Zahrnt 1971: 61, 95, 107; contra Gehrke (1985: 124), who believes it was democratic.

2.10 Heraclea, Area B: House types; early walls in black.

fifth century BC has reasonably high archaeological visibility. There are striking remains of domestic architecture from Classical sites such as Selinus and
Himera. Yet we should be cautious in ascribing the lack of early buildings in
Heraclea exclusively to site-specific factors such as the Hellenistic leveling of
the site, incomplete or improper excavations, or simply bad luck. For Heraclea
is not an isolated case. In fact, none of the Greek settlements established during the Classical period have yielded any significant archaeological evidence of
standardized houses, or any solid houses at all, dating from the first fifty years
after their foundation. The ubiquity of this lacuna shows that site-specific factors cannot be the only explanation. Pyxous, Kamarina, Chersonesus, Thurii,
Amphipolis, Lissos, Issa, Pharos – in none of these sites have the houses built
during the first 50–75 years after the foundation been unearthed. The same is
true for many other cities founded or re-founded during the Classical period,
for example Priene, a site that has been crucial in the study of Greek urban
planning.[19] Priene was unearthed from 1894 to 1899, a period when excavation techniques and pottery analysis were far less refined than they are today.
Hence, the chronology of the buildings was not based on a sound stratigraphic

[19] On the history of research, see Hoepfner, Schwandner 1994; Cahill 2002; Rumscheid 2014.

framework. Rather, the excavators simply *assumed* that the earliest structures they found coincided with the original layout of the city (the same holds true for many other settlements, e.g., Olynthus, excavated from 1928 to 1938). In spite of significant progress in excavation and dating methods, archaeologists have continued to base their reconstructions on similar assumptions. For example, Hoepfner and Schwandner have explained similarities in the size and layout of Classical and Hellenistic houses in Priene as the result of a master plan carried out immediately after the foundation.[20] However, new research in Priene has not confirmed the high chronology of the living quarters, i.e., their construction around the middle of the fourth century, when the city was allegedly established.[21] It seems that it took several decades until the residential quarters of the city were filled with houses. Moreover, the houses do not correspond to any fixed type. Rather, there seem to be different house types that coexisted alongside each other, although their chronology is not always clear.[22]

As to the decades immediately after 350 BC, when Priene was allegedly established, excavations have yielded extremely scarce and controversial data. The paucity of archaeological and epigraphic data has led Simon Hornblower to downdate Priene's re-foundation to the period of Alexander the Great (336–323 BC).[23] Again, this is not an isolated case. The scarcity of the archaeological evidence has fostered doubts about the foundation date of a series of Classical settlements such as Chersonesus, Lissos, and Heraclea.

For example, archaeologists working in Heraclea have emphasized the scarcity of material evidence from 433/2 to around 375/50 BC. Most of the materials dating from this period come from cult sites, especially from the Demeter sanctuary. On these grounds, Liliana Giardino has argued that initially Heraclea was not an actual city but an agglomeration of cult sites ("sacred landscape"). According to Giardino, Tarentum reclaimed the site and the territory by reactivating some of the pre-existing cult sites, but was unable to send enough settlers to set up a real city-state.[24] Likewise, Giampiero Pianu (1990: 247) concludes from the study of part of the South Necropolis that the site was very sparsely populated until about 370 BC when it finally "took off." In Pianu's opinion, between 433/2 and 370 BC, Heraclea was a sort of "fake city" characterized by acute *oliganthropia* (lack of people). Salvatore Bianco (1999: 56) also hypothesizes that the "real take-off" of the settlement only occurred after 370 BC.

However, our difficulties in tracing early settlement phases in Heraclea and other Classical colonies may depend on archaeological visibility rather

---

[20] Hoepfner, Schwandner 1994: 208–212.
[21] Hiller von Gärtringen 1906, p. xi.
[22] Rumscheid 2014.
[23] Hornblower 1982: 323–330.
[24] Giardino 2012.

2.11 Late fifth-century pottery from Heraclea (Giardino 2012: fig. 6).

than on demographic underdevelopment. Apart from some walls of the late fifth century mentioned above, there is further evidence of a settlement. The so-called "*deposito acromo*," a set of plain vases of the fifth century BC ritually deposited in the agora of Heraclea, suggests that the main square was laid out at a very early stage.[25] Pottery dating to the late fifth and early fourth century BC has been found scattered all over the Castello hill.[26] The pottery finds consist mostly of fragments of red-figure and black-glazed *skyphoi* and *craters* (Figure 2.11), but there is also some coarse ware pottery of the late fifth century. In the past, this kind of pottery was considered undatable. However, recent work by Francesca Silvestrelli has shown that some shapes in plain and banded wares can be dated more precisely based on stratigraphic excavations in Metapontum and its hinterland. Among these, there is a bowl type with a

[25] Gramegna 2015/16.
[26] Lo Porto 1961: 139; Hänsel 1973: 461 ("Fossa III" and "Strato 3"); Adamesteanu, Dilthey 1978: 521; Giardino 2012: 101–103.

flat rim, which is attested in Heraclea.[27] Moreover, during our excavations in 2015 we found some pits with materials of the late fifth to early fourth centuries BC below Hellenistic building remains on the Castello hill (Trench B). Besides red-figure and black-glazed pottery fragments, they contained fragments of coarse ware vases, including a large bowl of the type described above.

In the light of these discoveries, the hypothesis according to which the city was sparsely populated until about 370/50 BC should be revised. Pottery finds and contexts, Heraclea's coinage, and finds from sanctuaries point to the existence of a functioning polis from the late fifth century BC. Yet the fact remains that there are almost no building remains dating to that period. One wonders where and how the people of Heraclea lived. In my opinion, the scarce visibility of their dwellings depends on various factors. There are doubtless site-specific factors such as the leveling of some areas in the Hellenistic period. However, it should also be borne in mind that in newly established settlements the amount of rubbish, especially pottery, tends to be much smaller than elsewhere. As a result, we lack one of the most important types of evidence for recognizing structures and layers of the foundation period. Secondly, Heraclea had no quarries, and building stone had to be imported. In such a context, it is likely that the inhabitants reused old building materials when constructing new houses. Foundations walls in Heraclea are of limited height and in some cases may have been built on floor level, as in neighboring Metapontum.[28] Therefore, pebbles from obliterated walls could easily be reused without leaving any archaeological trace. Thirdly, it is likely that the dwellings of the first generation were extremely scanty and therefore left few or no detectable traces. This last point might explain why there is not one single Classical colony where the houses of the first generation are well-enough preserved to be visible in the archaeological record.

Except for Heraclea, this phenomenon is particularly evident in Kamarina. The date of the re-foundation (461/60 BC) is confirmed by the dating of some mid-fifth century tombs unearthed in the Passo Marinaro necropolis south of the city.[29] Yet the buildings excavated in the urban center date to the middle of the fourth century BC and later, i.e., about a century after the re-foundation and some decades after the Carthaginians besieged the city (405 BC). The house plots follow a regular grid, which is thought to go back to the 450s,[30] but this is a mere hypothesis, since no material traces of fifth century dwellings have been documented so far. As in Heraclea, the lack of good building stone in the area may have caused the reuse of building materials and the destruction of earlier settlement phases.

[27] Hänsel 1973: 454–457, fig. 31, no. 2–3.
[28] Courtesy Keith Swift and Francesca Silvestrelli.
[29] Lanza 1990; Salibra 2014.
[30] Mertens 2006: 351–352; Di Stefano 2014.

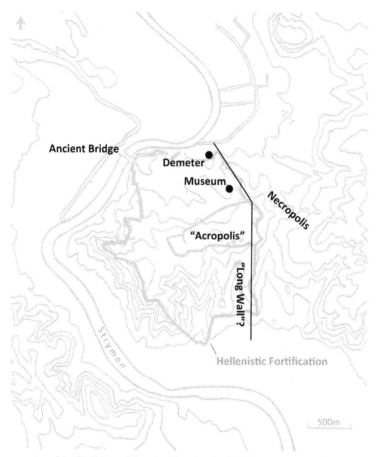

2.12 Amphipolis: Map of the site (drawing by R. Marino, *Parco Archaeologico di Paestum*, based on Lazaridis 1997).

Likewise, in Thurii, the remains of dwellings from the second half of the fifth century are lacking. Yet the importance of the city during this period is beyond doubt. Thurii was strong enough to start a war with Tarentum about possession of the territory of Siris immediately after its foundation, and the city's silver coins were widely distributed during the second half of the fifth century.[31]

The same holds true for Tyndaris. According to historical sources, Dionysius the Elder established the settlement in the early fourth century BC. Yet it is archaeologically invisible before the Early Hellenistic period.[32]

The case of Amphipolis is particularly revealing (Figure 2.12). The dating of the fortifications is unclear, but the visible remains are not much earlier than Late Classical/Hellenistic.[33] Remains of dwellings have been

---

[31] See Bugno 1999; Greco 2009.
[32] La Torre 2004; Spigo 2005.
[33] Lazaridis has dated the first phase of the fortification to the foundation period, but the archaeological evidence does not corroborate the dating – see for example Lazaridis 1997:

discovered in various parts of the urban center, but none of them pre-date the mid-fourth century BC.[34] Still, according to Thucydides, Amphipolis must have been a populous, well-structured fortified city from the 420s BC onward. In Thucydides' account of the city's surrender to Brasidas in 424/3 BC and the battle between the troops of Brasidas and Cleon in 422 BC (IV 102–109; V 6–11), several interesting facts emerge: Amphipolis had a large enough population to represent a considerable military force (indeed, prior to 422 BC, the city had endured Thracian attacks); some of its citizens lived in the countryside (IV 103,5); the town was protected by the so-called Long Wall stretching "from river to river" (i.e., from a point on the Strymon south of the settlement to a point north of it), which must have existed already in 424 BC (Thuc. IV 102), but had already been obliterated by the time Thucydides was writing (see V 10,6). Thucydides calls it a σταύρωμα in V 10,6, suggesting that it was a wooden palisade or stockade.[35] In 422 BC, Cleon deemed it necessary to attack the city walls with siege machines (V 7,5); yet no trace of the walls of this period have been detected by archaeological research. Indeed, the city described by Thucydides – the Long Wall, the dwellings, the agora – is completely invisible in the archaeological record, except for the wooden bridge over the Strymon, one of the few wooden structures from the Classical period that have survived to the present day.

As it turns out, many newly established colonies and *synoikismoi* of the Classical period have a lacuna in the archaeological record spanning several decades. It is important to bear in mind that this is typical of newly established settlements, and not of already extant sites. Entire living quarters of the late fifth century BC have been excavated in Selinus and Himera, while in fifth century BC colonies such as Heraclea, Amphipolis, and Chersonesus, nothing of the kind has come to light. In Olynthus there are numerous houses dating to before 349 BC, while we have little idea of the appearance of the living quarters of fourth century BC settlements such as Issa, Pharos, and Priene at the same time.

The idea that founding a city involved the construction of "type houses" should be discarded, at least as far as Classical colonies are concerned. Evidence from Olynthus, Kamarina, and Heraclea suggests that orthogonal streets and regular house plots were laid out in an early stage, but there is no positive evidence of standardized houses or any solid houses at all during the first fifty years after the foundation. After all, how should we expect private houses to have looked like, if more than ten years after the foundation of Amphipolis

---

31: "... [T]he first section of the wall belongs to the Classical period and is securely dated to between 424 and 422 BC by the narrative of Thucydides, who refers to the battle between Kleon and Brasidas before the walls of Amphipolis." See also Pritchett 1980: 298–300.

34 Lazaridis 1997: 47–48; Peristeri, Zographou, Darakis 2006.

35 The term usually refers to military camps: Thuc. VI 64,3; Xen. Hell. III 2,3.

the fortifications consisted of a wooden palisade? It is fairly unlikely that the settlers lived in stone houses while the city walls were made of wood. We have to imagine that the first generations lived in temporary wooden buildings that were only gradually replaced with solid stone houses of fairly regular shape. One of the few cases where archaeologists have actually found traces of such early wooden dwellings is Elea in southern Italy, a colony founded around 540 BC by Phocaean settlers. The first generation of settlers lived in wooden huts, as is demonstrated by the post holes found below some of the earliest solid houses in the lower city.[36]

LIVING IN TENTS AND HUTS

Classical colonies may have resembled early European settlements in North America such as Jamestown, the first permanent English settlement in America, established by the Virginia Company in 1607 as "James Fort." A wooden palisade surrounded the first settlement. It had a triangular form and extended for less than a hectare. Archaeological evidence of the early phases consists almost exclusively of postholes and holes dug into the ground. The settlers initially lived in tents and later in huts and timber houses.[37] Just like Jamestown, many Greek colonies may have evolved from simple tent camps. In this regard, a passage in Xenophon's *Anabasis* is revealing. When the Greek mercenaries on their way back from the Euphrates River arrived on the southern shore of the Black Sea, Xenophon considered founding a *polis* there. However, his men were opposed to the idea and when they came to a place suitable for the foundation of a city (a promontory with a natural harbor), they were anxious about Xenophon's attempts to carry out his plan:

> The men took up quarters *(eskénoun)* on the beach by the sea, refusing to encamp on the spot which might become a city; indeed, the fact of their coming to this place at all seemed to them the result of scheming on the part of some people who wished to found a city.
>
> (Xenophon, Anabasis VI 4,7, transl. C.L. Brownson, 1922)

Xenophon's companions refused to set up their tents *(skénein)* on a site suitable for a city, because this was obviously the way in which a city usually started. We may understand now why ancient texts dealing with the establishment of a colony never mention architects or construction workers. There were no specialized experts; everybody had to look out for himself. It is telling that the *geonomoi* in the Brea decree were not specialized surveyors or anything like that, but democratically chosen citizens (probably drawn by lot); in other words, they were amateurs.

---

[36] Krinzinger 1994: 24, fig. 11. See also Kuznecov 1999 on the Black Sea Region.
[37] Kelso 2005; Kelso *et al.* 2012.

The first solid buildings were not necessarily houses, but storage buildings. Among the oldest structures known from Megara Hyblaia, Selinus, and Himera there are so-called stone circles, circular platforms with a diameter of about 2–3 meters.[38] They usually lie in the corners of regular house plots, which later were covered with solid structures. The circular platforms were at first interpreted as small cult sites that delimited the house plots of the colonists.[39] However, parallels in mainland Greece and miniature objects from tombs suggest that they were the bases for granaries.[40] The importance of granaries in ancient Greece can hardly be overestimated. Charondas of Locri refers to the household community as *homosepyos* ("those who eat from a common granary"), and in a ritual text from Selinus (possibly Late Archaic), the term *homosepyos* has the same meaning.[41] The symbolic value of the *sipyos* (granary) might explain why the bases of the granaries in Megara Hyblaia, Himera, and Selinus were not demolished in later periods. In Selinus, there is evidence for ritual activities accompanying both the construction and the abandonment of the stone platforms. What is important here is that these structures are the only ones surviving from the beginnings of the colony. The dwellings were probably less solid and less meaningful on a symbolic level, and thus were erased during later phases.

The main concern of Greek colonists was probably not how to build the houses but how to divide up the land. The social status of the citizens largely depended on the ownership of land; houses could express that status, but we cannot even be sure of the importance of dwellings for the expression of social status in the fifth century BC.[42] Demosthenes, for example, claims that the Athenians of the Classical period did not consider domestic architecture as a matter of social prestige:

> Such was their rank in the world of Hellas: what manner of men they were at home, in public or in private life, look round you and see. Out of the wealth of the state they set up for our delight so many fair buildings and things of beauty, temples and offerings to the gods, that we who come after must despair of ever surpassing them; yet in private they were so modest, so careful to obey the spirit of the constitution, that the houses of their famous men, of Miltiades or of Aristeides, as any of you can see that knows them, are not a whit more splendid than those of their neighbours. For selfish greed had no place in their statesmanship, but each thought it his duty to further the common weal.
> (Olynth. 3,25–26, transl. J.H. Vince & M.A. Cambridge, 1930)

Demosthenes obviously exaggerates in order to make his point – the story of the good old days. However, it is significant that he attributes the attitude of

---

[38] A. Henning in Mertens, Hoesch, Dehl-von Kaenel 2003: 413–418.
[39] *Ibid.*
[40] Guzzo 2013.
[41] *Ibid.*
[42] Shipley 2005: 369–373.

the Athenians towards private housing not to laws or philosophic ideas, but simply to the "spirit of the constitution/city" *(ethos tes politeias).*

The evidence suggests that in the fifth and probably also in the fourth century BC the layout of dwelling houses in the colonies was a question of necessity rather than one of ideology and politics. The colonists needed shelter and, especially in the first few years, resources were limited. The initial dwellings would have been tents and huts while solid houses were constructed only a few decades after the foundation.

In archaeological terms, the early phases remain almost totally invisible, and we have little idea of the appearance of the dwellings of the first generation of colonists. However, it is possible to make some general assumptions about life in these settlements. In any unplanned, temporary settlement of tents or huts with hundreds or even thousands of inhabitants, the standards of hygiene are inevitably precarious. Beyond a population of a certain number of people, the only way to avoid this is by paving the streets and constructing drains and sewers. Of course, only developed settlements could have such facilities. The colonists who had to face the winter in tents and huts and whose survival depended on the first harvest had concerns other than building sewage systems. We might therefore want to look first at sanitation standards in developed settlements of the Classical period; the colonies hardly reached those standards, at least not in the beginning. If non-colonial settlements reach a standard X, it can be inferred that in the colonies, sanitation standards were below X.

In the past, archaeologists were quite optimistic about the standard X. Scholars readily accepted any evidence suited to support optimistic assumptions about Classical sanitation, no matter how isolated it was, because they wanted to believe that the Greeks lived in neat, clean cities.[43] Yet systematic analysis of text sources and archaeological data suggests that this was not the case and that the hygiene in many cities was actually quite precarious.[44] To begin with, latrines and sewage systems, as known from the Imperial period, are not attested for the Archaic and Classical periods. Archaeological remains of pipes for fresh water, drains for rainwater (i.e., at Rhodes, Corinth, Akragas, Metapontum, and elsewhere), and other plumbing fixtures prove, however, that the absence of latrines and sewers is not due to a lack of technical knowledge and capacity.[45] Although single households could eventually have proper pipes running into public drains in order to get rid of their sewage, as observed for example in Athens at the so-called Great Drain, the reason that most people did not have any need for

---

[43] Hiller von Gaertringen, Wilski 1904: 159; Hoepfner, Schwandner 1994: 320.

[44] See Owens 2011. The following paragraphs are partly taken from my contribution to this volume; I would like to express my gratitude to Olga Koloski-Ostrow for permitting me to reuse the parts here.

[45] Wilson 2000: 164–165.

such fixtures can be attributed to two main reasons. First, depositing sewage and manure in cesspits, on dunghills, or on the streets was obviously not considered an aesthetic or hygienic problem,[46] and second, the agricultural activities of many inhabitants created a demand for sewage as compost, which was collected and recycled. The earliest structures within settlements that can be related to the handling and removal of garbage, feces and sewage, are cesspits (koprones).[47] Until the fourth century BC, they were quite common in urban settlements. Koprones of the sixth to the fourth centuries BC have been found in Selinus, Athens, Euesperides (Libya), Stymphalos, and Halieis. Some are situated in courtyards, others in the streets.[48] Not all houses in these sites had koprones. Apparently, some households organized waste disposal by other means (dung heaps, etc.). Koprones situated in the street could have been used by several households. The apparent absence of cesspits might, in many cases, also be due to excavation techniques.

In the context of urban spaces, cesspits are a phenomenon of the sixth to the fourth century BC. In the fourth century, however, a new development takes place: the installation of drains, by which waste, feces, and/or sewage could be flushed from the inside of the houses into the open (alcoves or streets) where it ended in above-ground drains or in the gutter. Only in a few cases can these drains can be related to actual latrines or cesspits; more often they provided the possibility of disposing of anything liquid or semi-liquid, be it the contents of a chamber pot, kitchen waste, or anything else. Drains or latrines with drains leading into the open have been found in several sites. In Dystos on Euboea, in House J: entering the courtyard, the oikos and other rooms were situated on the right-hand side; to the left, there are two small rooms, in one of which two stone toilet seats were found. The seats are built into the wall, with a concave backrest carved into the square stones behind the seats. The drains of these toilets terminate on the outside of the wall beneath a large stone. The construction of the house can be dated to the fourth century BC as a result of an analysis of the building technique of the structure. The latrines cannot be a later alteration, since the stone used for the seats is part of the masonry.[49] In Thasos, House B of Îlot I, a small trapezoid room (no. 4) measuring little more than 4 square meters in size, was found with a kind of basin, from which sewage could

---

[46] In later times, however, domestic architecture and urban infrastructure increasingly became a subject of aesthetic discourse: Heracl. *Crit.* 1.1; 1.21; Strabo 14.1.37; see also: Kolb 1984: 122–122; Lauter 1986: 90; Wörrle, Zanker 1995: p. v. On manure management, see Forbes 2013.

[47] The terminus *kopron* for cesspits, meaning deposits and compost heaps for feces and other manure, is taken from ancient literature (Ault 1994: 198). The word *kopros*, from which *korpon* derives, can mean feces and garbage, but also manure. If a pit is lined with bricks and can neither be a cistern (i.e., because it could not hold water) nor a storage room or cellar, and if the filling is distinctly organic, this structure can be interpreted as a *kopron*.

[48] Zuchtriegel 2011b: 30.

[49] Hoepfner 1999: 353–366.

be flushed into the street (fourth century BC). This fairly rudimentary device consists of a stone slab that was inclined towards a drain. A similar installation was found in Room 1 of house A.[50] In Olynthus, different kinds of drainage arrangements can be observed. In the first place, terracotta basins were found which were interpreted by Robinson as "urinal and toilet seats,"[51] although it is more likely they represent sewage fixtures. The only completely preserved example was not found in its original context.[52] Another one, however, of which only the exit-pipe remains, is still *in situ:* it is inserted in a wall at ground level leading from the inside of the house into the street.[53] The diameter of the exit-pipe measures 0.08 meters. Other fragments of basins of this kind have been found in the House of Zoilos[54] and in a *stoa* in area A IV.[55] In the House of Zoilos, there is also a stone slab like the one in Thasos, inclined toward a small drain in the wall that ends on the street. The slab measures approximately 0.5 x 0.5 meters. The room ('Room 0') where it is located is situated next to the entrance and is rather small: 1.9 x 1.7 meters.[56] On the other hand, in some Olynthian houses the drainage of the courtyards led through a room out into the street. Considering that this drainage system was uncovered, it could thus be used to pour out liquids and flush them outside. The rooms in question are situated next to the entrance, and were probably some kind of "stable and kopron (…) where domestic manure for the suburban garden was collected."[57] Such rooms have been found for example in Houses A VI 5,[58] A VIII 4,[59] and A VIII 6.[60] In Olynthus, both wastewater and rainwater flow off mainly into open drains along the streets and into the alcoves between the houses.[61] An almost totally intact terracotta toilet seat, open at the bottom and hollowed out on one side to collect urine, was found in one of the alcoves, which might be the location where it had also been used ('primary refuse').[62] A drain into the open has also been found in Orraon (northwestern Greece). It belongs to the second half of the fourth century BC. The drainage of the court was divided into two separate channels, one of them running through the *oikos* with a fireplace, the other one through a stable or storage room (Room e).[63] If

---

[50] Grandjean 1988: 111, 177–178, 417–419, pl. 65, 88, supplement no 1.
[51] Robinson 1946: 179.
[52] Robinson, Graham 1938: 205; Robinson 1946: 178–182, pl. 156–157; Martin 1957: 71; Hoepfner, Schwandner 1994: fig. 75.
[53] Robinson, Graham 1938: 205–206, fig. 16.
[54] Robinson 1946: 163, pl. 133.
[55] Robinson, Graham 1938: 205; Robinson 1946: 93.
[56] Robinson 1946: 165, pl. 133, 135,2.
[57] Hoepfner, Schwandner 1994: 97.
[58] Robinson, Graham 1938: 104–105, pl. 98.
[59] Robinson 1946: 23, pl. 14.
[60] Robinson 1946: 23.
[61] See Robinson 1946: pl. 41, 52, 62–63, 73, 98, 110, 113, 124, 195–196.
[62] Robinson, Graham 1938: 205 n. 90.
[63] Dakaris 1986: 119–141, fig. 4–7, pl. 37b; Hoepfner 1999: 395–411. The drain in the *oikos* was possibly installed subsequently, cf. Hoepfner 1999: 408.

the sole intended purpose of this drainage system were to drain off rainwater, one channel would have been sufficient. Additionally, in the *oikos* there seems to be some kind of basin, connected to the drain. In Eretria, in house II there is a drain leading from a small room through the wall into the street; it has been interpreted as a latrine. The structure dates to the end of the fourth or the beginning of the third century BC.[64] In some houses in Euesperides, there seem to have been drains that ended in the streets too.[65]

Whatever was poured out or flushed from these drains ended up in the streets. The scope of the facilities mentioned here cannot therefore have been to improve the cleanliness of the streets. Rather, they facilitated daily life in the dwellings themselves. Furthermore, if drains lead into the streets or into the open, we have to assume that sewage could be deposited there by other means as well. As some households flushed sewage directly into the streets using drains, probably many others as well were allowed to do so without using plumbing (by carrying the sewage to these areas using vessels, chamber pots, and so on). Consequently, in cities like Olynthus streets and alcoves were regularly exposed to pollution; an impression that is confirmed by literary evidence speaking about defecating and urinating in the streets.[66] Inscriptions and regulations interdicting defecation in sanctuaries indicate *ex negativo* that the situation outside the sacred precincts was different. The evidence also suggests that concerns about defecating in the streets did not arise from the pollution of public space but from the possibility of being seen. If the "shamefulness" of being seen applied to women to a higher degree than to men, urinating women could also be the object of sexual arousal on the part of male beholders, as depicted on an Attic red-figure hydria in Paris.[67]

The situation changed when sewers and drainage channels were covered and connected to drains and latrines inside houses. However, these developments only began in the fourth century BC. Some subterranean drains from Thasos, running along the side of the street (whereas the later ones run in the middle of the streets), date to as early as to the fourth century BC.[68] In Priene, the subterranean canalization is considered as a part of the original city plan, but in the beginning it probably served merely to carry off rainwater, and only later were latrines connected to it.[69]

Throughout the Hellenistic period, drains and sewers in Heraclea were situated above ground (Figure 2.13). There was no systematic urban sewage system; underground drains were only built in certain parts of the city. As to the

[64] Reber 1998: 108–109, 139–140, fig. 164, 170.
[65] Wilson 2000: 166.
[66] For example Herodotus 2.35; Aristophanes, *Eccl.* 331–326; *Nubes* 1382–1390; *Pax* 9, 98–101, 157–166, 1265–1267.
[67] Kilmer 1993: no. R68 (Paris, Louvre G 51).
[68] Grandjean 1988: 429–430.
[69] Dörpfeld 1901: pl. 38.

2.13 Heraclea, Area A: Aboveground sewers in a Hellenistic habitation.

foundation period, it is doubtful if there were any sewers or drains at all. The urban street grid represented probably the only regular, standardized feature; apart from that, the settlement must have looked more like a slum than a planned city, especially after several days of rain.

NO HOUSES, NO HOUSEWIVES?

If scholars like Monika Trümper (2011) and John Bintliff (2014) are right in considering domestic space as a crucial element for the construction of social hierarchies (as I think they are), the lack of solid and standardized houses implies a lack of social determination. The temporary dwellings of the early years offered only very limited possibilities for codifying the position of subaltern household members through architectural features. This entailed rather indefinite social roles. The colonists could not rely on built structures in their households to define the role of women, children, and slaves (if they had any). They could, of course, rely on other means to enforce social hierarchies, but one of the most important ones was missing. This is particularly evident in the case of women. Attic vase paintings often show women indoors among servants with household and personal effects. From Penelope's "chamber" (ὑπερῷον) to the third story of Thornton Hall in Charlotte Bronte's *Jane Eyre*, there is a tradition of confining women symbolically to (and identifying them with) domestic space. Literary sources seem to suggest that in the Classical period the *gynaikonitis* (women's apartment) was usually situated in the upper floor.[70] On the other hand, recent research demonstrates that the limitation of female household members to specific indoor spaces was probably rather a male ideal than social reality. Marilyn Y. Goldberg (1999) has argued that everyday practice in Athenian houses was less codified and less separated along gender lines than text sources and images may suggest. In colonial settlements, however, the very existence of fixed spatial structures is doubtful. Tents and improvised wooden dwellings offered no stage for enacting female roles in the way that would have been done in Athens or other cities of mainland Greece. The absence of solid stone-built houses does not, of course, in itself mean an absence of material culture to separate spaces and people; tents work just as well, as for example in the case of Bedouin tents, but these are part of a tradition that for centuries has inscribed social order into this kind of dwellings. In the Greek world, social structure was linked to the structure of the house, at least at the level of ideology. We should bear in mind that even in Athens reality hardly corresponded to the ideal of Greek women as portrayed in Classical texts and in Athenian vase paintings.[71] However, in the colonies the gap between ideal and reality was even larger than in homeland Greece. Put simply, if the Greek woman was – at least ideally – defined through her life and work in the *gynaikonitis* and *oikos*, there were no Greek women in the colonies. Of course there may have been women from Greece, but some of the specific means of reifying traditional Greek femininity – namely certain types of domestic architecture – were lacking. To what extent this implied the emergence of less restrictive female identities remains unclear, but it must have had some impact.

It needs to be stressed that we know extremely little about the numbers of girls and women who actually emigrated to the colonies and how widespread intermarriage with local women was.[72] The textual sources (all written by men) provide no insight. At the same time, the intrinsic link between modern colonialism, exoticism, and sexism risks biasing our views of the role of women in ancient colonization. The issue of local and Greek intermarriage is particularly problematic, given that in modern times the native woman has become an archetype of male ideologies of colonization (see Conrad's *Heart of Darkness*). Whilst aware of such pitfalls, I believe that intermarriage between Greek settlers and local women was fairly widespread. Literary sources and foundation decrees of the Classical period never mention women among the contingents of settlers parting for a new colony.[73] It is therefore likely that in many cases the settlers married local women. Admittedly, arguments *ex silentio*

---

[70] Lys. I 9; Men., Sam. 230. See Hoepfner, Schwandner 1994: 238–239.

[71] Goldberg 1999; Trümper 2011.

[72] Shepherd 1999; 2012.

[73] There are a few isolated references to Archaic colonization, such as the priestess Aristarche who "conducted" the Phocaeans to Massalia: Strabo IV 1,4.

are always of limited value, but the complete absence of women in the texts (especially official ones) is noteworthy. At the same time, the archaeological data seems to confirm that intermarriage was quite common.[74]

Some extremely interesting evidence comes from Chersonesus, where at least ten grave stelae (out of about seventy) dating from the fourth century BC have non-Greek names. The stelae all belong to married women. The traditional view that they were local Taurics has been questioned by Paula Perlman (2011) who stresses that in several cases men with Greek names gave non-Greek names to their children. Moreover, the non-Greek names attested in Chersonesus are not typically Tauric names; indeed, some of them seem to originate in Asia Minor:

> If the non-Greek names tell a story, than it is not the story of inter-marriage between Greek colonists and the Taurics of Crimea. Instead, the non-Greek names point to contact with Asia Minor as we might expect for a colony of Heraclea Pontica, and they attest the diffusion of foreign cults.
>
> (Perlman 2011: 393)

Perlman is certainly right to question the idea that women with non-Greek names were local Taurics. However, it is still necessary to explain why Chersonesean women – wherever they actually came from – were represented as non-Greeks through their names to an extent unparalleled in mainland Greece. It is doubtful that the non-Greek names reflected the actual place of origin of their bearers, considering that both Greek and non-Greek names are found within a single family. Rather than places of origin, the names of Chersonesus seem to reflect hybrid identities in a context where the boundaries between Greek and non-Greek were not always clear.

As we have seen, during the early years, many colonial settlements lacked the architectural features that reenacted Greek femininity in the traditional way of homeland Greece. At the same time, the inscriptions from Chersonesus demonstrate that female names embodied hybridity rather than Greekness. This suggests the idea that in colonial settlements femininity was defined in less restrictive terms than in mainland Greece. The situation is not unlike that described by Gillian Shepherd for Archaic Magna Graecia and Western Sicily on the basis of burial evidence.[75]

While in Chersonesus men with Greek names gave non-Greek names to their daughters, in Heraclea a different kind of hybridization can be observed. Here, freed slave women, presumably of non-Greek origin, bear Greek names. As in Chersonesus, this is a period that dates to several decades or even centuries after the foundation. At Heraclea, there is no clear evidence for slaves

[74] Shepherd 2012.
[75] Shepherd 2011; 2012.

in the early phases of the colony. The emission of silver coins from as early as the late fifth century BC[76] and the use of imported Carparo stone from the Salento region for the fortifications[77] suggest that the city's economy was flourishing during the first half of the fourth century BC. The presence of household and public slaves is hardly surprising in such a context.[78] However, only from the late fourth century onward is there positive evidence of the existence of slaves: excavations in the Demeter sanctuary have yielded at least six bronze tablets with inscriptions which, according to G. Maddoli, refer to freed slave women (Figure 2.14).[79] The inscriptions date from

2.14 Heraclea, sanctuary of Demeter: *Manumissio* inscription (?) and iron chains (Gertl 2012: fig. 10).

the late fourth and third centuries BC and are written in local Doric dialect. It appears that the names of the freed women are Greek (for example, "Philoxena dedicates herself to Demeter ..."). Yet it is unlikely that they were local women from Heraclea. A bronze sculpture depicting "horses and women captured in a war with the Messapians" (Paus. X 10,6), donated by the citizens of Tarentum to the sanctuary of Apollo in Delphi hints at the origin of the majority of slaves in Magna Graecia. In Classical Greek city-states, slaves were usually foreigners (non-Greeks, but also Greeks). However, the slave women of Heraclea speak the local Doric dialect when they step into the public arena. This is perfectly logical, given that the local community was supposed to acknowledge their new status. As in Chersonesus, names and dialects reflect fluid and hybrid identities, rather than places of origin.

SKIRTS AND BOOTS

Female identities were mirrored in ritual activities, seen for example in the sanctuary of Demeter at Heraclea, which dates back to the very beginning of the colony.[80] Women played a central role in the cult of Demeter, not only in the urban center but also in the extraurban sanctuary of Conca d'Oro. Excavations at Conca d'Oro have yielded an inscription dating to the third

---

[76] Siciliano 2008 with bibliography.
[77] Neutsch 1967: 110–118; Tagliente 1986a: 129.
[78] Uguzzoni, Ghinatti 1968: 143–144. (Ghinatti assumes a limited number of household and agricultural slaves for the fourth century BC).
[79] Maddoli 1986; Gertl 2012: 136. Sceptical Sartori 1992.
[80] Otto 2008; Gertl 2012.

or second century BC that reads: "Philemena, daughter of Nikon, and her children and grandchildren to Demeter as a vow." As Luisa Prandi emphasizes, the text points to female agency.[81] Philemena appears as mother and grandmother, with particular emphasis on reproduction as a crucial issue in colonial societies. Unfortunately, virtually nothing is known about birth and childbearing in Classical colonies – I will discuss some evidence from the *necropoleis* in the following chapter. With regard to the notion of hybridity, it is interesting to note that the sanctuaries of Demeter in Heraclea and Conca d'Oro have yielded considerable numbers of terracotta figurines showing Artemis Bendis, a Thracian goddess whose cult had been introduced into Athens at the end of the fifth century BC.[82] During the second half of the fourth and the early part of the third century BC, images of Artemis Bendis were extremely popular in Magna Graecia, especially in Taranto and Heraclea. The goddess – a hybrid of the Thracian goddess Bendis and Greek goddess Artemis – is depicted as a female figure with leather boots, knee-length robe, and a Phrygian cap made of lion-skin. Many images show her holding a bow in her left hand, and sometimes she holds a fawn, a torch, or other objects in her right hand (Figure 2.15). In the second half of the fourth century BC, Artemis Bendis was one of the most popular themes for terracotta figures in southern Italy. Figurines depicting the goddess have been found all over the region, in both Greek and indigenous settlements.

In Heraclea, Artemis Bendis figurines often seem to be associated with doors and gates. Near the west gate of the Castello hill, a votive deposit with hundreds of figurines representing Artemis Bendis has been unearthed,[83] and near the entrance of the sanctuary of Conca d'Oro, more than a dozen figurines of Artemis Bendis were ritually deposited.[84] Likewise, figurines of Artemis Bendis were found near the entrance to the urban sanctuary of Demeter.[85]

The rural cult site of Conca d'Oro was apparently some sort of annex of the sanctuary of Demeter in the urban center, as Massimo Osanna has argued based on finds and structural remains.[86] Coins, pottery fragments, and terracotta figurines show that the cult site at Conca d'Oro was established between the late fifth and early fourth century BC, and not around 350 BC as previously thought.[87] During the field survey carried out in 2012, we found a votive deposit (HE25) situated on an ancient road that connected Heraclea with Conca d'Oro and Santa Maria d'Anglona (Figure 2.16). This deposit also contained fragments of terracotta statuettes representing Artemis Bendis and a female figure with

[81] Prandi 2008: 129.
[82] Osanna 2008: 63–64; Otto 2008: 82; Gertl 2012: 132.
[83] Lo Porto 1961: 138–139; Neutsch 1967: 163.
[84] Rüdiger, Schläger 1967: 341; Curti 1989; Osanna 2008: 63.
[85] Otto 2008: 82.
[86] Osanna 2008: 63.
[87] Cf. the coins published in Rüdiger 1969: 172–180.

polos, possibly Demeter. Both types have close parallels in Conca d'Oro.[88] Apparently, the site of the deposit was situated on the road from Heraclea to Conca d'Oro and Santa Maria d'Anglona, and might indicate ritual processions connecting the two cult sites (to this day the latter site is the culminating point of a yearly procession in honor of the Madonna of Anglona).[89]

As we have seen, statuettes of Artemis Bendis appear in the urban center and in the countryside at sites where female rituals took place. At the same time, Artemis Bendis embodied hybridity more than most other deities, and represented an unconventional model of femininity: a nomadic hunting goddess, an ethnically mixed virgin who lives in the wild. The figure of Artemis Bendis combines the idea of hardship and primitivity with freedom and resistance against the order

2.15 Conca d'Oro: Demeter and Artemis Bendis figurines (Osanna, Prandi, Siciliano 2008: fig. 42).

of the *oikos*. This is precisely the theme of Euripides' *Hippolytus*, staged in Athens in the year 428 BC. Clearly, Artemis is a signifier of the world outside the polis. In southern Italy, and especially in a relatively young polis like Heraclea, she could also be a signifier of the beginnings of the polis. In a colony where tents and huts were only gradually replaced by solid and standardized stone houses, Artemis as a female figure who lives outside the world of the *oikos* may have appeared less exotic and different than in Athens or Corinth. Assuming that the grandmothers and great-grandmothers of the women who dedicated statuettes of Artemis Bendis around 350 BC were brought up in tents and huts and lived in a town without sewers and drains, the goddess dressed in a skirt and boots may

[88] Zuchtriegel 2012b: 149–150, fig. 9 & 10.
[89] On the procession and possible pagan origins, see Rüdiger, Schläger 1967: 340 note 1.

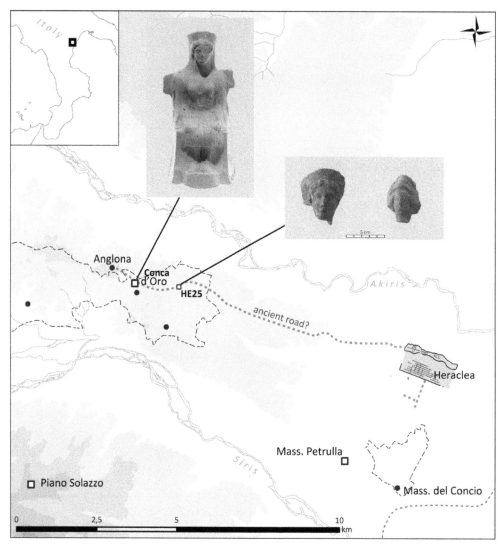

2.16 Road from Heraclea to Conca d'Oro with votive deposit HE25.

not have been exclusively or primarily a counterpoint to Greek womanhood, but also an element of memory and, arguably, a role model. I do not want to play down gender hierarchies and exploitation in ancient Greece, but it seems to me that the experience of hardship and disorder that characterized many colonial settlements during their early phases may have contributed to the emergence of alternative female role models. This could explain the immense popularity of Artemis Bendis in southern Italian colonies and in inland sites that were undergoing comparable migration and colonization processes, as we shall see in Chapter 6. In such frontier communities where the walls of women's rooms and courtyards had yet to be built and where every hand was needed to reclaim and cultivate land, girls and women probably had more contact with the reign of Artemis than elsewhere in the Greek world.

THREE

TOMBS: VISIBILITY AND INVISIBILITY IN COLONIAL SOCIETIES

While the previous chapter examined the settlers' way of life, this chapter investigates how they expressed social difference at the level of ritual through burial rites and funerary customs. I also aim to explore the relationship between the social order of the urban center (*polis*, city) and the symbolic order of suburban cemeteries (*necropolis*, city of the dead).

Greek cemeteries have often been seen as a mirror of the polis. For example, Hoepfner and Schwandner have argued that the introduction of standardized house plots and "type houses" was accompanied by the introduction of sumptuary laws and standardized grave monuments. According to Wolfram Hoepfner, the cemeteries of Classical settlements were marked by a high degree of modesty and uniformity, as was the case in Athens during the middle of the fifth century, and again during the late fourth century BC (so-called type burials).[1] However, the existence of type burials has never been verified on the ground in any colony or *synoikismos* of the Classical period. A major problem is that only a few sites have yielded significant numbers of tombs; furthermore, excavations were either carried out a long time ago, as at Kamarina, or have not yet been published, as at Amphipolis and Chersonesus.[2] In particular, the early phases are scarcely attested. As in the case of early dwellings, this lacuna can be interpreted in various ways: either there were only a few people

---

[1] Hoepfner 1989; Hoepfner, Schwandner 1994: 312–313.
[2] See Lanza 1990 on the excavations conducted by Paolo Orsi at the necropolis of Kamarina; Posamentir 2007; 2011 on Chersonesus.

living in the colonies, or the tombs were of such a kind that they do not show up in the archaeological record.

What is quite clear is that the "cities of the dead" did not simply reproduce the social order of the cities of the living. In some cases, the *necropoleis* actually seem to subvert or compensate for the male-dominant order of the polis. At Heraclea, and arguably at other sites too, children and girls received special attention, and I will try to offer a possible explanation. But first, we have to return to the problem of visibility.

BURIAL TYPES, CHRONOLOGY, AND VISIBILITY

At Heraclea, out of more than 1,500 tombs, 350 of which are published, only one dates to the last third of the fifth century BC. About 1–2% of the published tombs date to the years 430–370 BC, a period covering about 7% of the cemetery's lifespan.[3] The only burial dating to the last third of the fifth century is the so-called Tomb of the Policoro Painter (hereafter called the Policoro tomb). No more than five burials are known from the early fourth century BC: four cremations consisting of a single vase serving as an urn (Figure 3.1) and one inhumation with a black-glazed cup, a bronze helmet, and a bronze belt.[4] The number of tombs increases during the period 350–325 BC, and reaches a peak in the last quarter of the fourth century BC. Out of 43 tombs dating to 350–325 BC, 13 contain only one vase (30%). From 325 to 300 BC, the tombs with no more than one vase represent 17% (16 out of 96).[5] Thus, there seems to be a general trend from one or a few grave goods to several grave goods. The burials containing many grave goods are often inhumations.

The percentage of inhumations increases over the years, but this may be a false impression. Archaeologists tend to recognize only those burials that contain grave goods or, as in the case of cremations, are deposited in an urn. However, there may be other graves that are very hard to recognize or even completely invisible. Excavations in the Southern Necropolis of Heraclea have yielded several inhumation burials without grave goods (Figure 3.2).[6] As at Chersonesus (see Chapter 2), some of them may belong to the first or second generations of settlers, although this cannot be demonstrated. Considering that most of the early cremation burials have yielded no more than one vase, it would not be surprising if there were also burials without any grave goods. The fact that so few burials from the late fifth century BC are known is not

---

[3] Calculations based on Pianu 1990.
[4] Pianu 1990; Lanza 2012; Bottini, Lecce 2015.
[5] Pianu 1990: 245.
[6] Crupi, Pasquino 2015: 102 (11 tombs without grave goods out of 45 tombs in the Via Salerno necropolis).

3.1 Heraclea, South Necropolis: Cremation burial with red-figure amphora (tomb 53 in via Avellino) (Pianu 1990: pl.VI 1–2).

necessarily a sign of demographic underdevelopment (called *oliganthropia* in the ancient written sources), as has been argued in the past.[7] A significant number of burials from the years 433–350 BC may be invisible because they contained no pottery or other objects. The lack or paucity of grave goods could be due to poverty, but also to ideological reasons. Cultural patterns and sumptuary laws may have restricted burial rites and the use of grave goods. Heraclea's mother-city Tarentum adopted burial restrictions earlier in the fifth century BC. In the aftermath of a defeat against the Iapygians and the introduction of democracy around 470 BC, burial customs in Tarentum underwent a drastic change.[8] During the Late Archaic period, the elite had buried their dead in chamber tombs with rich sets of Athenian banquet vases and other prestigious grave goods. After 470 BC, chamber tombs disappear and standardized burials with few or no grave goods become common. Apparently certain forms of ritual consumption and the display of wealth in general were considered problematic. As before, most burials are inhumations, but there is no emphasis on wealth, gender, or social status. Only very few tombs contain any grave goods at all, usually an Athenian *lekythos*, an *alabastron*, or a fibula in

[7] Pianu 1990: 247.
[8] Greco 1981; Dell'Aglio 2015.

3.2 Heraclea, South Necropolis: Crouched burial without grave goods (Lanza 2015: fig. 12).

the case of some female burials (Figure 3.3).[9] It is not before the end of the fifth century that the number and quality of grave goods in Tarentum increase again. From the late fifth century BC onward, high quality red-figure vases are used as grave markers for some tombs. As lavish burials reappear only after the 430s BC, the Tarantine colonists who arrived at Heraclea presumably brought extremely modest burial customs with them.

HEROES AND MORTALS ...

During the first fifty to seventy years of Heraclea, one tomb stands out in terms of the number and quality of grave goods: the Tomb of the Policoro Painter (Figure 3.4). Even in "normal" cemeteries of the Classical period there are hardly any comparable burials. The Policoro tomb was discovered in 1963 after having been partially destroyed and plundered. It consisted of a cavity of 2.32 x 0.76 meters oriented roughly north-south. The interior was painted in white with a red stripe running along the wall; two large stone slabs covered the tomb (Figure 3.5). The grave goods included seven *hydriai* (six red-figure, one black-glazed), five *pelikai* (all red-figure except for one black-glazed), two red-figure *kotylai*, and five more black-glazed vases: a type C *kylix*, two small

9   Lippolis 1994: 137–140.

3.3 Inhumation burial from Tarentum, fifth century BC (Dell'Aglio 2015: fig. 7). (Courtesy of *Archivio fotografico della Soprintendenza Archeologia, Belle Arti e Paesaggio delle Province di Brindisi, Lecce e Taranto.*)

cups, and two small jugs. Table 3.1 with a list of the grave goods is based on Degrassi's catalog (1967). The Policoro Painter has not yet been attested elsewhere, and nothing is known about where he came from or where his workshop was based. On the other hand, the workshop of Amykos (Table 3.1, no. 3) was definitely based in Metapontum.[10]

The vases date the tomb to the late fifth century BC, although caution is required given that there may have been other objects which have been lost. The vases from the tomb were all confiscated from private houses where they had been illegally brought. The tomb group as it is presented today in the National Archaeological Museum at Policoro is the result of meticulous restoration work. According to the construction workers who were building an apartment on the site of the tomb and who were present during its discovery, the largest of the *hydriai* (no. 2) was placed in the center of the chamber and contained human bones, which have been lost.[11] The available data suggests that this is a cremation burial, although parts of the skeleton were not completely burnt.

The Policoro tomb was situated near the eastern edge of the so-called southern plateau at some distance from the East Necropolis (fourth to third centuries BC), which was situated in the plain below the plateau (see Figure 2.1).[12]

[10] Silvestrelli 2005.
[11] Degrassi 1967: 196.
[12] Tagliente 1986b.

3.4 Heraclea: Vases from the Tomb of the Policoro Painter (elaboration G. Gramegna, based on Degrassi 1967).

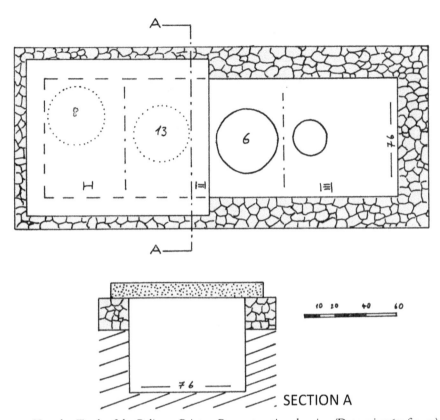

3.5 Heraclea, Tomb of the Policoro Painter: Reconstruction drawing (Degrassi 1967: fig. 57).

However, the tomb was not completely isolated, as some meters to the south a fossa tomb was excavated (tomb 2: Figure 3.6). Just like the Policoro tomb, it had been plundered, but the police did recover some grave goods: a red-figure *pelike* (proto-Apulian according to Degrassi), a black-glazed cup, a plate, and a red-figure *oinochoe* (proto-Apulian). We do not know where these finds are today as all attempts to trace them have failed. About ten meters northeast of the Policoro tomb, two further burials were found: tomb 3, which is said to have contained fragmented vases and the remains of an infant skeleton, and tomb 4, a fossa grave covered with four limestone slabs containing the remains of a child's skeleton and a small jug decorated with vertical red stripes.[13] As in the case of tomb 2, the finds are untraceable. In his publication of the Policoro tomb, Nevio Degrassi (1967) mentions yet another tomb which was discovered nearby. Unfortunately, it is not included in any topographical plan, and there are no photographs or drawings. The tomb contained "a group of unpainted amphorae brimming with the burnt bones of adults and children"[14] and therefore must have been multiple burials or *polyandrion*. The pottery finds

[13] Degrassi 1967: 196–197, note no. 7.
[14] Degrassi 1967: 196.

TABLE 3.1 *The Tomb of the Policoro Painter*

	Vases	Vase paintings and references
1	Red-figure hydria, h. 43.8 cm (Policoro Painter?)	Young couples, ballgames (shoulder); Silenus, youth, and young women (Degrassi 1967: 207–8)
2	Red-figure hydria, h. 57.8 cm (Creusa Painter)	Wedding preparations on the shoulder (Degrassi 1967: 210–12)
3	Red-figure hydria, h. 52.4 cm (Amykos Painter)	Youths, young women, and Eros on the shoulder (Degrassi 1967: 208–10)
4	Red-figure hydria, h. 44.5 cm (Policoro Painter)	Amazonomachy Amazon killed by naked youth with spear; above Sarpedon carried away by winged demons (Degrassi 1967: 197–202)
5	Red-figure hydria, h. 44.3 cm (Policoro Painter)	Medea fleeing on winged chariot, Jason with sword, dead children, and paidagogos (Degrassi 1967: 204–7)
6	Red-figure hydria, h. 44.4 cm (Policoro Painter)	Pelops on chariot with four horses, on the left Aphrodite, on the right Hippodameia (Degrassi 1967: 202–4)
7	Black-glazed hydria, h. 43.5 cm	(Degrassi 1967: 226)
8	red-figure pelike, h. 39.8 cm (Policoro Painter)	A: Two warriors flanked by two women, identified as Eriphyle, Amphiaraos, Polyneikes, and Harmonia from left to right B: Four mantle youths (Degrassi 1967: 221–23)
9	Red-figure pelike, h. 40.6 cm (Policoro Painter)	A: Dirke pulled under the bull by Amphion and Zethus B: Four cloaked youths (Degrassi 1967: 223–25)
10	Red-figure pelike, h. 44.5 cm (Karneia Painter?)	A: The Herakleidae led by Iolaos taking refuge at an altar, on the left a herald (from Athens), on the right Athena Promachos B: Four naked youths in the palestra (Degrassi 1967: 212–17)
11	Red-figure pelike, h. 45.0 cm (Karneia Group?)	A: Poseidon (identified in a graffito as POSDAN) with trident and another male figure (Hermes?) riding on horseback B: Athena with shield and helmet on a chariot with female charioteer, small olive tree on the left (Degrassi 1967: 217–21)
12	Black-glazed pelike, h. 44.0 cm	(Degrassi 1967: 226)
13	Red-figure skyphos, h. 17.0 cm	A: Woman with cist B: Silenus with tambourine (Degrassi 1967: 225–6)
14	Red-figure skyphos, h. 17.0 cm	A: Naked youth with strigilis B: Silenus (Degrassi 1967: 226)
15	Black-glazed type C kylix, h. 10.0 cm	(Degrassi 1967: 227)
16	Black-glazed Bolsal, h. 4.4 cm	(Degrassi 1967: 227)
17	Black-glazed Bolsal, h. 4.9 cm	(Degrassi 1967: 227)
18	Black-glazed jug, h. 7.3 cm	(Degrassi 1967: 227)
19	Black-glazed jug, h. 7.5 cm	(Degrassi 1967: 228)

and the bones are untraceable. The
Policoro tomb and the other tombs
probably lay outside the city walls,
although the precise plan of the fortification walls is unknown.

The Tomb of the Policoro
Painter is so named because Nevio
Degrassi believed that the Policoro
Painter himself was buried there.[15]
Others have argued that the tomb
belonged to a female member of
the local elite, possibly a priestess,
based on the fact that *hydriai* were
typically "female" vases and that
most of the myths depicted on the
vases have female protagonists.[16]
Furthermore, it has been observed
that two vases refer to Athens in
important ways: *pelike* no. 10 shows
the Herakleidae in Athens and *pelike*
no. 11 shows Athena and Poseidon
on their way to the contest about
Attica (Figures 3.7 and 3.8). On
these grounds, Giampiero Pianu has
suggested that the person buried
in the Policoro tomb originated in
Athens and had come to Heraclea via Thurii.[17]

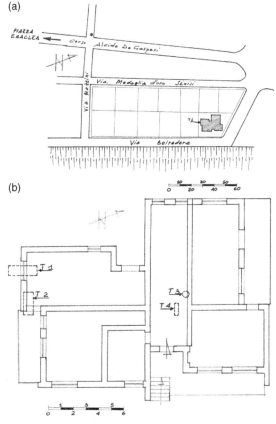

3.6 Heraclea: Tomb of the Policoro Painter (T1) and neighboring tombs (Degrassi 1967: fig. 46).

However, it remains to be explained why no comparable burials are known
from Athens, nor from any other Classical polis.[18] The Policoro tomb is unique.
It is true that the use of *hydriai* has parallels in cremations in Athens, Kamarina,
Tarentum, and Chersonesus. For example, in Chersonesean elite burials of
the fourth century BC, bronze *hydriai* were used as cinerary urns,[19] and in
Kamarina several Classical tombs contained two or three *hydriai* (bronze, black-
glazed and/or red-figure *hydriai*).[20] In Tarentum, a number of tombs dating to
the second half of the fifth century contained one *hydria*, which makes them

[15] Degrassi 1967: 231.
[16] Pianu 1989. Trendall 1989: 22 wonders "whether the set from the Policoro tomb might not
have been specially commissioned for someone who had a particular fondness for Euripidean
drama or had possibly been himself an actor."
[17] Pianu 1989; 1997.
[18] Cf. Kunze-Götte, Tancke, Vierneisel 1999.
[19] Carter 2003: 95.
[20] Lanza 1990.

3.7 Tomb of the Policoro Painter: Vase no. 11, side A (Degrassi 1967: pl. 66).

special, given the absence of grave goods in most of the other tombs of this period.[21] No doubt the use of *hydriai* as funerary vases was widespread in Classical Greece but as far as I know there is no burial in any Greek city of this period with a similar number of *hydriai*, *pelikai*, or *amphorae*. The quantity and quality of the vases from the Policoro tomb recall fifth century Athenian *Opferrinne* assemblages, e.g., the so-called bride's service from the Kerameikos necropolis (c. 430 BC), although the ritual is quite different.[22]

In terms of ritual practices, a close parallel to the Policoro tomb comes from Poseidonia or Paestum on the Tyrrhenian Coast of southern Italy.[23] In the agora of Poseidonia, archaeologists discovered a subterranean chamber measuring 3.55 x 3.85 meters (Figure 3.9). It had a ridged roof that was originally covered by an earthen tumulus.[24] Judging from the finds, the subterranean chamber was built around 510 BC. Inside, the excavators found six bronze *hydriai* and two bronze *amphorae* lined up along the walls which contained the remains of a viscous liquid, perhaps honey, as well as a black-figure *amphora* with a depiction of the apotheosis of Herakles (Figure 3.10). Five iron spits *(obeloi)* were placed on a low stone basis in the center of the chamber.

Mario Torelli has long pointed out the parallels with the Policoro tomb.[25] Indeed, the vase shapes and quantities are extremely similar, with the important difference that the underground chamber in Poseidonia contained no human bones or ashes. Some scholars have interpreted the complex as a cult site dedicated to a female deity.[26] However, Emanuele Greco, who has conducted new

---

[21] A. D'Amicis, in Lippolis 1994: 150–151.
[22] Houby-Nielsen 1996: 49.
[23] Cf. M. Torelli, *Dibattito*, in Siritide e Metapontino 1998: 322.
[24] Greco 2014.
[25] *Op. cit.* See also Bottini 1992: 97, who stresses the tomb-like character of the monument.
[26] Kron 1971 (female heroic cult); La Rocca 1972/3: 443–444 (Aphrodite Nymphia).

excavations around the chamber (first discovered in 1954), believes that it was the cenotaph of the legendary founder of Poseidonia (or of the mother-city Sybaris?).[27] The underground chamber lies in the agora – the place where one would expect the *heroon* of the city founder. What is more, it was not accessible and was completely hidden beneath the tumulus, a typical feature of tombs rather than sanctuaries.

Mario Rausch (2000) points out an interesting parallel that ultimately supports the hypothesis that the underground chamber in Poseidonia was the *heroon* of the city founder, although Rausch himself does not admit this. As he emphasizes, the subterranean chamber, the presence of honey, wine (amphora), and iron spits recall rituals performed in honor of the *Tritopatores* ("third fathers") in Selinus, which

3.8 Tomb of the Policoro Painter: Vase no. 11, side B (Degrassi 1967: pl. 67).

are described on a bronze tablet found in one of the suburban sanctuaries of the city.[28] This does not mean that the underground chamber in Poseidonia was a *Tritopatreion*, as Rausch believes. The *Tritopatreion* in the Kerameikos necropolis of Athens, which is the only one yet to be excavated, looks totally different from the *heroon* of Poseidonia.[29] However, there are parallels in terms of ritual and religious beliefs which may help to shed light on the broader context. Just like the sanctuaries of the "third fathers," the underground chamber in Poseidonia was apparently dedicated to a heroic figure belonging to a past generation.

The same may be true for the Policoro tomb. In my opinion, the parallels between the *heroon* of Poseidonia and the tomb in Policoro suggest that the latter was some kind of heroic burial. However, it was not the *heroon* of the city founder of Heraclea as the Greeks used to bury the official founder of a colony

---

[27] Greco 2014. See also Greco, Theodorescu 1983: 74–79; Bottini 1992: 97–103 (*heroon*).

[28] Rausch 2000; *lex sacra* from Selinus: Jameson, Jordan, Kotansky 1993: 29–37, 63–73 (*melíkarta* = honey drink).

[29] See Knigge 1988: 103 fig. 97.

3.9 Paestum: Underground chamber in the agora. (Courtesy of *Parco Archeologico di Paestum*.)

(if there was one) in the agora. Besides Poseidonia, such "(pseudo-)burials" have been discovered in the agora of Cyrene and Selinus. Thucydides's account of Amphipolis demonstrates that the tradition of burying the city founder in the agora continued well into the fifth century BC.[30] Another example is fourth century Kassope, where a monumental chamber tomb has been interpreted as the *heroon* of the city founder. It is situated inside the walls, though not in the agora; its dating is unclear.[31]

Geophysical prospection and new excavations suggest that the agora of Heraclea was situated on the Castello hill east of *insula* I.[32] On the other hand, the Policoro tomb is located far from the agora in a marginal zone among other tombs. At least one of them must be roughly coeval, as it contained early Apulian red-figure ware (the finds are lost so this cannot be proven). It would be useful to know more about the multiple burial found in the vicinity, but all attempts to trace the finds have failed. It might have been a public monument created after some catastrophic event. Degrassi says it contained bones of children which means that it was not a warrior tomb. The individuals buried here might have died in an attack on the settlement, from famine, or from an epidemic.

[30]   Thuc. V 11,1.
[31]   Hoepfner, Schwandner 1994: 141–144; Koukouli-Chrysanthaki 2002: 69–73.
[32]   Osanna *et al.* 2015 (who reject the location of the agora by G. Pianu 2002).

3.10 Paestum, underground chamber in the agora: Bronze hydriai and black-figure amphora. (Photo F. Valletta/G. Grippo, courtesy of *Parco Archeologico di Paestum*.)

Evidently, the Policoro tomb was situated in a burial area, though maybe a special one. Multiple burials and public grave monuments often lie on important roads or in central areas of a necropolis. We do not know much about the topography of the area, as it was built over in the 1960s and many finds were lost, but it is likely that a road passed nearby.[33] This may explain why some special burials were located here and not in the so-called East Necropolis at the foot of the plateau.

Who then was the person buried in the Policoro tomb? According to Degrassi and Pianu, the vase paintings show that the owner of the tomb had close connections with Athens, or may even have come from there. They stress that some of the mythological scenes on the vases have parallels in Euripidean drama, although what is depicted on the vases was not always visible on stage. For example, the killing of Dirke by Amphion and Zethus was not enacted on stage but reported by a messenger.[34] Furthermore, if a myth appears on southern Italian vase paintings and in a play by Euripides, this does not necessarily prove any direct relation. However, two vases explicitly refer to Athens: the contest for Attica between Athena and Poseidon (*pelike* no. 11: Figures 3.7 and 3.8) and Iolaos with the Heracleidae supplicating for protection in Athens (*pelike* no. 10). The two images could be read as anti-Dorian propaganda: Poseidon, who was widely worshipped in the Peloponnese (and in Tarentum) and who is denoted by his Dorian name "Posdan" on the Heraclean pelike, is defeated by

[33] Quilici 1967: map IV.
[34] Degrassi 1967: 230–231; Trendall 1989: 22.

Athena, as in the contest between the two for the possession of Attica, Athena's gift to the Athenians (the olive tree) prevails over the horses of Poseidon. To leave no doubt about the meaning of the image from Policoro, the vase painter added a small olive tree beneath Athena's chariot. Likewise the myth of the Heracleidae, especially in its Euripidean version (dating to the 430s BC), could be read as propaganda for Athens and against Sparta: the Athenians protect the children of the Doric hero Herakles from their own kin, King Eurystheus of Mycenae.[35]

As mentioned before (Chapter 1; cf. Diodorus XII 36,4), Tarentum founded Heraclea by adding settlers of Tarentine origin. In other words, Tarentum reinforced an existing community. This community must have been the joint colony founded by Tarentum and Thurii some years before. Thus, the Thurian colonists who were already living in the area probably stayed there. In the past, archaeologists were quite optimistic about finding Thurian and Athenian traditions in the material culture of Heraclea, for example on coins, which would have corroborated the role of Thurii in the foundation of Heraclea. However, Aldo Siciliano now interprets the earliest coins of Heraclea as anti-Thurian propaganda.[36] At the same time, new research confirms that the material culture of Heraclea closely resembled that of its mother-city Tarentum, as the production of clay figurines and the use of imported Carparo stone may illustrate.[37] Nowadays, the Athenian elements in the Policoro tomb appear more isolated than ever. But perhaps this is precisely what explains the unique character of the tomb. As we have seen, in terms of ritual, the closest parallel so far known is the heroon of Poseidonia. Yet the Policoro tomb lies among other tombs and therefore cannot be the heroon of the official founder of the city. In other words, it is likely that the person buried here played a crucial role in the foundation period, although she/he was not honored as the official founder. The Athenian elements in the vase paintings suggest that the owner of the Policoro tomb had an Athenian/Thurian background, and that background might have prevented the city of Heraclea from honoring her/him as a founder hero.

... AND SOMETHING IN-BETWEEN?

The data from Heraclea does not support the hypothesis that there were only two kinds of tombs in Classical settlements, especially in those that were democratic: standardized type burials outside the walls and the founder's *heroon* in the agora. We have seen that there was also something in-between.

[35] Pianu 1997.
[36] Siciliano 2008: 99–100.
[37] On the *pinakes*, see Bianco, Crupi, Pasquino 2012.

Among the earliest tombs of Heraclea at least three categories can be distinguished: inhumations without grave goods, cremations with a single vase, and the Policoro tomb.

Interestingly, in Thurii there is a comparable range of tomb categories. South of Thurii, about forty mounds are scattered over the countryside; they were once the only visible monuments in the area, as the ancient city was hidden under thick alluvial layers not far from the mouth of the River Crati (ancient Crathis) in the middle of a wide coastal plain. Between 1879 and 1899, four mounds were excavated.[38] It turned out that they were tumuli of the Classical period. Unfortunately, the pottery finds were lost. However, preliminary reports in *Notizie degli Scavi* 1879 and 1880 as well as notes and drawings from the nineteenth-century excavations give some insight into the stratigraphy and chronology of the tumuli.[39] The *timponi*, as they are called in the local dialect, were distributed over an area about 8 kilometers in length southeast of Thurii. It is not known with any certainty how many of them are burial mounds and how many are just natural mounds or palaeodunes. We also have little idea where the other cemeteries of Thurii lay and how they looked.

The first tumulus (the so-called *Timpone piccolo*) is a collective burial, which recalls Classical tumuli in the Kerameikos necropolis of Athens with groups of tombs overlying each other. Originally, the *Timpone piccolo* measured about 16 meters in diameter and was five meters high. The upper layers yielded remains of four inhumation burials without any grave goods, all oriented eastwards. About 1.5 meters below the surface the excavators noted burnt bones and ashes, probably the remains of cremation burials. The subsequent layer was deep black and contained two other inhumation burials. However, the most important discoveries were yet to come: It turned out that the tumulus covered an older and much smaller tumulus that partially incorporated another small tumulus. Each of the small tumuli contained a stone cist with skeletons that were partially burnt (semi-cremation). One of the tumuli is said to have contained another inhumation burial, but there is no further data to verify this. The stone cists contained no grave goods, except for three Orphic gold tablets placed next to the right hand of the deceased (the tablets were sent to Naples where they are still preserved). The earthen layers around and on top of the tombs yielded numerous pottery fragments. The available data suggests that the "Small Tumulus" was erected in the fourth century BC.[40]

As we have seen, this tumulus was built on top of three extraordinary tombs, two of them in stone coffins and containing Orphic gold tablets. Angelo Bottini has long emphasized the heroic character of these burials which are

---

[38] Guzzo 2005.
[39] Cf. Coscia 2012.
[40] Bottini 1992: 27–51; Coscia 2012.

clearly different from "normal" burials around and on the tumuli.[41] The other burials had neither stone slabs to protect them nor individual grave goods. Obviously, there was a clear distinction between the older, heroizing burials and later burials on the tumulus. The latter are further divided into inhumations and cremations, which were the more expensive ones. Pottery fragments from various layers show that collective rituals accompanied the building of the tumulus. The people buried in the Small Tumulus may have belonged to the same family or clan, but there is no way to prove this.

According to Bottini, the so-called Orphic gold tablets belonged to people who were initiated in Orphic or Dionysian cults *(mystai)* and whose tombs were deliberately separated from the urban necropolis.[42] However, as we do not know other tomb areas around Thurii, it is difficult to say how exceptional and marginal the *Timponi* actually were.

Timpone no. 4 was also a collective burial. The excavation report mentions human bones and teeth mixed with fragments of pottery and metal objects.[43] By contrast, the biggest tumulus (*Timpone grande*) seems to have contained only one tomb. Although archaeologists excavated a large portion of the "Great Tumulus" with a diameter of 28 meters and a height of 8 meters, they discovered only a single burial. It was placed in the center at ground level and consisted of a stone cist (2.43 x 1.32 meters) containing ashes, cremated bones, and a human skull (oriented westward). Again, Bottini speaks of a semi-cremation, which he interprets as a ritual imitation of death through a lightning strike, and thus of apotheosis.[44] The remains were covered with a cloth of white linen, not spoiled by fire or ashes and perfectly conserved at the moment of the opening of the tomb. Finds of metal fittings further show that the deceased lay in a wooden coffin. The excavators also found two small wooden boxes decorated with palmettes, silver plaques, and a stylus.[45] The stylus was found on the chest of the deceased, and fragments of gold plaques on her/his head (possibly a crown). Two Orphic gold tablets with incised letters were found next to the skull. Like the other gold tablets from Thurii, they contain prayers and directions for the soul of the deceased to reach the realm of Persephone.

According to the excavation reports, the Great Tumulus consisted of 13 layers. The lowermost layer contained ashes, charcoal, and wooden remains. Descriptions of (lost) pottery finds suggest that the tumulus dates to the late fifth century BC, although this should be treated with caution. The excavators

---

[41] Bottini 1992: 63.
[42] Bottini 1992: 63–64.
[43] *Notizie degli Scavi* 1880: 153.
[44] Bottini 1992: 48–49.
[45] Bottini 1992: 47.

mention "Classical burials" arranged around the Great Tumulus, but no further data is available.[46]

At the center of another tumulus, the so-called *Timpone Paladino*, the excavators found a stone cist that tomb raiders had already plundered. As this became clear, the excavation was continued elsewhere. Thus, it remains unknown whether the Paladino tumulus contained other burials besides the plundered chamber tomb at the center. Pottery fragments found during the excavation date to the fifth century BC.

As we have seen, at least two tumuli, the *Timpone grande* and *Timpone Paladino*, date to the second half of the fifth century BC. It is likely that the individuals buried in the cist graves at the center of these tumuli were leading figures in the foundation period of Thurii. Walter Burkert even suspects that the *Timpone grande* was the tomb of the Athenian Lampon, who led the colonists together with another Athenian named Xenokritos (Diodorus XII 10). However, Lampon returned to Athens, where Thucydides (V 19) mentions him on the occasion of the peace of Nikias. He might have come back to Thurii before his death, perhaps after the failure of Athenian intervention in Italy, which he actively promoted,[47] or during the reign of the Thirty Tyrants,[48] but this only remains speculation. Lampon was known as a soothsayer linked to the cult of Demeter and Kore and to Pythagorean philosophy. This, of course, would fit in with the *Timpone grande* burial: the Orphic gold tablets from the tomb refer to Demeter and Kore; the use of linen is typical of Pythagoreans who were not allowed to dress in wool; the isolated position of the tumuli might express the isolated position of *mystai* in the community.

At the same time, Lampon cannot have been the official founder hero of Thurii. In 434/3 BC, the Thurians engaged in a *stasis* (upheaval, civil war) about the issue of who should be honored as the official founder of the city. The colonists from the Peloponnese were on one side and the Athenians on the other. Eventually, they convened to consult the oracle of Delphi; the Pythia proclaimed that they should worship "the god himself" (Apollo) as the *ktistes* (founder) of Thurii (Diodorus XII 35). At this point, neither Lampon, who definitely died after 434/3 BC, nor anyone else could be honored as the official founder and be buried in the city.[49]

Whoever was buried in the tomb of the *Timpone Grande*, it should be clear that she/he was a leading figure who received special honors after her/his death. It is not excluded that the leading figures of a colony also included women, as suggested by a passage in Strabo (IV 1,4) referring to the priestess

[46] *Notizie degli Scavi* 1879: 252.
[47] Scholion to Aristoph., Cl. 332 ("Lampon was also much active in politics. He appeared to be introducing oracles continuously about the colony of Thurii").
[48] On Lampon, see Podlecki 1998: 88–91.
[49] Nafissi 2007.

Aristarche and her role in the foundation of Massalia. The same holds for other heroic burials in Classical colonies such as the Policoro tomb. Less important individuals, even though members of the elite, were cremated and buried in bronze vessels or red-figure vases. There is something heroic about these tombs too, but unlike the stone cist tombs of Thurii and the Policoro tomb, they have many parallels in other Greek necropoleis and in indigenous sites of the period, e.g., in Roccagloriosa, Irsina, and Timmari. Another burial category consists of inhumations in simple pits without any grave goods. Inhumations of this category are known from Tarentum, Thurii, Heraclea, and Chersonesus Taurica; they probably belonged to citizens who received a formal burial but without special honors. The possibility of identifying burials belonging to subaltern groups, which are even less visible in the archaeological record, is fairly low.[50]

Kamarina is another Classical site that has yielded inhumations without grave goods. Yet the overall picture is different here, as a large number of rich tombs dating to the first fifty years after the foundation have come to light. Between 1904 and 1909, more than 1,600 tombs were unearthed. In the years 1972–1973, another 407 tombs were excavated.[51] Today, Kamarina is the Classical settlement with the best-known necropolis spanning the fifth and fourth centuries BC. Unfortunately, the excavation reports provide almost no information about the spatial organization of the tombs.

However, the data from Kamarina positively contradicts the hypothesis that democratic settlements were characterized by standardized type burials. Ritual practices and grave goods in fifth century Kamarina have close parallels in other Classical necropoleis in Sicily, especially in Gela and Akragas.[52] As in the case of Tarentum and its colony Heraclea, homeland traditions determined burial customs far more than democratic or egalitarian ideologies. From the earliest phase of the colony, both cremation and inhumation burials are attested. Many early cremations (third quarter of the fifth century BC) are quite modest and contain few or no grave goods – for example, SEP.619 with some plain vases, or SEP.671, an inhumation burial "in the bare earth."[53] On the other hand, there are quite exceptional cremations from the same period; for example, tomb SEP.567, which contained an unpainted stamnos and three other vases, including a black-glazed Bolsal.[54] Tomb SEP.1131 is another outstanding cremation. It contained a bronze hydria which is 40 cm high and dates to the middle of the fifth century BC, two kylikes, and two alabastra.[55] Some cremations recall early cremations in Heraclea, although the finds from Kamarina are

---

[50] On slave burials in Greece, see Kurtz, Boardman 1971: 198–199; Esposito, Pollini 2013.
[51] Salibra 2014 with bibliography.
[52] *Veder greco* 1988.
[53] Tomb numbers as in Lanza 1990.
[54] Lanza 1990: 21.
[55] Lanza 1990: 105–106.

much better preserved. Tomb SEP. 578 contained a large Athenian red-figure hydria filled with ashes and bones. The vase paintings show the departure of a warrior and are probably the work of the Peleus Painter.[56] Tomb SEP.615 consisted of a red-figure stamnos dating to the second half of the fifth century BC and containing the only known cremation of a child from Kamarina. Furthermore, the excavations yielded cremations deposited in red-figure craters: SEP.1145, SEP.1252, and SEP.1478. Among the early tombs, there is also an exceptional inhumation, tomb SEP.1222, dating to the last quarter of the fifth century BC. It was covered by four stone slabs forming a ridged roof. The body of the deceased had been laid out on a terracotta sarcophagus on a sort of bier, as suggested by four iron legs found inside. The tomb included three red-figure hydriai, an olpe, two lekythoi, and a lamp. The hydriai have been attributed to the Painter of the Louvre G443, the Christie Painter, and the Naples Painter, respectively.[57]

Among the tombs of Kamarina, a multiple burial (tomb SEP.1621) from the middle of the fifth century is particularly interesting since it dates to the first generation of the Classical colony. The excavation reports mention the remains of what might have been an *ustrinum* (cremation site), in the middle of which a small pit had been dug into the rock. Inside the pit, the excavators found a black-glazed bell crater 40 cm high covered with a roof tile and filled with "burnt bones belonging to several skeletons."

In some tombs, grave goods included fibulae and cloak pins typical of indigenous communities in eastern Sicily.[58] Such objects seem to point to cultural intermixing and intermarriage, but further analysis is needed to substantiate this hypothesis.

Apart from a broad spectrum of grave goods, the necropolis of Kamarina has yielded one of the earliest examples of a grave *naiskos* with a marble sculpture. It dates to the last decades of the fifth century BC.[59] Given that marble works are extremely rare in Classical colonies, the naiskos in Kamarina is noteworthy. Both grave goods and grave markers clearly distinguish the necropolis of Kamarina from other colonial cemeteries of the period. A possible explanation for this shall be provided later on in this volume (see Chapter 7).

The extraordinary character of the necropolis of Kamarina becomes clear if it is compared to Amphipolis: Based on the published data, the necropolis of Amphipolis, which was an Athenian colony, has yielded less Athenian imports than that of Kamarina.[60] The settlers of Amphipolis buried their dead in simple pits that recall the burial practices at Thurii and Heraclea. Finds of

---

[56] Beazley 1968: 1041 no. 11; Lanza 1990: 23–24.
[57] Lanza 1990: 120–121.
[58] Lanza 1990: 188.
[59] Ghisellini 2010: 290–292.
[60] Lazaridis 1983: 38–39; 1984: 40–41; 1997: 72–73; Koukouli-Chryanthaki 2002: 57–59.

iron nails suggest that in some cases they used wooden coffins.[61] As at Athens and Thurii, pottery is found both inside and around the tombs. In some cases, aboveground grave markers are documented. They usually consist of terracotta tiles forming small roofs (*kalyvites*); from the fourth century BC onwards, individual tombs had marble stelae. During the first two generations of the colony, grave goods are extremely scarce and modest. Some tombs contained Athenian white-ground lekythoi while others had no grave goods at all. Only a small number of tombs have yielded more expensive vases, e.g., an Athenian red-figure crater showing ephebes running a torch-race, dating to the last quarter of the fifth century BC. Among and beneath tombs of the fifth and fourth centuries BC, archaeologists have found inhumations in rectangular pits and cremations without any grave goods.[62] These extremely modest burials probably date back to the first generations of the colony. Given the variety of burial types attested in the late fifth century BC, the necropolis of Amphipolis points to social differentiation rather than to egalitarian burial ritual.

Excavations near the museum, in an area inside the ancient walls, led to the discovery of a tomb that has been identified as the heroon of Brasidas, the official founder hero of Amphipolis after 422 BC. The tomb lies in the courtyard of a fourth century building and consists of two cavities: one contained a silver *larnax* with bones and a golden wreath; the other held pottery fragments, which have been interpreted as votive objects (Athenian red-figure and black-glazed *skyphoi*, bowls, plates, *kantharoi*, lamps, and fragments of other vessel forms). Most of the material is unpublished. Analyses of the bones from the cremation burial suggest that the buried person was a 35- to 45-year-old man.[63] This age would fit Brasidas. However, scholars who have seen the unpublished materials believe that the tomb dates to about a century after Brasidas's death.[64]

Overall, the cemeteries of Classical colonies offer a relatively broad spectrum of burial types and ritual practices. This, of course, corresponds to the general situation in the Greek world, though with two important exceptions: First, the cist graves of Thurii and the Policoro tomb have no direct parallels in homeland cemeteries, and second, the extreme simplicity of many early burials with few or no grave goods seems to be typical of colonial settlements.

Similar characteristics emerge, however, from the analysis of burials in newly established settlements that were not colonies but *synoikismoi*, such as Olynthus. The idea of type burials does not seem to apply here, although most burials were extremely basic. Out of 600 excavated burials, 53 are cremations – 47 of which contained grave goods that clearly distinguished them

[61] Lazaridis 1983: 39.
[62] Lazaridis 1983: 39.
[63] Koukouli-Chrysanthaki 2002: 60–73.
[64] See Mari 2010: 409–410 (with bibliography).

from other burials. Among the cremations, the percentage of infant burials is much lower than the general average. Furthermore, "cremations contained more pottery than other objects in comparison with inhumations, and the pottery was mainly of the less ordinary kind" (Robinson 1942: 146, 144–157). In other words, cremations generally belonged to upper class adults.

The 540 inhumations offer an equally heterogeneous picture (Robinson 1942: 158–173). As the excavators have pointed out (Robinson 1942: 174), "[n]ot all graves contained furniture. Only a little more than 60 per cent of them contained any objects at all, and often the objects were no more than poorly-made little saucers." Furthermore, "[h]alf of the adult inhumations were protected by terracotta roof tiles, the remainder being buried in stone or wood coffins or without any rigid protection" (Robinson 1942: 158).

A third category of burials is represented by a sole chamber tomb discovered about 1,040 meters west of Olynthus. It was plundered long ago (possibly in antiquity), but pottery fragments found during the excavation suggest that it was built in the late fifth or early fourth century BC.[65] Beside the pottery, the excavations have yielded some small fragments of bronze petals, beads, gilded jewelry, and "many fragments of very thin bronze sheet, flat or slightly rounded, gilded on both sides, of which the total area preserved was about fifty or sixty square centimeters."[66] As at Thurii, the tumulus lies at some distance from the urban center. The bronze sheet from Olynthus does not have any engraved letters and it is not known whether it had anything to do with mystic or Orphic beliefs, but the parallels are intriguing.

NON-GREEK BURIALS

In most settlements, the numbers of archaeologically visible burials – including those without any grave goods – remain low during the early years. It is often difficult, or even impossible, to distinguish between female and male burials. Evidently, the archaeological record is not representative of the entire community. Archaeologically visible tombs probably represent only a small segment of the population. Even the most modest inhumations may belong to citizens and elite-members who received a formal burial, though without grave goods, and not to subaltern groups. This is also the case for non-Greeks whose burials have been discovered in Chersonesus, Kamarina (?), and Heraclea in Lucania. These people were neither slaves nor peasants. They seem to be members of non-Greek elites who had established contacts with the Greek settlers or had become Greek citizens.[67] In other words, indigenous burials point to ethnic intermixing at an elite level; they do not reflect subaltern identities.

[65] Robinson 1942: 117–124.
[66] Robinson 1942: 123.
[67] Cf. accounts on "hellenized barbarians" as analyzed in Moreno 2007: 146–169; Hall 2002: 221.

In the early years of Chersonesus Taurica (late fifth century BC), alongside typically Greek burials in a supine position, there are some crouched burials, which have close parallels in non-Greek inland settlements.[68] Neither the spatial distribution of the tombs nor the grave goods (scarce or totally absent in both groups) point to any hierarchical distinction between supposedly Greek and Tauric burials. It seems that the colony originated as a mixed settlement of Greeks and locals of equal status.[69] Of course, there may have been slaves (locals and/or Greeks), but they do not appear in the necropolis.

At Heraclea, a crouched burial without grave goods was excavated among some Hellenistic tombs in the so-called southern Necropolis (see Figure 3.2).[70] The general context suggests that it may date to the fourth or third centuries BC. In spite of the indigenous burial type and the absence of grave goods, I doubt that the person buried here was a slave or a servant. As inscriptions from the sanctuary of Demeter suggest, names of slaves were usually Hellenized (see Chapter 2). In general, the cultural identity of slaves did not command much respect in the Greek world. Thus, it is highly unlikely that slaves received a formal burial of a non-Greek type. Rather, the crouched burials of Heraclea and Chersonesus belonged to non-Greeks who had a relatively high social status, although it is impossible to tell whether they were Greek citizens.

At Heraclea, only one crouched burial is known, but there may have been many more individuals with a non-Greek cultural background. In the fifth century BC, indigenous burial customs in southern Italy underwent a drastic change. In many areas, burials in a supine position replaced crouched burials, a process usually ascribed to the arrival or ethnogenesis of the "Lucanians." Many Lucanian tombs are not distinguishable from Greek tombs of the same period, as both regularly include Italiote black-glazed and red-figure vases, which were produced by itinerant workshops roaming between coastal and inland areas. The population of Heraclea might have included non-Greeks without them being archaeologically visible through specific burial customs. Some burials, despite being "normal" inhumations, are likely to belong to indigenous individuals as they contain special objects, most notably armor and weapons. Interpreting such objects as ethnic markers is of course debatable. Some scholars utterly reject any possibility of tracing ethnic identities in Classical burials of southern Italy.[71] I would agree that grave goods are of no use if ethnicity is defined as a biological category. However, if ethnicity is considered as a cultural construct that may undergo change and hybridisation (as I think it should be), then material culture certainly is significant.[72] Literary sources show that

---

[68] Belov 1950; 1981; Zedgenidze, Savelja 1981.
[69] Carter 2003: 22.
[70] Lanza 2015: 96–97.
[71] Nowak 2009; 2014.
[72] Díaz-Andreu García 2005; Shepherd 2011; 2013: 549–552.

ethnicity as a cultural category was crucial for the self-perception of southern Italian communities during the Classical and Hellenistic periods.[73] Under certain circumstances, clothes, weapons, and pottery may have contributed to the construction of collective or individual identities, though phenomena that are less visible in the archaeological record, such as body treatment and ritual, were probably much more important.

At Heraclea, five tombs with armor and/or weapons are currently known.[74] They date to the fourth and early third centuries BC and probably belonged to individuals with an indigenous background – I will discuss some of them in Chapter 6. The presence of non-Greeks ultimately complicates the social structure of the colonies. The fact that some of them adhered to traditional burial customs shows that they saw themselves as different from the Greek settlers.

MARGINALITY AND CENTRALITY

In the past, archaeologists have paid little attention to the spatial organization of ancient cemeteries, but this has begun to change. For example, Claire Lyons (1996), Gillian Shepherd (2007), and Francesco Quondam (in Luppino *et al.* 2010) have used spatial analysis to study identity and ritual in Archaic Sicily and southern Italy. Recently, scholars have started to apply similar approaches to the analysis of Classical cemeteries, though not in the colonies.[75]

We still know extremely little about the spatial organization of colonial cemeteries of the Classical period, especially during their early phases. In many cases, there is no data at all; in other cases, the excavation data has remained unpublished. Some new data is now available from Heraclea, where Mariafrancesca Lanza (2012) has analyzed a group of tombs in the so-called Southern Necropolis. Most of them date from the late fourth to the second century BC, but the spatial pattern that emerges here may be older.

At first sight, the spatial organization of the Southern Necropolis recalls the situation in mainland Greece. The tombs at Heraclea form clusters separated from each other by about ten to hundred meters (Figure 3.11). Lanza has identified more than seventy such clusters. In several cases, excavations have proved that the space between two clusters actually contained no burials. Although many tombs have been destroyed or plundered during construction work since the 1950s, there can be no doubt that the necropolis was organized in clusters. The tomb clusters appear to be distributed along two main axes, probably ancient roads crossing the necropolis. The earliest tombs of the Southern

---

[73] Adamesteanu 1972; Bottini 1999; Musti 2005: 261–284.
[74] Neutsch 1967: 160; A. Bottini, in Piranomonte 2001: 91.
[75] Sporn 2013.

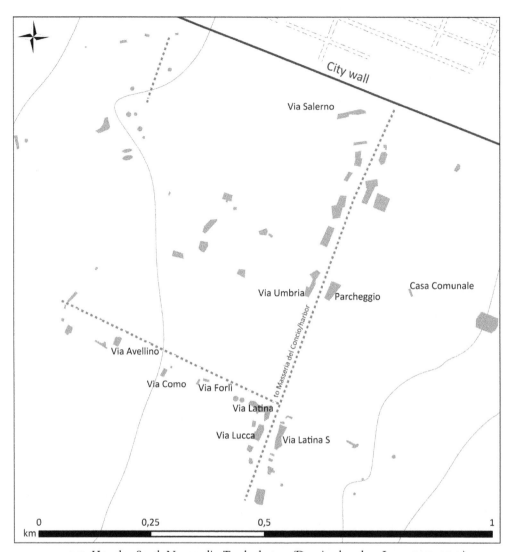

3.11 Heraclea, South Necropolis: Tomb clusters. (Drawing based on Lanza 2012; 2015.)

Necropolis, which date to the late fifth and the first half of the fourth century BC, belong to two separate clusters situated at a distance from each other. Given that many tombs of the early phases remain invisible, more than one cluster may date back to the late fifth or early fourth century BC.[76]

Lanza has looked closely at a cluster in Via Umbria and concludes that it was subdivided into several nuclei of tombs that probably corresponded to family groups (Figure 3.12). More recently, Giuseppina Crupi and Mariadomenica Pasquino (2015) have noted similar subdivisions in a cluster excavated in Via Salerno in 2009.[77]

[76] Lanza 2012: 182–185.
[77] On family groups in Western Greek cemeteries, see Carter 1998; Shepherd 2007: 99.

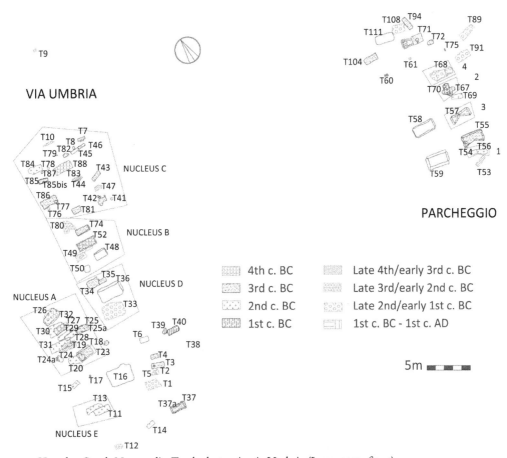

3.12 Heraclea, South Necropolis: Tomb clusters in via Umbria (Lanza 2012: fig. 5).

Lanza identifies four nuclei in the Via Umbria cluster (A, B, C, D), each one comprising about five to fifteen burials. The earliest burials, which date from the late fourth century BC, normally lie in the center. Some nuclei were in use until the second century BC. In the Via Salerno cluster, Crupi and Pasquino distinguish six nuclei dating from the late fourth to the second century BC (Figure 3.13). While the nuclei may represent small family groups, the clusters probably reflect clans or neighborhoods. In a fourth/third century inscription from Heraclea – known as the Heraclea Tablets (IG XIV, 645) – the name of each citizen is followed by his father's name and two signets, one of which seems to refer to his family or clan, while the other may refer to a larger unit, probably a *phyle*, *phratria*, or similar.[78] I believe that the tomb clusters reflect such units.

Clusters and nuclei containing different age and gender groups are a characteristic feature of many Classical cemeteries. They are found at Tarentum (although less clearly), Thurii, and Athens, where groups of tombs are arranged

[78] Uguzzoni, Ghinatti 1968: 125–129.

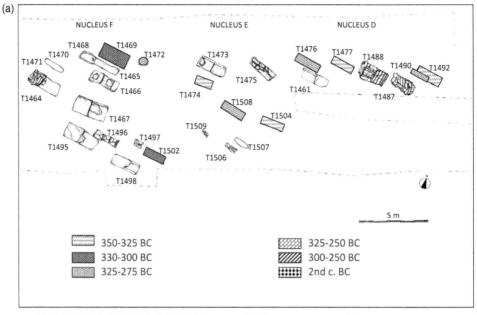

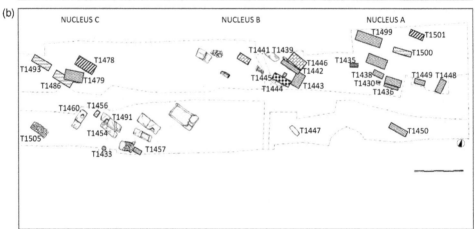

3.13 Heraclea, South Necropolis: Tomb cluster in via Salerno (Crupi, Pasquino 2015: fig. 3 & 4).

over burial mounds, forming distinctive clusters. The excavation of a large
burial mound (so-called Southern Tumulus) at Athens led to the discovery of
a Helladic tomb at its center. From the late sixth century BC onwards, several distinct tomb nuclei including both inhumations and cremations spread
over the slopes of the Southern Tumulus.[79] In the second half of the fifth century BC, the Athenians began to enclose groups of burials in so-called *periboloi*,

[79] Knigge 1976.

monumental precincts, which were often made of marble stone and belonged to rich families, as is demonstrated by inscriptions, sculptures, and grave goods.[80]

As should be clear by now, tomb clusters and nuclei are not typically colonial features. Yet there is something distinctive about the nuclei at Heraclea, since in several cases the oldest burial, which lies in the middle of the nucleus, belongs to an infant or a girl. To my knowledge, this is not a common phenomenon in the Greek world although future research may change this picture.

At the center of nucleus A in Via Umbria, we find two inhumation burials dating to the end of the fourth/beginning of the third century BC. One of them (tomb 27) had been plundered; the other (tomb 19) belonged to a child, as is suggested by the presence of a tintinnabulum bearing the depiction of a sleeping boy in a cradle. During the third century BC, three more tombs were added to nucleus A, and during the second century/beginning of the first century five more were added.[81] The neighboring nucleus B was formed around a cist grave of a girl from the middle of the fourth century BC (tomb 52). The grave goods are relatively rich and comprise two red-figure lekythoi and a lekanis, an alabastron, a golden ring, a small box, and a terracotta figurine representing *Aphrodite hoplismene*, i.e. armed Aphrodite (Figure 3.14).[82] Between the late fourth and the second century BC, twelve more tombs were placed around this tomb, including two relatively rich male inhumations. Nucleus C seems to consist primarily, if not exclusively, of infant and child burials.[83] Tomb nuclei of infants are known from other parts of the Greek world, for example on the Southern Tumulus in the Kerameikos of Athens where a group of *enchytrismoi* with skeletons of infants and children has been excavated.[84] Lanza identifies a fourth nucleus (D) which consists of four tombs although the one in the center had been plundered.

Thirty meters east of the Via Umbria cluster, another tomb cluster was found (via *Umbria-parcheggio*). Lanza suggests dividing the twenty burials excavated here into four nuclei, but I wonder whether the whole cluster could be interpreted as a single family nucleus with tomb 67 at the center. Tomb 67 dates to the third century BC and is a multiple burial consisting of a cremation and two inhumations, presumably of children or infants, although this is not clear from the excavation report. The tomb was covered by a crouched burial (tomb 70), which might belong to a person of non-Greek origin as argued above.[85]

[80] Closterman 2013.
[81] Lanza 2012: 187–188.
[82] Lanza 2012: 188.
[83] Lanza 2012: 190.
[84] Knigge 1976: 13.
[85] Lanza 2012: 193–194.

3.14 Heraclea, South Necropolis: Tomb 52 in via Umbria (Lanza 2012: fig. 8).

Excavations in the Via Salerno cluster have demonstrated that nucleus A formed around a burial of a mother and her newborn child from the second half of the fourth century BC (tomb 1500). Between the last quarter of the fourth century and the second half of the second century BC, at least ten tombs were added to this nucleus. Three of them belong to newborn babies, and three to young girls. As in Via Umbria, the girls' tombs have yielded unusually rich grave goods. Nucleus B in the Via Salerno cluster consists exclusively of infant burials, while nucleus C also has a girl's tomb at the center, distinguished by a particularly rich set of grave goods (tomb 1486). Crupi and Pasquino argue that the objects allude to the girl's wedding, as she probably died unmarried. Nuclei D and E have no clear boundaries and it is unclear whether they actually have been two separate nuclei or rather a single one. The southern part of nucleus F seems to be concentrated around a tomb with two newborn babies (tomb 1497), though this should be treated with caution as the bones have not been analyzed.

In many Greek cities, children and particularly young girls received special burials. However, the phenomenon is particularly evident in colonial cemeteries from the Archaic to the Classical periods.[86] Moreover, the fact that tombs of children and girls at Heraclea are found at the center, and date to the earliest phase of family nuclei is exceptional. It is unclear whether this method of organizing burial clusters goes back to the early phases of Heraclea or whether it was an innovation of the second half of the fourth century BC. Whatever the case, the period when girls' tombs become archaeologically visible is the same as the one when Philemena dedicates a bronze sheet on behalf of herself, her children, and grandchildren in the sanctuary of Demeter at Conca d'Oro.[87] In both cases, female members of the community are symbolically located at the center of lineage and kinship.[88]

[86] Shepherd 2013: 545.
[87] Cf. Prandi 2008: 128.
[88] Cf. Shepherd 2007: 100.

It is hardly surprising that the death of babies and children was considered worthy of special ritual attention, especially in a colony where the death toll among the youngest is likely to have been higher than elsewhere. What is unusual against the background of Classical Greek polis ideology is that these tombs should have become points of reference for entire family nuclei. In the light of the literary sources, this is entirely unexpected. Classical authors are not known for their love of children; in fact, some of them openly despised marriage and parenthood, either because they had other ideals, or because they considered educating and bringing up children a risky endeavor.[89] The interest of Greek political theory in children is almost entirely restricted to their future role as citizens. Reproduction is what matters; childhood and child bearing in themselves are of no interest.[90] It is also striking that a large number of texts and images portray children as sexual objects.[91] While some sources discuss motherhood, though mostly from the viewpoint of men, I can think of no explicit passage on fatherhood in Classical literature. The fact that male authors show so little interest in themes such as parenthood and childhood should be seen in the context of a culture that was described as "infanticidal" by Lloyd de Mauss in his famous 1974 study on the history of childhood.

In the context of colonization and urban planning, children became important when it came to obtaining the "right number" of citizens in a city-state.[92] Ancient authors discuss this issue almost exclusively with regard to male citizens, and not with regard to the entire population. Ancient texts suggest that in colonial settlements, demography was perceived as something that required awareness and control — not only at the moment of the foundation, but also long afterward.[93] Presumably, demography continued to be an issue at Heraclea as the colonists multiplied and new settlers arrived well into the fourth century BC.[94] In some way or another, the community had to face the problem of the "right number," be it in terms of overpopulation or be it in terms of a decreasing population. With regard to ideology and culture, however, this mainly concerned reproduction and not children as such.

At first sight, Athenian vase-paintings seem to give more importance to children than political philosophy.[95] Based on an analysis of Athenian red-figure pottery, Martina Seifert (2011) has argued that children were actively involved from a young age in specific rituals within the oikos and the phratria. However, it should not be forgotten that most of these vase paintings come

[89] See Democritus, Fragm Diels. 276. See also Dasen 2004.
[90] Cf. Plato, Rep. 460b–461e; Aristotle, Pol. 1266b, 1337a–1342b.
[91] Lear 2015.
[92] Plato, *Republic* 460b–461e; *Laws* 745c–747e.
[93] *Ibid.*
[94] Cf. Vokotopoulou 1991: 81–83 (people asking the oracle of Dodona whether they should go to Heraclea).
[95] Crelier 2008; Seifert 2011.

from funerary contexts. As at Heraclea, the importance and centrality of children within the community emerges in the sphere of death. I wonder whether such symbolic representations may really be taken as evidence of children's central role in society. Perhaps burial rituals simply compensate for, and therefore indirectly confirm, the social marginality of children. There is a striking contrast between the marginal role of children in life and their prominence in death. This contrast also emerges in Jason's behavior in Euripides' *Medea*: on the one hand, Euripides depicts him as a poor, uninvolved father, while on the other, he appears most desperate after the death of his children:

JASON: Alas, how I long for the dear faces of my children, to enfold them in my arms.

MEDEA: Now you speak to them, now you greet them, when before you thrust them from you.

(verses 1399–1402, transl. D. Kovacs)

Are these the voices of two migrants, translated into myth? Whatever the case, the centrality of men in terms of demography and ideology contrasts with the centrality of children and girls and with the marginality of certain male inhumation burials in the Southern Necropolis at Heraclea. The transition from one social position (the marginal living child) to another (the centrality of the dead child's burial) may have originated in the notion of being responsible for the death of children and young women who had little or no possibility to make decisions about their lives. Such a sense of responsibility and guilt is more likely to develop in colonies and migrant families than elsewhere. In Euripides, Jason feels responsible only when his children are already dead; he demands to bury them in a city where he had not provided them with a secure place when they were still alive.

The decision to emigrate is seldom easy, as is illustrated in inscriptions found in Greek oracle sanctuaries, for example at Dodona. Among many others, the inscriptions include a man named Nikomachos who asks whether he should emigrate to Tarentum or to Heraclea (fourth century BC). We do not know what the answer was and how he decided, but any decision of such an importance could lead to self-doubt and remorse if it entailed, albeit only indirectly, the death of a child. The importance and centrality of children and young girls in the necropolis of Heraclea probably do not reflect their social position in life, but quite the opposite: Since their lives were subordinated to demographic and economic necessities, their death may have provoked, beside grief and despair, a feeling of guilt on the part of other family members. The tombs do not convey the voices of children and girls, but those of male adults who lived and expressed themselves in a colonial world.

FOUR

FIELDS: COLONIAL DEFINITIONS OF EQUALITY

In the previous chapters, I argued that domestic architecture and burial customs in Classical colonies reveal traces of economic hardship, social stress, and complex relations. The data positively contradicts the hypothesis that Classical settlements were characterized by standardized houses and tombs as expressions of equality and democracy. In this chapter, I argue that equality, which was crucial at the level of ideology, was first and foremost a question of land property and land use. Land distribution defined equality in the colonies and determined its limitations and peculiarities.

When in 2012 the *Scuola di Specializzazione in Beni Archeologici* of Matera (SSBA) started a field survey in the territory of Heraclea, one of our main goals was to find out more about rural life and land use in a Classical colony (Figure 4.1). However, after analyzing all the published data and conducting three field survey campaigns (2012–2014), we still have extremely little data regarding the period 450–350 BC. In past excavations and extensive field surveys, not a single habitation or tomb dating to this period was recorded. As far as the 2012–2014 field survey is concerned, out of 28,300 pottery fragments, not more than five (three skyphoi and two bowls) can be dated with any certainty to 450–350 BC (Figure 4.2).[1] They come from sites that have

---

[1]   I share the position held by R. Witcher in his paper on "Broken pots and meaningless dots..." (2006), but I do not agree – like some colleagues – that dot maps should be abandoned *tout court*. In my view, dot maps can still be useful if used as part of a broader range of analytic tools, including analysis of on-site pottery assemblages and off-site materials. However, in the

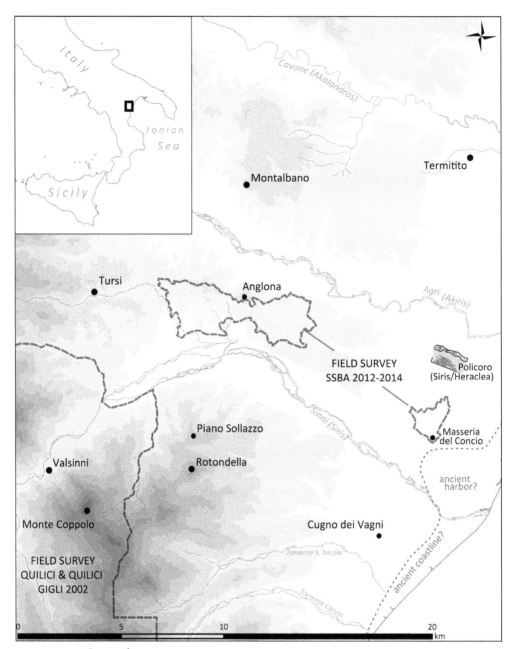

4.1 Surveyed areas, 2012–2014.

yielded considerable amounts of Hellenistic pottery (HE36/37, HE81, HE181, and HE209). Another site (HE91) has yielded two bowl rims that might be early fourth century BC (Figure 4.2), although the dating is not entirely clear.

case of the outer chora of Heraclea, off-site materials are extremely scarce; during our survey, we mapped them individually. By contrast, the higher density of off-site materials in the area around the urban center was systematically documented within each field spot.

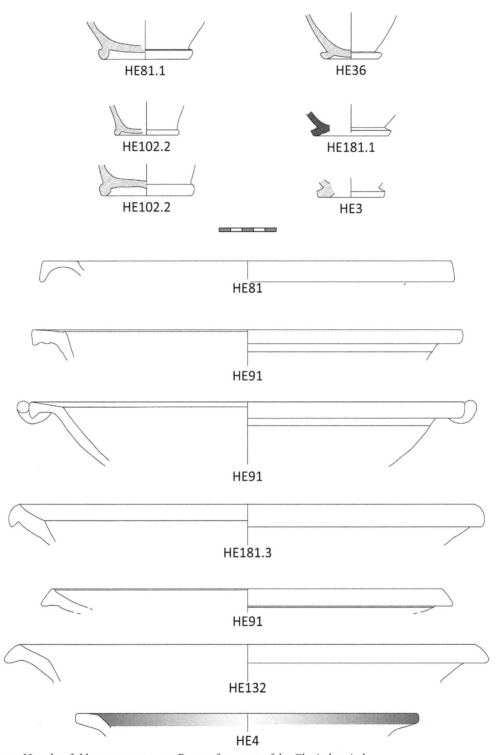

4.2 Heraclea, field survey 2012–2014: Pottery fragments of the Classical period.

HE91 was identified in the midst of excavation material from a modern canal which makes it difficult to assess the type of site.

To sum up, we do not know of one single site that was occupied exclusively during the Classical period. As a result, it is unclear whether and how roof tiles of the Classical period can be distinguished from later phases, which makes it difficult to recognize Classical phases on sites without diagnostic pottery finds. All that can be said is that three or four Hellenistic farmsteads have yielded a few pottery fragments dating to the early fourth century BC (Figure 4.3).

This is even more surprising if we consider that during the same period the chora of neighboring Metapontum was covered with farmsteads and rural burial areas. If we compare the density of rural habitations and tombs calculated on the basis of our field survey with the density of rural sites in the chora of Metapontum (based on Carter, Prieto 2011), the difference between the two territories becomes clear: For about 80–100 years after the foundation of Heraclea, rural sites, especially tombs, are practically absent in the archaeological record. The density of rural sites only reaches the level of Metapontum around 325 BC (Figure 4.4).

Geological and post-depositional processes can be ruled out as possible explanations, as there is little difference in this regard between the territory of Metapontum and that of Heraclea. Both are characterized by marine terraces with good archaeological visibility and large river valleys (Bradano, Basento, Cavone, Agri, Sinni) where no sites were found since everything is covered by thick alluvial layers – which is of course a phenomenon that concerns the Classical, Hellenistic, and Imperial periods alike. Furthermore, the material culture in both territories was very similar during the fifth and fourth centuries BC. Excavations and field surveys in the chora of Metapontum give an idea of how habitation sites of the Classical period appear in the archaeological record;[2] the fact that comparable evidence is so scarce in the chora of Heraclea is significant. It may be explained by the actual absence of rural habitation sites or the different nature of rural sites which makes them invisible in the archeological record.

EARLY RURAL SANCTUARIES

While rural habitation sites are missing or remain invisible during the first decades of the colony, a number of cult sites are attested from the very beginnings of Heraclea. One of the first cult sites to be established in the territory was the sanctuary of Piano Sollazzo. It is situated some distance from the urban center, above a valley that would later separate the Heraclean territory from the Lucanian territory around Mt. Coppolo (cf. Figure 4.3 and Chapter 6).

---

[2]   Carter 2008; Carter, Prieto 2011.

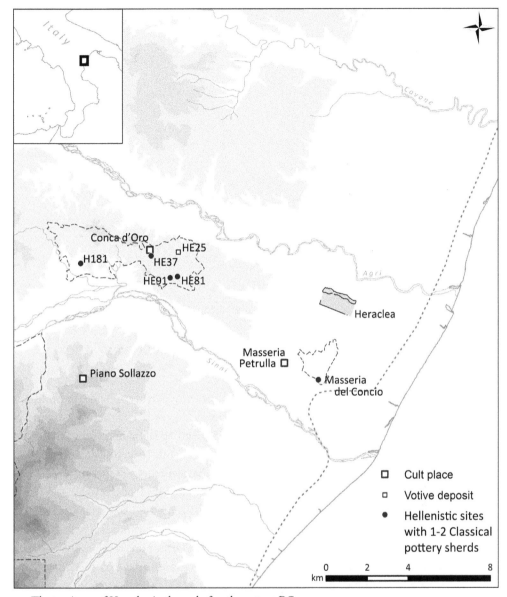

4.3 The territory of Heraclea in the early fourth century BC.

The evidence consists mainly of pottery and terracotta statuettes, but find-ings of pebbles point to the existence of one or more buildings. The materials were scattered over an area of about 30 x 30 meters. Distribution analysis sug-gests that most of the Classical and Hellenistic finds come from two separate votive deposits, which were scattered by plowing and can only partly be recon-structed. Published pottery finds suggest that the site was frequented as early as the seventh/sixth century BC, i.e., during the occupation of Siris by Ionian settlers. Among the Archaic finds there are fragments of *coppe a filetti*, Ionian cups, and Corinthian amphorae. The site may have been a sanctuary as early as

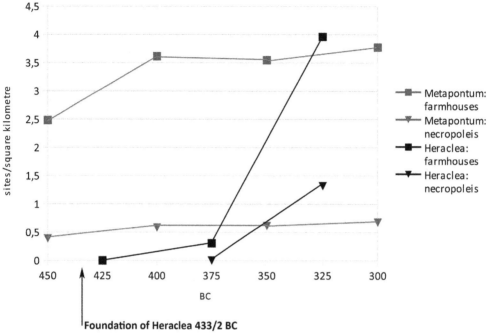

4.4 Density of rural sites at Heraclea and Metapontum, 450–300 BC.

the Archaic period, although there is no clear evidence of Archaic cult buildings or votive terracottas.[3] More than five-hundred terracotta statuettes and *pinakes* dating to the middle of the fifth to the third century BC demonstrate that from the foundation of Heraclea, Piano Sollazzo was definitely a cult site. Among the earliest terracottas, there is a series of *pinakes* (votive reliefs) depicting a male figure reclining on a *kline* and a female figure sitting at his feet (Figure 4.5).[4] These pinakes are not distinguishable from Tarentine products of the same period. It is likely that they were made at Tarentum or at Heraclea with molds brought from Tarentum.[5] Excavations in Tarentum have yielded hundreds of similar pinakes, while some isolated examples come from Metapontum and its territory. Most Tarantine examples come from votive deposits in the Classical necropolis, as well as from cult sites in the city and its territory.[6] At Heraclea, on the other hand, pinakes were not used in funerary rituals but are attested at several urban cult sites, namely in the Favale votive deposit south of the Varatizzo valley and in a deposit in Area B on the Castello hill. The reclining figures are now usually interpreted as citizens celebrating a ritual banquet, although some scholars have

---

[3] Berlingò 1994: 553; A. Casalicchio, *Appendice: I materiali ceramici*, in Crupi, Pasquino 2012: 327–335.

[4] Crupi, Pasquino 2012.

[5] Crupi, Pasquino 2012: 309–311.

[6] Lippolis, Garraffo, Nafissi 1995: 51–53; Poli 2010a.

4.5 Piano Sollazzo: Terracotta pinakes (Crupi, Pasquino 2012: fig. 4).

preferred to interpret them as local heroes or divinities.[7] Whatever the case, pinakes are not linked to the cult of one specific deity. Rather, they seem to be connected to certain rituals, given that the number of cult sites at Heraclea where such pinakes were found is fairly limited.

As well as the large number of pinakes, excavations at Piano Sollazzo have yielded terracotta figurines of young men with horses, which can be interpreted as Dioscuri, and young men sitting on various other animals.[8] These also have close parallels in Tarentum. Furthermore, terracottas depicting Silenoi and tragic masks and dozens of miniature vessels were found.

Piano Sollazzo is not the only rural sanctuary that goes back to the early years of the colony. The sanctuary of Demeter at Conca d'Oro may date back

7   Lippolis *et al.*, *op. cit.*
8   Poli 2010b; Crupi, Pasquino 2012: 314–317.

to the late fifth/early fourth century BC, as is suggested by finds of coins and terracotta figurines.[9] Similarly, the sanctuary of Masseria Petrulla, possibly dedicated to the Nymphs, has yielded fragments of red-figure pottery dating to the early fourth century BC.[10] Of course, these materials may have been deposited in the sanctuaries long after being produced,[11] but the combination of various types of evidence suggests that rural sanctuaries spread relatively early in the history of Heraclea.

The presence of rural sanctuaries from an early period contrasts with the absence or invisibility of farmsteads and tombs. Finds analysis suggests that at least two or three rural sanctuaries were established simultaneously with, or shortly after, the foundation of Heraclea. It remains unclear who frequented them, and there may well have been visitors from indigenous areas. However, the rural sanctuaries appear as outposts of Heraclea both from a political and religious perspective. They testify to the presence and interest of the community in the countryside.

If we combine data from excavated sites, especially cult sites, with our survey data, the countryside of Classical Heraclea appears in a new light. In the past, the paucity or lack of evidence of rural sites was often seen as a sign of economic and social underdevelopment. For example, Filippo Coarelli has interpreted the spread of rural habitation sites during the later fourth century BC as the result of a democratic revolution in Heraclea that put an end to some sort of oligarchic underdevelopment. According to Coarelli, the dense occupation of the countryside in the late fourth century BC stemmed from a "democratization of the chora."[12] Salvatore Bianco and Liliana Giardino, who argue that the urban center of Heraclea was underpopulated until 370/50 BC, believe that the spread of rural sites during the second half of the fourth century reflected the belated take-off of the polis as a whole.[13]

At this point, I would like to stress two points: First, there is some evidence for early settlement phases at Heraclea, as mentioned above (Chapters 2 and 3). In the second quarter of the fourth century, Heraclea was already a lively urban center. Second, the study of pottery assemblages from the 2012–2014 field survey shows that the number of sites increases significantly only during the last third of the fourth century BC (Chapter 5). Clearly, around 370/60 BC, the central place had developed into a fortified urban settlement, but only some forty to fifty years later do rural habitation sites become visible in the archaeological record. Heraclea was not generally underdeveloped; instead, what emerges is a contrast between the developing urban center and the "empty"

[9] Cf. Rüdiger 1969: 192–193; Zuchtriegel 2012b: 150.
[10] Battiloro, Bruscella, Osanna 2010.
[11] Osanna 2008: 52.
[12] Coarelli 1998: 285.
[13] Bianco 1999: 56; 2000: 812–813; Giardino 2012: 92–93, 111–112.

countryside. This kind of emptiness may be interpreted in various ways: There may have been no, or only very few, rural sites, or there were sites but they do not appear in the archeological record because they were too scanty to leave any recognizable traces. In any case, the situation was clearly different from neighboring Metapontum. In the territory of Heraclea, the presence of stable farmsteads of the kind attested around Metapontum in the late fifth and early fourth century BC can be excluded.

As I argue here, the settlement pattern that emerges from the study of Heraclea and its territory reflects the egalitarian ideology of Classical Greek colonists. On the other hand, the spread of farmsteads and rural necropoleis is not due to democratization and development, but simply to the break-up of the egalitarian structure that characterized the first two or three generations.

EQUAL IN WHAT?

The ideology of equality that shaped Heraclea in its early phases may be described as follows: The colonists were first and foremost landowners and agriculturalists, and they lived mainly in the urban center and not in the countryside. The notion of equality applied to land property but also to the place of residence, which had to be the same for all. With regard to equality, land property and urbanity were crucial issues, whereas standardized houses and tombs had symbolic importance at most. The important questions were how much land one got (and how much land one household could manage), and how close to the agora one lived. The importance of land property and urban residence emerges from literary and epigraphic sources, but also from the archaeological evidence at Heraclea and other Classical colonies.[14]

To begin with, in the text sources the crucial issues were always agriculture and land ownership. The settlers went for land, not for other resources or trade opportunities. This is nothing new: David Hume could "not remember a passage in any ancient author where the growth of the city is ascribed to the establishment of a manufacture,"[15] and archaeological data from Greek colonies of the fifth and fourth centuries BC fully coincides with this impression.

The most detailed account of land distribution in a Greek colony is included in the foundation decree of Korkyra Melaine on the island of Korčula (Croatia).[16] The inscription consists of several fragments found in a Roman cistern near the modern village of Lumbarda on the eastern side of the island. Based on letter-forms, the text can be dated to the late fourth or early third century BC.[17]

[14] Greco 1981; 1982; Osanna 1992: 144.
[15] Quoted from Finley 1973: 137.
[16] Syll.³ 141. Cf. Graham 1964: 42–43.
[17] Lombardo 2005.

The following translation is from Cahill (2002: 219–220, partly altered):

Good fortune. When Praxidamos was recorder *(hieromnemon)*, (in the month of) Ma[chaneus, an agreement of the oikis]ts of Issa and of Pyllos and his son Dazos. [The oikists wro]te this up and the people decreed it.

The first (colonists) [who took possession of the la]nd and who built the walls of the city will receive: of the fortified city, a house p[lot, on each] together with his portion; of the (land) o[utside it (i.e. the walled city), the same (colonists) will receive] a 'first allotment', (consisting of) [of the best land] three plethra, of the other (types of land), the (fixed) portions.

(The magistrates) shall write up [–] as each (colonist) received by lot. [One] and a half plethra (of land) shall be inalienable, for them and for their [offspring]. Those who come later shall receive: of the [city, one house plot, and] of the undivided (land), four and one-half plethra. Th[e magistrates shall swear neve]r to make a redistribution of the city or of the territory [in any way. If a magistrat]e proposes or a private citizen advocates anything contrary to wh[at has been decreed, let him be deprived of civic rights, and his prop]erty confiscated, and [whoever kills him will go] unpunished …

(two lines missing)

[– if the p]eople dec[ree –]

These people took possession of the coun[try and fortifi]ed the city:

(Tribe of) [Dyma]nes	(Tribe of) [Hylleis]	(Tribe of) Pamphyloi
[Ar]ch[e]laos son of Mesodamos	Hera[kleidas son of Theot]imos	Onasimos son of Kephalos
…	…	…

(there follows a list of 200–300 more names)

As becomes clear, each settler received a land lot in the chora but lived within the city walls. The same holds for Thurii during its early years, as Diodorus shows (XII 10–11, quoted in Chapter 1). One of the reasons for the civil war in Thurii was that the Sybarites had "portioned out the land lying near the city among themselves, and the more distant land to the newcomers." This was problematic because the land close to the city was the best, as it was easier to get there from the urban center, where the colonists lived. The Brea inscription also emphasizes the importance of land distribution, a task entrusted to ten *geonomoi*, one from each Athenian phyle.[18] None of this is surprising against the backdrop of Classical Greek text sources which tend to attribute greater importance to agriculture while despising craft production and trade. It is likely that those who went to live in a colony did so in order to become

---

[18] IG I³ 46.

landowners. It could be argued that the land lots of Korkyra Melaina were too small for the settlers to live off. However, while the inalienable part of the "first allotment" and the plots assigned to "newcomers" are actually quite small, the size of the *mere* (portions) allotted to each of the first settlers is unclear.[19] They may well have been large enough to feed a family.

Theoretically, all settlers – at least those belonging to the first generation – received not just land, but equal shares of land. David Asheri has frequently emphasized this point,[20] but more recent studies have questioned the hypothesis that land lots in Greek colonies were of equal size.[21] It is certainly true that there is little evidence of equal land distribution in Archaic colonies. The term *kleros* (lot), which implies some kind of equality, is used in the sense of allotment or piece of land only from the fifth century onwards (Hdt., Thuc.). In *The Odyssey* (VI 10), we hear that Nausithoos "divided the fields" (ἐδάσσατ' ἀρούρας), but this does not necessarily imply any *equal* land division. The Spartan *homoioi* may have been equals in terms of land property from a very early stage.[22] However, as Paul Cartledge has argued, *homoioi* may not mean equals but rather similar,[23] and Stephen Hodkinson's work shows that there was actually little economic equality among the Spartans.[24] Inheritance practices were more or less the same as elsewhere in Greece, except that daughters could inherit a half-share (as in Gortyn). This means that even if there should have been an initial moment when land shares were equal (which may be doubted), it would not have remained that way for long. There is good reason to believe that the tradition that Lycurgus divided the land into equal lots was invented in the third century BC by the kings Agis IV and Cleomenes III in order to justify their radical proposals aimed at reforming Spartan society.[25]

From the fifth century BC onward, the evidence is more abundant. Equal distribution of land, as in the case of the first settlers of Korkyra Melaina, appears to have been common practice at least from the second half of the fifth century BC. Thucydides (I 27,1) reports that in the year 435 BC, the Corinthians announced that anyone who wanted to could participate in the colonization of Epidamnos "on the basis of equality and parity" (ἐπὶ τῇ ἴσῃ καὶ ὁμοίᾳ), and Diodorus claims that shortly after 443 BC the people of Thurii divided the land "on equal terms" (ἐπ'ἴσης). Given the context, expressions such as ἐπ'ἴσης must refer to equal land division. The Athenian cleruchy on Lesbos, which was undoubtedly egalitarian, ultimately confirms this. As

[19] Cf. Lombardo 1992: 179.
[20] Asheri 1966.
[21] Hennig 1989; Gallo 2009.
[22] See the discussion in Hennig 1989: 30.
[23] Cartledge 2009: 9–10.
[24] Hodkinson 2002.
[25] Cartledge 2009: 110–119.

Thucydides (III 50) reports, the Athenian cleruchs did not take care of their *kleroi* individually, but received a sort of rent from the former owners who continued to cultivate the land:

> The Athenians also demolished the walls of the Mitylenians, and took possession of their ships. Afterwards tribute was not imposed upon the Lesbians; but all their land, except that of the Methymnians, was divided into three thousand allotments *(kleroi)*, three hundred of which were reserved as sacred for the gods, and the rest assigned by lot to Athenian shareholders, who were sent out to the island. With these the Lesbians agreed to pay a rent of two *minai* a year for each allotment, and cultivated the land themselves.
>
> (transl. E.P. Dutton, 1910)

Surprisingly enough, Luigi Gallo has argued that this would not imply the creation of equal allotments.[26] In my opinion, however, the egalitarian nature of the cleruchy emerges clearly from the fact that each shareholder received an equal amount of money from his lot, although we are unfamiliar with the way in which the rent was exacted in practical terms. If there had been no division of the land in equal lots (whether real or virtual), the same sum would have been exacted for small and large estates, which would of course be absurd.

In the case of Lesbos, the cleruchs were shareholders rather than settlers; in the case of Epidamnos, they virtually acted as investors who joined in an economic venture. According to Thucydides (I 27,1), the Corinthians proclaimed that "any who were not prepared to sail at once, might by paying down the sum of fifty Corinthian drachmae have a share in the colony without leaving Corinth." The result was that "great numbers took advantage of this proclamation, some being ready to start directly, others paying the requisite forfeit" (Transl. J.M. Dent, 1910). It is likely that those who paid a fixed sum to participate on equal terms in a colonial expedition expected to be given equal shares of land. The foundation decree of Cyrene also guarantees equality. However, the inscription, which purports to be original but in its preserved form dates to the fourth century BC, might be projecting ideas of the Classical period onto the early history the city.[27] There may never have been an equal distribution of land in Archaic Cyrene, but beyond doubt this was what was expected by people in the fourth century BC. By the Classical period, equality had become a central issue, and it was primarily a question of land distribution.

CITY WALLS

Besides land ownership and the equal distribution of land, another crucial issue emerges from the written sources: the attempt to ensure that the entire

[26]   Gallo 2009.
[27]   SEG IX 3. Cf. Graham 1964: 41–42.

community lived in the urban center. The most striking example is again Korkyra Melaina, where each colonist received a house plot *(oikopedon)* within the city walls. The privileged position of the first settlers – who received larger land lots than the others, as we have seen – is justified by the fact that they built the walls. Together with land distribution, fortifying a place to live in is one of the main concerns of the colonists. Korkyra Melaina is not the only example where this emerges: While written sources on Classical colonies very rarely refer to the construction of temples, public buildings and houses (let alone type houses), the building of fortifications is frequently mentioned. Hagnon built Amphipolis "so as to be conspicuous from the sea and land alike, *running a long wall across from river to river*" (Thuc. IV 102,3). When the Spartans founded a colony at Trachis, "*they fortified anew the city*, now called Heraclea, distant about four miles and a half from Thermopylae and two miles and a quarter from the sea, and commenced building docks, closing the side towards Thermopylae just by the pass itself, in order that they might be easily defended" (Thuc. III 92,6). The settlers of Thurii, "having found not far from Sybaris a spring called Thuria (…) and believing this to be the place which the god had pointed out, *threw a wall about it*, and founding a city there they named it Thurii after the spring" (Diodorus XII 10,6). "The Parians, who had settled Pharos, allowed the previous barbarian inhabitants to remain unharmed in an exceedingly well fortified place, while they themselves founded a city by the sea *and built a wall about it*" (Diodorus XV 13,2).[28] Other examples could be added. Recent scholarship has emphasized the symbolic value of fortifications,[29] but in many cases the colonies had actual need of them. For example, Thurii, Amphipolis, and Pharos were attacked shortly after their foundation. It was therefore preferable for the settlers to live in a fortified town rather than in the countryside. However, there was a further reason why the colonists would rather live in the urban center: only those who lived in or close to the urban center could fully exercise their citizen's rights. On the other hand, moving to the country often meant facing social downgrading and gradual exclusion from political participation, as will be seen in Chapter 5.

CLASSICAL COLONIES AS "ACKERBÜRGER POLEIS"

The model that emerges from both written sources and archaeological field-work is that of an egalitarian community of landowners living in a fortified urban center.[30] It is debatable whether this model already existed in the Archaic period, especially as far as equality is concerned, but the evidence is quite clear for the Classical period, at least in theory. To describe this model, I shall use the

[28] Transl. J.D. Dent, 1910 (Thuc.), and C.H. Oldfather, 1989 (Diod.), slightly altered.
[29] An overview of new approaches can be found in Lorentzen *et al.* 2010.
[30] Cf. Asheri 1966; Faure 1981: 95.

term "Ackerbürger polis," a term coined by Max Weber.[31] An *Ackerbürger* is an owner of land *(Acker)* who lives in a town *(Bürger)*. Ackerbürger polis refers to a city-state where this description applies to most, if not all, citizens.

Weber's model of the Ackerbürger polis has never been very popular among classicists. Recently, Mogens Herman Hansen has attempted to revive it by emphasizing the role of town-based agriculture in the Classical period. I would like to quote Hansen's thesis no. 24 from *95 Theses About the Greek Polis in the Archaic and Classical Periods:*

> Pace Moses Finley, Max Weber's *antike Stadt* as an ideal type is a very valuable model when applied to the Greek *polis* of the fifth and fourth centuries. Because of his 'primitivistic' view of the ancient economy it was Finley who argued that Weber's *Idealtypus* or 'model' of *die antike Stadt* did not fit the over one thousand middle-sized and small *poleis*. The investigations conducted in the Polis Centre indicate that Weber's ideal type of city does fit even small *poleis*: the Classical *polis* (in the sense of state) was a self-governing (but not necessarily independent) political community invariably centred on a *polis* (in the sense of town). Many *poleis* were so big that it was impossible for all inhabitants to know one another, whereas in most cases the number of adult male full citizens was small enough to allow the *polis* (in the political sense) to be a face-to-face society. A considerable number of townsmen were farmers who had their home in the city but their fields in the hinterland (*Ackerbürger*). The town was enclosed by a defense circuit and centred on an *agora* in which the inhabitants supplied themselves with a substantial part of the necessities of life, often produced in the hinterland but sometimes imported from abroad.[32]

While it is still the subject of debate whether, and to what extent, cities in mainland Greece were Ackerbürger poleis, the archaeological evidence from Heraclea and other Classical colonies shows that in colonial settlements the majority of citizens were Ackerbürger.

As we have seen, a number of rural sanctuaries were established in the hinterland of Heraclea immediately after the foundation of the colony. They show that the territory was part of the religious, and arguably the economic and political structure of the colony. The reason why the colonists were interested in the countryside can only have been fertile soils and pastures, as other resources were missing. At the same time, artisanal production remained scarcely developed way into the second half of the fourth century BC, as will be seen in Chapter 7. Although the colonists lived in the urban center, there is little doubt that the territory was the main resource of the colony. Many citizens probably

---

[31] Weber 1909; 1921. Cf. Hansen 2004.

[32] Published on the website: www.copenhagenpoliscentre.info/ (27 November 2014). Cf. Hansen 2004.

worked the land themselves, although it cannot be excluded that some leased their land to non-landowners, who may not have been citizens and may have lived, at least periodically, in ephemeral, archaeologically invisible dwellings in the countryside.[33] With regard to the early phases, I believe that such forms of dependent labor were not very common. The availability of land, combined with the often-lamented *oliganthropia* (lack of people), did not favor the development of dependent labor and land leasing. Many had no other choice than using the available workforce, including their own labor, to survive the first few years.

The concentration of this population of agriculturalists struggling for survival in the urban center is suggested not only by the lack of rural habitation sites, but also by the nature of the urban settlement, especially the fortifications. It is not known exactly when the Castello hill in Heraclea was fortified – probably several years or decades before the southern quarter, which was fortified in the second quarter of the fourth century BC.[34] The stone blocks used for the foundations of the city walls are made of Carparo stone, which means that they were imported from the Salento region, probably via Tarentum. The entire coast area between Metapontum and Heraclea lacks decent quarries. If the colonists did not want to use local molasse conglomerate of extremely poor quality or sandstone from the area of Monte Coppolo, which is very hard to work (unlike the Lucanians in the fourth century BC, it was never used by the Greeks on the coast), they had to use pebbles and mud-bricks or import building stone. Pebbles and mud-bricks were used for the houses, imported Carparo stone for the fortifications – at least for the foundation walls. The stone blocks were probably carried by ship to the harbor of Heraclea, which was situated on the mouth of the Sinni River. From there they had to be transported with heavy carts over a distance of more than three kilometers to Heraclea.

By the second quarter of the fourth century BC, the walled area comprised about 140 hectares (see Figure 2.1). Of this area, about 68 hectares were suitable for house building: 22 hectares on the Castello hill (12.5 hectares west of the agora and 9.5 hectares east of it) and not less than 46 hectares in the southern quarters. The walled area therefore offered space for a large population, at least theoretically. Geophysical prospection and excavations in Selinus show that in the fifth century BC the living quarters of the city comprised about 2,500 house plots spreading over 70 hectares. The estimated urban population is 14,000–19,000, which would mean an average of 200–270 inhabitants per hectare.[35] If we take this as a guide, we may conclude that fourth

[33] On this type of labor force, see Foxhall 1990.
[34] Tagliente 1986a: 129.
[35] Zuchtriegel 2011a.

century Heraclea offered space for about 13,000–18,000 inhabitants. The city may never have had so many inhabitants, but it was laid out in such a way that it *could* offer space for up to 18,000 people. At the same time, 18,000 is about the total number of people that could live off the city's territory as reconstructed for the late fourth century BC on the basis of site distribution and spatial analysis (see Chapter 6). The total area of the territory amounts to about 320 square kilometers. Based on historical data from sixteenth- to nineteenth-century Italy, the Peloponnese, and some Greek Islands, I estimate that ancient Greek farming allowed carrying capacities of up to around 50 persons per square kilometer.[36] If we take this figure as a guide, the total number of people who could live off the chora would be around 17,000, which approximates to the 18,000 that could live in the urban center. Of course, these are only rough estimates, but the walled center generally seems to have offered enough space for the maximum number of people that could live off the territory.

One of the reasons why modern scholars have questioned the model of the Ackerbürger polis is that they consider the distances between dwelling places and fields to be excessively large if the cultivators lived in nucleated settlements rather than in isolated farmsteads on or close to their fields.[37] However, such views are not at all convincing. First, we need a reasonable assessment of the distances involved. Figure 4.6 shows a cost distance analysis for the chora of Heraclea based on a slope model generated from a digital elevation model (DEM) with an accuracy of 20 meters.[38] Given the lack of data on ancient streets, bridges, and fords in the area, large rivers are factored in with an additional "cost" of 30 minutes across the board. The results have been checked against empirically measured walking distances, which confirm our data. However, the values should not be taken literally with regard to specific cost paths, especially in mountain areas.[39]

We can now compare the data sets generated from cost distance analysis and ethnohistorical estimates on carrying capacity in order to answer two questions (Table 4.1): (1) how many square kilometers could be reached from Heraclea in a given amount of time; (2) how many people could live off this area?

As the table shows, the area reachable within a four hours' walk would be sufficient to feed the maximum number of inhabitants of the urban center (close to 18,000). It is perhaps no mere coincidence that the sanctuary of Piano Sollazzo is situated on the border of the four-hour radius from the urban

---

[36] Ruschenbusch 1978: 8–9; Malanima 1999: 87–90; Corvisier, Suder 2000: 32–35; Zuchtriegel 2012a: 277.

[37] See the discussion in Hansen 2004.

[38] Calculation based on: 0–20% slope: 4 km/h (value 25); 20–30%: 2.86 km/h (value 35); 30–40%: 1.3 km/h (value 75); > 40%: 0.4 km/h (value 250). The values for elevated slope percentages are based on calculations for Alpine hiking trails.

[39] Geitl, Doneus, Fera 2008.

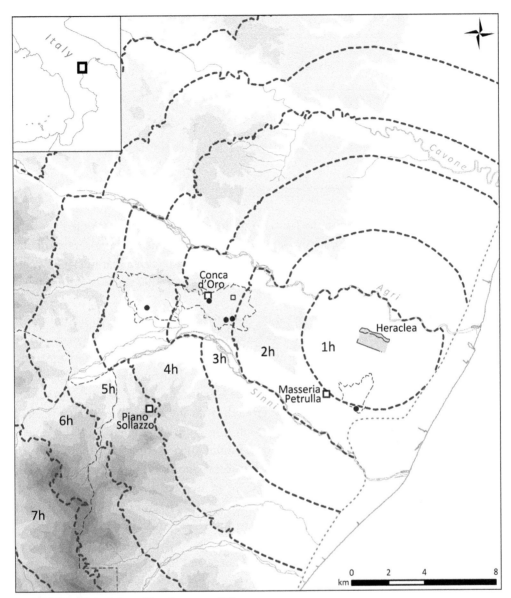

4.6 Walking distances from Heraclea, c. 375 BC.

center, i.e., on the border of the territory that would suffice for the maximum number of settlers/urban farmers who could live in the walled center.

Of course, the pattern that emerges from spatial analysis and carrying capacity estimates should not be confused with actual land use in a given historical moment. Ethnohistorical evidence makes it quite clear that land ownership and agricultural labor were extremely complex matters, and Ancient Greece is no different.[40] Yet the fact that stable rural habitation sites and rural necropoleis

[40] Foxhall 1990.

TABLE 4.1 *Walking distances and carrying capacity at Heraclea*

Walking distance	Reachable area (square kilometers)	Carrying capacity (number of people estimated)
1h	35.6	1,780
2h	99.9	4,995
3h	206.9	10,345
4h	341.6	17,080
5h	523.2	26,160
6h	737.9	36,895

are not attested before the last third of the fourth century BC, while the urban center offered space for a large population, suggests that the model of the Ackerbürger was at least partially implemented. I imagine that the landowners and their families were based in the walled center and cultivated their fields from there.

This, of course, would mean that some of them walked three or four hours one-way to reach their fields. Whether Greek farmers would regularly cover such distances is highly controversial among scholars.[41] Today archaeologists and historians have only limited access to empiric data on pre-industrial farming, which might explain why opinions vary drastically. Some assumptions objectively are based on questionable grounds, as in the case of the frequently cited five-kilometer limit suggested by John Bintliff. As Bintliff argues, "[c]atchment theory (cf. Vita-Finzi & Higgs 1970; Bintliff 1999c) suggests that a distance of around five kilometers or, better, a walk of one hour, provides a useful limit to regular intensive cultivation, except in unusual historical circumstances." Beyond this limit, "urban farmers were largely replaced by those living in rural nucleations and farms."[42] The cited work of Vita Finzi and Higgs (1970) concerns *Prehistoric Economy in the Mount Carmel Area of Palestine: Site Catchment Analysis*.[43] Its applicability to ancient Greece and Italy is highly debatable, especially since empirical data from more recent periods offers a different picture. Way into the twentieth century, the majority of southern Italian peasants lived in so-called agrotowns. In the 1930s, Carlo Levi noted that farmers in southern Italy would get up several hours before sunrise during certain periods of the year to reach their fields, covering distances of up to four hours one-way.[44] During a field campaign in the chora of Siris-Heraclea in September 2013, we interviewed 68-year-old Salvatore Taio from Tursi, a town not far from Policoro/Heraclea. He told us that until the 1950s, local farmers from Tursi,

---

[41]   Cf. the discussion in Schuller, Hoepfner, Schwandner 1989: 40.
[42]   Bintliff *et al.* 2007: 136.
[43]   Published in "Proccedings of the Prehistoric Society London" 36: 1–37.
[44]   *Cristo si è fermato a Eboli*. Torino: Enaudi, 1945.

including his own family, walked two to three hours to reach their fields in the area of Santa Maria d'Anglona (about 8 kilometers as the crow flies), where they cultivated primarily cereals and legumes, but also olives. Vineyards and orchards were situated within a narrow radius of less than five kilometers from the town, as they require intensive maintenance. Equally, Francesco Riscatti from Matera reports that until the 1950s his grandfather used to cover the distance between his house in Matera and his leasehold at Timmari/Rifeccia – 18 kilometers – with a mule cart. When he had to work on the fields, he would get up at four or five o'clock in the morning to go to Rifeccia where he arrived after a four-hours trip. At Rifeccia there was an old *masseria* (estate) owned by a wealthy family of Matera where Riscatti and other tenants could stay overnight if necessary. A few kilometers before Rifeccia, the road crossed a river; there was no bridge, only a ford, where the carts would often get stuck, which is why the area was known as *Rifeccia puttanella* (bloody Rifeccia). The farmers cultivated mainly grain, legumes, and tobacco in this area. Vineyards and olive groves were situated closer to the town.[45] A similar situation has been observed in Greece where, during the Methana peninsula survey, archaeologists talked to locals who walked up to six hours to take care of olive groves and fields; they often stayed several days in the open or in temporary stone huts *(kalivia)* while working their fields.[46] The idea that pre-modern societies were generally characterized by a high percentage of country dwellers[47] depends perhaps on northwestern European perspectives. In southern Italy and in many parts of Greece, nucleated settlements were common throughout the middle ages. The *paese* (town) offered protection from invaders and bandits, and its *piazza* was the center of social and cultural life. In the light of these accounts from Italy and Greece, it appears possible that distances of up to four hours between habitations and fields were covered in ancient Greek city-states.

The case of Heraclea shows that during the first decades of the colony, the settlers preferred living in the walled center, despite having to face long walks to their fields. Similar conclusions can be drawn from field surveys and excavations in other Classical colonies. For example, the number of rural sites in the chora of Thurii remains very low until the first half of the fourth century BC, when it rises sharply. In some areas, the foundation of Thurii even led to a slight drop in the number of rural sites, at least those that are visible in the archaeological record.[48] The population, which was fairly large judging

---

[45] This was referred to me in 2014 by Francesco Riscatti. The name of his grandfather was Francesco Paolo Riscatti.

[46] Forbes 2007: 80.

[47] For example Hanson 1995; Horden, Purcell 2000 (according to the authors, usually not more than about 10% of the total population around the Mediterranean lived in cities – but see Hansen 2004; 2006: 29).

[48] Carafa, Luppino 2011: 178–179.

from literary sources, seems to have been concentrated in the walled center. In Chersonesus, the earliest farmsteads date to the middle of the fourth century BC, fifty or seventy years after the foundation.[49] The rural territories of Issa and Pharos remained largely empty until the Imperial period; here too, the majority of the population probably lived in the fortified urban center.[50] The only exception is Kamarina, where two farmsteads just outside the walls seem to have been established around the middle of the fifth century BC, in other words shortly after the resettlement of the site in 461 BC.[51] As already mentioned, the lack of rural sites does not necessarily mean that the countryside was empty. There may have been ephemeral structures that are not visible in the archaeological record, though the fact remains that in most Classical colonies farmsteads of the type known from other Greek territories are not attested during the early phases.

ARCHAEOLOGICAL EVIDENCE OF LAND DIVISION

Traces of regular grids in the territories of Kamarina, Chersonesus, and Pharos suggest that the land lots of the colonists were standardized to ensure equality in land ownership.

In Kamarina, ancient rubble walls and roads delimit regular parcels which must have been part of a larger grid (Figure 4.7). At least three of them were occupied by Classical farmsteads. The parcels measure 270 by 210 meters equaling 5.76 hectares, enough to feed a family, though perhaps too much work for a small family consisting of two to four adults and teenagers. Given that the parcels are oriented in the same way as the urban grid, they are thought to date back to the refoundation of Kamarina in 461 BC.[52] In fact, Diodorus (XI 76,5) mentions a land distribution on this occasion.

The peninsula of Tauric Chersonesus near modern Sevastopol is the best-preserved example of ancient Greek land division (Figure 4.8).[53] Roads and rubble walls delimit rectangular parcels that spread over 110 square kilometers and were mapped as early as 1786 by a Russian military engineer. Aerial and satellite photography make it possible to identify over four-hundred parcels consisting of rectangles of about 630 by 420 meters, i.e., 26.5 hectares, though deviations are frequent.[54] Each parcel was subdivided into six lots of about 4.4 hectares. More than 2,200 such lots have been identified.

---

[49] Nikolaenko 2006: 160–162.
[50] Gaffney, Kirigin 2006 (a field survey on the island of Issa yielded no Classical and only three Hellenistic sites); Kirigin 2006: 76–85.
[51] Di Stefano 2000: 693, 704 (the finds are unpublished).
[52] Di Stefano 1993/4: 1379; 1996; 2000; Mertens 2006: 352–354.
[53] Müller 2010: 125–151 with bibliography.
[54] Nikolaenko 2006.

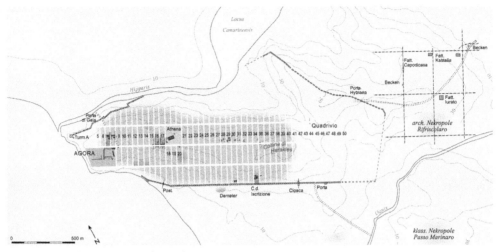

4.7 Kamarina (Mertens 2006: fig. 625).

Scholars still debate the dating of the land division in Chersonesus. Based on excavation data, the parcels must have existed by around 300 BC, though they might be much older or even date back to the foundation period of Chersonesus (420s BC). It is unclear whether the rubble walls and paved roads along the parcels used already existing land divisions, or whether they radically changed the structure of the landscape. Moreover, on the eastern edge of the peninsula of Sevastopol (Lighthouse Point), there are parcels with a slightly different orientation which seem to be part of an older division, although the absolute dating is again unclear.

The lots were under intensive cultivation, as a large number of regular terraces and ditches show. Whether these were vineyards, as some scholars argue, is unclear, given that terraces and ditches, besides being notoriously undatable, are not necessarily indicators of vine cultivation. From the late fourth century BC onwards, Chersonesean transport amphorae are attested in many sites around the Black Sea; Chersonesus appears to have exported large quantities of agricultural products (again, wine is likely to be among them, but there is no clear evidence of this given the lack of chemical analysis of the amphorae).[55]

During the fourth century BC, Chersonesus seized control of the area of Kalos Limen and Kerkinitis in the north. Subsequently, the fertile land along the coast of the Tarkankut Peninsula was divided into regular lots similar to those in the chora of Chersonesus (the chora of Chersonesus is sometimes called "nearer chora" as opposed to the "distant chora" in the north).[56]

By 300 BC Chersonesus was democratic, as noted from a long inscription known as Oath of Chersonesus. This would fit the division of the chora into

[55] Müller 2010: 187–189.
[56] Cf. Ščeglov 1986, especially p. 155–156.

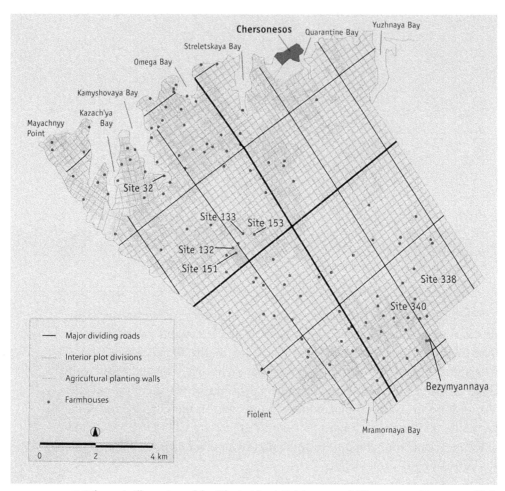

4.8 Schematic illustration of the Classical land division around Chersonesus. (Courtesy of J.C. Carter.)

equal-sized lots although unfortunately the issue of when exactly democracy was introduced in Chersonesus is just as unclear as the dating of the allotments. Sergey Saprykin (1994) suggests that the land was redistributed after a democratic revolution in the fourth century BC, but there is no reliable evidence to support this view. What is certain and what may shed new light on the history of Chersonesus is that a hundred years after the foundation the majority of the citizens and landowners still lived in the walled center, as their grandfathers and great-grandfathers had done. The number of land lots on which farms were built is extremely low, and the farms themselves are all relatively late (second half of the fourth century/early third century BC). Hence, the majority of land lots were presumably owned and cultivated by urban dwellers.

Another example of Greek land division is the chora of Pharos (Figure 4.9), although dating is even more difficult here than in Chersonesus. As has been shown by aerial photography, rubble walls and roads, some of which are still

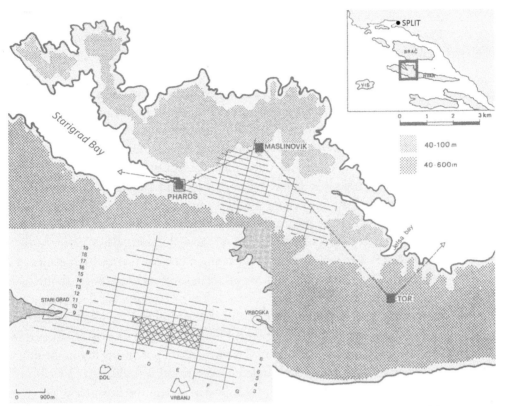

4.9 Pharos: Land division and watch towers (Chapman, J.C., Bintliff, J., Gaffney, V., Slapšak, B. (eds.). *Recent Developments in Yugoslav Archaeology*, fig. 9.3 & 10.3. Oxford: BAR).

in use, divide the plain east of ancient Pharos (modern Starigrad) into regular parcels that measure roughly 180 by 900 meters and were interpreted either as following a 1 x 5 Greek stadia module or a Roman 5 x 25 actus module. Based on spatial analysis, Zoran Stančič and Božidar Slapšak (1988) claim to have ended the "long and vexed discussion of the origin of the Pharian cadastral system," arguing that the basic unit of measurement was a Greek stadium of 181.2 meters, equaling 600 feet (1 foot being 0.302 meters).[57] The authors conclude that the parcels go back to the pre-Roman period of Pharos, probably to the earliest phase of the colony. GIS analysis also suggests that the entire grid was created around a central measure point *(omphalos)*.[58] What remains to be explained is why the grid in the territory of Pharos does not have the same orientation as the urban street grid, as at Metapontum and Kamarina. Another question is how the parcels of 180 by 900 meters were subdivided. In some parcels, there are traces of subdivision walls and ditches, but their dating is completely unclear. In total, at least eighty parcels of the 1 x 5 stadia size

[57] Stančič, Slapšak 1988: 194; the results were later confirmed: Slapšak 2001.
[58] Kirigin 2006: 76–85.

are known. If it is assumed that each of them was subdivided into five land lots measuring one square stadium (3.3 hectares), the total amount of land lots would have been about four hundred, which were all reachable from the urban center on foot in under 2.5 hours (see Figure 4.9).[59]

A total number of about 400 lot holders and citizens (Ackerbürger) would be in line with the relatively small urban center of approximately ten hectares. If we take the figures proposed for fifth century Selinus as a guide, ten hectares offered space for up to 2,700 inhabitants; if we take Hansen's figures, we get numbers between 1,500 and 3,000 inhabitants. On the other hand, the 400 lot owners did not live alone but must have had families, which according to a rough estimate included 4.6 to 7.5 persons (where 4.6 is the minimum value below which the population would begin to shrink, while values around seven apply to households with one or more domestic slaves or servants).[60] Thus, we get a number between 1,800 and 3,000 for the total population. In other words, the maximum number of urban dwellers coincides with the total number of agriculturalists (landowners and their families) as calculated on the basis of the land lots. As in the case of Heraclea, such estimates do not necessarily correspond to any given moment in the history of these sites; rather, they show that in Classical settlements all farmers could potentially live in the urban center, and all urban dwellers could be farmers.

This brings us back to Tauric Chersonesus, where the situation is less clear. Judging from the development of the necropoleis, the urban center originally covered an area of 27 hectares (corresponding to the area east of Volodymir's Church) and was enlarged in the Hellenistic period until it covered approximately 75 hectares. In Table 4.2, I again compare estimates on the urban population with agricultural households (lot holders plus families). I assume here that the 2,200 land lots attested in the chora correspond to 2,200 households with an average of 4.6 to 7.5 household members (children, women, slaves, free men).

As to the Classical period, the data from the countryside does not match those from the urban center. The urban area of 27 hectares could hold about 1,100 households at the most, whereas there are 2,200 land lots. The walled center was too small for 2,200 lot holders and their families, and since there are no other settlements in the area, they cannot have lived elsewhere. Only from the Hellenistic period, when the urban center covered an area of 75 hectares, was there enough space for all the lot owners and their families. It is therefore likely that the allotments in their preserved form originated in the Early Hellenistic period, although they might of course be an enlargement or modification of older allotments going back to the foundation period. In fact, traces

---

[59] Cf. Gaffney, Stančič 1991: 80.
[60] Hansen 2006: 61–63; Zuchtriegel 2011: 118–119.

TABLE 4.2 *Urban and rural spaces and demography at Chersonesus*

Urban area	Calculating 150 to 300 inhabitants per hectare (cf. Hansen 2006)	Calculating 4.6 to 7.5 members for 2,200 households/ land lots
Classical (27 hectares)	Space for c. 4,000 to 8,000 urban dwellers	10,120 to 16,500
Hellenistic (c. 75 hectares)	Space for c. 11,000 to 22,500 urban dwellers	

of earlier allotments are documented in various parts of the Chersonesean territory, although they cannot be dated precisely.[61]

COLONIZATION AND GEOMETRY

The efforts needed to create regular grids such as the ones preserved in Kamarina, Chersonesus, and Pharos can hardly be overestimated. The land had to be surveyed, which was no easy task in a time when surveyors did not have topographical maps, binoculars, and optical levels.[62] Land measurement is actually the origin of all geometry, for geometry literally means land measurement, as Herodotus emphasizes (II 109).[63] The Greeks were aware of this etymology until much more recent times. The *Introduction* to a work on measurement attributed to the mathematician Heron of Alexandria (first century AD?) begins with the words:[64]

> The first geometry, as old legend learns us, occupied itself with the measurements and divisions of fields, whence it was also called geometry. The idea of measurement was found by the Egyptians because of the flood of the Nile. For it made many fields that were visible before the flood invisible by the flood, and many fields became visible again by the going down of the water where it was impossible any more that everyone recognized his possessions: for

[61] Nikolaenko 2006: 156.

[62] Krause 1998; Prieto 2004.

[63] Tradition has it that at the door to Plato's Academy the phrase Μηδείς ἀγεωμέτρητος εἰσίτω μου τὴν στέγην was engraved, and although the relevant sources are about a thousand years after Plato's lifetime, there may be some truth in it: cf. Joannes Tzetzes, *Chiliades* VIII, 973 (12th century) for the full citation; see also Joannes Philoponus' sixth century commentary on Aristotle's *De Anima* (in *De An.*, *Comm. in Arist. Graeca*, XV, ed. M. Hayduck, Berlin 1897: 117, 29) as well as Elias' commentary (also sixth century) of Aristotle's *Analytics* (in *Cat.*, *Comm. in Arist. Graeca*, XVIII, pars 1, ed. A. Busse, Berlin 1900: 118, 18). The phrase is usually translated as "Let no one ignorant of geometry come under my roof." However, for the Greeks of the Classical period, the word "geometry" had a double sense. The phrase could also be translated as: "Let no one ignorant of land measurement come under my roof." Plato was, if not a Pythagorean, certainly strongly influenced by Pythagorean tradition: cf. Horky 2013.

[64] Bruins 1964: 80.

this the Egyptians invented the measurement of the land left by the Nile. (transl. E.M. Bruins, 1964)

In Classical Greece, geometry was often associated with colonization, as a passage in Aristophanes' *Clouds* (201–5) shows:

STREPSIADES	What's this?
STUDENT	Geometry.
STREPSIADES	What's it useful for?
STUDENT	Measuring out land (γῆν ἀναμετρῆσαι).
STREPSIADES	Land in cleruchies?
STUDENT	No, all of it.
STREPSIADES	You are telling me something clever (ἀστεῖον), for this invention is democratic (δημοτικὸν) and useful (χρήσιμον).

Strepsiades' answer at the end of the quoted passage alludes to the use of geometry by the urban ruling class (the *asteioi* as opposed to rural and uninformed groups) to gain control over agricultural land as part of democratic (meaning, imperialist) policies. Measuring out land was the first step toward colonizing it.

The oldest example of Greek land division on the ground is Metapontum. Analysis of the land division of Metapontum confirms the connection between equality, agriculture, and citizenship as hypothesized in this book.

Traces of regular features, the so-called division lines, which were first identified in the 1950s,[65] cover an area of 17 kilometers along the coastal plain and up to 10 kilometers inland.[66] As excavations directed by Joseph C. Carter have shown, the division lines are ancient drains that "had the principal function of collecting water from the surface of the chora and, where possible, of directing it away from the fields towards the natural drainage of the river valleys. They were in a number of cases flanked by roads, as has become clear in the excavations at Pantanello and elsewhere."[67]

There are two grids that differ from each other by about 20°. The drains and roads in the northern part of the chora (Bradano-Basento zone) are oriented NW-SE, the ones in the southern part (Basento-Cavone zone) being roughly E-W. Transversal division lines are visible in some sections of the Bradano-Basento zone. They do not form rectangles but trapezoids with an acute angle of 80°.

GIS-based analysis by Alberto Prieto shows that the distances between the division lines range between 184 and 235 meters in the Bradano-Basento zone and between 231 and 261 meters in the Basento-Cavone zone. As regards orientation, the majority of the lines do not deviate by more than of 1–2° from the mean,

[65] Schmiedt, Chevallier 1959 (aerial photographs were taken principally in 1954–1955; in addition, the authors analyzed older photographs provided by military services); Adamesteanu 1973.
[66] Prieto 2005: 10–20; Carter, Prieto 2011: 1027–1133.
[67] Carter, Prieto 2011: 1037.

although single segments deviate by as much as 5–7°. Deviations in distance and orientation are often caused by natural features such as valleys and watercourses. Although attempts to perceive sophisticated mathematical principles at work should be taken with great caution,[68] Prieto stresses that "the generally coherent arrangement of the longitudinal features (i.e., the obvious attempt at parallelism) indicates that the anthropically-directed portion of the Metapontine landscape organization was probably conceived (and even executed) as a unified project."[69]

Carter interprets the division lines as evidence of a distribution or redistribution of land based on egalitarian principles.[70] This is indeed the only plausible explanation, as emphasized above. The idea that these features served other purposes, like the assessment of tax classes, is unconvincing. If there were any regular per capita taxes at all in sixth and fifth century Greece (which may be doubted), taxes and liturgies were probably based on crop yields, as in the case of the Athenian *pentakosiomedimnoi*, and not on field sizes.[71]

It was originally thought that the land distribution goes back to the first generation of settlers who came to Metapontum, but there is nothing to substantiate this early dating. As excavations have not yielded any datable materials, the chronology of the land distribution depends on indirect evidence, especially tombs aligned along some of the division lines. The oldest of these tombs date from around 480 BC when the division lines must have already existed.[72] It cannot be excluded that they were created several years or even decades earlier, but there is no reason to assume that they were much older.

The period between 525 and 475 BC, during which the land division was carried out, is highly significant in the history of Metapontum. However, what this meant in practical terms is controversial. Carter now considers the years 525–575 BC a period of crisis, which only ended in the early Classical period (called "rebirth" or the "happiest years").[73] The results of the crisis were, according to Carter, a drastic decline in the number of rural sites, a fall in the number of votive offerings in the sanctuaries, and the fact that no new temples and *stoai* were built between 525 and 475 BC.[74] The construction of many kilometers of water drains and roads along parallel lines would have been a huge undertaking which Carter doubts could have been carried out under such circumstances. He therefore suggests down-dating the division lines to after 475 BC.[75]

---

[68] Prieto 2005: 128–136.

[69] Prieto 2005: 138.

[70] Carter, Prieto 2011: 768–769.

[71] On the question of taxes, see Möller 2007; Lyttkens 2013: 96–117.

[72] Carter 2008: 150: "… [L]a linea di divisione precedentemente scavata dall'ICA nel 1984, che era fiancheggiata da una parte della necropoli di Pantanello e poteva essere datata (sulla base di circa ottanta sepolture presenti su ciascun lato) non posteriormente al 480 a.C. circa …"

[73] Carter, Prieto 2011: 745.

[74] Carter, Prieto 2011: 727–9, 734–5.

[75] Carter and Prieto (2011: 768–770) argue that although the land division might have begun in the early fifth century BC, the striking of coins showing the river god Acheloos in the

However, as Carter himself has admitted, a number of tombs aligned along the division lines show that the parcels must date to before 480 BC.[76]

As I argue here, the crisis of 525–475 BC, if considered to be a period of innovation, development, and social change, could be a possible explanation of the division lines rather than a reason to revise their dating. According to the Ackerbürger model proposed earlier in the chapter, it is not surprising that a redistribution of land was accompanied by a drop in the number of rural habitation sites. Rural populations in Classical city-states were marginalized and excluded from political and cultural participation; only urban dwellers could participate fully in political activities and military training in the *asty*. In the *Politics* (1305a), Aristotle argues that in the past many Greek cities were ruled by oligarchs and tyrants "because the common people lived on their farms busily engaged in agriculture." The wealthy and powerful were also called *asteioi* (urban dwellers), because they alone were able to spend most of their time on social and political activities in the urban center. The poor were not *asteioi* insofar as they were forced to work for their living, whether in the fields or in a workshop. Unsurprisingly, the word *agroikoi* (rural dwellers) had a pejorative connotation.[77] Although some scholars have different views, I argue here that a high number of rural dwellers is not a feature of democratic, but of aristocratic and oligarchic societies.[78]

In Metapontum, a peak in the number of rural sites was reached around the middle of the sixth century BC.[79] During this period, there was a high degree of specialization and social stratification, which is typical of aristocratic regimes and tyrannies. Rural burials in the mid-sixth century BC show that some inhabitants of the countryside possessed relatively high economic and social status. However, the richest and most extraordinary tombs were found near the urban center, where the aristocratic elite and perhaps the 'tyrant' and his family were buried.[80]

At the same time, small landowners and farmers lived in the countryside. They continuously faced the risk of social and economic downgrading, given that partible inheritance (whereby male children received equal shares of the land) was common in most cities and probably also in Metapontum. If

mid-fifth century BC "almost certainly commemorated the successful completion of the whole project". See also Uggeri 1969, who has suggested that Aristeas, a pupil of Pythagoras, began the construction of the parallel drains and roads around 466 BC.

[76] Carter 2008: 150.

[77] See Liddell, H.G., Scott, R., Jones, H.S. 1996. *A Greek-English Lexicon, 9th edition: With a revised supplement*, s.v. *asteios* and *agroikos*. Oxford: Oxford University Press.

[78] There might be exceptions like Locri Epizephiri where the local aristocracy maintained a firm hold on the land and apparently avoided the creation of rural settlements: Osanna 1992: 234–237.

[79] Carter, Prieto 2011: 677–726.

[80] De Siena 1999: 233–236; Carter, Prieto 2011: 699–700, 725–726; Bottini, Graells, Vullo, forthcoming.

compared with rural habitation sites of the fifth century BC, the rural sites of the mid-sixth century appear relatively heterogeneous with regard to the quantity and quality of finds.[81] The rural population was characterized by a high degree of social stratification, which may have contributed to inner tensions and upheaval, leading to a redistribution of land.

Many of the *staseis* (upheavals) attested during the Late Archaic period in Magna Graecia, e.g., in Sybaris (511 BC), Croton (c. 509 BC), Kyme (504 BC), and Tarentum (c. 473 BC), originated in tensions between the *demos* (ordinary people) and local aristocracies. In Sybaris, Croton, and Kyme, the sources mention the expulsion of rich landowners and the redistribution of land.[82] Something of the sort may have happened in Metapontum during the Late Archaic period.[83] The drop in rural sites in 525–475 BC could be the result of the social and political emancipation of rural dwellers who moved to the city to benefit fully from the newly acquired political rights. It is impossible to check this hypothesis against the archaeological data from the urban center of Metapontum, since extremely little is known about the city's living quarters. What we do know is that a new *ekklesiasterion* (assembly place) was built in the agora during the second half of the sixth century, and was renovated in the first half of the fifth century (the chronology is based on preliminary reports).[84] The Late Archaic *ekklesiasterion* could hold up to 7,500 people, probably about the total number of male citizens. This suggests that a high percentage of the citizens regularly participated in public meetings and assemblies by this time. Many of them may have benefited from the land redistribution.

Interestingly, the drop in the number of rural habitation sites towards the end of the sixth century is particularly drastic in one of the most fertile areas of the entire territory of Metapontum, the so-called Central Plateau. This area appears to have been almost completely deserted in the Late Archaic period.[85] If there had been a crisis characterized by economic difficulties and demographic decline, one would expect the most fertile areas to be among the last to be abandoned. The fact that the drop in sites is particularly drastic here suggests that these areas remained under cultivation, but that the cultivators now lived in the urban center rather than in the countryside as before.

To assess the true nature of Metapontum's Late Archaic crisis, another fact needs to be considered: The epigraphic and archaeological data suggests that after the destruction of Sybaris in 510 BC, Metapontum controlled the territory of ancient Siris (later Heraclea), which had already been destroyed around the middle of the sixth century BC (Chapter 1). This means that the

---

[81] Carter, Prieto 2011: 699.
[82] Robinson 1997: 37–38, 76.
[83] Carter, Prieto 2011: 738–741.
[84] Mertens 2006: 161–163; 334–337.
[85] Carter, Prieto 2011: 732.

total area of agricultural land controlled by Metapontum roughly doubled (judging from later evidence, the territory of Siris measured about 300–320 square kilometers).[86] These were ideal circumstances for a land reform, as wealthy aristocrats who had to give away portions of their land could be compensated with land in the newly occupied territory of Siris. At the same time, the city of Metapontum needed to enforce military and political control over a huge territory. This was even more challenging since indigenous communities in Pisticci and Chiaromonte were rapidly growing.[87] As a result of the land redistribution, a larger part of the male population could pay for military equipment (panoply) and participate in military training in the urban center. Thus, the city could hope to cope with the new situation.

Interestingly, there was a clear distinction between the chora of the city and the annexed territories in the south. Figure 4.10 is a cost distance analysis of the region carried out using the same parameters described earlier in this chapter. It shows that almost the entire territory of Metapontum[88] was reachable on foot in less than four hours. Division lines are attested exclusively within this area of four or a maximum of five hours' walking distance. No traces of division lines have been found south of the River Cavone in the territory of ancient Siris. If the division lines resulted from a land redistribution in favor of a new group of urban hoplites/citizens, the reason why no lines are attested south of the River Cavone should be clear: It would have been difficult for the hoplites/landowners of Metapontum to cultivate land lots in a walking distance of more than five hours from the urban center where they lived. The land south of the River Cavone was, in every sense, beyond the reach of the Ackerbürger community and its egalitarian standards. It had to be exploited in a different way, and the archaeological data does indeed show that it was structured differently.

Our field survey and excavations in and around Heraclea show that there was a variety of settlement types. The site of ancient Siris (later Heraclea, present-day Policoro) has yielded fifteen typically Metapontine tombs of the early fifth century BC, evidence of ritual activities and temples, and a large number of pottery fragments in various pits and layers in the settlement.[89] Policoro probably served as some kind of minor center in the area. Further south at the site of Cugno dei Vagni, excavations have led to the discovery of a small village consisting of 12 oval huts dating to the sixth/fifth century BC (unpublished).[90] During our field survey, we found isolated farmsteads and tombs as well as possible cult sites in the countryside. The Late Archaic pottery from these sites

[86] Zuchtriegel 2012a: 277.
[87] Bottini, Lecce 2013; Bottini 2013.
[88] On the extension of the territory of Metapontum, see Osanna 1992; Carter 2008.
[89] See Berlingò 1986: 118, on the tombs, most of which are on display in the museum of Policoro; Rescigno 2012b on the cult sites.
[90] Bianco 2000: 810–811.

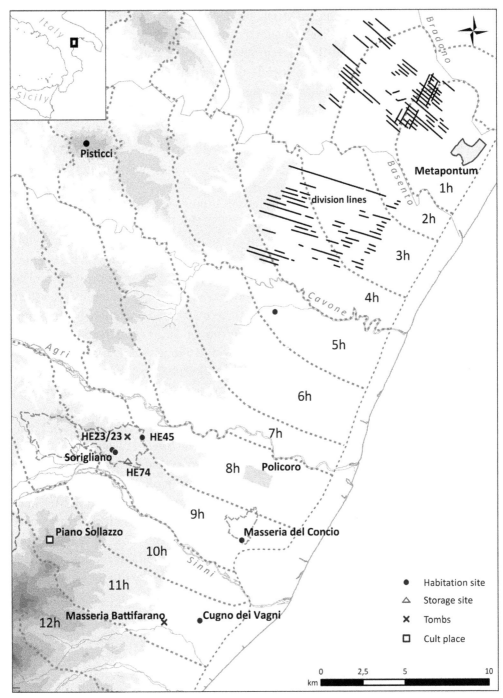

4.10 Walking distances from Metapontum and sites around Policoro, c. 500 BC.

has close comparisons in Metapontum, whereas indigenous pottery is practically absent. This does not mean that we have to exclude the presence of indigenous individuals or even groups of people living in the territory, but the hegemonic culture was apparently that of Metapontum. An inscription written in Metapontine dialect and found in the territory of Metapontum lists the property of a goddess "on the River Siris," thus confirming the Metapontine dominion over Siris.[91]

However, there is a clear distinction between the rather loosely organized territory around ancient Siris and the territory around Metapontum which was divided by drains and roads into standardized parcels. The latter required an almost incredible amount of technical knowledge and energy. Much later, in the late fourth/early third century BC, the Heracleans called a geometer from Naples to measure the plots in the sacred lands of Athena and Dionysus.[92] This shows that measuring out land was a task for specialists. It is extremely unlikely that as complex a project as the regular division of the Metapontine landscape could be carried out without the help of experts around 500 BC.[93] It is tempting to think of Pythagoras who established a school in Metapontum at the end of the fifth century BC, but this remains a mere hypothesis.[94]

The physical reification of the land division through streets, canals and/or rubble walls required a huge amount of labor. As Joseph Carter (2003: 24) has pointed out, building the stone-paved roads and walls that divide the chora of Chersonesus "was one of the most ambitious projects ever undertaken by a single polis."

Surveying the land and building the infrastructure would have been pointless if the land had been unequally distributed. Some individuals such as the official founder of a colony may have received more than others. On the other hand, settlers who arrived some time after the foundation may have received smaller parcels than the "first settlers," as for example at Korkyra Melaina.[95] However, these cases have to be viewed against the backdrop of widespread practices aimed at egalitarian land distribution. Expressions such as "in equal parts" should be interpreted as references to equal land distribution, especially if they refer explicitly to the chora (cf. Diodorus in the case of Thurii).

SUBSISTENCE, SURPLUS, AND FAMILY FARMS

The land-lots in Kamarina (5.8 hectares), Chersonesus (4.4 hectares), and Pharos (3.3 hectares?) are relatively small. In particular, the latter are very close to the

---

[91] Osanna 2012a: 35.
[92] See IG XIV 645, I 187.
[93] See also Aristoph., Birds 995–996, where the mathematician Meton offers to measure and divide the land in Cloudcuckooland; Xenophon (Memorabilia IV 7,2) suggests that measuring out a parcel was something not everybody was capable of.
[94] On Pythagoras, see Minar 1942; Dillon, Hershbell 1991.
[95] Syll.[3] 141, lines 9–11.

absolute minimum for feeding a family, as is suggested by medieval and early modern data from central Europe.[96] There may have been colonies where the land lots were too small to survive. Based on data from early modern Italy and Greece, it can be estimated that at least 1.8 hectares per adult were needed.[97] Average households of 4 to 8 persons needed about 7 to 14 hectares. It would appear that the land-lots at Kamarina, Chersonesus, and Pharos were a sort of minimum income that had to be supplemented in some way. The same holds for Korkyra Melaina, where the inalienable land of the first settlers was 1.5 plethra, while newcomers received 4.5 plethra. If a plethron was 100 feet by 100 feet as elsewhere in the Greek world, 1.5 plethra would correspond to 0.14 hectares, while 4.5 plethra would be 0.40 hectares – certainly not enough to feed a family.

The settlers therefore had to exploit agricultural resources beyond the parceled, equally divided land around the urban center. They had to engage in animal breeding, forestry, and land reclamation in the outer chora *(eschatià)*. In a relatively short time span, such activities undermined the egalitarian system based on equal-sized land lots, as ancient authors were well aware. Aristotle (Pol. 1266a) observes that egalitarian laws usually concerned land property and criticizes Phaleas for considering no other types of property:

> And also we cannot approve what Phaleas has said about equality of property, for he makes the citizens equal in respect of landed estate only, but wealth also consists in slaves and cattle and money, and there is an abundance of property in the shape of what is called furniture; we must therefore either seek to secure equality or some moderate regulation as regards all these things, or we must permit all forms of wealth.
>
> (Aristotle, Pol. 1267b, transl. H. Rackham, 1944)

Unlike land property, wealth in "slaves, cattle, and money" was something that could not be distributed equally, even according to someone like Phaleas. In Plato's ideal colony, described in the *Laws* (745e–d), all settlers receive equal lots. To avoid inequality, the lawgiver "must cut each lot in two and join two pieces to form each several allotment, so that each contains a near piece and a distant piece, – joining the piece next the city with the piece furthest off, the second nearest with the second furthest, and so on with all the rest." Furthermore, the lots have to be equal in terms of yield and value:

> And in dealing with these separate portions, they must employ the device we mentioned a moment ago, about poor land and good, and secure equality by making the assigned portions of larger or smaller size.
>
> (Plato, Laws 745d, transl. R.G. Bury, 1967/8)

Plato divides the citizens into four property classes *(timémata)*. He (744b) claims that "it would indeed be a splendid thing if each person, on entering the

[96] See Rösener 1985: 207–214.
[97] See above and Ruschenbusch 1978: 8–9; Malanima 1999: 87–89.

colony, had all else equal as well," but he admits that this is impossible, because "one man will arrive with more possessions (χρήματα) and another with less." As indicated by LSJ, the word *chremata* (possessions) can refer to "goods, property, money, gear, chattels," but also to sheep and cattle, as becomes clear from expressions like πρόβατα καὶ ἄλλα χρήματα (sheep and other *chremata*). It is in this context that Plato introduces the concept of "symmetrical inequality" which is crucial for his notion of justice and equality:[98]

> … it is necessary for many reasons, and for the sake of equalizing chances in public life, that there should be unequal valuations, in order that offices and contributions may be assigned in accordance with the assessed valuation in each case, – being framed not in proportion only to the moral excellence of a man's ancestors or of himself, nor to his bodily strength and comeliness, but in proportion also to his wealth or poverty, – so that by a rule of symmetrical inequality they may receive offices and honors as equally as possible (ἰσαίτατα τῷ ἀνίσῳ συμμέτρῳ), and may have no quarreling. For these reasons we must make four classes, graded by size of property …
>
> (Plato, *Laws* 744b-c, transl. R.G. Bury, 1967/8)

A citizen may increase his property "by discovery or gift or money-making, or through gaining a sum exceeding the due measure by some other such piece of luck," although in the ideal polis of the *Laws* no citizen shall possess more than four times the value of the original lot (744d–e). At the same time, no citizen shall have less than the value of the original lot which is considered the "threshold value of poverty" (πενίας ὅρος). The allotments at Kamarina, Chersonesus, Pharos, and Korkyra Melaina corresponded to such a poverty threshold. I tend to believe that economic equality in Classical colonies was restricted to the distribution of relatively modest land lots. Settlers who arrived with some wealth could easily outperform those who arrived with little or nothing. Animal husbandry was particularly important in this context. Metapontum and Heraclea, for example, became regional trade centers for sheep and wool.[99] It is likely that in the early phases of a colony, the wealthy were not allowed to accumulate large estates, but they were free to invest their *chremata* in animal husbandry. According to Aristotle's *Politics* (1305a), the oligarchs of Archaic Megara distinguished themselves through the possession of large herds; when Theagenes attempted to overthrow them with the support of the people, he began by "slaughtering the cattle of the wealthy which he captured grazing by the river." The story shows how important animal husbandry was in the political economy of ancient Greek city-states.

---

[98] Moore 2012: 91.
[99] Cf. Meo 2011; 2012; 2015.

If colonial egalitarianism was limited to the distribution of relatively small land lots, this might explain social differentiation in early tombs, as observed in Kamarina, Amphipolis, Heraclea, and Chersonesus. With regard to mainland Greece, Lin Foxhall (2002: 218) refers to the "paradox of substantial inequalities in landholding juxtaposed to the notion of political equality in poleis where landholding and citizenship were linked in various ways"; in the case of Classical colonies, we might be appropriate to refer to the paradox of substantial equality in landholding juxtaposed to inequalities in other types of possession and ritual/funerary representation. In the long term, land distribution had little impact on social and economic equality, especially if the land lots were too small to feed more than four or five persons. Under such circumstances, the crucial question was how much *chremata* a settler brought with him. In other words, the seeds of inequality sprouted immediately. Those who had little more than their land lot (presumably the majority of the colonists) were under considerable economic stress, especially if they had to walk three or four hours to reach their fields. Crop failures and the devastation of fields in the case of war would have hit them particularly hard.[100]

In this context, cultivating land on one's own was certainly out of the question. Sowing and harvesting were activities that required the work of several people, and processing the crops was equally labor-intensive. In Classical Greek colonies, having a family was therefore not a question of personal preference, but a matter of survival as in most agrarian economies. In a newly established colony, it was difficult to find free laborers to help out, as a free man could become a landowner himself. Thus, having a family was even more important than elsewhere: women and children were the main agricultural workforce for colonists who had only a few slaves, or none at all. Under such conditions, the struggle for survival may have led to the break-up of traditional hierarchies based on gender, age, and status (slave/free citizen), although the male citizens had a privileged legal status. In Theophrastus' *Characters* (VI 2–3), a hardworking farmer is caricatured as someone who "distrusts his friends and relatives, but discusses the most important things with his *oiketai* and tells hired laborers everything from the assembly." In Classical colonies, it is not unlikely that the majority of the citizens were hardworking farmers. As I have argued in Chapter 2, images of Artemis Bendis, which were widespread at Heraclea and its hinterland, embodied female agency in traditionally male spheres of activity. The agency of women in colonial societies also seems to emerge in Plato, who advocated gender equality in his imaginary colonies Kallipolis (in the *Republic*) and, to a lesser degree, Magnesia (*Laws*). Perhaps Plato had a colonial frontier society in mind when writing this. Tellingly, he bases his views on women and children not on arguments about justice, but rather on usefulness and

---

[100] On agricultural "survival," see Gallant 1991; Groot, Lentjes, Zeiler 2013.

"everyday life." He argues that "if it were ordained that every practice (πάντα ἐπιτηδεύματα) is to be shared in common by women as well as men, it would be better for the happiness (εὐδαιμονία) of the city" (Laws 781b).[101] According to LSJ, epitédeuma can mean "pursuit, business, custom" as well as "everyday habit, way of life." For Plato, this included not only labor and business, but also warfare and politics. At the same time, the Laws insist on male privileges at the level of civic and political rights. Women are not allowed to inherit or own land. Plato's ideas concerning women in the Laws have been defined as incongruous.[102] Such a critique is doubtlessly justified in terms of ethics or logic. Historically, however, the emancipation of women in the sphere of epitedeúmata (work, business) and their exclusion from land ownership are congruent with the social and economic structure of Classical colonies. Politically, the colonies consisted of male landowners, but they had no chance of survival without the help of women and children.

---

[101] Transl. R.G. Bury, 1967/8.
[102] Samaras 2010: 196.

FIVE

FARMS: THE END OF EQUALITY?

The spread of isolated farmsteads and villages in Greek landscapes is often interpreted as a sign of economic growth and prosperity. On the other hand, a fall in the number of rural sites is usually considered a sign of crisis. Some scholars have even interpreted the establishment of isolated farmsteads as an indicator of democratic tendencies. For example, Victor Hanson (1995) has argued that the very emergence of the Greek polis was intrinsically linked to the diffusion of the family farm which, according to Hanson, represented the economic and cultural backbone of the hoplite class, the citizens who had the means and time to serve in the heavy infantry. In Hanson's analysis, the roots of Western civilization and democracy are linked to the family farm.[1]

In the case of Heraclea, the increase in the number of rural sites during the fourth century BC has been interpreted as the result of a "democratization of the chora." According to Filippo Coarelli, the emergence of numerous rural dwelling sites originated from a democratic redistribution of land around 350 BC.[2]

However, the results presented here do not support such views. If egalitarian and democratic models involved living in nucleated settlements (Ackerbürger polis), the dissolution of such a settlement pattern through the emergence

---

[1] Critical observations in Foxhall 2002: 210–218.
[2] Coarelli 1998: 285.

of isolated farmsteads may be interpreted as a rupture of egalitarian and democratic structures.

FROM RURAL SITES TO RURAL DWELLERS

In Heraclea, this seems to be confirmed by the analysis of rural sites of the Early Hellenistic period. As the number of archaeologically visible, stable habitation sites and rural necropoleis increased from around 330 BC, the picture offered by the archaeological record is an extremely heterogeneous rural settlement pointing to increasing social stratification (Figure 5.1). This emerges very clearly from the analysis of rural habitation sites, whereas data concerning rural burial sites is less abundant, since rescue excavations of Classical and Hellenistic burials in the countryside are unpublished and the possibilities of identifying burials in a field survey are limited. On the Ionian Coast, it is particularly difficult to detect Classical and Hellenistic tomb areas through field survey, given the frequency of tombs *a cappuccina* (i.e., tombs covered with roof tiles) which makes it impossible to use roof tiles as a criterion for the distinction between burials and habitation sites. Surface finds do not always indicate whether we are looking at a small habitation site or a group of burials. In the 2012–2014 field survey at Heraclea, we used the absence of cooking ware as well as the high percentages of fine ware as indicators of burial sites. Sites where fine ware was either absent or associated with considerable numbers of roof tiles, coarse ware, *pithoi*, and cooking ware were interpreted as habitation sites. The latter usually yielded considerably more finds than sites interpreted as burial places (up to 1,000, whereas burial places usually yielded fewer than a hundred fragments).

Some habitation sites were characterized by a broad spectrum of classes. The pottery classes documented here comprise Laconian roof tiles, black-glazed pottery, coarse and plain ware, cooking ware, and *pithos* ware. Among these sites are HE3 and HE7 on Figure 5.2, where the (visibility-corrected) distribution of the major classes in a portion of the area surveyed in 2012–2013 is shown. The activities that presumably took place at such sites range from the storage and processing of agricultural products, as attested by finds of oil presses (Figure 5.3), mortars and pithoi, to food preparation and rather sophisticated modes of consumption, as suggested by black-glazed and red-figure banqueting vessels (Figure 5.4). Sites of this kind are often situated on slopes close to natural springs. In some cases, hypothetical burial sites were found nearby. There is little doubt that these sites were farmsteads that served as permanent dwellings.

Some of the smaller sites interpreted as farmsteads also yielded a broad spectrum of pottery classes, e.g., HE9 and HE34 in Figure 5.2. In some cases, the lower artifact density at these sites, as well as their relatively small size, might

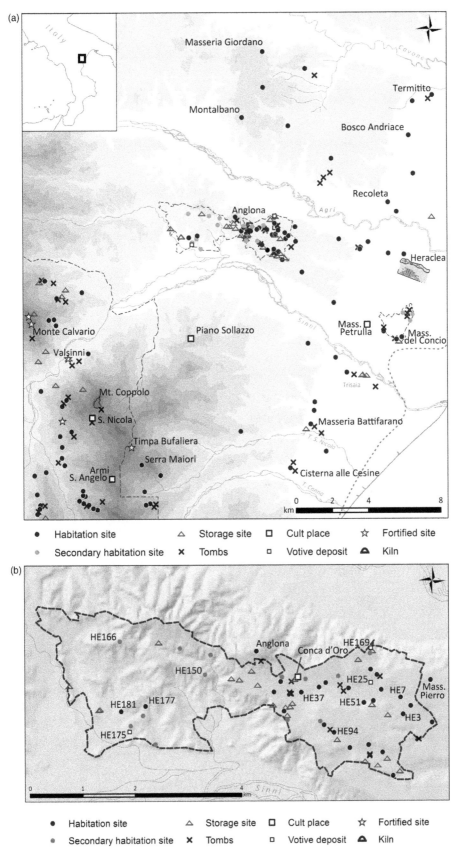

(a)

Masseria Giordano

Montalbano

Bosco Andriace

Termitito

Recoleta

Anglona

Heraclea

Monte Calvario

Piano Sollazzo

Mass. Petrulla

Mass. del Concio

Valsinni

Trisaia

Mt. Coppolo

S. Nicola

Masseria Battifarano

Timpa Bufaliera

Serra Maiori

Armi
S. Angelo

Cisterna alle Cesine

0   2   4   8
km

● Habitation site   △ Storage site   ☐ Cult place   ☆ Fortified site

● Secondary habitation site   ✕ Tombs   ▫ Votive deposit   ◬ Kiln

(b)

HE166

Anglona

Conca d'Oro

HE169

HE150

HE25

HE7

Mass. Pierro

HE181   HE177

HE37

HE51

HE3

HE175

HE94

0   1   2   4
km

Sinni

● Habitation site   △ Storage site   ☐ Cult place   ☆ Fortified site

● Secondary habitation site   ✕ Tombs   ▫ Votive deposit   ◬ Kiln

5.1 The territory of Heraclea, c. 325 BC.

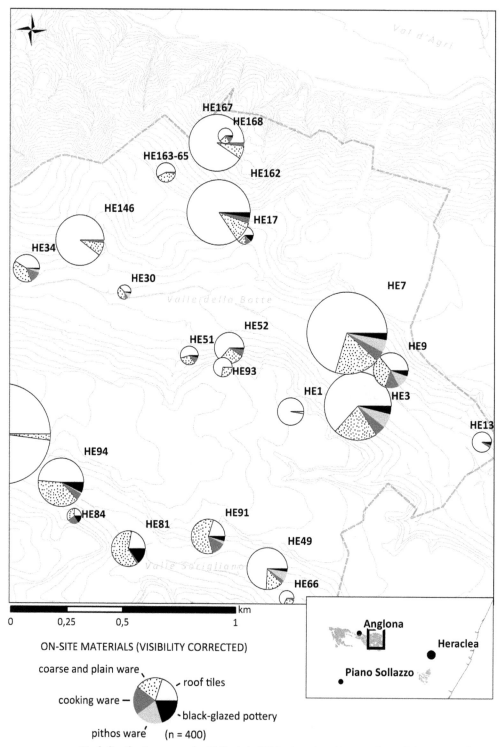

5.2 Find distribution on early Hellenistic habitation sites in a portion of the surveyed area, 2012–2013.

5.3 Oil press from site HE3.

stem from post-depositional processes and/or scarce visibility, although on the whole such factors are not likely to have determined the picture since conditions were often the same as in the case of large farmsteads. Furthermore, there are a number of small sites that have not yielded any fine ware at all. Some of them, e.g., HE1 and HE93 (Figure 5.2), may have been storage facilities or outbuildings that belonged to farmsteads in the vicinity or to households in the urban center. This is also suggested by the fact that HE1 and HE93 are situated on a plateau, i.e., in an area with no direct access to natural springs. Here, water had to be taken from wells or cisterns, if there were any, or carried from springs on the slopes below the plateau. However, access to fresh water might have been secondary if the buildings served primarily as storage facilities for agricultural produce and tools.

Surprisingly, some small- and medium-sized sites have also yielded kitchen ware (HE146, HE163-65). The presence of cooking pots and pans indicates that people lived here, at least periodically. Whether they were agricultural slaves or Greek citizens who had their principal residence elsewhere, or citizens who could only afford a relatively modest style of life, remains uncertain. In any case, the diversity of sites testifies to social stratification. The rural population did not consist of a homogeneous, egalitarian group of farmers, but of a variety of social groups, some of whom lived in very modest conditions whereas others enjoyed relatively high living standards.

5.4 Pottery assemblages from site HE7.

A high degree of social stratification is also suggested by excavations of Early Hellenistic farmsteads (Figure 5.5). On one hand, at Panevino we have an example of a small family farmhouse of c. 100 square meters consisting of not more than two or three rooms.[3] A small oven or kiln was installed at the back of the building. The farmhouse was built around 300 BC; during the second century BC it was replaced by a slightly larger building consisting of two rooms. Some (unpublished) tombs found nearby suggest that the building was permanently inhabited by its owners, who were buried on the site.

On the other hand, at Bosco Andriace a huge building of c. 800 square meters has been excavated, with more than ten rooms and a central courtyard.[4] The materials are in large part unpublished, but on the basis of preliminary excavation reports the complex can be dated to between c. 300 and 200 BC. The dating corresponds roughly to the first phase of Panevino. Finds of large pithoi indicate that the rooms on the western side of the central courtyard were used for storage. A room south of the courtyard has been interpreted as a kitchen; a sewer from the courtyard passed through it. The finds include numerous amphorae, loom weights, and fragments of black-glazed pottery and kitchen ware.

We therefore have two farmsteads dating to the same period but they are totally different in layout and material culture. The survey data discussed above suggests that contrasts like those between the two sites of Panevino and Bosco Andriace were by no means exceptional and characterized the entire territory during the Early Hellenistic period.

[3]   Bini 1989: 16; Bianco 2000: 813–815.
[4]   De Siena, Giardino 2001: 151–153; Giardino 2003: 188; Russo 2006: 171.

focolare

Panevino, phase 1

10 m

Panevino, phase 2

pithos

pithoi

courtyard

pithoi

kitchen

bath

Bosco Andriace

5.5 Excavated farmsteads in the territory of Heraclea.

THE HERACLEA TABLETS AND THE ECONOMY OF INEQUALITY

To get an idea of what it meant to be agriculturist farmer in this period, we can rely on a unique piece of evidence – the so-called *Heraclea Tablets*; these two bronze tablets with Greek inscriptions date to the late fourth or early third century BC and have a Latin inscription from the first century BC on the back.[5] Only the Greek texts are of relevance here. The inscriptions were found in 1732 near the River Cavone by a farmer who was plowing a field. Tablet I is completely preserved, whereas Tablet II is fragmentary. The Greek texts record two occasions on which a group of magistrates entrusted by the *demos* of Heraclea reclaimed sacred lands in the Akiris River valley (modern Agri). The lands, which belonged to the sanctuaries of Dionysus and Athena, had been illegally occupied and many of the old boundary stones (*horos* stones) had disappeared. The Heraclea Tablets describe the remeasurement, division, and leasing of the lands to individual citizens. As Alberto Prieto (2005: 21) has emphasized, the Heraclea Tablets "are unique among Greek juridical texts because they contain the most detailed textual

[5] Uguzzoni, Ghinatti 1968; Prieto 2005: 66–92.

description of an organized landscape anywhere in the Greek world, one of the earliest of its kind."

The Heraclea Tablets do not contain any precise information about where the tenants lived, although there are references to buildings in some of the plots. However, the Tablets do confirm the hypothesis that egalitarian structures were breaking up as some communities specialized in agriculture during the Early Hellenistic period while others did not. Like the settlement pattern, the Tablets reflect the effects of social stratification and economic differentiation. An analysis of the text suggests that during this period, agriculture at Heraclea was characterized by phenomena such as specialization, investment, social stratification, and regional trade, as also indicated by the archaeological evidence. Judging from the Tablets, by the late fourth/early third century BC, the polis of Heraclea had given up any attempt to equalize access to agricultural land; the polis actually seems so have promoted specialization and cash cropping, as I will argue in the following pages. My argument is based on a revision of the surface measurements used in the Tablets.

In the Heraclea Tablets, the most frequent unit is the *schoinos*, a term that has been interpreted in various ways. However, one thing is acknowledged by all scholars and is beyond doubt: 1 *schoinos* corresponds to 30 paces *(oregmata)* and 120 feet *(podes)*. The foot used at Heraclea was the Doric foot of 0.327 meters, as Liliana Giardino has demonstrated based on excavation data from the urban center.[6] What is important is that in the Tablets the conversion *1 schoinos = 30 paces = 120 feet* applies for both length and area measurement units of the same name.

Most scholars who have commented on the Tablets have assumed that the schoinos as a measurement of area was a squared schoinos, i.e., 120 feet x 120 feet = 14,400 square feet.[7] Consequently, the foot (as a measurement of area) used in the Tablets cannot be a square foot (as just mentioned, 1 schoinos equals 120 feet). A possible solution to this problem would be that in the Heraclea Tablets 1 *pous* measured 1 foot x 120 feet and one *oregma* 4 feet x 120 feet, as proposed by Max Guy and others (Figure 5.6).[8] But in this case, the foot as a measurement of area would be based on the schoinos, which would appear odd in the context of ancient Greek metrology.

As early as 1855, Richard Lepsius proposed an alternative interpretation – it was not taken into account in any of the later commentaries on the Tablets but I believe it definitely merits attention. Unlike other scholars, Lepsius did not base his reconstruction on the idea of a squared schoinos, but on the *pous* as a unit of measurement of area, arguing that the latter cannot be understood as a square foot since a square foot of c. 0.3 x 0.3 meters would be far too small

[6] Giardino 1998: 185.
[7] Franz 1853: 706; Quilici 1967: 180–186; Guy 1998; Gabba 2006.
[8] Guy 1998: 261–262.

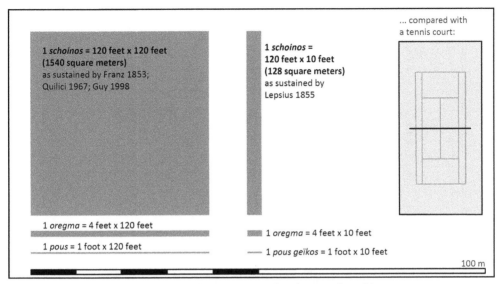

5.6 Hypothetical reconstruction of the *schoinos* mentioned in the Heraclea Tablets.

to be used in the context of field measurement.[9] According to Lepsius, the foot in the Tablets ought to correspond to a larger unit for measuring surface area, namely the *pous geïkos* (land foot) which in some cases could be abbreviated and simply be called *pous*.[10] The *pous geïkos* measured 1 foot x 1 *ákaina* (perch) of 10 feet (in some sources 12 feet), i.e., 10 or 12 square feet.[11] On these grounds, a schoinos would be a rectangle of 10 feet x 120 feet = 1,200 square feet, which is less than a tenth of a squared schoinos of 14,400 square feet (Table 5.1).

In the context of ancient Greek metrology, the reconstruction by Lepsius appears much more coherent than reconstructions based on squared schoinoi. There is yet another argument in favor of Lepsius that I would like to add. The lease contract regarding the lands of Athena in Tablet II indicates that fifty *schoinoi* equal one *gyas*, which was another unit of area measurement.[12] The Greek term *gýas* (Doric) or *gýes* (Attic) refers to the part of the plow that connected the plowshare to the yoke.[13] Like the Roman *iugerum* (yoke), a *gyas* would have corresponded roughly to an area plowable in one day. As known, a *iugerum* amounts to about 0.25 hectares. At any rate, 0.7 hectares is about the maximum area a man could plow in a day.[14] However, a *gyas* of 50 square schoinoi would amount to a huge area of more than 7 hectares whereas, on

[9] Lepsius 1855: 96–98. A *pous* as a unit of area measurement can also refer to a square foot (see for example Plato, *Men.* 82c.).
[10] Lepsius 1855: 97–98.
[11] Hultsch 1854: 36–37, 186–187; *Tab. Her.* IV.
[12] Uguzzoni, Ghinatti 1968: 181–182.
[13] Gow 1914: 266–270.
[14] Müller 1967: 93.

TABLE 5.1 *Heraclea Tablets: plot sizes, rents, and yields*

| | | | | | | | | | | based on Lepsius 1855 (schoinos = 120 feet x 10 feet) | | based on Franz 1854, Gui 1998 et al. (schoinos = 120 feet x 120 feet) | |
	1	2	3	4	5	6	7	8	9	10	11	12	13
lot	special features	total area (schoinoi)	cultivated area (schoinoi)	vineyards (schoinoi)	vineyards (%)	vineyards rent in 5 years (medimnoi)	annual rent (medimnoi)	annual rent in barley (kg)	area needed to grow barley for rent (ha)	hectares	rent in barley (kg) per hectare	hectares	rent in barley (kg) per hectare
Dionysus 1	building	847	201	?			57	896	1.4	10.8	83	130.4	7
Dionysus 2		773	273	no			40	629	1.0	9.9	64	119.0	5
Dionysus 3		849	312	no			35	550	0.8	10.9	51	130.7	4
Dionysus 4	vineyard	849	308	?			278	4,370	6.7	10.9	402	130.7	33
Dionysus total:		*3318*	*1094*				*410.0*	*6,445*	*9.9*	*42.5*	*152*	*511.0*	*13*
Athena I		138	133.5	4.5	3.3	269	53.8	846	1.3	1.8	479	21.3	40
Athena 2		139	123	16	11.5	695	139	2,185	3.4	1.8	1,228	21.4	102
Athena I	building?	59.5	51.25	8.25	13.9	446	89.2	1,402	2.2	0.8	1,841	9.2	153
Athena II	building	72	63.5	8.5	11.8	632	126.4	1,987	3.1	0.9	2,156	11.1	179
Athena III		74	66.5	7.5	10.1	630	126	1,981	3.0	0.9	2,091	11.4	174
Athena IV		83	68	15	18.1	630	126	1,981	3.0	1.1	1,864	12.8	155
Athena A	road	68.5	62	6.5	9.5	856	171.2	2,691	4.1	0.9	3,069	10.5	255
Athena B	building	66	59.5	6.5	9.8	458	91.6	1,440	2.2	0.8	1,704	10.2	142
Athena C		70	63.5	6.5	9.3	306	61.2	962	1.5	0.9	1,074	10.8	89
Athena D		54.5	48	6.5	11.9	235	47	739	1.1	0.7	1,059	8.4	88
Athena E		71	64	7	9.9	580	116	1,824	2.8	0.9	2,007	10.9	167
Athena F		38.5	30	8.5	22.1								
Athena total:		*934*	*832.75*	*101.3*	*10.8*	*5737*	*1147.4*	*18,037*	*27.7*	*11.5*	*1,574*	*137.9*	*131*

the basis of Lepsius' hypothesis, a schoinos would amount to a relatively small area of about 0.64 hectares. This is much closer to what one would expect for a "yoke."[15]

Finally, it should be borne in mind that at Athens 300 plethra (about 30 hectares) were considered a large estate, as sources referring to the possessions of Alcibiades, Phainippos, and other wealthy Athenians demonstrate.[16] If a schoinos were 120 feet x 120 feet, the allotments in the lands of Dionysus would be about four times the size of the estates of the Athenian elite.[17] Such allotments would simply be too large to be managed by individual tenants. This ultimately supports Lepsius's hypothesis of schoinoi measuring 120 feet x 10 feet. Therefore the idea of square schoinoi should definitely be abandoned.

What consequences does this have for the interpretation of the Heraclea Tablets? Firstly, the question of the correct localization of the sacred lands can be viewed in a different light. Reconstructions based on squared schoinoi involve certain unresolved problems, e.g., the island in the River Akiris mentioned in Tablet I, which is estimated to be two or three kilometers long.[18] The estates bordering the lands of Dionysus would be equally large.[19] Reconstructions based on rectangular schoinoi of 10 feet x 120 feet appear much more realistic, although the precise location of the lands remains uncertain (Figure 5.7).

More importantly, the ratio between plot size, yield, and rent changes: In the Heraclea Tablets, the rent is numeralized in *medimnoi* (1 *medimnos* corresponds to about 52.4 liters[20]). The rent had to be paid in barley, even though the tenants cultivated other crops. We are unfamiliar with the precise rules by which crop yields other than barley (vine, orchards, legumes, etc.) were converted into barley. We are therefore unable to specify the precise ratio between yield and rent. However, the yield-rent ratio can be approximately reconstructed in some instances. The rents vary considerably depending on which crops were cultivated. Relatively low rents were due for cereals, whereas orchards and olives had higher rents, and the most expensive rents were due for plots with vineyards.[21] What makes it impossible to get precise numbers is the lack

---

[15] In eighteenth-century Prussia, 0.65 hectares corresponded to a *Pommerscher Morgen* (Pomeranian acre, literally "morning"), an area manageable by one man in a day (Müller 1967: 93). Jameson, Runnels, van Andel (1994: 388) give 0.3 hectares for a day's work. It should be added here that in Late Antiquity, some authors mistook a *gyas* for a plethron (100 feet x 100 feet: Hesych. quoted in Hultsch 1854: 315; *Etym. Magn.* s.v.: "50 *gyai* are 50 *plethra*"). This kind of confusion would be understandable if a *gyas* measured 0.64 hectares, but not if it measured 7 hectares. On similar measurement units in the Byzantine and Ottoman world (stremma, dönüm), cf. Foxhall 2003: 81–83.

[16] Isager, Skydsgaard 1995: 78. See Plato, *Alc.* 123c; Lysias XIX 29.

[17] See the reconstructions in Quilici 1967: 180–186.

[18] IG XVI, 645, I, 38.

[19] On the location of the sacred lands, see Prieto 2005: 214, fig. 2.6.

[20] According to the Sicilian-Attic *medimnos* (Sartori 1967: 43). Whether or not the Laconian *medimnos* had a higher capacity, as Hultsch hypothesized (1862: 260), remains unresolved.

[21] Kamps 1938: 77–81; Uguzzoni, Ghinatti 1968: 206–211.

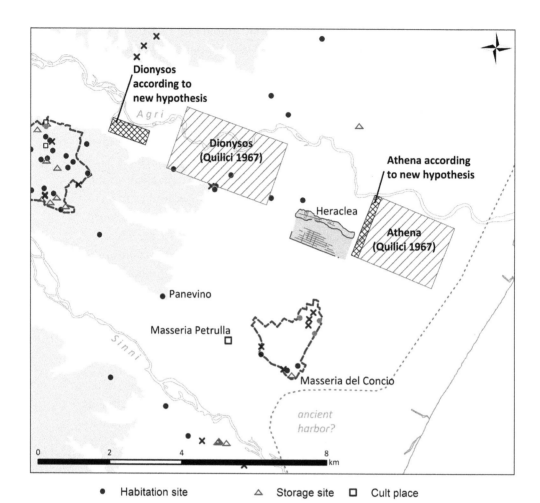

5.7 Hypothetic location of the lands of Athena and Dionysus mentioned in the Heraclea Tablets.

of detailed information for a number of features. For example, in the lands
of Dionysus there are extensive areas of "maquis, uncultivated land, and oak
trees"; it is unclear, however, to what extent these areas contributed to calculat-
ing the rents. In plot 1, the presence of such areas seems to lead to a relatively
high rent, but the fact that plot 3, though much bigger than plot 2, yielded a
lower rent shows that the calculation also depended on other factors not speci-
fied in the Tablets (Table 5.1). The same holds true for the lands of Athena: for
example, plots III and IV are charged equally, although plot IV has twice as
large a vineyard as plot III. It seems that vineyards generally gave rise to much
higher rents than other types of cultivation. In fact, according to a rough estimate, the rent for vineyards was about twenty times the average.[22]

[22] Uguzzoni, Ghinatti 1968: 204–208.

However, we can try to estimate how much land was necessary to produce the amount of barley that had to be paid for each plot, although it is of course unclear where the barley was actually grown.[23] It might have been grown directly on the plot or somewhere else. As column 9 in Table 5.1 shows, in the lands of Dionysus about a tenth of the area of each plot was needed to produce the annual rent, except for plot 4 which contained vineyards and therefore has to be considered separately. Considering that plots 1–3 do not contain significant portions of vineyards, olive groves, etc., and thus may have served primarily for the cultivation of grain, it can be estimated that the rent corresponded in this case to about 10% of the actual yield. This is in line with other cases such as the lands of Zeus at Locri which were let for one tenth of the yield.[24] Again, it turns out that the idea of square schoinoi of 120 feet x 120 feet is highly improbable, since the rents would be extremely low, namely about 1% in plots 1–3 of Dionysus (Table 5.1).

The picture changes in the allotments with vineyards belonging to the lands of Athena which were situated in the vicinity of the town and therefore suited to intensive exploitation. According to our calculations, the areas needed to produce the rent there exceeded the total area of the plots, except for plot 1 (Table 5.1). This means that the contract obliged the tenants to ameliorate the land, not only by prescribing actions such as planting a certain number of vines and olive trees,[25] but by the very conditions of the contract. If the tenant of plot 2 in the lands of Athena decided to cultivate barley, the yield would not have sufficed to pay the rent. He had to exploit the lands as much as he could. In practice, the tenants of the allotments in the lands of Athena needed to possess other land where they could produce the barley to pay the rent. The point of renting these plots was to gain so much profit from the cultivation of vines, fruit trees, etc., that one could afford to produce or purchase enough barley to pay the lease. The yield of vineyards could be further increased through polyculture, i.e., by growing beans, pulses, and vegetables between the rows of vines, or around the field. Almond, fig, or other fruit trees on the field boundaries could provide further crops without interfering with the vines; (sub-)renting the land to shepherds after the grape gathering was another possible source of income and helped to fertilize to the land. All these methods are well attested ethno-historically, and once more underscore the complexity of tenancy end agricultural practices.[26]

---

[23] On the basis of Sallares 1991: 389, an average yield of 650 kilograms of barley per hectare appears plausible. Considering that the product was probably stored with spelt for better conservation (see Pliny, Nat. hist. XVIII 304), a liter would have corresponded to about 0.3 kilogram of pure barley: see Cappers, Neef 2012: 86, 226, 383, 391. If the Tablets prescribed that the rent was to be paid in *krithá kathará* ("clean barley": IG XIV, 645 I 103), this probably refers to the removal of the spikes rather than of the spelt.

[24] Costabile 1987: 114.

[25] See for example IG XIV, 645 I 114–116.

[26] Foxhall 1990: 104–108.

Nonetheless, renting the plots in the lands of Athena did involve certain risks, for example a fall in wine prices. Suppose the spread between the prices of wine and barley began to shrink: in such a case, the tenant of plot no. 2 in the lands of Athena would sooner or later start to lose money. Renting these lots meant speculating on a rise or at least on the constancy of wine prices.

The analysis of the contracts shows that the polis as a lessor of the sacred lands was not interested in supporting landless citizens and their families; rather, it maximized the rent by letting the lands to those who already had certain resources, or investors who were able to generate higher yields. It is true that the rent in the lands of Athena was due only after five years,[27] but this was of little help for landless citizens. Rents of 630 medimnoi and more (c. 33,000 liters) were more than the "little man" could afford. It is difficult to imagine that a family like the one living on the Panevino farm could meet the requirements of the contracts, especially in the lands of Athena. Only relatively rich households possessed enough pithoi, silos, and storage rooms to handle such quantities (Table 5.1).[28]

WERE RURAL FARMERS SECOND-CLASS CITIZENS?

The situation that emerges from excavations, field survey data, and the analysis of the Heraclea Tablets is characterized by differentiation and specialization processes that left the rather primitive economy of the Ackerbürger colony behind. The emergence of a class of rural dwellers led to the break-up of the closeness that characterized the original settlement and entailed important sociocultural and political transformations within the community. What developed here from the second half of the fourth century BC onward was not, as some have argued, a democratization of the chora but quite the opposite.[29] Henceforth, a significant part of the population would choose (or was obliged) to live in the chora and be buried there. Even if there had been ephemeral, archaeologically invisible dwellings in the countryside during earlier phases, the sites of the later fourth century reflect a new kind of rural economy and lifestyle. One main reason for this new phenomenon might be that these people were under economic pressure and needed to react in some way. Moving into rural areas allowed them to intensify agricultural production and to increase their income. Living in the countryside meant minimizing the distance between their home and workplace and consequently having more time and energy for agricultural activities. Many of them were probably citizens who for economic reasons left the community of *politai* in the *asty* (walled center) and abandoned the way of life that had characterized the early years

---

[27] IG XIV, 645 II 35.
[28] On storage capacities of Classical farmsteads, see Foxhall 2009.
[29] Cf. Coarelli 1998: 285.

of the colony. However, the new class of rural dwellers that emerged around 330 BC may also have included non-citizens and indigenous groups who were already living in the countryside without being archaeologically visible. These, then, became part of a new class of rural dwellers who adopted economic and social practices which make them archaeologically visible.

Ancient authors were aware that living in the countryside often led to social downgrading and gradual exclusion from political participation. For example, Aristotle observes that farmers who have small properties are often too busy to meet in the assembly, and concludes with regard to the "best state" that "the citizens must not live a mechanic or a mercantile life (for such a life is ignoble and inimical to virtue), nor yet must those who are to be citizens in the best state be tillers of the soil (for leisure is needed both for the development of virtue and for active participation in politics)."[30] Luciano Canfora has pointed out that even during the heyday of Athenian democracy, the majority of *georgoi* (farmers) were only sporadically present in the assembly and had practically nothing to say: when they attended the assembly, they did not so much participate as resort to "yelling and insulting."[31] In Plato's *Laws* (756b–e) the lower classes are exempted from regular attendance, whereas members of the upper classes are fined in case of absence. The fact that residing in the country meant exclusion from political life is also suggested by Theophrastus' *Characters* (XXVI 6), where the oligarch blames Theseus for "having given more weight to the *demos*" by promoting the synoecism of Athens. The very emergence of specialist farmers is considered a typical feature of oligarchic, nondemocratic economies by Aristotle (Pol. 1329a):

> ... it remains to consider whether everybody is to take part in all of these functions (for it is possible for the whole of the people to be at once farmers and craftsmen and the councilors and judges), or whether we are to assume different classes corresponding to each of the functions mentioned, or whether some of them must necessarily be specialized and others combined. But it will not be the same in every form of constitution; for, as we said, it is possible either for all the people to take part in all the functions or for not all to take part in all but for certain people to have certain functions. In fact these different distributions of functions are the cause of the difference between constitutions: democracies are states in which all the people participate in all the functions, oligarchies where the contrary is the case.
>
> (transl. H. Rackham, 1944)

In a city-state founded as a community of socially and economically equal landholders who lived in the urban center (referred to here as Ackerbürger), the emergence of a specialized class of farmers living in the countryside

---

[30] Pol. 1328b–1329a (transl. H. Rackham, 1944). On Greek concepts of citizenship see Mossé 1993.

[31] Canfora 2011: 82–83, analyzing Aristophanes, *Acarn.* 20–39.

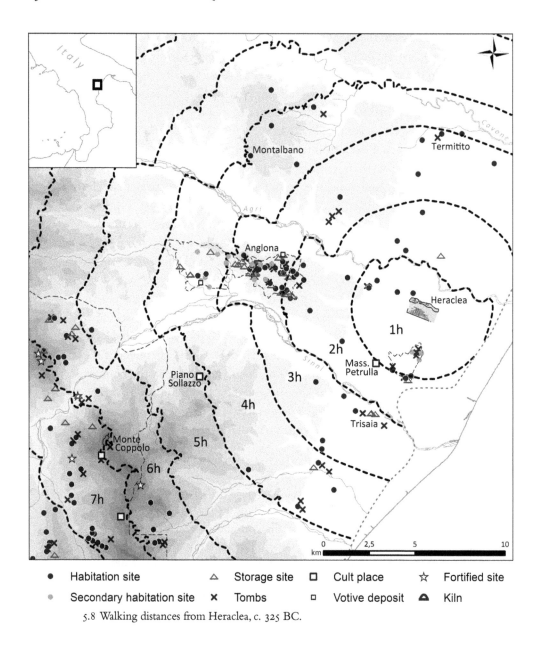

| • | Habitation site | △ | Storage site | ◻ | Cult place | ☆ | Fortified site |
| • | Secondary habitation site | ✕ | Tombs | ◻ | Votive deposit | ⬮ | Kiln |

5.8 Walking distances from Heraclea, c. 325 BC.

represented a new development that interfered with the egalitarian structure of the original community. Although farmers who lived up to four hours' walking distance from Heraclea (Figure 5.8) could attend the *alia* (as the assembly was called there) once in a while (given that they had the right to do so), they could not go to the city every day to participate in *symposia* (banquets), *hetairiai* (parties), trials, commissions, and other activities at the core of the political life in a Classical polis. Likewise, this rural population could hardly attend the gymnasium regularly and was thus excluded from one of the most important practices of Greek manhood.[32] According to Aristotle, agricultural work and athletics were simply two separate worlds: in the "best state," the gymnasium of the older men is situated on the agora where *georgoi* and *banausoi* (farmers and artisans) have no access unless summoned by the magistrates.[33]

Living in the urban center and taking care of one's fields some kilometers away in the countryside may have been stressful, but it was doubtless possible, as outlined in the previous chapter; by contrast, living several hours from the urban center and participating actively in the political, social, and cultural life of the urban center was practically impossible. What I would like to stress here is that participation was not only a question of political rights, but also of living conditions. The political, ethnic, and cultural structure of the rural population may actually have been very heterogeneous. At the same time, the rural dwellers faced economic and living conditions that tended to exclude them from active political participation in the polis, whatever their juridical or social status. This is maybe not so self-evident today, as rural dwellers are motorized and connected with the world via newspapers, the internet, etc., but it reflects the experience of most pre-modern societies. As recently as the 1950s, this was still the case. Antonio Gramsci and other pre-war theorists had assumed that southern Italian peasants who lived in nucleated settlements and worked the fields of rich landowners could be enfranchised through the allotment of land and the building of dwellings on the parcels.[34] As this became reality thanks to the land reform of the 1940s and 1950s (Figure 5.9), the new settlement pattern led to a number of unforeseen sociocultural problems which contributed to the partial failure of the reform, as pointed out by local historians such as Michele Orsini from Palagiano (Apulia, southern Italy). One of the problems was a profound sense of isolation and exclusion on the part of the rural dwellers:

> As before, the farmers lacked any security in the selling of their products. Often they would await the period of harvest with anxiety; the gain which recompensed them for their labor was expected with so much preoccupation, because the market was dominated by the merchants who fixed the prices as they liked. Attempts to form cooperatives failed soon. That the beneficiaries were obliged to reside on the land turned out to be a problem. The peasants in Palagiano as elsewhere in Apulia could hardly bear the displacement from the urban center. They were used to returning to town after work, and after supper, though tired, to meet on the *piazza* or at the barber's or the saddler's shop where they chatted and exchanged news. In the country, they found themselves suddenly thrown into total isolation far from the town where they had lived for years; without social contacts they were forced to live in isolated houses far from each other (...). Anyone who had no means of transport was completely isolated.

[32] Cf. Pritchard 2013.
[33] Cf. Aristotle, Pol. 1330a.
[34] Gramsci [2007].

5.9 *Case coloniche* in the area of Policoro (ancient Heraclea), around 1960. (Courtesy of Comune di Policoro.)

> (…) At Conca d'Oro, the 'center' of the area concerned by the agrarian reform, the settlers would meet to enjoy some company whenever they could, listening to the radio or playing cards. During such short absences in the evening, the houses were looked after by the women who awaited the return of their husbands with anxiety, since streets and courtyards were pitch-dark. The children suffered more than anybody from the displacement from town. They had neither comrades to play with nor places to meet … (Orsini 2008)[35]

The *case coloniche* (colonist houses) of Conca d'Oro were about 8 kilometers from the town of Palagiano. As I have argued above, until the 1950s many

[35] As cited on the webpage: www.palagianonline.it/paese/index.php?option=com_content&view=article&id=574:la-riforma-agraria-&catid=24:il-lavoro&Itemid=100 (12/11/2014: "Nessuna tutela ebbe, ancora una volta, l'agricoltore nella vendita dei suoi prodotti; spesso il periodo del raccolto che doveva essere atteso con ansia, per i ricavi delle vendite, compenso giusto per le sue fatiche, veniva atteso con tanta preoccupazione, essendo il mercato in balia dei commercianti che ne stabilivano il prezzo a loro piacimento. Tentativi di costituzione di cooperative naufragarono prestissimo. Risultò negativo l'obbligo, per gli assegnatari, di risiedere in campagna. Gli agricoltori palagianesi come in genere, quelli pugliesi, mal sopportavano l'allontanamento dal centro abitato. Erano abituati, dopo il lavoro, a rientrare in paese e, dopo la cena, anche se stanchi, si incontravano in piazza o nelle botteghe del sellaio o del barbiere dove discorrevano e si scambiavano notizie. (…) Chi non aveva un mezzo di trasporto proprio era completamente tagliato fuori dal contesto sociale del paese. (…) A Conca d'Oro, dove era stato ubicato il 'Centro' per il nostro territorio interessato alla Riforma Agraria, gli assegnatari, pur di stare un po' insieme si incontravano, quando potevano, per ascoltare la radio o giocare a carte. La sera, durante queste brevi assenze, le abitazioni, venivano lasciate alla custodia delle mogli che aspettavano con ansia, il rientro dei mariti, essendo le strade e le corti delle case, al buio totale. Chi soffriva più di tutti l'allontanamento dal paese, erano i ragazzi. Non avevano più compagni con cui giocare, né posti per incontrarsi …")

peasants walked distances of 8 kilometers and more to reach their fields. As the quotation demonstrates, this does not mean that similar distances were regularly covered in the opposite direction, i.e., from country to town. One apparent reason was that the settlers would have had to leave their families alone and walk one or two hours in the dark. Another reason is probably that unlike agricultural labor, socializing in the *paese* is principally a contingent activity that cannot be scheduled. Of course rural dwellers would go to town on special occasions (festivities, assemblies), but full participation obviously required more than that. It involved "hanging out" with other people, chatting and discussing all kinds of issues; therefore it required a sort of regular availability for interlocution on the part of the community members. A farmer living in the country might walk to town to get his hair cut at the barber's shop, buy tools, etc., but in the strict sense he could not hang out in town. For hanging out is principally something undesigned, whereas walking several kilometers presupposes some kind of design or intention, even if it is only to visit the town. In other words, even a farmer who comes to town offhandedly is confronted with the question, "Why are you here?" Whereas those who live in town are simply there. The conditions of communication are not the same.

Admittedly, accounts from southern Italy before and after the agrarian reform are of limited value for the reconstruction of Classical Greek colonies. There is a comparable analysis for eighteenth- to nineteenth-century Locorotondo in Puglia where people moved away from the paese without this being perceived as a loss or social downgrading.[36] Yet the cited passages from Xenophon, Plato, Aristotle, and Theophrastus, among others, suggest that the sociocultural situation of rural dwellers in ancient Greek colonies might have been comparable to that of Italian peasants in Pagliano and many other rural areas. At any rate, I can think of no preindustrial society where rural and urban dwellers were really equal in terms of cultural and political participation.

Processes of social stratification, as in Early Hellenistic Heraclea, are also evident in the territory of Tauric Chersonesus, although this may not seem so at first glance. As mentioned above, the land division in its visible form dates to the second half of the fourth century BC, although it may partly go back to an older, less extensive division system. This suggests that the citizen body had maintained (or reestablished) an egalitarian order as late as three or four generations after the foundation. When the division system was created or enlarged in the second half of the fourth century, the citizens had not only equal-sized land lots but were also in large part concentrated in the urban center. It is true that more than 140 rural sites dating to between the second half of the fourth century and the early third century have been documented in the territory of Chersonesus, some of

---

[36] Galt 1992. The explanation might lie in the kind of crops that were cultivated. In the case of Locorotondo, the cultivation of high-value cash crops like grapes, the trade in which was not dominated by local elites, gave farmers some kind of autonomy.

which have also been excavated. However, there are no tombs in the so-called nearer chora, i.e., the area covered by the division walls. It seems that the majority of the citizens had their main residence in the urban center, where they were also buried, as indicated by tombs and painted stelae described in Chapter 3. Moreover, there is a considerable number of land plots where the existence of buildings can definitely be excluded. Hence the question arises: Who lived in the farmsteads of Chersonesus? Most farmsteads at Chersonesus were built around a central tower and protected by a fortification wall. They usually had considerable storage facilities. Therefore it has been argued that the farmsteads were not owned by individual citizens, but by groups of citizens or maybe even by the polis itself.[37] The buildings may have been used as temporary lodgings during harvest time and/or as storage facilities. Interestingly, the picture changes in the distant chora (territories more than 60 kilometers north of Chersonesus), where rural settlements and isolated farmsteads were permanently inhabited as indicated by tombs found in the vicinity of habitation sites.[38] It is important to note that these areas were probably controlled by Chersonesus from around 360 BC, as agreed by most scholars.[39] Hence, we have to imagine that the rural settlement of the second half of the fourth century BC was divided into two different socioeconomic units: the nearer chora which was owned and managed by the citizens living in the town, and the distant chora which was cultivated by people living scattered in the countryside. While the territory around Chersonesus continued to be structured according to the model of the Ackerbürger polis, the lands beyond the grid and the annexed territories to the north around Kalos Limen and Kerkinitis were characterized by rural habitation sites serving as permanent dwellings. Excavations at Panskoye I, a site northeast of Kalos Limen, have brought to light various Early Hellenistic buildings in a fortified enclosure as well as an enormous complex with central courtyard (U6) situated nearby. In the necropolis north of the settlement, both Greek and Taurian burial rites and grave goods are attested.[40] This indicates that the ethnic, cultural, and economic structure of the community was different from that of Chersonesus, where burial rites and grave monuments of the Early Hellenistic period were typically Greek, and recall models from mainland Greece.[41]

WINE AND OIL: THE END OF EQUALITY AND THE BEGINNINGS OF AN ECONOMIC BOOM

As in Lucanian Heraclea, the expansion of the rural settlement at Chersonesus coincided with social stratification, but also with an unprecedented economic

[37] Nikolaenko 2006: 163.
[38] Stolba, Rugov 2012.
[39] Ščeglov 1986: 155–156; but see Carter 2003: 25 ("from about 300 BC").
[40] Stolba, Rugov 2012.
[41] Posamentir 2011.

boom. In the Early Hellenistic period, Chersonesus started to produce large amounts of transport amphorae, which were stamped with the names of local magistrates *(astynomoi)* and are therefore easily recognizable.[42] The amphorae produced at Chersonesus contained probably wine that was shipped along the coasts of the Black Sea. As is known, the northern shores of the Black Sea were not suited to olive cultivation, although wild olives are attested in some areas.[43] At the same time, the plots around Chersonesus are full of what has been interpreted as indicators of vineyards (rows of stonewalls and terraces), although it must be stressed that this is by no means certain.[44] The features discovered in the plots of Chersonesus do point to intensive agriculture, but a number of gaps in the evidence make it impossible to say with certainty what was cultivated there in specific periods. Unfortunately, a study on the distribution of Chersonesean amphorae is still lacking. It would be very interesting to see where the wine or whatever the nature of the produce contained in these amphoras were consumed.

The high degree of specialization and intensive agriculture might also explain the prohibition of grain exports in the Oath of Chersonesus mentioned earlier: the inhabitants used their land-lots mainly to produce wine and other cash-crops for export at the cost of not producing enough grain to feed the population.[45] It is assumed that the distant chora served primarily to ensure the supply of grain to the central-place. Like Heraclea in Lucania, Early Hellenistic Chersonesus was characterized by regional trade, specialization, and cash cropping.

Similar phenomena can be observed in many other regions, too. During the Late Classical and the Early Hellenistic periods, large estates that specialized in olive and wine production emerge in Attica, Macedonia, the Aegean, and in colonial areas in southern Italy, Sicily and the Black Sea Region.[46] The same holds true for many regions outside the Greek world, such as Punic Ibiza and Spain.[47] The rupture with the past is particularly drastic in Classical foundations such as Heraclea and Chersonesus, where economic transformations occurred against the backdrop of a totally different way of life: that of the Ackerbürger colony (though only partially, in the case of Chersonesus). The model of the Ackerbürger polis represents the real peculiarity of Classical colonies; the Early Hellenistic boom led to a general assimilation of settlement and economic patterns in the entire Greek world and beyond. Yet the abandonment of the Ackerbürger model does not always coincide with the Early Hellenistic boom.

---

[42] Stolba 2005a.
[43] Cordova, Lehmann 2006.
[44] Yanuchevitch, Nikolaenko, Kuzminova 1985; Nikolaenko 2006.
[45] See Stolba 2005b.
[46] Lohmann 1993: 194–219; Jameson, Runnels, van Andel 1994: 383–394; Osanna 2000; Adam-Veleni, Poulaki, Tzanavari 2003; Foxhall 2009; Carter, Prieto 2011: 809–868.
[47] van Dommelen, Gómez Bellard 2008.

At Thurii, for example, the emergence of isolated farmsteads seems to date back to the first half of the fourth century (two or three generations after the foundation), i.e., several decades earlier than at neighboring Heraclea. On the other hand, in some fourth century colonies such as Issa and Pharos, rural habitation sites remain almost totally invisible throughout the Hellenistic period. Relatively small communities like the Adriatic colonies of the fourth century BC could obviously preserve the structure of an Ackerbürger polis for several centuries. The decline of the Ackerbürger model was probably reinforced by economic developments in the Early Hellenistic period, but it could have begun much earlier (as at Thurii) or may have failed to appear even after the end of the Classical period.

In the light of the original structure of most Classical colonies, the emergence of rural dwelling sites represented a rupture and maybe even a sort of failure. Although the stable occupation of the countryside seems to have contributed to a certain type of growth and prosperity, it did not necessarily lead to a situation where all community members could improve their economic condition and social status. Permanent rural dwellers represented a new group who at least partially had to endure social downgrading and exclusion from political life, as outlined above.

Neither in the colonies nor in other Greek city-states did rural populations develop sufficient class consciousness to become a significant political factor. Within the hegemonic discourse, this population appears as an object either of derision and mockery or, especially in the Hellenistic period, of bucolic and romanticizing literary imagination *(eidyllia)*.[48] Classical sources refer to spontaneous solidarity in affairs of daily life and agriculture, but never of politically conscious activities on the part of peasants.[49] This voicelessness of the rural population ultimately confirms their subaltern status. The urban center obviously remained the only point of reference from which meaning and power flowed, while the countryside served at best as a rhetorical or artistic counterpoint from which no genuine reaction was to be expected. The fact that many urban dwellers were also farmers, and given the social and economic heterogeneity of the rural population, undoubtedly contributed to this situation. There was no clear distinction between urban consumers and rural producers, as in modern cities. The fact that many urban dwellers were also landholders and agriculturists meant that farmers who lived in the countryside did not distinguish themselves through any specific and exclusive role in society, namely providing food for the city, since they shared this function with large parts of the urban population. A wealthy landowner would often possess a country

---

[48] Kolb 1984: 125–126; Schmitz 2004: 435.
[49] Schmitz 2004: 423–444. See also Aristotle, *Pol.* 1319a.

house in addition to his primary residence in town.[50] Thus, peasants were not really defined by anything that they possessed or did, given that everything they possessed and did was also possessed and done by any Ackerbürger living in town; they were basically defined by the lack of something, namely the possibility of living in town. The very term *georgos* (farmer) was probably coined only in the fifth century BC, whereas originally everybody was a farmer to some extent, so there was no need for a specific term for this condition.[51] In newly founded colonies, this situation continued as late as the fifth and fourth centuries BC, as I have tried to argue in Chapter 4. If everybody was a farmer, being a poor farmer simply meant being poor without any further attributes.

[50] See Isager, Skydsgaard 1995: 67, who assume that Xenophon Oec. 9,3 refers to the "town-house" of Ischomachos, "where the farm buildings are located elsewhere."
[51] Schmitz 2004: 434–436.

SIX

MOUNTAINS: THE LIMITS OF GREEKNESS AND CITIZENSHIP

In the Classical period, relations between colonists and local populations were extremely varied, very much as they had been in the Archaic period. Literary sources refer to violent conflicts accompanying the establishment of Classical colonies (Thurii, Amphipolis, Pharos), but there are also accounts of cases where Greek settlers and locals collaborated, as in Emporion and Korkyra Melaina.[1] The foundation decree of Korkyra mentions the "settlers from Issa" together with "Pyllos and his son Dazos," apparently local Illyrian rulers with whom some kind of agreement had been made.[2] In Emporion on the east coast of Spain, Iberians and Greeks collaborated in the creation of the New Town *(Neapolis)* around 500 BC, although the two communities appear to have remained physically and politically separated.[3]

WHAT WERE THE GREEKS DOING ON THE COAST?

In violent conflicts, Greek contingents were often victorious when fighting at sea or with support from the sea, as for example in Eion (Thuc. VII 107,1), Pharos (Diod. XV 13,4), and along the coast of southern France (see Strabo

---

[1] As C. Dougherty (1993: 158) has observed, military violence is rarely mentioned in colonial myths or legends, though "hints of a level of discomfort with this violence" can be detected in the texts.

[2] Syll.³ 141, lines 1–2. The names are thought to be of Illyrian, Macedonian or Iapygian origin.

[3] Sanmartì 1993; Oller Guzmán 2013.

IV 1,5 on Massaliote naval power). On the other hand, Greek armies suffered a series of catastrophic defeats when they advanced from the coast into inland areas. In the third century BC, Tauric Chersonesus seems to have survived thanks to its harbor, as Scythian groups had seized almost the entire territory of the city.[4] According to Herodotus (VII 170,3), the most terrible defeat ever suffered by Greeks (*phonos hellenikos megistos*) took place when the Tarantines advanced inland to attack the Iapygians in the 470s BC. About a decade later, in around 465/4 BC, a contingent of 10,000 settlers sent to Enneahodoi (later Amphipolis) was defeated by the Thracians at Drabeskos, about 20 kilometers inland.[5] As long as the Greeks operated on the coast, they had access to logistic options that were out of reach for most of the groups living in the hinterland of the colonies. Seafaring techniques (Greek, but also Phoenician and Etruscan) continued to define power relations along the coasts of the Mediterranean and the Black Sea, including military hegemony, but also trade and exchange in the widest sense. This process continued throughout antiquity and the Middle Ages, and it had probably started long before the fifth century BC.[6] As soon as the Greeks moved inland, things changed drastically. We might speak of military supremacy on the part of the Greeks, but it was based on naval power and therefore strictly limited to coastal areas.

Yet, seafaring and military power contributed indirectly to the transformation of areas far inland. Similar phenomena emerge in the history of the transatlantic slave trade from the seventeenth to nineteenth centuries, although the general context is different. It has been observed that many Africans were not captured by European slave traders, but by competing local groups. However, the driving force behind it were the Europeans on the coast, as Chinua Achebe pointed out in a lecture at Bard College, New York:

> You'll find all kind of fancy statements about the Africans selling themselves. In fact, one professor of history at Stanford was saying not so long ago on television that the Europeans did not do this, they were on the coast, they didn't go inland; the Africans brought their brothers down to the coast. And I want to ask him: What were the Europeans doing on the coast of Africa, thousands of miles from their homes?[7]

Of course, the transatlantic slave trade and Greek colonization are very different in many aspects, but it may be useful to keep this example in mind when asking the question: What were the Greeks doing on the coast? Classical Greece imported large numbers of slaves from the Black Sea region and Thrace;[8] they

---

[4]   Stolba 2005b: 302–303, with bibliography.
[5]   See Thuc. I 102,2; Diod XI 70,5.
[6]   Cf. Horden, Purcell 2000: 133.
[7]   See www.youtube.com/watch?v=mNdjcFOoVi8
[8]   See Miller, M.C. 1997. See also Polybius, Hist. IV 38 ("... [T]hose commodities which are the first necessaries of existence, cattle and slaves, are confessedly supplied by the districts

cannot have only come from a small strip of land along the Black Sea coast where Greek colonies were established. As Nadežda A. Gavriljuk (2003) has shown, the Greek slave trade heavily influenced the economy and the culture of communities living far from the coast in the steppe north of the Black Sea.

In this light, the archaeology of Greek colonization should look not only at the colonies themselves, but also at the entire hinterland, i.e., all those areas which maps showing Greek colonization (including Figure 1.1) usually represent as blank spaces.[9] In the context of Classical archaeology, filling in these blank spaces often means leaving the traditional limits of the discipline behind. Considering that the archaeology of inland settlements in regions like Lucania, Illyria, Thrace, Scythia, etc., is no less complex than the history and archaeology of any Greek region studied by Classical archaeologists for over a hundred years, much work remains to be done. In this chapter, I shall again use Heraclea in Lucania and its hinterland as a case study with the objective of contextualizing the colony within a broader regional settlement pattern (Figure 6.1). How does the picture of the settlement change if we try to fill in the blank spaces along the banks of the River Siris?

The inland mountains around Heraclea rise sharply from the coast, especially in the south towards Calabria. Unlike most parts of Apulia, inland Basilicata and Calabria are mountainous, partly alpine, regions. Mountains as high as 800 meters above sea level rise within a distance of 14 to 20 kilometers from the Heraclean coast. The highest among them is Monte Coppolo (890 meters above sea level), on top of which lay a fortified settlement dating to between the fourth century BC and the Imperial period. A field survey conducted by Lorenzo Quilici and his team on the slopes of Monte Coppolo and neighboring mountains revealed numerous small sites dating to between the Bronze Age and the Middle Ages (see Figure 5.1).[10] Still further inland, habitation sites of the fourth/third centuries BC were discovered in areas more than 1,000 meters above sea level.[11]

Such areas were traditionally considered as marginal and detached from Mediterranean connectivity, but there are an increasing number of studies that tend to question such views. In *The Corrupting Sea*, Peregrine Horden and Nicholas Purcell (2000) suggested reconsidering the history of mountain regions around the Mediterranean and abandoning the stereotype of isolation and marginality:

> Mountain societies can no longer be characterized, as they were by Braudel, primarily in stark Malthusian terms: of cultural and economic

round the Pontus in greater profusion, and of better quality, than by any others," trans. E.S. Shuckburgh); Strabo, Geogr. VII 3,12.
[9] Cf. Hodos 2006.
[10] Quilici, Quilici Gigli 2002.
[11] Roubis *et al.* 2015.

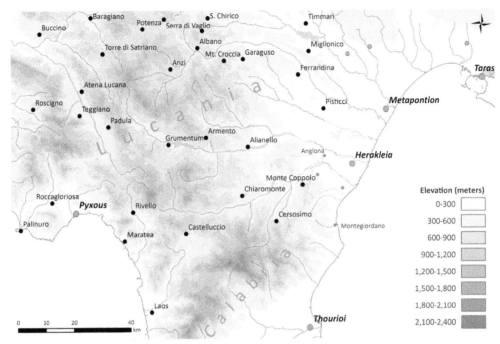

6.1 Lucania during the fourth century BC.

poverty and isolation, with the pressure of expanding population on scarce, overwhelmingly agrarian, resources being relieved in the last resort only by permanent emigration. Mountain microecologies, like almost all microecologies, are parts of greater ecological networks (as Braudel conceded, but with regard only to transalpine trade routes and to a few other, somewhat picturesque, examples). This interdependence is, more-over, especially pronounced where the fragmentation is most intense. Mountains can seem hostile and marginal areas; yet they are actually closely integrated into the patterns of production and communication that abut them. That explains why mountain zones unexpectedly – and even paradoxically – become regions with wide internal coherence and close contact and interchange across what appear, to the outsider, to be formidable physical obstacles. (Horden, Purcell 2000: 80–81)

Ancient Lucania may serve as a test case to understand the role of mountain areas around the Mediterranean and the nature of coast-inland interaction during the Classical and Hellenistic periods.

When Heraclea was founded in 433/2 BC, many inland settlements were undergoing drastic transformations. Until the fifth century, inland sites consisted of loose agglomerations of huts and tombs (compounds). In Basilicata, the best known example of this settlement type is Torre di Satriano near Potenza.[12] The polycentric settlement of Torre di Satriano was separated from neighboring

---

[12] See Osanna, Vullo 2013.

settlements by vast areas where no, or only very few traces of, habitations have been detected. It therefore appears to have been a kind of central place that must have been characterized by some sort of collective identity and organization.[13] During the sixth and fifth centuries BC, indigenous sites in the hinterland of the coast such as Chiaromonte, Alianello, and Pisticci were probably not so different from Torre di Satriano, although in the case of Chiaromonte and Alianello, the tombs are not situated among the houses, as in Torre di Satriano, but in burial grounds outside the settlement.[14] This may reflect a higher degree of spatial (and perhaps political) organization. However, after the conquest of Siris by the Achaeans in 560 BC (probably under Sybarite leadership) and again after the destruction of Sybaris in 510 BC, none of the inland communities seized the opportunity to expand into the coastal zone. As the archaeological and epigraphic evidence suggests, it was Metapontum that took control of the territory of Siris in this period (see Chapter 4). Despite a relatively high degree of political organization, the inland communities appeared to have no interest in taking control of the coastal area during this period. This scenario would change from the later fifth century BC onwards.

A "BLACK HOLE" IN THE ARCHAEOLOGICAL RECORD?

From the central decades of the fifth century BC onward, inland communities tend to fade from view in the archaeological record.[15] This moment marked the beginning of a rather enigmatic period that culminated in around 360/50 BC with the emergence of a new settlement pattern, accompanied by new burial customs and a completely different material culture. These phenomena have been related to the arrival or emergence of a new ethnic group, the Lucanians (Lucanization), a people of Samnite origin according to ancient authors (cf. Strabo VI 1,3). The archaeological data does not allow us to trace the process of Lucanization in detail, and the textual sources are rather ambiguous. Only from the 350s are the Lucanians securely attested in the literary evidence; earlier references are doubtful and should be treated with caution.[16]

There is, for example, the story of the Brettioi, who appear in Calabria during the Classical period. Strabo (VI 1,4) describes them as subaltern revolters (in Lucanian the term *brettioi* means runaways, as Strabo believed) who first "merely tended flocks for the Leucani, and then, by reason of the indulgence of their masters, began to act as free men, at the time when Dion made his expedition against Dionysius and aroused all peoples against all others."[17] On

---

[13]   Osanna 2013: 46–49.
[14]   On settlement patterns and burials, see Bianco 1996.
[15]   Bottini 1999.
[16]   Musti 2005: 270. The earliest secure reference is Isocr., *On the Peace* 50, dated to 356 or 352 BC.
[17]   Transl. H.L. Jones, 1924.

the other hand, the Greek historian Antiochus, who wrote in the late fifth century BC, never mentions the Lucanians, but fragments attributed to him refer to the Brettioi. Evidently, Antiochus had some information about developments in inland Calabria and Basilicata, although he has a different perspective from that of later sources including Strabo.[18] Relations between Lucanians and Brettioi may be unclear, but the scarceness or ambivalence of the evidence does not necessarily imply that the inland mountains were empty during the later fifth and the first half of the fourth century BC. Archaeologically, parts of the inland population had always been invisible. At Early Iron Age and Archaic sites such as Torre di Satriano, Garaguso, and Chiaromonte, where local elites are plainly visible in the archaeological record, the existence of peasants and herdsmen is only indirectly deducible.[19] If the emergence of the Leukanoi and Brettioi was linked to the emancipation of formerly subaltern and therefore invisible groups, as some scholars have argued, and/or involved large-scale migration and unstable settlement forms, as others argue, there is little chance of tracing these processes in the archaeological record.[20] At the same time, we do have some evidence indicating that during the second half of the fifth century inland communities interfered with colonial settlements on the Ionian Coast in important ways. This indirectly confirms the vitality of the inland regions during this phase. Just as astrophysicists infer the presence of invisible black holes through their interaction with other matter and with electromagnetic radiation, we may infer the presence of the Lucanians as early as the late fifth century through their interaction with Greek settlements on the margins of inland Lucania.

Polyaenus (II 10), for example, who wrote in the second century AD, describes the Spartan general Cleandridas fighting the Lucanians in the period of the foundation of Thurii.[21] Polyaenus may have used the term Lucanians anachronistically to refer to local populations who in a later period were known as Lucanians,[22] but this does not mean that the whole story about Cleandridas

[18] Musti 2005: 261–284; Isayev 2007: 11–21.

[19] See Osanna, Vullo 2013.

[20] Torelli 1993; Isayev 2007: 13–16 doubts the reliability of the sources; unlike Torelli, Pontrandolfo (1982: 7–19) considers the Lucanians descendants of local populations and confutes the migration hypothesis.

[21] "Cleandridas, after the Thurians under his command had defeated the Lucanians, led his men back to the field of battle. He pointed out to them, on the spot where they had stood, the close and compact manner in which they had fought, and he told them that it was because of this that they had won the victory; but the enemy, who left their posts and loosened their ranks, had been unable to withstand their united attack. Meanwhile, the Lucanians rallied and advanced against him with a considerably larger force. Cleandridas retreated to a confined and narrow spot, where the enemy could not make use of their superiority in numbers, but his own men could extend their front to an equal length. By this manœuvre he defeated the Lucanians a second time." (transl. R. Shepherd, 1793)

[22] Musti 2005: 271.

fighting local groups near Thurii in the fifth century BC should be ignored. A site discovered recently at Rose near Cosenza suggests that inland communities of the Late Archaic and Classical periods were much better organized than previously assumed. The excavations yielded numerous Greek pottery imports dating to between the sixth and fourth centuries BC as well as remains of a monumental stone building from the fifth century BC.[23]

Recent work by Angelo Bottini and Lucia Lecce shows that Heraclea also interfered with inland communities as early as c. 400 BC, as also suggested by the literary sources. Bottini and Lecce (2015) have demonstrated that the earliest of a small number of Italic tombs at Heraclea dates to around 400 BC, rather than to the second half of the fourth century BC as previously believed.[24] The tomb (T. 1188) is situated in the West Necropolis of Heraclea and contained a skeleton in supine position, a black-glazed cup (c. 400 BC), a bronze helmet (second half of the fifth century), and a bronze belt of Samnite type (Figure 6.2). This type of belt is first attested in sixth-century BC Apulia, from where it spread during the fifth century BC to other regions of southern Italy, reaching its widest distribution in the fourth century BC.[25] It is not only the helmet and the "Samnite belt" that distinguish tomb 1188 from other tombs of the same period, but also the combination of a relatively rich set of grave goods with an inhumation burial. As pointed out in Chapter 3, during the early phases of Heraclea cremation burials were usually richer than inhumation burials, although they are still rather modest in comparison to burials from other sites. Tomb 1188 is one of the richest burials from this period; it certainly did not belong to an ordinary mercenary, particularly since mercenaries in southern Italy only became important from the late fourth century BC onwards. Instead, tomb 1188 can be considered an elite burial belonging to a person identified as an Italic warrior.

Strabo (VI 3,4) reports that when the Tarantines fought a "war against the Messapians for the possession of Heraclea," they had "the cooperation of the king of the Daunians and the king of the Peucetians." It has been suggested that the war *peri Herakleias* mentioned by Strabo took place before the establishment of the city and was fought for the possession of the territory of Siris.[26] In this case, Strabo would have used the name of Heraclea to indicate the territory which would belong to the city after the events mentioned in the passage. The man buried in tomb 1188 may have been a leading figure among the non-Greek allies of Tarentum and/or Heraclea in this period.

There is yet another reference to Lucanian or other non-Greek warriors in early Heraclea: On the red-figure pelike with Poseidon and Athena fighting

[23] Taliano Grasso, D'Alessio 2014.
[24] Bottini, Lecce 2015.
[25] Romito 1995.
[26] Sartori 1967: 22–23.

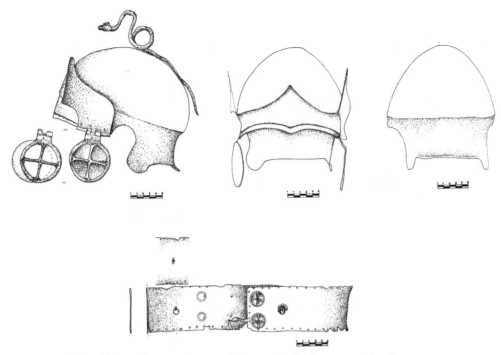

6.2 Bronze belt and helmet from tomb 1188 at Policoro (Bottini, Lecce 2015: fig. 8).

for the possession of Attica from the Tomb of the Policoro Painter (see Table 3.1, no. 11, and Figure 3.7), Poseidon and his companion wear wide belts; Poseidon's belt is held in place by crosswise chest straps. Belts of this kind, which are not known from homeland Greek vase painting, clearly recall "Samnite belts" found in southern Italian tombs. In particular, Poseidon's belt with chest straps recalls a bronze corslet of the second half of the fourth century BC found at Laos, which was a Lucanian settlement during this period.[27] The interpretation of the vase-paintings from the Policoro tomb is rather complex, and the allusion to Lucanian costumes on pelike no. 11 cannot be easily deciphered. Nevertheless, the depiction does indicate a certain awareness of inland populations and their way of life on the part of Greek elites and artisans as early as 400 BC.

The Poseidon pelike from the Policoro tomb and the bronze belt from tomb 1188 in the western necropolis are among the earliest finds testifying to the use of "Samnite belts" in the area.[28] The colonies seem to have been involved in some of the processes going on in the inland regions, although it remains uncertain what part they actually played in ethnic and/or social transformations during the late fifth and the early fourth centuries BC. The situation

[27] Settis, Parra 2005: 418 no. III.218.
[28] Cf. Romito 1995.

is comparable to that on the Tyrrhenian coast, given that the Greek colony of Poseidonia/Paestum is one of the sites where the process of Lucanization – whatever this meant in practical terms – first became visible in the archaeological record. From the second half of the fifth century BC, the material culture and burial rites of the city underwent a profound change. Most notably, many male burials from this period contain weapons and "Samnite" bronze belts, which distinguish them from burials in other Greek colonies.[29] Oscan inscriptions and modifications in the burial pattern leave little doubt that by the fourth century BC the city had become in large part Lucanized, or, as Aristoxenus of Tarentum put it, barbarized:[30]

> Aristoxenus, in his book entitled *Promiscuous Banquets*, says: "We act in a manner similar to the people of Paestum who dwell in the Tyrrhenian Gulf; for it happened to them, though they were originally Greeks, to have become at last completely barbarised, becoming Tyrrhenians or Romans, and to have changed their language, and all the rest of their national habits. But one Greek festival they do celebrate even to the present day, in which they meet and recollect all their ancient names and customs, and bewail their loss to one another, and then, when they have wept for them, they go home."
>
> (transl. C.D. Yonge, 1854)

It is still the subject of debate whether the "barbarization" of Poseidonia was the result of a Lucanian conquest, as Strabo (VI 1,3) suggests, or rather the final outcome of a slow "infiltration of new groups into the territory."[31] Whatever the case, it is interesting that the Lucanians first become visible on the margins of what would later be called Lucania, i.e., in the Greek colonies on the coast. As far as can be inferred from the scarce evidence, the emergence of a Lucanian identity was characterized by expansive and highly transformative processes, suggesting something akin to colonization from the inland toward the coast rather than a decolonizing movement, in the sense of a recovery of traditional settlement sites and cultural practices.[32]

CHANGING MEDITERRANEAN LANDSCAPES

As archaeologists, we can only describe the results of these processes. Around 360/50 BC, numerous new central-places – known as *oppida* – become visible in the archaeological record. Some of them occupy sites that had been inhabited in the early Iron Age and the Archaic period (e.g., Torre di Satriano, Serra di Vaglio, Arpi, Timmari), while others are established on sites that have yielded

---

[29] Cipriani, Longo, Viscione 1996; Cipriani 2000; Torelli 2003; Crawford 2006.
[30] Quoted in Athenaeus XIV 632a.
[31] Isayev 2007: 144.
[32] See Asheri 1999.

6.3 Fortification wall of Serra di Vaglio. (Courtesy of *Archivio fotografico della Soprintendenza Archeologia, Belle Arti e Paesaggio della Basilicata.*)

little or no older evidence (e.g., Tricarico, Cersosimo, Monte Coppolo).[33] They all share a series of features:

1) They were situated on hilltops or mountains from which the territory could be monitored.

2) Unlike the Archaic settlements in the region, Lucanian *oppida* were fortified. They usually had an outer wall as well as one or two inner walls that created a sort of acropolis within the walled area (Figure 6.3).[34]

3) In several cases (e.g., Rossano di Vaglio, Torre di Satriano, Timmari) extra-mural sanctuaries were found several hundred meters from the settlements on the slopes beneath the walls. Given that these sanctuaries were often situated close to natural springs, it is assumed that water played an important role in ritual activities. The sanctuaries were often dedicated to female deities such as Mefitis, who in some cases was identified with Aphrodite.[35]

4) The territories around the hilltop settlements were characterized by isolated farmsteads and small groups of tombs.[36]

During the third century BC, many settlements were abandoned or profoundly transformed as a result of Roman intervention. The settlements that continued to be inhabited after the first half of the third century BC lost their function as central-places, except for Potenza and Grumentum which served as Roman administrative bases in the region.[37]

---

[33] For a catalog of sites, see Barberis 1999; De Gennaro 2005.
[34] For a recent summary, see Henning 2011.
[35] Battiloro, Osanna, forthcoming.
[36] Osanna 2010b.
[37] On third-century Lucania, see Lo Cascio, Storchi Morino 2001; Horsnaes 2002; Gualtieri 2003; Osanna 2012b.

From the archaeological point of view, social change in the inland areas during the Late Classical and Early Hellenistic periods can be described mainly in terms of urbanization and economic development. In some cases the walled areas of the *oppida* reached considerable dimensions, as for example in Civita di Tricarico (c. 40 hectares) and Serra di Vaglio (c. 100 hectares). Judging from excavations and geophysical prospection conducted on some sites, the *oppida* were more than just refuge forts housing a few storage and administrative buildings. At least some of them, such as Serra di Vaglio, Pomarico Vecchio, and Civita di Tricarico, contained extensive residential quarters and production areas. The settlement of Civita di Tricarico is particularly well known due to a long-term fieldwork project which started in 1988. Some important results of the excavations on the site have recently been presented by Olivier de Cazanove, Sophie Féret, and Annamaria Caravelli (2014). As Cazanove points out, the urban area – which was subdivided by two interior walls into an acropolis (with temple), an upper settlement, and a lower settlement – was never completely covered with buildings. Areas covered with buildings alternated with areas where no traces of buildings were found which may have served as fields or pastures.[38] Yet Cazanove rejects the idea of a polycentric settlement consisting of various nuclei, as attested at Archaic sites in the region. He underlines the fact that streets running across large areas within the settlement created a grid, which appears, if not orthogonal, at least pseudo-orthogonal.[39] He also notes that the various built-up areas are orientated in a fairly uniform manner. Cazanove argues that it would be more appropriate to speak of living quarters, or *bande bâtie*, than of nuclei. He suggests that the settlement of Civita di Tricarico originated not as a heterogeneous, mixed agglomeration of dwellings, but as a planned, "colonial" settlement.[40]

The excavations at Tricarico provide new insights into the organization of household activities and craft production in Lucanian hilltop settlements. For centuries, the peoples of inland Basilicata had produced and used traditional so-called matt-painted pottery as well as impasto and coarse ware pottery. In addition, a limited number of elite households used imported Athenian, East-Greek, and colonial pottery.[41] As a result of the process of Lucanization, the material culture changed completely. In the course of the fifth century BC, matt-painted pottery shapes were largely replaced by red-figure and black-glazed pottery. Unlike other communities such as the Daunians in northern Apulia, the inhabitants of fourth century BC Lucania did not continue to produce traditional subgeometric fine ware pottery. During the second half

[38] Cazanove, Féret, Caravelli 2014: 233.
[39] Cazanove, Féret, Caravelli 2014: 234.
[40] Cazanove, Féret, Caravelli 2014: 25.
[41] Osanna, Vullo 2013.

of the fifth century BC, the Greek colonies on the Ionian Coast (especially Metapontum and Tarentum, see Chapter 7) had begun to produce Italiote red-figure pottery. From there the production of red-figure pottery spread throughout the entire region. Greek workshops moved inland and new workshops were established in non-Greek areas.[42] From the first half of the fourth century BC, it becomes increasingly difficult and often even impossible to distinguish between Greek and indigenous red-figure and black-glazed pottery. Italiote red-figure pottery became the commonly used fine ware in both Greek and Lucanian areas, leading to the abandonment of traditional shapes, styles, and techniques, except for occasional reminiscences.[43] The process of Lucanization ultimately turned the use of Greek visual language from being a privilege of the elite into a ubiquitous mass phenomenon that supplanted traditional forms of expression. In this light, the history of Italiote red-figure vases in Lucania also represents the history of a transformation of traditional versions of cultural diversity that were partly homogenized and integrated within new hybrid forms – a form of Mediterranean globalization that some individuals and groups may have perceived as a cultural loss, while others gained socially and economically.[44] What can be observed here is a truly Hellenistic development in the sense of Hellenic culture and/or idiom becoming hegemonic in non-Greek communities.[45] In Lucania, Hellenism became a widespread cultural and social phenomenon from around the midfourth century BC for reasons that still remain largely unknown. Traditional explanations for the origins of Hellenistic art and culture that focus on Alexander the Great and the political transformations in the East do not apply in this context, given the lack of direct links between southern Italy and the events taking place in the eastern Mediterranean. As I will argue here, the emergence of Hellenism in southern Italy depended above all on agricultural and economic developments. As on the coast, these developments went handin-hand with social stratification.[46]

As excavations in Tricarico and other Lucanian settlements have shown, craft production usually took place inside private houses. Even isolated farmsteads would often have a small kiln nearby to produce roof tiles and pottery for domestic use. In Civita di Tricarico, black-glazed pottery, coarse ware, and tiles were produced within private households. The House of the Molds (*maison des moules*) in the upper settlement below the acropolis has yielded

---

[42] See Bottini 2001; Silvestrelli 2004; 2005. See also the comments in Lecce, L., Bottini, A., Todisco, L. 2007 & 2016. *CVA* Matera (Italy, vol. 73, 82), Rome: L'Erma di Bretschneider.

[43] Carpenter, Lynch, Robinson 2014.

[44] Morris 2003.

[45] Cf. Isayev 2007: 41–54.

[46] On the Hellenistic West, see Prag, Crawley Quinn 2013; on "Hellenistic economies," see Archibald, Davies, Gabrielsen 2011.

numerous terracotta molds that can be dated on stratigraphic grounds to before the second half of the third century BC. The workshop that operated here produced statuettes of actors, animals, female figures, divinities such as Eros and Aphrodite, sea monsters, and terracotta ornaments for funerary use.[47] The style and iconography of the figurines recall Tarantine products of the third century BC.

The houses themselves are relatively large (c. 200 square meters in the case of the House of the Molds, others are even larger). Most houses in Tricarico consist of a *pastas* or portico with a series of rooms opening onto it. Such a layout has parallels in the Greek and Roman world, but not in Lucania, although the situation may change in the future as more settlements are brought to light. Judging from finds distributions, the terracotta molds from the *Maison des moules* were stored in an attic or first floor above the pastas, while the other rooms served primarily as living spaces. In general, no clear distinction between the houses of artisans and those of others can be made on the basis of the ground plans and/or materials. It seems that in many households craft production was simply one of various activities. A similar picture emerges from excavations in the urban center of Laos, where silver and bronze coins were made inside an inhabited house.[48] This kind of organization recalls Archaic elite dwellings such as the so-called *anaktoron* in Torre di Satriano, the house of the local ruler of the community around 500 BC.[49] However, the social position of artisans in Tricarico and their place in the household are unclear. Did they belong to the family, and if so, were they servants or free men? Or were they itinerant artisans hosted by the owners of the houses? Whatever their position, the style and quality of their products are practically indistinguishable from that of coastal workshops.

The archaeological evidence suggests that Lucanian *oppida* were not organized according to the model of the Ackerbürger polis, which continued to influence Greek colonization throughout the fourth century BC (Issa, Pharos, Korkyra Melaina). In inland Lucania, the establishment of fortified hilltop settlements was accompanied by the spread of isolated farmsteads in the countryside. This means that rural dwellers were not a belated split-off from the urban community, as in Greek colonies of the Classical period, but an integral part of the social structure as it emerges in the archaeological record from around the middle of the fourth century BC. An intensive field survey at Torre di Satriano has revealed a network of farmsteads in the territory, and other field surveys in the region suggest that the phenomenon was virtually ubiquitous.[50] The layout and appearance of the rural sites can be reconstructed on the basis

[47] S. Féret, M. Dewailly in Cazanove, Féret, Caravelli 2014: 176–177.
[48] Cantilena, Munzi 2001.
[49] Osanna, Vullo 2013.
[50] Osanna 2010b.

of a series of rescue excavations in Basilicata and northern Calabria.[51] The buildings unearthed were relatively large and often had a central courtyard and storage rooms. Tombs discovered in the vicinity of some farmsteads resemble the tombs from suburban necropoleis around the central-places. Male burials often contain bronze belts and weapons, as well as red-figure and black-glazed banqueting pottery, and sometimes also *strigileis*, suggesting that the male inhabitants of the farmsteads saw themselves as warriors and symposiasts. As Ilaria Battiloro and Massimo Osanna have argued, suburban sanctuaries at Torre di Satriano, Timmari, etc., may have been used for ritual banquets and ritual gatherings of the rural population.[52] The inhabitants of the countryside were described as a new middle class of landowners/warriors who represented the backbone of Lucanian economic and military power.[53] When ancient authors mention Lucanian armies numbering ten thousand and more, we have to imagine that many of them were rural dwellers.[54]

What is important here is that in inland Lucania, military organization, urbanization, and rural settlement developed together from the earliest phases, whereas at Heraclea and other Classical colonies on the coast the emergence of rural settlements was a distinct and belated phenomenon. Thus, although Lucanian and Greek farmers of the fourth and third centuries BC had much in common, Lucanian rural dwellers had a different social background from their Greek neighbors. It is true that in both cases the countryside was structured around an urban center, and both Lucanian and Greek farmers were influenced by macroeconomic processes leading to agricultural intensification and settlement diversification. Yet they confronted these processes from different starting points. Unlike Greek farmers, Lucanian farmers were not faced by a demeaning loss of urbanity, since wherever they came from, it was probably not a city. They may not have belonged to the elite within their communities, but they did lack the background of social downgrading of many Greek rural dwellers.

CLOSE NEIGHBORS

One of the new fortified centers to emerge in the inland mountain area during the fourth century BC was situated six hours' walk from Heraclea on Monte Coppolo (see Figure 5.8), from where almost the entire Greek territory could be monitored (Figure 6.4).[55] The walled area comprised about 14

---

[51] Russo 2006.
[52] Battiloro, Osanna, forthcoming.
[53] Torelli 1993: xv–xvi.
[54] See for example Diod. XIV 12, where there is a description of a Lucanian army of thirty thousand foot soldiers and four thousand cavalry.
[55] On Monte Coppolo and its territory, see Quilici 1967: 92–111; Quilici, Quilici Gigli 2002: 79–136.

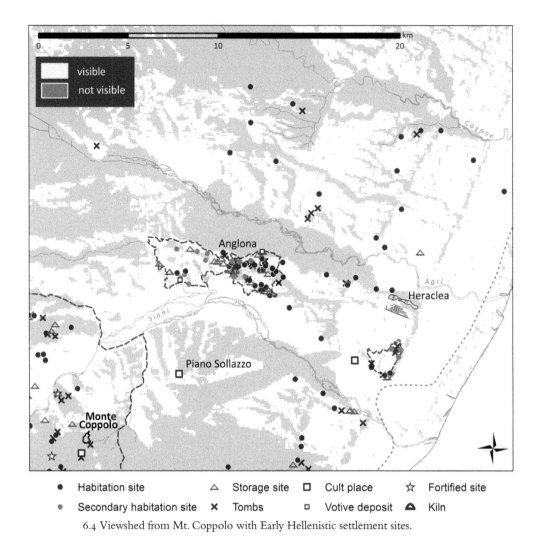

6.4 Viewshed from Mt. Coppolo with Early Hellenistic settlement sites.

hectares, five or six of which are suitable for building, the remainder being too steep.[56] The fortification walls consisted of local arenite and were about 3 meters thick. On the southern slopes of the hilltop, where the only trafficable access to the settlement lay, there was a gate of Scaean type protected by a tower (Figure 6.5). The highest part of the walled area was occupied by a fortified acropolis, within which the remains of two rectangular stone buildings have been identified. Aerial photography has revealed the existence of an orthogonal street grid in the lower city. A series of field surveys carried out in the walled area have yielded pottery dating to between the fourth century BC and the Imperial period.

[56] The numbers in Quilici, Quilici Gigli 2002: 122 (10.7 hectares and 40–50 hectares respectively) appear to be mistaken.

6.5 Mt. Coppolo: Tower on the southern side of the city wall (partly reconstructed).

During a field survey directed by Lorenzo Quilici and Stefania Quilici Gigli, a considerable number of sites were documented in the countryside around Monte Coppolo (Figure 6.6). It is assumed that the necropolis of the central-place was situated below the south gate. San Nicola on the southeastern slopes of the mountain might have been a suburban sanctuary, as is the case for other hilltop settlements in the region.[57] The site lies near a natural spring on an ancient road that passed south of Mount Coppolo. A high density of finds was noted in an area of about 1 hectare, comprising black-glazed and banded pottery (fourth/third centuries BC), cooking ware, plain ware, pithoi, roof tiles, and Terra Sigillata (first/second century AD, though one plate seems to be as late as third/fourth century AD). Although no clear indicators of ritual activities have been found, e.g., terracotta votives, the topographic features (slopes, spring, road) recall other Lucanian sanctuaries.[58]

The picture that emerges from the analysis of archaeological sites and geographic features in the territory of Monte Coppolo is typical of Lucanian settlements. Farmsteads and secondary sites which may have been temporary shelters or storage buildings spread over the mountains and hills around a

[57] Quilici, Quilici Gigli 2002: 55–61.
[58] Quilici, Quilici Gigli 2002: 61.

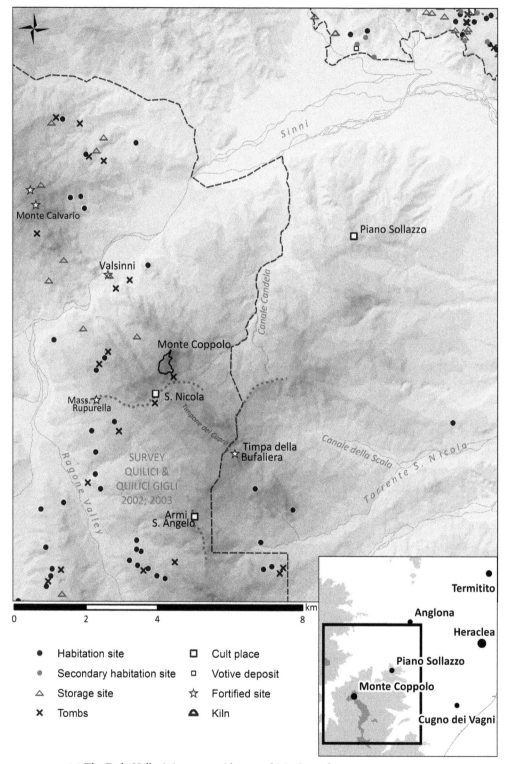

6.6 The Early Hellenistic countryside around Mt. Coppolo.

fortified central place. In many cases, small burial sites were identified near the farmsteads. Some of them have yielded weapons and/or armor, objects that are absent in rural burials in the coastal area around Heraclea.[59] As one moves farther southeast from Monte Coppolo, the farmsteads tend to form small agglomerations or villages that may have served as subcenters in marginal zones of the territory.

According to current research, it seems that rural settlements did not extend to the hills east of Monte Coppolo. A strip of land without habitation sites separated the farms in the inland mountains from those spreading throughout the lower areas around Heraclea. In the Early Hellenistic period, this zone corresponded to the border between the two territories, as clearly emerges from a series of observations. First, on the inland side the border was protected by fortifications at Timpa della Bufaliera and Timpa del Ponto. Both are situated on land-routes leading from the coast into the mountains. Timpa del Ponto is a small rock on the River Sinni near the medieval village of Valsinni. Quilici documented the remains of a rectangular building on top of it, which he interpreted as a watch tower, while nearby he noted a pear-shaped silo dug into the rock.[60] Silos of this type were used from the ancient period until the Middle Ages and beyond as granaries and storage facilities for legumes.[61] If they were hermetically sealed, grain and legumes could be stored for a long time. Pottery fragments found on the site date from the fourth to the third/second centuries BC. Local farmers report having found tombs along the modern road south of the site. The strategic position of Timpa del Ponto is quite clear. Anyone going up the River Sinni from the coast had to pass by this site, since there are steep mountains on both sides of the valley. In the Middle Ages, this led to the establishment of the castle of Valsinni (where the fifteenth-century poet Isabella Morra lived) and a customs-post.

Another route led from the area south of the Siris River up to the hills around Rotondella and Nova Siri south of Piano Sollazzo (see Figure 6.6). The hills in this area were separated from the mountain massif of Monte Coppolo by two steep valleys, one of which passes beneath the hilltop of Piano Sollazzo and runs north into the River Sinni (Canale Candela), while the other one runs southeast into the San Nicola Creek (Canale della Scala). Today, the road leading inland runs over a ridge that forms a watershed between these two valleys, and it must have already run this way in antiquity. On the western end of the ridge, where it merges into the mountain massif of Monte Coppolo, the road forks. One way leads northwest up to Monte Coppolo; the other leads southwest toward the farmsteads and villages around Armi Sant'Angelo,

[59] For bronze finds from Massa and Timpone del Ponto (Samnite belt?), see Quilici, Quilici Gigli 2002: 28–29 no 5; 231 no. 1–2.
[60] Quilici 1997: 241–244; 251–256; Quilici, Quilici Gigli 2002: 26–29 no. 5.
[61] Cf. Zuchtriegel 2012a: 278–281.

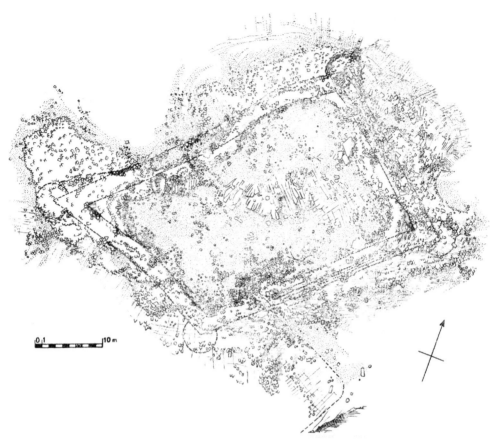

6.7 Timpa della Bufaliera: Late Classical/Early Hellenistic fortress (Quilici 1967: fig. 169).

and from there on to Cersosimo. Before the road reaches a small high plain north of Armi Sant'Angelo, it passes between the slopes of Timpone del Capro (860 m asl) and a steep hill south of it named Timpa della Bufaliera (780 m asl), on top of which the remains of a small fort can be seen. Rubble walls with a thickness of 3 meters form a trapezium of about 30 x 20 meters with round towers in the corners (Figure 6.7). The entrance lay on the southern side where it was hidden from the road. The material recorded by Quilici in the 1960s includes a black-glazed salt nap of the late fourth century BC.[62] When I visited the site in 2013, the walls were in such a bad state that the existence of towers and the thickness of the walls could no longer be verified. However, some plain and black-glazed pottery fragments found between the roots of a fallen tree confirmed Quilici's dating.

The fort of Timpa della Bufaliera belonged to Monte Coppolo, as is evident from its topographical position. It lies on the inland side of what I interpret as the border zone between Greek and Lucanian territory. Moreover, it is situated

---

[62] Quilici 1967: 91 fig. 187. Cf. Morel 1981: 213, tab. 68.

on the northern part of the massif of Monte Coppolo and Timpone del Capro. If it had been a Greek border fortress, as has been suggested,[63] the Lucanians would have been able to overlook it entirely – a strategically disadvantageous position that is quite unlikely. Lastly, the walls of the fortress are made of local arenite stone like the walls of Monte Coppolo. As far as is known, the Heracleans never used this type of building stone.[64]

Having passed the border fort of Timpa della Bufaliera, the road proceeds southwards over a massive ridge that separates the Ragone Valley in the west from the coastal area in the east. In the middle of the ridge looms a solitary crag called Armi Sant'Angelo, which today is accessible only by climbing. On top of it, Quilici noticed the remains of a rectangular structure measuring about 30 by 30 meters, as well as fragments of roof tiles and pottery.[65] Two black-glazed plates recorded by Quilici seem to date to the late Hellenistic period (potentially the first half of the first century BC). When I visited the site in 2012 I noticed a foot of a black-glazed cup datable to the third century BC. Considering that the position on top of the crag is unsuited to a farmstead, Quilici interpreted the structure as a cult site that may also have served as a watch tower, emphasizing the presence of well-dressed stone blocks and fine ware.[66]

Another fortified site was identified on the western slopes of Monte Coppolo (Masseria Rupurella), further downhill on the road coming from the sanctuary of San Nicola. If Quilici is right, the site housed a watch tower guarding access to the settlement from the upper part of River Sinni.[67] Given that the Lucanians were by no means a unified, homogeneous people, a watch tower on this side of the mountain would make sense.

As for the Heracleans, they could survey the border zone from the Hellenistic village on the hilltop of Santa Maria d'Anglona and from the sanctuary of Piano Sollazzo. The latter is situated on the western edge of a plateau (*piano*), from where Canale Candela and the eastern slopes of Monte Coppolo are visible. The geographical position of the sanctuary also enabled intervisibility with Santa Maria d'Anglona and Heraclea. The sanctuary of Piano Sollazzo was established immediately after the foundation of Heraclea, as already mentioned in Chapter 4. Why were the settlers so eager to occupy this strategic position? One explanation may be that the mountains around Mount Coppolo were settled as early as the fifth century BC, although this is not visible in the archaeological record. Unfortunately, this cannot be verified given the current state of research, although the site of Piano Sollazzo suggests that there were

[63] Osanna 1992: 113 no. 27.
[64] Zuchtriegel 2012b: 153.
[65] Quilici 1967: 36–40 no. 27; Osanna 1992: 113–114 no. 28.
[66] Quilici 1967: 40 ("*luogo di culto, con valore anche militare*").
[67] Quilici, Quilici Gigli 2002: 61–63, no. 31.

communities to whom the inhabitants of Heraclea and its territory wanted to signal their presence.

ROOF TILES AND LOOM WEIGHTS

In the Early Hellenistic period, when the territories of Monte Coppolo and Heraclea were dotted with dwellings and groups of tombs, the two territories maintained some distinctive features despite the economic and cultural entanglement that characterized this period. Such small differences shed some light on the living conditions on both sides of the border. For instance, Lucanian and Greek farmsteads had different roofs. During our survey in the territory of Heraclea, we noted that sites of the Early Hellenistic period yielded no flat roof tiles or *stroteres*, but only curved Laconian tiles. Only sites that continued to be used into the second/first centuries BC yielded flat as well as curved tiles, indicating that Laconian roofs were gradually replaced by Corinthian ones from this period onwards. By contrast, flat tiles were found on nearly all habitation sites around Monte Coppolo dating to the fourth/third centuries BC, i.e., from the so-called Lucanian period (*periodo ellenistico-lucano*). Figure 6.8 shows only sites that were abandoned after the Early Hellenistic period. Although the precise chronology of most sites and the nature of the finds mentioned in older publications is unclear, comparison of our survey data with that of Quilici & Quilici Gigli 2002 provides a clear picture. The roofs of the farmsteads looked different on each side of the border zone, and this also holds true for the two central-places. While flat tiles from Early Hellenistic mountain sites have close parallels in the fortified settlement of Monte Coppolo, excavations at Heraclea suggest that Laconian roofs prevailed until the middle/late Hellenistic period.[68]

Surprisingly enough, the mountain dwellers used a more sophisticated technique than the Heracleans on the coast. Flat tiles are more difficult to fire, since they are bigger, and unlike Laconian roof tiles they need to be produced to standardized dimensions in order to allow them to fit. Furthermore, flat tiles can only be used together with curved tiles to cover the joints (*stroter* and *kalypter*), whereas one type of tile is sufficient in the case of a Laconian roof.

Another small difference that sheds light on the living conditions in the hinterland of Heraclea regards wool production and weaving. The way in which the people of Monte Coppolo protected their borders toward the coast suggests that they were not always on good terms with the polis of Heraclea. Livy mentions that Alexander the Molossian "liberated" Heraclea from the Lucanians, maybe on occasion of a threat rather than an actual conquest of the city, as there is no trace in other textual sources or in the archaeological record.[69] However, military conflicts did not prevent the two communities from

[68] Quilici 1967: 92–111; Quilici, Quilici Gigli 2002: 79–136.
[69] Sartori 1967: 22–23; Prandi 2008: 16.

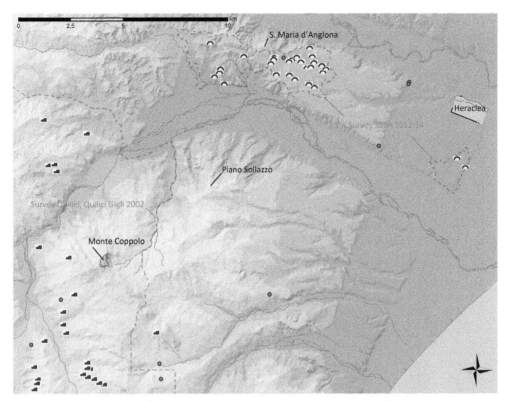

Sites frequented only in the Early Hellenistic period: ⌒ only Laconian roof tiles ◢ Laconian and flat roof tiles ● no data

6.8 Roof types at Early Hellenistic sites around Heraclea and Mt. Coppolo.

establishing trade contacts. Ancient accounts of conquests and battles between Greeks and Lucanians are only one side of the coin. The other side is that inland Lucania was strongly interconnected with neighboring regions. Lucania appears to have been an integral part of what has been called the Hellenistic *koiné* of southern Italy.[70] Finds of Heraclean bronze coins and miniature vessels of the same type as those used in the cult sites of Piano Sollazzo and Favale suggest that Monte Coppolo was in close contact with the Greek colony of Heraclea.[71]

In the economy of the region, wool and textile production were a key factor, as is clear from a variety of sources. Judging from archaeobotanical and archaeozoological data, animal husbandry and especially sheep breeding played an important role in inland Basilicata during the Hellenistic period.[72] Through the Greek harbors of the region, especially Tarentum, wool was available to a huge market expanding over considerable parts of the Mediterranean. As Late Hellenistic and Early Imperial written sources demonstrate, Tarentine textiles

[70] Isayev 2007: 26–28; Osanna 2010b.
[71] See Quilici, Quilici Gigli 2002: 126.
[72] Mercuri *et al.* 2012.

6.9 Heraclea, Area B: Loom weight types (Meo 2015: fig. 2).

(which Roman authors call *Tarentina*) became famous all over Italy.[73] On the basis of literary and archaeological evidence, Francesco Meo (2012; 2015) has argued that from the Early Hellenistic period, Heraclea was also involved in textile production and trade. Analysis of loom weights and other finds from Area B on the Castello hill shows that in some of the houses two looms were used simultaneously, suggesting that textiles were produced for sale rather than for their own use. The vast majority of weaving materials found in the houses consist of discoidal loom weights (*oscilla*) which produced tighter woven fabrics than traditional pyramidal weights (Figure 6.9).[74] In Tarentum and probably elsewhere, the weavers were women who processed the wool on commission, as can be deduced from literary sources and inscriptions.[75]

[73] Morel 1978. Cf. Pliny, Nat. Hist. XIX 2; Varro, R.R. II 2,18; Strabo VI 284; Col. VII 2,3.
[74] Meo 2012.
[75] Mele 1997; Meo 2012: 268.

As our field survey suggests, this kind of commercial weaving was concentrated in the urban center: few rural sites have yielded loom weights.[76] Excavation data supports this, since even large farmsteads like the one at Bosco Andriace possessed only one loom. Although the raw material obviously came from the countryside, the processing of surplus wool was concentrated in the urban center. But where exactly did the wool come from? In the territory of Heraclea, zones suited to sheep farming can be found toward the inland mountains, in the area of Piano Sollazzo and Santa Maria d'Anglona.[77] As we have observed during our field survey, the rural settlement changes toward the outer chora or *eschatià* west of Anglona: the site density diminishes, and while in the inner chora many farmsteads lie on slopes beneath natural springs, in the *eschatià* a number of sites have been identified on hilltops and ridges in a position with better visibility of the surrounding areas (Figure 6.10). This is typical of areas characterized by sheep farming.

But even if the *eschatià* was used primarily for sheep rearing, it may be doubted that it supplied enough wool for the weaving industry in the urban center. It is therefore likely that the inland mountains supplied a good portion of the raw material.[78] At the same time, wool production and weaving in inland areas were not organized in the same manner as in the chora of Heraclea. Unlike sites in the Greek territory, many Late Classical/Early Hellenistic rural sites around Monte Coppolo yielded pyramidal loom weights as were already used in the Early Iron Age (Figure 6.11).[79] Discoidal loom weights are extremely rare here. Among the few discoidal weights found around Monte Coppolo, two were made of perforated pottery fragments,[80] indicating that although the technical advantages of discoidal loom weights were known, regular production had not developed. The commercial weaving at Heraclea was obviously not practiced in the Lucanian hinterland; textile production remained a traditional household activity carried out by family members. However, surplus wool from the inland areas found a natural outlet in Heraclea with its specialized weaving industry and harbor. The mountain dwellers may have had better roofs on their houses, but the Heracleans on the coast made warmer fabrics.

The role of textile production and trade in Lucania opens up new perspectives on the interpretation of loom weights found at Heraclean cult sites. This is especially the case for Santuario del Vallo, a sanctuary where more than 70 loom weights have been found, many of them decorated. It has been suggested

---

[76] Early Hellenistic sites with loom weights: HE9, HE68, HE81, HE155, and HE198. HE94 (pyramidal loom weight) has also an Archaic phase. HE204 and HE209 yielded both pyramidal loom weights and oscilla, while HE205 yielded one pyramidal loom weight.

[77] Roubis 2015.

[78] Meo 2015; Zuchtriegel 2015.

[79] Quilici, Quilici Gigli 2002: 178–181 no. 238–240; 238–236 no. 18–27; 247 n. 28; 247–248 no. 30; 248 no. 31; 255–256 no. 44.

[80] Quilici, Quilici Gigli 2002: 248 no. 31; 250–253 no. 39.

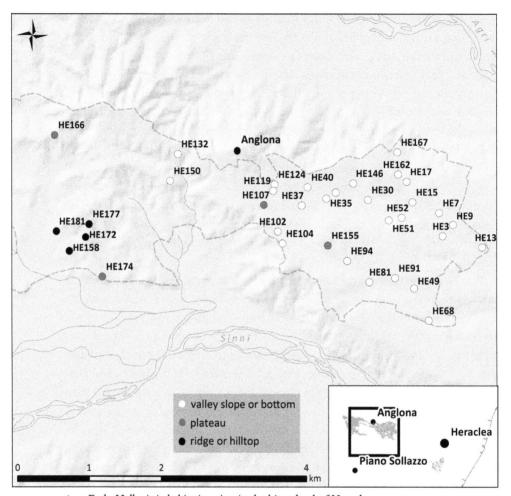

6.10 Early Hellenistic habitation sites in the hinterland of Heraclea.

that the loom weights were brought here during rituals focusing on femininity and initiation,[81] but I wonder if this is really likely in a period when weaving had turned into a specialized industry performed by paid laborers. Maybe in the Late Classical and Early Hellenistic periods the use of loom weights as votive gifts was linked to the wool trade rather than to femininity and *rites de passage*. Notably, during the first phase (late fourth century BC?) of the sanctuary, the main building in the center of the sacred precinct appears to have been a squarish cult structure that recalls the form of Lucanian temples. Was this then a Lucanian sanctuary in a Greek polis? We do not know with certainty which divinities were worshipped in the Santuario del Vallo, but Artemis Bendis seems to have played an important role. As mentioned earlier, Artemis Bendis was also very popular in inland Lucania. In the Doric-Laconian tradition, the

[81] D'Esposito, Galioto 2012: 155.

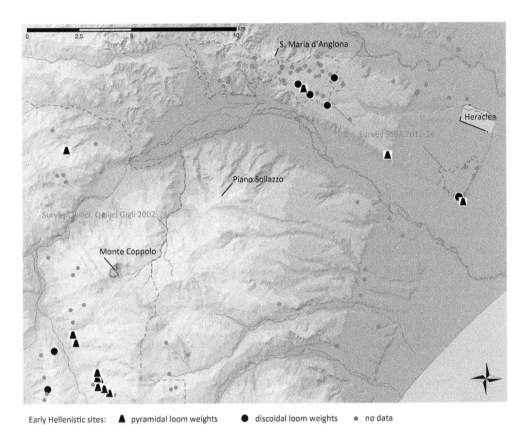

Early Hellenistic sites: ▲ pyramidal loom weights   ● discoidal loom weights   ● no data

6.11 Loom weight types at Early Hellenistic habitation sites around Heraclea and Mt. Coppolo.

goddess was associated with animal husbandry and pastoralism, for example at the sanctuary of Artemis at Karyai.[82] On these grounds, I wonder whether the Vallo Sanctuary at Heraclea served as a sort of branch office for the wool trade between Greeks and Lucanians, although this cannot be proven on the basis of available evidence. Whatever the case, such an interpretation would explain the high number of loom weights found there.

WINE AND OIL IN LUCANIA

If it is accepted that wool was one of the most important products exported from the inland areas, the question arises: what products did the Lucanians receive in return from the Greeks? The answer is not that simple. As mentioned above, black-glazed and red-figure vases were produced both in inland and coastal areas. Hence, Greek vases – whatever that meant at that time – had lost their function as exclusive gifts and export goods in these areas. A product that might still have found a ready market was wine. It is true that local communities

[82] Baudy 1999: 233.

in Basilicata cultivated vines from a very early period, and macro remains of *vitis vinifera* testifying to vineyards were found at several Early Hellenistic sites in Lucania, for example at Roccagloriosa and Pomarico Vecchio.[83] But apart from the fact that indigenous wines were of low quality in comparison with Greek ones, the mountainous countryside permitted only very limited yields. It is unlikely that the Lucanians could produce enough wine to meet local demand that had increased dramatically due to the emergence of a new middle class whose members celebrated Greek-style banquets, as outlined earlier.

The same is true for olive oil. Judging from finds of *lekythoi*, *unguentaria*, and *strigileis* in inland tombs and houses, the new Lucanian middle class consumed considerable amounts of oil (Figure 6.12).[84] Yet the climatic conditions in the inland mountains were even less suited to olive cultivation than to vineyards. Accordingly, oil presses and other finds pointing to olive cultivation are extremely rare in inland Basilicata,[85] whereas at Heraclea oil presses made of Carparo stone (which had to be imported) were found both in the chora and in the urban center (see Figure 5.3). Oil was highly valued and sold well, as suggested by a passage from Leonidas of Tarentum (*Ant. Pal.* VI 300,3) who calls it *euthesauron* (easy to store). The demand for oil and wine on the part of inland communities may have contributed in important ways to agricultural specialization and intensification processes at Heraclea, as described in the previous chapter. This brings us back to the Heraclea Tablets (cf. Chapter 5). As emphasized before, the rents for vineyards were about twenty times as high as the average rent for grain fields. The reason for this must have been that wine sold so well that the leaseholders could hope to make some profit despite the high rents. On the basis of estimated values, most of the plots in the lands of Athena yielded around 2,000 liters per year, but some may have yielded more than 4,000 liters (Table 6.1).[86] Such quantities certainly exceeded the private needs of the leaseholders. Clearly, at least part of the wine produced here was for sale. At the same time, the diffusion of Greek-style banqueting among the rural populations of inland Lucania created a market for wine unparalleled in earlier periods.[87] It is quite likely that the two phenomena were interrelated.

The situation in Tauric Chersonesus was probably similar in many aspects. As Christel Müller has argued, large parts of the city's wine production were sold to non-Greek communities in the northern Black Sea region.[88]

---

[83]   Nava, Osanna, De Faveri 2007: 285; see also Lentjes 2013.

[84]   Russo 2006: 174; Mandić, Vita 2015.

[85]   Mercuri *et al.* 2012 have found *Olea europaea* at Difesa S. Biagio in the hinterland of Metaponto. For Lucania see D'Andria, Roubis 1999; Brun 2010: 430–431.

[86]   On the basis of Columella (cited in Ruffing 1999: 396), I estimate an average yield of 2.1 liters per square meter.

[87]   On the relationship between social change and consumption of "foreign" food and beverages (especially alcohol) see Dietler 2010: 186–203. Cf. Horden, Purcell 2000: 209–220.

[88]   Müller 2010: 187–189.

(a)

(b)

6.12 Sant'Arcangelo: Female burials Cicchelli T. 33 (a) and Mastrosimone T. 63 (b) (Mandić, Vita 2015; pl. 7).

As we have seen, the Heraclea Tablets prescribed that the rents were to be paid in barley to the public granary *(damosios rhogos)*. The polis of Chersonesus was also interested in accumulating grain, as suggested by the Oath (see Chapter 5). In the case of Heraclea, it seems that the polis promoted the cultivation of vineyards not because it had an interest in the product itself, but because in this manner the amount of public barley could be multiplied without adding new lands to the public domain. Paradoxically, turning a grain field into a vineyard increased the amount of barley that the polis received for letting sacred lands in return for payment of rent. As I have sought to argue, the type of agricultural intensification that accompanied such processes entailed a series of social phenomena such as the increasing stratification and marginalization of rural dwellers who specialized in agriculture.

TABLE 6.1 *Heraclea Tablets: vineyards and yields in the lands of Athena*

lot	area (schoinoi)	vineyards (schoinoi)	vineyards (square meters)	estimated yield (liters)
Athena 1	138	4.5	576	1,210
Athena 2	139	16	2,048	4,301
Athena I	59.5	8.25	1,056	2,218
Athena II	72	8.5	1,088	2,285
Athena III	74	7.5	960	2,016
Athena IV	83	15	1,920	4,032
Athena A	68.5	6.5	832	1,747
Athena B	66	6.5	832	1,747
Athena C	70	6.5	832	1,747
Athena D	54.5	6.5	832	1,747
Athena E	71	7	896	1,882
Athena F	38.5	8.5	1,088	2,285
total:	*934*	*101.3*	*12,960*	*27,216*

An increasing demand for grain on the part of the public sector may have originated for various reasons. For instance, Heraclea may have exported grain to areas that suffered from shortages *(sitodeia)* attested on various occasions during the Hellenistic period.[89] The importance of grain exports at Heraclea seems to be confirmed by the discovery of more than twenty underground silos in the zone of the harbor, although the dating of these structures is not entirely clear.[90] The polis may have also accumulated grain to distribute it cheaply or free of charge among poor citizens.[91] However, one of the most important reasons for accumulating grain was the need to have provisions available in the case of war. Besides the raids of Dionysius II of Syracuse, the conflicts with inland communities represented a major threat to Heraclea. New developments in warfare, especially long and extensive military campaigns like the ones conducted by Alexander the Molossian, Pyrrhus, etc., would have been impossible without huge staple food provisions.[92] Hence, the data suggests that Lucanian military power and consumption habits, which were both related to the emergence of a rural middle class, strongly influenced the Greek communities on the coast. Put simply, wine was sold to the Lucanians, while grain was used to feed the armies fighting the Lucanians and other enemies: the two markets were growing constantly between the fourth and the third centuries BC, and required a reaction on the part of the Greek communities living on the coast.

[89] Pazdera 2006: 165–171; Hansen 2006: 30; Berthelot 2012.
[90] Zuchtriegel 2012b: 278–281.
[91] Pazdera 2006; Moreno 2007.
[92] Cf. Briant 1994.

HOW TO BE GREEK

How, then, did this economic interdependence affect the social geography of the Greek colonies? One of the major changes regards cultural and ethnic identities: As they ventured inland, the inhabitants of Early Hellenistic Heraclea would have encountered not the Other, but barbarians who were, in a manner of speaking, turning Greek.[93] This is evident not only from material culture, where Lucanian and Greek farmsteads are hardly distinguishable, but also from the fact that the Lucanians coined money and introduced alphabetic writing. Some evidently spoke and wrote Greek.[94] If, on the other hand, "Greekness" during the Classical period was largely defined through the Other (the Barbarian), as Jonathan Hall has argued,[95] the very definition of Greekness must have undergone a crisis when the Other turned Greek to the extent seen in Late Classical/Early Hellenistic Lucania.

As the cultural distinction between Greeks and Barbarians began to blur in southern Italy and elsewhere, other ways of distinguishing Greeks from non-Greeks became important. Archaeologists have long emphasized the importance of the gymnasium in the Hellenistic world as a place of reaffirmation of Greekness.[96] Hellenistic gymnasia were not only places where a certain way of life was cultivated, but also acted as archives: the question of being enrolled or not reestablished the boundary between Greeks and non-Greeks.

In terms of practices associated with Greekness, the rural population of Heraclea was both dangerously distant from the urban center and dangerously close to the Lucanian territory. Again, this is not simply a question of political rights and birth status. In fifth century BC Greece, the very act of moving away from the coast to inland areas was regarded as a potential threat to Greekness, as suggested by Herodotus's (IV 108) story of the inhabitants of Gelonus, a fortified town in the inland north of Olbia with Greek cult sites and a large fortress built entirely of wood. As Herodotus points out, "the Gelonoi were by their origin Greeks, who left their trading ports to settle among the Boudinoi [a local Scythian tribe]; and they speak a language half Greek and half Scythian."[97]

As we have seen, the vicinity of Greek and Lucanian farmers was not only a spatial phenomenon, but also an economic one. As argued above, sheep rearing

---

[93] Cf. Hall 2002: 196 on *mixellenes* and the Classical Greek notion of "culture" which presupposed that "... barbarian populations might through cultural convergence become more Hellenic."

[94] Poccetti 1989; Parente 2009.

[95] Hall 2002: 172–205, especially p. 179 ("The invention of the barbarian antitype provided a completely new mechanism for defining Hellenic identity. In the Archaic period, Hellenic self-definition was 'aggregative.' (...) Now, Hellenicity was defined 'oppositionally' through differential comparison with a barbarian outgroup.")

[96] Delorme 1960: 425; Cohen 1978: 36.

[97] Transl. A.D. Godley, 1920. On archaeological data from the hinterland of Olbia, see Bujskich 2006.

was important in both inland regions and the *eschatià*. Therefore the empty zone between the Greek and Lucanian territories should not be imagined as a sort of buffer zone, but rather as a space for non-stable forms of economic exploitation, especially pastoralism. Assuming that the wool from this rural area was processed and traded in Heraclea, the Lucanians and the inhabitants of the *eschatià* were united by economic interests and at the same time opposed to the urban center that controlled the processing and selling of the raw material. Furthermore, the Greek farmers produced goods that must have been in high demand in the inland regions, namely wine and oil.

The constant contacts in the hinterland must have aroused the suspicion of the urban elite. Like other colonial cities, Heraclea was probably concerned about economic transactions that did not pass through and were uncontrolled by the urban center. Concerns of this sort also emerge from the so-called Oath of Chersonesus (IOSPE I² 401): the citizens swore not to "betray to anyone whomsoever, whether Greek or barbarian, Chersonesus, Kerkinitis, Kalos Limen, the other forts, and the rest of the chora, which the people of Chersonesus inhabit or inhabited" and not to "sell grain suitable for exportation which comes from the plain, nor export grain from the plain to another place, except to Chersonesus."[98] It was apparently difficult to control the sale of products beyond the borders (hence the oath), and the rural population was suspected of acting on its own account and of ignoring the necessities of the urban center. Moreover, the inhabitants of the outer chora were also suspected of fraternizing with neighboring communities. Aristotle (Pol. 1330a) mentions that "some people have a law that the citizens whose land is near the frontier are not to take part in deliberation as to wars against neighboring states, on the ground that private interests would prevent them from being able to take counsel wisely."[99] This is ascribed to the fact that the inhabitants of distant parts of the chora were suspected of "neglecting hostility against neighboring/bordering people."[100]

In Chapter 5, I argued that community members living in marginal zones of the chora were gradually excluded from certain practices (political, athletic, and social activities) that embodied Greekness. It is likely, though less well-documented in the sources, that marginalization also affected the Greekness of women living in the outer chora. As Jonathan Hall (2002: 195) has observed, in Classical Greece "transhumant subsistence strategies" as well as "the right of women to dispose of alienable property and to act as heads of families" could mark out certain areas as "more primitive and thus more 'barbarian.'" In other words, if women in the *eschatià* had to take over the leadership of

---

[98] Transl. Th.F. Lytle.
[99] Transl. H. Rackham, 1944.
[100] Arist. Pol. 1330a.

the household when men were absent, they risked appearing less Greek and more barbarian. This might have been the case when men were occupied with intensive agriculture, trade, or animal husbandry. Paradoxically, the participation of men in political or athletic activities in the urban center, about four hours' walk away, entailed a certain degree of alienation from the Greek model of life on the part of female household members, as they had to act as heads of the family in the meantime.

In a cultural context where Greekness had to be constantly affirmed through certain political, cultural, and physical practices, the position of the inhabitants of the outer chora inevitably became ambivalent. After all, what was considered Greek here and what was considered barbarian? The kind of ambivalence and hybridization that characterized these areas has not yet received much attention, though it merits further investigation, as Lin Foxhall has suggested. During a survey near Bova in southern Calabria, in the mountains halfway between Rhegion and Locri, Foxhall and her colleagues identified a number of Classical sites where the material culture "appears to be 'Greek', whatever that really meant in practice."[101] Foxhall observes further:

> It is also not clear at present how 'Greek' were the 'Greeks' living in the Bova countryside. It seems likely that the inhabitants of the Umbro Greek site considered themselves to be 'Greek' but whether the citizens of Rhegion and Locri considered them to be 'Greek', or even part of (or 'having a share in', as Greeks would have expressed it) one of the two poleis, remains an open question. Also, whether there is a vertical dimension to 'Greekness' is a question which needs further investigation – does it fade beyond a particular altitude to be replaced by indigenous identities? (Foxhall *et al.* 2007: 26)

The situation at Heraclea seems to confirm Foxhall's hypothesis that Greekness faded as one moved inland, although I think that in this case Greekness was not replaced by indigenous identities – for what would that have meant in fourth century Lucania? – but by hybrid ones. As becomes evident in the long run, hybridity reveals its spatial dimension against the backdrop of the Classical model of the polis as it emerges from the foundation of Heraclea and other colonies: because of the fundamental nexus between Greekness, citizenship, and centrality (Ackerbürger polis), marginality and decentralization inevitably led to hybrid identities, in the sense that the rural population approached, both literally and metaphorically, the "barbarians living in the surroundings" (Aristotle).

Coming from the urban center to one of the farms in the *eschatià*, travelers would have seen the inland hills dotted with Lucanian farmsteads overshadowed by the oppidum of Monte Coppolo (Figure 6.13). Turning around, they would

---

[101] Foxhall *et al.* 2007: 25.

6.13 The Valley of the River Sinni with Piano Sollazzo (center) and Mt. Coppolo (right) in the background, from northeast (site HE86 near Anglona).

have noticed similar hills dotted with Greek farmsteads and tombs. Landscape and settlement patterns were hardly distinguishable. While boundary sanctuaries such as Piano Sollazzo may have reinforced the limits of the Greek chora, habitation sites reveal the ambivalence of Greekness and the limits of the polis. However, it should not be forgotten that the places of marginality and ambivalence were also the places where violence first erupted. Violent conflicts, even though usually controlled by the polis, initially affected the rural territories, both Greek and Lucanian. Hybridity and economic entanglement on the one hand and the threat of violence, enslavement, devastation, and looting on the other coincided here. If we try to imagine what life was like in the chora, we should take into account these aspects as well. The reason why anyone would face the various risks of living in the countryside was probably economic pressure. In social and cultural terms, there was little to gain, at least from the viewpoint of hegemonic discourse. Colonial ideology and practice (habitation patterns, cultural reaffirmation of Greekness, etc.) implicated that rural dwellers, especially in remote areas, were *per definitionem* socially and culturally marginalized.

SEVEN

WORKSHOPS: *BANAUSOI* IN THE COLONY

When Adolf Furtwängler (1893) discovered that much of the red-figure pottery found in southern Italy was produced in local workshops, he assumed that Thurii and Heraclea played a key role in the transmission of techniques and styles from Athens to Magna Graecia.[1] But was the foundation of Thurii really crucial in this context? The earliest southern Italian red-figure vases come from the Ionian Coast and its hinterland (the so-called Lucanian group) and from Apulia (Apulian group). Both groups reveal strong Athenian influence on forms and iconography. The Pisticci Painter, who seems to have introduced red-figure pottery to southern Italy (440s BC?), used the forms, motifs, and subjects from Athenian painters such as the Christie and Achilles Painters.[2] In the late fifth century BC, the Amykos and Cyclops Painters worked in the tradition of the Pisticci Painter, who may well have trained them.

WORKSHOPS IN COLONIAL SETTLEMENTS

In the 440s BC, Athenian colonists had come to Thurii and probably also to Heraclea by way of the joint colony Siris. Against this backdrop, Furtwängler's assumption that red-figure vase-painting was brought to southern Italy by

---

[1] Furtwängler 1893: 151–152.
[2] Cf. Mannino 1996; Denoyelle 2007.

Athenian potters and painters who moved to these two places does appear plausible.

However, in 1973 archaeologists discovered a kiln containing fragments by the Amykos Painter in Metapontum.[3] Wasters and broken vases made by the Creusa and Dolon Painters, two immediate followers of the Amykos Painter, were found nearby. Nowadays, there is little doubt that the Pisticci and Cyclops Painters also worked in Metapontum, at least for some time during the late fifth and early fourth centuries BC. While early Lucanian red-figure pottery was apparently based in Metapontum, the earliest Apulian workshops, which were established shortly after the emergence of early Lucanian red-figure pottery, were almost certainly located in Tarentum where the most important pieces come from. It has to be admitted, however, that in Tarentum no kilns or wasters dating to the late fifth and fourth centuries have come to light so far.

By contrast, the fifth century colonies of Thurii and Heraclea have yielded only small quantities of early southern Italian red-figure pottery. There is no evidence for red-figure workshops in Thurii.[4] As mentioned in Chapter 3, the burial mounds south of the city contained some red-figure pottery, probably of Athenian production. Judging from the excavation reports, the number of vases was rather limited compared to Athenian burials of the period. A few red-figure vases dating to around 400 BC have been found during excavations in the urban center, including an early Apulian bell-krater that has been attributed to the Hearst Painter, one of the earliest vase painters in the Apulian tradition.[5] At Heraclea finds of early southern Italian red-figure pottery are limited to a few skyphoi and fragments of kraters from various parts of the Castello hill (see Figure 2.11), a late fifth century skyphos ascribed to the Policoro Painter from the sanctuary of Demeter, and the vases from the Tomb of the Policoro Painter (see Figure 3.4).[6] Several of these vases were clearly imported from Metapontum, such as a skyphos by the Creusa or Dolon Painter from the eastern edge of the Castello hill,[7] and two hydriai by the Amykos and Creusa Painters in the Policoro tomb (no. 2 & 3). Two bell kraters, one of which may be attributed to the Amykos Painter and the other to the Tarporley Painter, were found in the extraurban sanctuary of Masseria Petrulla.[8] Whether the Policoro Painter was based in Heraclea, as suggested by Arthur D. Trendall,[9]

[3] Silvestrelli 2005: 113 with bibliography.
[4] Guzzo 1997: 379.
[5] Cf. *Notizie degli Scavi* 95, III supplement, 1970, fig. 136–139, 143; Trendall, Cambitoglou 1978: 29 (Sybaris no. 12850–12853).
[6] Lo Porto 1961: 139 (mentions sporadic finds of krater fragments attributed to the Pisticci or Amykos Painters as well as to the Tarporley Painter and the Painter of the Birth of Dionysus); Giardino 2012: 101–103, fig. 6.
[7] Hänsel 1973: 457, 461, 468, fig. 43.
[8] Battiloro, Bruscella, Osanna 2010: 244–249 (vase attributions courtesy of F. Silvestrelli).
[9] Trendall 1989: 21.

remains unclear. Although many excavations have been conducted in Heraclea and its hinterland over the last few decades, only one more vase by the Policoro Painter has come to light since the discovery of the Policoro tomb in 1963 (the skyphos from the sanctuary of Demeter mentioned above). Of course the overall picture may change through future excavations, but two facts are beyond doubt: First, the most important early Lucanian workshops were located in Metapontum, and second, Heraclea imported products from there during the late fifth and early fourth centuries BC.

In my opinion, it is no mere coincidence that early Lucanian red-figure workshops are attested in Metapontum rather than in Thurii or Heraclea. There are several reasons why potters and painters would have settled in Metapontum and Tarentum rather than in one of the new colonies, even though many came from Thurii's mother-city Athens or had connections with Athenian workshops. One reason is that the agrarian and egalitarian structure of fifth-century colonies would not have attracted artisans and craft production remained underdeveloped during the early years of these colonies. In other words, the distribution of early Lucanian red-figure pottery workshops, as it appears today, probably reflects historical phenomena and is not simply the result of accidental discoveries.

The lack of evidence for early southern Italian red-figure workshops in Thurii and Heraclea is not an isolated phenomenon. Indeed, except for Kamarina which I shall discuss separately, no Classical colony has yielded any evidence of specialized craft production during its early years. In most Classical colonies, specialized workshops only become archaeologically visible several decades after their foundation. Heraclea eventually did develop into a center for pottery and terracotta production, but not before the second half of the fourth century BC. In this period, traces of pottery production can be found over large parts of the city. There is no evidence of a separated potters' district or *kerameikos* as in Metapontum, Athens or Selinus (Figure 7.1).[10] Instead, production areas were distributed over the entire city. From the late fourth century BC onward, numerous pottery kilns were built in Area A on the Castello hill, some in private houses and others in the open. Eight were restored and left *in situ*, but the excavation report mentions about fifty further kilns that are no longer visible (Figure 7.2).[11] In addition, the excavators found more than two hundred fragments of terracotta molds, most of which are still unpublished.[12] The largest number of molds were found in rooms 6 and 7 of insula IV. The two rooms were part of what may have been a separate apartment in the southeastern corner of a large peristyle house. The molds found here

[10] Bentz *et al.* 2013.
[11] Barile 1983/4: 8.
[12] Adamesteanu 1970: 485; Orlandini 1983: 505–507; Giardino 1996.

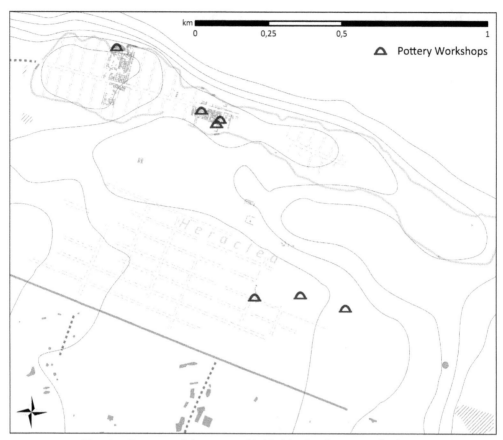

7.1 Heraclea: Pottery workshops, second half of the fourth century/third century BC.

date from the last decades of the fourth to the early second century BC. They represent a variety of types including Artemis Bendis – seated and standing female figures, some of which recall Early Hellenistic Aphrodite statuettes – Herakles, and various male figures.[13] On the slopes of the Castello hill south of Area A, the excavators discovered a waste deposit with numerous fragments of terracotta statuettes and molds. The finds include a terracotta pestle *(impastoio)* with an inscription reading, "Onasimos is beautiful" (ΟΝΑΣΙΜ[ΟΣ] ΚΑΛΟΣ).[14] Likewise, in Area B, pottery and terracotta production is only attested from the second half of the fourth century BC onward. In the 1960s archaeologists noticed numerous fragments of Artemis Bendis statuettes in the area.[15] Excavations in the years 1973/4 uncovered the remains of several kilns in an open area later occupied by a large house in insula VI. Among the finds were pottery wasters, terracotta molds for discoidal loom weights, and statuettes

13   Ceccatelli 1975/6: 257–258; Barile 1983/4: 185.
14   Neutsch 1967: 134.
15   Neutsch 1967: 133–134; 163–164.

7.2 Heraclea, Castello Hill, Area A: Pottery workshop in insula 4, rooms 6 and 7. (Courtesy of *Archivio fotografico della Soprintendenza Archeologia, Belle Arti e Paesaggio della Basilicata*.)

resembling those from the central quarter.[16] The workshops in Area B were active throughout the third century BC.

Other pottery workshops were discovered in the southern quarter of the city in via Napoli and close to the hospital of Policoro. The kilns of via Napoli were located in open areas. Analysis of wasters and pottery deposits has shown that plain wares and internally glazed wares typical of Hellenistic Heraclea were produced here during the third century BC. The kiln excavated near the hospital was part of a house dating to the late fourth or third century BC.[17]

A similar situation can be observed in various other colonies of the Classical period. In Chapter 2, we looked at painted grave stelae from Chersonesus. In mainland Greece, similar grave stelae were used from the fifth century BC, but in Chersonesus they are not attested before the second half of the fourth century BC. The mass production of Chersonesean transport amphoras began around the same time.

[16] Giardino 2012: 110.
[17] Calvaruso 2012; Giardino, Calvaruso 2015.

A similar pattern may be found in Issa (founded around 385 BC): there is evidence for workshops that produced painted grave stelae and Gnathia-style pottery, but again production only began in the late fourth century BC.[18]

The colonies of Heraclea, Chersonesus, and Issa were founded between the fifth and the early fourth centuries BC, but specialized craft production in each one of these settlements is only attested from the second half of the fourth century onward. Was craft production in these colonies therefore linked to a general intensification of production and trade during the Early Hellenistic period? This may indeed be the case, though only to a certain extent. For there are several aspects in this process that are typical of newly founded settlements and they cannot be ascribed to macroeconomic trends. In old colonies such as Metapontum, Tarentum, Locri, Selinus, Epidamnos, Olbia, and Pantikapaion, to name just a few, craft production is attested throughout the fifth and early fourth centuries BC. This shows that the belated emergence of specialized craft production in Classical colonies is not simply the result of general developments in the Greek world. Nor is the underdevelopment of craft production in Classical colonies typical of Greek colonies in general. In mixed settlements and colonies of the seventh century BC, craft production played a key role from the outset. In several cases, the very establishment of a settlement or colony was linked to craft production and trade, as for example in Ischia, Incoronata, Policoro, and Berezan. Judging from the material evidence, artisans and merchants were among the first Greeks to arrive in these places and to establish relations with non-Greek populations living in the area. The contrast with Classical colonies could hardly be sharper.

CHANGING ECONOMIC AND POLITICAL CONTEXTS

The changing role of craftsmanship in colonial settlements from the seventh century to the fifth and fourth centuries BC can be ascribed to two main factors: (1) technological and logistical innovations, and (2) ideology. In the seventh century BC, migration and colonization lowered population pressure in mainland Greece, but these were not state-led, coordinated processes. They should be viewed as a series of individual initiatives led by aristocratic leaders who provided ships and essential resources.[19] This is not exactly what modern scholarship has defined as "trade before the flag," or economic exploitation preceding political and military subjection. Yet trade and craftsmanship did play a crucial role in the early phases of Greek colonization, and there are at least several superficial analogies with the trade before the flag model. By contrast, it would be absurd to speak of trade before the flag with regard to

---

[18] Milićević Bradač 2007: 51.
[19] Osborne 1998.

fifth and fourth century BC colonies. Not surprisingly, trade before the flag has never been considered a useful model for Classical colonization. This may illustrate how profoundly things changed from the seventh to the fifth century BC. During the rather spontaneous initiatives of the early periods, trade and craft production were often fundamental for the creation of fruitful relationships with local rulers who were interested in Greek knowledge and products. In such a context, artisans could expect some appreciation and support on the part of colonial elites. On the other hand, during the Classical period the foundation of a colony was usually conducted by a mother-city that was pursuing its own political interests and strategies. This could involve state-led military campaigns, such as at Epidamnos and Amphipolis. The participants in these campaigns could expect to benefit from the administrative infrastructure of the founder city. For example, they may have hoped that the mother-city would provide assurances that the land-lots would really be of equal size. The crucial role of administrative support and infrastructure from the mother-city emerges from the foundation decree of Brea, an inscription found in Athens (the findspot in itself is revealing and testifies to the crucial role of the mother-city). In the decree the Athenian assembly determines that land distribution in Brea should be carried out by ten *geonomoi*, one from each phyle. Finally, a special magistrate is appointed to "pay out the money," probably some kind of start-up package for the settlers.[20] In the case of Epidamnos (435 BC), those who could not participate in the military campaign, for whatever reason, were allowed to deposit a fixed sum of 50 drachmas (Thuc. I 27). It is likely that in return they counted on being given an equal share of land, i.e., a standardized land-lot (see Chapter 4).

As should have become clear, Classical colonization was strongly conditioned by a series of technical and economic developments. The notion of equality was linked to monetization, as is clear in the case of Epidamnos, but also in the case of Lesbos. Of course this cannot have been the case in the seventh and early sixth centuries BC, when there was no coined money. In the Archaic period, the social status of the settlers depended far more on the capabilities and skills they possessed. In the Classical period, money made it possible to express social status in abstract numbers. Thus, the social and economic standing of the colonists could be standardized and equalized. The settlers now became shareholders who invested a fixed amount of labor and/or money to obtain certain entitlements. For example, at Korkyra Melaina the first settlers who took possession of the land and fortified the town were entitled to receive equal shares of the best land, whereas those who arrived later and did not collaborate in the riskiest parts received smaller allotments. At the same time, technical innovations in field measurement made it possible to guarantee

---

[20] IG I³ 46, 34–35. Cf. Malkin 1994b.

equality in land property not only in theory but on the ground. However the accounts of Spartan *homoioi* and other egalitarian landholder communities of the early Archaic period are interpreted, the surveying techniques available at that time did not allow great accuracy in the distribution and assessment of land. Excavations at Megara Hyblaia suggest that the Greeks were able to lay out orthogonal city grids as early as 700 BC,[21] but there is no evidence that they were able to do the same for the countryside as a whole.

The importance of technical and economic innovations for the history of Greek colonization can hardly be underestimated. Equality, as defined by fifth and fourth century authors, would not have been possible without field measurement techniques and money. Equality and democracy have a material and a technical dimension. In the fifth century it had become possible to standardize the investment (in money) and the share of the settlers (by measuring out equal lots). This was crucial for the conceptualization of equality as something measurable and as a concrete objective of political discourse.

On the other hand, the written sources reveal a profound contempt for craft and mercantile activities from Herodotus onwards.[22] As a result, the main goal of those who participated in the foundation of a colony was to become an independent landowner. Money and logistics made it possible, while ideology made it desirable. As I have tried to demonstrate, Classical colonies were organized as Ackerbürger polis; consequently, what a colonist desired more than anything else was to become an Ackerbürger. It is likely that an artisan who managed to participate in the foundation of a colony attempted to improve his social status by becoming a landowner/farmer rather than by continuing to practice his previous trade for which he had been despised by the urban elites in his city of origin.

Moreover, Classical colonies provided hardly any profitable markets for the products of specialized artisans, especially during the early phases. The case of southern Italian red-figure pottery discussed earlier is quite revealing. During the second half of the fifth century BC, red-figure pottery was used in various ways: for symposia and domestic use, dedications in sanctuaries, grave goods. Red-figure pottery may have been regarded as inferior to silver vessels, yet it was not cheap.[23] In the late fifth century BC, an Athenian red-figure vase might have cost a drachma, in other words a day's wages.[24] Supposing that a set of symposia vases included several cups, amphorae, jugs, a crater, and so forth, this was not affordable for everyone. In their early years, most Classical colonies were not ready for large-scale consumption of red-figure pottery known from other sites such as Athens, Gela, Akragas, Selinus, or Tarentum.

[21] Mertens 2006: 63–72.
[22] See Burford 1972: 28–36; Lloyd 1993: 196–199.
[23] Gill, Vickers 1990; Vickers 2004.
[24] Cf. Sparkes 1991: 63.

After all, how should colonists who lived in temporary huts and were struggling for survival celebrate luxurious symposia? The material culture of the
early phases of the colonies is relatively modest. During the first two or three
generations of Heraclea and Thurii, red-figure pottery is extremely scarce in
domestic contexts. As for funerary use, some early tombs at Heraclea contained
only one vase, while others had no grave goods at all. Such puritan funerary
customs would not have attracted specialist artisans. The same is true in the
case of ritual activities in sanctuaries, judging from the small number of early
southern Italian red-figure vases found in the sanctuaries of Heraclea.[25] It is
doubtful that a red-figure pottery workshop would have found enough buy-
ers in Heraclea or Thurii. Specialist artisans probably fared much better in
older colonies like Metapontum and Tarentum. There they could rely on a
steady demand as well as on a local tradition of craftsmanship. New research
by Martine Denoyelle and Francesca Silvestrelli has shown that the first generation of red-figure workshops in Metapontum drew heavily on the local pottery traditions of the first half of the fifth century BC, although vase-paintings
were inspired by Athenian models.[26] The local tradition was the groundwork
on which new techniques and styles could be built up. This was not the case
at Thurii or Heraclea.

THE BIRTH OF THE POLIS OUT OF THE SPIRIT OF CRAFTSMANSHIP

If artisans had little reason to move to new colonies, or did so in order to
become agriculturalists rather than continue working as artisans, another question arises: How could the colonies have survived? After all, craftsmanship was
essential for the survival of a colony. Classical philosophers were well aware
that the ideal of political and economic autarky could only be achieved if
the polis possessed all the crafts required to supply all essential needs. In the
Republic (369b–c) Plato attributes the very origins of the polis to certain fundamental needs *(chreiai)* that have to be fulfilled through specialist workers such
as farmers, builders, weavers, shoe makers, and so forth.

   The picture painted here by Plato is rather anachronistic. In the eighth and
seventh centuries BC, the presence of certain raw materials and specialized
craftsmen would indeed have been indispensable in a new settlement. But by
the fifth century BC the situation had changed. As a result of the diffusion of
writing, the use of coined money, and innovations in the fields of military and
seafaring techniques, the Greek city-states had developed into highly effective
administrative organizations. Greek city-states were now capable of establishing overseas settlements whose main function was to offer land to those who

[25] Cf. Neutsch 1968: 774–775, fig. 27 a–b, fig. 20c; Giardino 2012: 101–103.
[26] Silvestrelli, forthcoming.

had none and to produce grain for homeland Greece.[27] The colonies could survive without specialist artisans, as the mother-cities were able to provide craft products in exchange for grain and/or political and military support. Thus, not only did the colonies offer an opportunity to get rid of poor citizens by giving them new social and economic opportunities; they also created new sales markets for the mother city's craft products. This is obvious in the case of Athenian red-figure vases which were exported to Thurii and Amphipolis. The establishment of local red-figure workshops would have provoked a decrease in Athenian exports, and the same is probably true for many other products which are less visible in the archaeological record, e.g., fabrics, leather, armor, iron tools, and so forth. In fact, there are no traces of local red-figure pottery production in the early years, as we have seen above. The data from Heraclea leads to similar conclusions. As already observed, the early coinage of the city closely recalls the coinage of Heraclea's mother city Tarentum. Maybe the earliest Heraclean coins were made in Tarentum, although this cannot be proved. Whatever the case, the artisans who struck the first coinage of Heraclea came from the mint of Tarentum.[28] Apparently, it was the mother-city that provided the know-how and probably also the raw material.

Recent excavations at Heraclea have yielded further data regarding the city's coinage. It seems that bronze coins were struck in Insula I in Area A on the Castello hill, an area partly excavated in 1968–1970. During the excavation campaign in 2014, we found the remains of what may be considered to be the mint of Heraclea during the Late Hellenistic period (Figure 7.3).[29] Since only the Hellenistic layers were brought to light, the date when the mint started operating remains unclear.

The mints of Athens and Thessalonike were located near the agora, that of Rome on the forum. The situation at Heraclea is similar. Geophysical prospection conducted in 2013 east of Insula I revealed a large area without traces of building measuring about 150 meters in length.[30] In the 1960s Dinu Adamesteanu had already suggested that this was the agora of Heraclea on the basis of aerial photographs.[31] Our research has confirmed this hypothesis.

Insula I, where the mint was located, was a public building in the agora. It differs from other insulae in Area A in important ways: it is oriented in a slightly different manner and its internal structure does not resemble that of other residential areas. The building complex was connected to the agora by a large portico on the eastern side. In the southern part of the portico, a group of plain vases of the fifth century BC were ritually deposited in three

[27] Moreno 2007; Prieto, Polleichtner 2007.
[28] Siciliano 2008.
[29] Osanna *et al.* 2015.
[30] *Ibid,*
[31] Adamesteanu 1969: 211.

7.3 Heraclea, Castello Hill, Area A: Late Hellenistic mint in insula I (excavations 2014).

pits beneath the foundation walls.[32] Other votive materials, mostly terracotta statuettes, have been found inside the building complex. Stone capitals made of *pietra tenera* (Tarantine stone) dating to the third century BC testify to one or more monumental building phases.[33] Furthermore, excavations during the 1960s yielded a fragment of a bronze tablet bearing the name of an *ephoros*, the highest-ranking magistrate in the city.[34] The combination of the various types of evidence makes it highly probable that this is a public building.[35] The mint fits well into this picture. The building complex may have been the official residence of the *ephoroi* and/or of other magistrates of Heraclea.

It appears that the mint of Heraclea was not located in a separate building as in Athens, but in the courtyard of a public building. The excavations in the courtyard, which was flanked by a small portico, have revealed three small pits in the ground, on the bottom of which dozens of bronze coin blanks, numerous metal waste products, and some coined bronze were found. One of the pits also contained the remains of coal and ashes.

It would appear as if during the Late Hellenistic period the casting of bronze blanks and probably other activities took place in the courtyard of a public building. In this context, minting was probably a sporadic activity scheduled in accordance with economic necessities. The fact that the coiners were

[32] Adamesteanu, Dilthey 1978: 517.
[33] Rescigno 2012a.
[34] Ghinatti 1980.
[35] Cf. Adamesteanu 1969: 211; Osanna 2008: 28.

7.4 Heraclea: City wall on the southern side of the Castello Hill, excavations around 1965 (Neutsch 1967: pl. 8.1).

working in a courtyard of a public building made it possible for the magistrates of the city to supervise the work closely. The way in which the mint was organized, with coiners who probably came from other cities in the region, suggests that craft production in Heraclea continued to depend largely on external know-how and manpower.

Tarentine influence is particularly evident in Heraclean craft production and coinage, during the early years, but Tarentum continued to play a crucial role in craft production at Heraclea throughout the fourth and third centuries BC. As we have already seen, the early votive terracottas found in the urban center and in the sanctuary of Piano Sollazzo closely resemble Tarentine products of the period (see Chapter 4). If they were not imported from Tarentum, they were produced at Heraclea with molds from Tarentum (the fact that there are no traces of local workshops before the second half of the fourth century BC suggests that terracotta was at least partly imported).[36]

Tarentine workshops probably also built the city walls of Heraclea during the first half of the fourth century BC. While the Lucanians used local arenite from the area around Monte Coppolo when they fortified their settlement during the second half of the fourth century, the Heracleans imported Carparo stone from the region around Tarentum (Figure 7.4). Dozens or even hundreds of men were presumably working in the quarries around Tarentum to provide the building stone. In addition, coachmen and shippers were needed to transport the blocks to Heraclea. It is likely that they were based in Tarentum. The same is true for the stonemasons who dressed the blocks and erected the walls, as suggested by a series of marks on some of the blocks used in the city walls and at Masseria del Concio near the harbor (Figure 7.5).[37] The precise function of the marks is unclear, but the fact that similar marks were used during

[36] Lo Porto 1961: 138; Dell'Aglio 2015: 68–69.
[37] Neutsch 1967: 162.

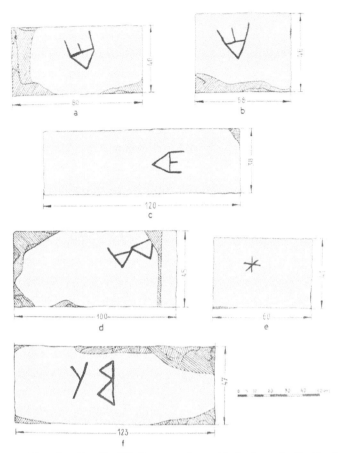

7.5 Heraclea, Castello Hill: Stone marks on blocks from the fortification wall (Neutsch 1967: fig. 9).

the construction of the new fortification of Tarentum around the middle of the fifth century BC (Figure 7.6) demonstrates that the builders of the walls of Heraclea had a Tarentine background.[38]

Once the walls were erected, there was little to do at Heraclea for stonemasons and builders. Except for the fortifications, the use of blocks or other dressed stone elements is extremely rare in Hereclea in the fourth century BC. It is therefore likely that the stonemasons either returned to Tarentum or became agriculturists at Heraclea.

In the third century BC stonemasons working in Heraclea still came from Tarentum or were trained there, as is shown by several capitals made to adorn a building in Insula I. The building stone used for the capitals (known as *pietra tenera*) was imported from Tarentum, and the stonemasonry clearly reflects Tarantine workmanship.[39] In Tarentum, the development of local traditions can be traced

[38]   On Tarentum see Lo Porto 1992: 13–14, tab. IX.
[39]   Rescigno 2012a.

7.6 Tarentum, city walls: Stone marks (Lo Porto 1992: pl. IX).

quite closely. By contrast, at Heraclea there is no evidence of a local stonemasonry tradition in the period between the building of the city walls in the early fourth century BC and the emergence of monuments made of *pietra tenera* in the urban center and in the necropoleis during the third century BC. It seems therefore that for a long time after the foundation, the colony relied on artisans and know-how from the mother-city. When craft production spread to Heraclea from the second half of the fourth century BC, the city maintained close economic ties with Tarentum, as shown by the import of *pietra tenera* and the Tarentine origin of the capitals.

DEPENDENT COLONIES

The colony's economy depended heavily on the mother-city, especially during the first three generations. It was the mother-city whose economic support made it possible for the colonists to organize their community as an Ackerbürger polis specializing in agriculture. The colonists could do without local craft production centers because the mother-city provided all the essential goods. In the case of Brea, the mother-city Athens even seems to have paid out some kind of start-up package to the colonists. It is likely that as soon as the colonies started to produce an agricultural surplus, mother-cities like Athens, Tarentum, or Syracuse demanded some sort of recompense for the financial, logistic, and military aid they were offering. The arrival of the Athenian fleet at Thurii in 413 BC is an example of just such recompense.[40]

It is obvious that the model of the Ackerbürger polis could only be implemented with economic support from the mother city or other external

[40] Thuc. VII 33,5–6.

partners. By analyzing the archaeological evidence, I arrive at roughly the same conclusions as Thomas Figueira in his 2008 paper, where he defines colonization as "an important political tool during the Classical period, since reordering and recolonising communities provided more resources, manpower and taxes to their initiators."[41]

It is obvious that the ideal of economic and political autarky was hardly achievable under such circumstances. Colonies consisting predominantly of agriculturalists simply could not survive unless they were supported by a larger network or political entity that offered a market for agricultural produce and provided raw materials and manufactured products such as coins, weapons, iron tools, fabrics, painted pottery, and so forth. This is the great paradox of Classical colonization: at first sight many Classical colonies appear to be rather primitive agricultural communities, but in most cases they were actually part of larger networks. In spite of, or rather because of, their primitive economic structure, the colonies contributed to economic and political entanglement in the ancient Mediterranean.[42] The colonies specialized in a specific economic sector (agriculture), and specialization always implies complexity. The Athenian colonies and cleruchies of the fifth and fourth centuries BC illustrate this particularly well, as Alfonso Moreno has shown.[43] The data analyzed here suggests that the Athenian colonies were not an isolated case: the same sort of interdependence characterized other Classical colonies.

The economic and political context in which Classical colonies existed was not always controlled by the mother-cities. The Adriatic colonies of Issa and Pharos received starting aid from Syracuse; Issa was a colony of Syracuse while Pharos was a colony of Paros. Both colonies were organized as Ackerbürger poleis. Pharos, in particular, remained an agricultural settlement of urban farmers for several centuries, as I have argued earlier (Chapter 4). The colony maintained the structure of an Ackerbürger polis even when Paros and Syracuse were facing political and military problems and were forced to cease providing support. During this period, local networks may have helped Pharos maintain its agricultural economy. The colony may have imported metal from the Balkans in return for wine, oil, textiles, and other products. During the fourth century BC, the culture of inland Illyria underwent profound changes. There was an increase of imports from Greece and other regions in central and southeastern Europe. Furthermore, locally produced fibulae and pottery forms recall Greek and Macedonian models.[44] It is reasonable to infer that the demand for perishable products *à la grecque* may have increased as well.

---

[41] Figueira 2008: 507.

[42] On the relationship between entanglement and social stratification in the ancient Mediterranean, cf. Morris 2003.

[43] Moreno 2007.

[44] See Benac, Čović 1957:113–115 (Glasinac Phase Vb: 350–250 BC). Most of the archaeological material is still unpublished. Some tomb groups from non-Greek islands and inland

As in other cases, in the case of the Greek colonies on the coast of Croatia, the diffusion of elements of Hellenistic culture in the inland may have favored the preservation of seemingly primitive agricultural settler communities. I use the word "seemingly" because if these communities were producing wine, oil, or textiles for Illyria, they actually were part of a complex network of exchange.

INDEPENDENT ORPHAN-COLONIES?

As I have tried to argue, the economic and social structure of Classical colonies depended on the mother-city or other supporters. But what about colonies that had no mother-city? If it is true that the model of the Ackerbürger polis presupposed a power network (usually controlled by the mother-city), colonies that had no such network had to follow a different model. Indeed, the evidence suggests precisely this: the colonies which, on the basis of the archaeological record, fit less well into the model of an Ackerbürger polis are those that had no mother-city to help them maintain the status of an agricultural community. The best known example is Kamarina. The distinctive feature of Kamarina is evident not only at the level of craftsmanship and trade, but also in other fields. The data suggests that where an imperial network was missing, a community of urban farmers could not subsist.

Excavations at Kamarina brought to light several pottery workshops and kilns situated around the urban center on sites with access to clay deposits and fresh water.[45] One of the kilns was situated northeast of the city on the River Hipparis, at a site where terracotta statuettes were produced as early as the first half of the fifth century BC – in other words, before the refoundation of Kamarina in 461 BC. Marcella Pisani (2008) has demonstrated that from around 430 BC the site was again occupied by a workshop that produced terracotta statuettes. Most of the statuettes and molds found here represent the goddess Artemis or a female figure holding a piglet as known from many sanctuaries of Demeter, but other themes also appear. During the fourth century BC, the workshop started to produce plain and banded pottery and black-glazed pottery inspired by Athenian shapes. The workshop was abandoned around 340/30 BC. The production of plain and black-glazed pottery some sixty years or more after the foundation is unsurprising, while the production of terracotta statuettes as early as one generation after the foundation stands out against the backdrop of other Classical colonies. As always, future excavations may change this picture. But on the basis of what we know today, the relatively early emergence of specialized craft production at Kamarina seems to

settlements with Greek pottery imports and imitations of the fourth century can be seen in the Museums of Zagreb and Split (see Sanader 2009: 16, fig. 7).

[45] Di Stefano 2012.

reflect a distinct historical situation. This is even more likely as Kamarina differs from most other Classical colonies in two further aspects. Firstly, Kamarina is the only colony where rural farmsteads are archaeologically attested from the foundation period (see Chapter 4). The spread of farmsteads during the first generation of the colony contrasts with what we observe in other colonies of the Classical period. Secondly, the Kamarinaian tombs of the second half of the fifth century BC display no parallels with any other Classical colony. Numerous Athenian imports point to trade connections from the very beginning of the settlement. While other Classical necropoleis were rather modest, the tombs of Kamarina tend to display wealth and status through grave goods and monuments. Kamarina apparently does not or not fully apply to the model of an agricultural Ackerbürger colony. There is no reason to doubt Diodorus' assertion that the land was allotted in equal parcels in 461 BC, as this seems to be confirmed by the archaeological data. However, the polis of Kamarina was obviously organized in a more complex way than other settlements which were basically communities of farmers living together in the urban center and cultivating their fields from there. This also emerges quite clearly from the distribution of pottery kilns which were situated in particularly suitable zones from an early period. By contrast, in an agricultural colony like Heraclea they are distributed randomly within the residential quarters (see Figure 7.1). Craft production and trade were fostered from an early phase in Kamarina, and the emergence of rural habitation sites indicates that, at the same time, some of the settlers specialized in agricultural production. We may assume that this kind of specialization and division of labor between farmers and artisans created the wealth that made it possible to import large quantities of red-figure vases from Athens.

There are several reasons why the settlers of Kamarina might have been less inclined than others to follow the model of the Ackerbürger colony which depended largely on other cities (generally the mother-city) for the supply of craft products. Many settlers from 461 BC probably originally came from Kamarina, where they had been displaced during the first half of the fifth century BC. In 461 BC, the urban area and the countryside were radically reorganized according to egalitarian standards, but many settlers still remembered the place where they had lived until about two decades previously when Gelon destroyed the city and transferred the inhabitants to Syracuse, granting them citizenship there (484 BC).[46] In 461 BC, the role of the mother-city Gela was probably restricted to advocating the return of the original inhabitants of Kamarina and their descendants. Gela never appears as the official mother-city in the sources. When referring to the refoundation of 461 BC, Thucydides uses the term *katoikizein*, thus implying some sort of reorganization or enlargement

---

[46] Cf. Hdt. VII 156,2; Thuc. VI 5,3.

of an existing community rather than the foundation of an entirely new community.[47] Diodorus (XI 76,5) refers to "Geloans who originally inhabited Kamarina" parceling out the land (μετὰ δὲ ταῦτα Καμάριναν μὲν Γελῷοι κατοικίσαντες ἐξ ἀρχῆς κατεκληρούχησαν). Unlike Heraclea, Issa, and other colonies that remained loyal to their mother-cities for a fairly lengthy period, Kamarina behaved in an independent manner from very early on. Against the will of Gela and Syracuse, the city formed an alliance with Leontinoi and Athens in 427 BC.[48] The Kamarinaians even waged war against Gela during this period until a truce was signed in 424 BC.[49] On this occasion, it was agreed that Kamarina should receive the city of Morgantina in return for a sum of money to be paid to the Syracuseans.[50] Although Kamarina eventually sided with Syracuse and Gela during the Athenian invasion of Sicily, it should be obvious that the city acted on its own account from the beginning. Kamarina clearly differs from typical Ackerbürger colonies such as Heraclea, Chersonesus, Issa, or Pharos which initially consisted of nucleated agricultural communities with minimal craft production.

Another colony where division of labor and specialization may have played an important role from the beginning is Amphipolis. The city was established in a strategic position on the slopes of Mount Pangaion where important silver and gold mines were exploited during the Classical period. The mines and Thracian wood, leather, and slaves were probably the main reason why the Athenians went there in the first place. However, only a small part of the settlers were Athenians; many settlers came from Argilos and various other places in the region. The defection of 424 BC deprived the city of any support from the mother-city during a very early stage of its development. It is doubtful that its new ally Sparta was prepared to step into the breach to provide economic support. Like Kamarina, Amphipolis acted independently from an early phase. The archaeological data does currently make it impossible to tell when specialized workshops and trade began to appear in Amphipolis. However, there is an interesting detail mentioned by Thucydides in his account of Brasidas's capture of the city. As Thucydides reports, Brasidas and his men arrived at the bridge over the River Strymon north of Amphipolis on a stormy winter night before sunrise:

> Brasidas easily overcame the guard, owing partly to the plot within the walls, partly to the severity of the weather and the suddenness of his attack; he then crossed the bridge, and at once was master of all the land that the Amphipolitans inhabited outside the walls. The passage of the

---

[47] VI 5,3: καὶ αὖθις ὑπὸ Γέλωνος ἀνάστατος γενομένη τὸ τρίτον κατῳκίσθη ὑπὸ Γελῴων. On the meaning of *katoikizein* in this passage see Casevitz 1985: 168, 172–173.

[48] Thuc. III 86,2; VI 75,3.

[49] Thuc. IV 58.

[50] Thuc. IV 65,1.

river was a complete surprise to the citizens within the walls, and many of those from outside were taken, while others fled into the town.

(IV 103,5–104,1, transl. after B. Jowett, 1881)

As this and other passages show, Amphipolis had a large fortified center. Yet a considerable number of the population lived in the countryside. The fact that the events reported by Thucydides took place in winter shows that the rural dwellers were based there permanently and not only periodically for harvest time. As I have argued before (Chapter 4), in other Classical colonies the settlers were initially concentrated in the urban center. In such cases, the occupation of the countryside several generations after the foundation may be interpreted as a result of social stratification and specialization. As far as Amphipolis is concerned, it is impossible to verify the existence of rural habitation in the archaeological record, as no systematic field surveys have been carried out.[51] In any case, it would not be surprising if Amphipolis resembled Kamarina in this respect.

Neither Kamarina nor Amphipolis really fit the model of a nucleated agricultural community (Ackerbürger colony). They differ in important ways from sites like Heraclea and Pharos. In Kamarina, excavations have brought to light farmsteads and workshops dating to the early phases and tombs with extraordinarily rich inventories of Athenian vases pointing to intensive trade. In Amphipolis, literary sources suggest that a considerable part of the population lived outside the city walls from the beginning.

The two sites do have something in common: neither could rely on a mother-city that provided goods and services lacking in an agricultural community. From this perspective, the cases of Amphipolis and Kamarina ultimately confirm the hypothesis that agricultural colonies depended on wider networks. When no such network existed, the model of the Ackerbürger colony could not work. Colonies like Kamarina or Amphipolis had no choice but to develop trade and craft production and to promote the division of labor within the community.

[51] Mari 2010: 408.

EIGHT

CLASSICAL GREECE FROM A COLONIAL PERSPECTIVE

Subalternity is not a special feature of Classical colonization, nor is the evidence of subaltern groups in Classical settlements any less scarce or ambiguous than elsewhere. Yet the way in which subalternity was implemented and experienced in Classical colonies is distinctive. Both the ideology of equality and cultural hybridization on the margins of the Greek world created specific conditions for subalternity and social visibility.

Ideologically, equality in the colonies was strictly limited to the citizen elite. It was defined in terms of equal landownership and citizenship, meaning active participation in political, cultural, and military activities in the urban center. In practical terms, the citizens were owners of equal-sized land-lots in the countryside living within the walled center. Archaeological and epigraphic evidence shows that most colonial settlements were laid out according to such a model: Especially in their early phases, these settlements were Ackerbürger colonies, i.e., communities of urban farmers/citizens. Craft production and trade were poorly developed (Chapters 4 and 7).

The Ackerbürger colony depended on the work of subaltern groups to compensate for the shortcomings of an economic system that was based entirely on landownership and agriculture. Yet colonial communities based on Greekness, citizenship, and equality left no space for different identities to emerge within the hegemonic discourse. All those who were not male citizens and landowners (women, artisans, non-Greeks, servants and slaves, children, tenants, rural dwellers) were excluded from the group of equals and thus largely invisible. This contributed to the condition of voicelessness and subalternity of these groups (Chapters 5 and 6).

Eventually, cultural hybridization began to undermine the oppositions that constituted the ideology of the Ackerbürger colony (citizen vs. noncitizen, Greek vs. barbarian, urban vs. rural, etc.). However, hybridity did not become a distinct culture and ideology in its own right, and thus remained highly ambiguous: it undermined elite culture, yet confirmed it at the same time.[1] Take language as an example: if the colonized use the language of the colonizing elite, they thereby subscribe to the cultural tradition of the colonizers; if they use alternative languages, the number of people capable of understanding could be much smaller and they risk not being heard. More generally speaking, if nonelite groups adopt the strategies of colonial elites (as embedded in economy, education, administration, politics, culture) this means submission, at least to a certain degree, to the hegemonic discourse; if they do not, they risk not having any impact at all.

Classical colonies were exposed to certain forms of hybridization that were typical of colonial areas. The struggle for survival and the lack of resources favored the break-up of traditional role models, especially in the case of women, children, and slaves. I have argued that this is eventually expressed in ritual, and that Artemis Bendis embodied female agency in colonial communities and frontier societies (Chapter 2). Likewise, burial ritual and votive offerings emphasize feminity and childhood since reproduction was a critical issue for these societies (Chapter 3).

The link between subalternity and hybridity is particularly clear in the case of rural populations. The political and cultural structure of the Ackerbürger colony excluded them from active participation, and thus contributed in important ways to the status of subalternity which was more pronounced in the colonies than in homeland communities. Although rural populations grew economically and demographically and their visibility increased, they remained excluded from elite status. On the one hand, they undermined the limits of citizenship and Greekness insofar as they represented an indeterminate category midway between citizens and noncitizens, Greeks and barbarians, urban and mountain dwellers. On the other hand, it is precisely this state of "inbetweenness" and cultural hybridity that ultimately confirms the idea of purity.[2] In Classical colonies, cultural hybridity was largely a characteristic of subaltern groups, while the citizen elite stuck to the cultural model of Greekness (Chapters 5 and 6).

---

[1] This process has been conceptualized by Bhabha 1994.
[2] On the links between concepts of hybridity and purity see Bhabha 1994 and, with regard to archaeology, Stockhammer 2012; Pappa 2013.

COLONIZATION AND CLASSICAL CULTURE

Authors like Herodotus, Aristophanes, Thucydides, and Xenophon who had direct knowledge of colonial settlements (Thurii, Eion, Amphipolis, etc.) were doubtless familiar with the way in which social hierarchies were created and enforced in the colonies. This may seem quite different from arguing that colonization and the experience of subalternity shaped Classical Greek culture as a whole – and yet that is the point I am trying to make in this chapter.[3]

There are many fields in which Classical Greek culture reveals the traces of colonization and subalternity in the colonies. As an example, I shall try to explore here how colonial practices affected political philosophy which was emerging as a new field in fifth- and fourth-century BC Greece. Political philosophy would have arguably developed differently without the background of colonization and subalternity described in the previous chapters.

Classical approaches to subalternity and political theory can be divided roughly into two major trends. On the one hand, philosophers from Hippodamus to Plato focused on the role played by subaltern groups in the polis. They tried to resolve the problem of social inequality by developing class systems in which every group had several specific functions. As Hannah Arendt has argued, these philosophers, in particular Plato, basically replace political action – which is always unpredictable – with the "fabrication" of political systems. Just like an artisan who fabricates something, Plato's "law giver" is supposed to create a stable political system.[4] It is probably no mere coincidence that this idea of fabricating political communities according to philosophical principles originated in a world where colonization and city foundations were a frequent occurrence. As we shall see, links between political philosophy and colonization actually emerge on various levels.

Things began to change in the fourth century BC: The idea of dividing the entire community into classes disappears, and the perspective is narrowed to elite citizens.[5] This emerges particularly clearly in Aristotle's *Politics*. From Aristotle onward, issues of social classes and subalternity are no longer considered crucial. As I will argue here, this development was due to the monetization of social relations and the divergence of social and physical spaces in the colonies. The entire development of political philosophy in the fifth and fourth centuries BC is only fully understandable against the backdrop of colonization.

---

[3]   I paraphrase Said here, when he states (1978: 11): 'I doubt if it is controversial, for example, to say that an Englishman in India, or Egypt, in the later nineteenth century, took an interest in those countries, which was never far from their status, in his mind, as British colonies. To say this may seem quite different from saying that all academic knowledge about India and Egypt is somehow tinged and impressed with, violated by, the gross political fact – and yet *that is what I am saying* in this study of Orientalism.'

[4]   Arendt 1958: 181–199.

[5]   Ober 1991; Leyden 1994.

POLITICAL PHILOSOPHY BEFORE PLATO

Phaleas of Chalcedon and Hippodamus of Miletus stand at the beginning of a philosophical tradition that reveals a series of colonial references if looked at more closely. I am aware that the question of when they lived is extremely controversial, which is why a few observations about chronology are required. Hippodamus of Miletus was probably born before 500 BC, since he was involved in the planning of the Piraeus and went to Thurii (founded 444/3 BC) later in his life. It is unlikely that he collaborated in the planning of the new urban center of Rhodos in 408 BC, as reported by Strabo XIV 2,9.[6] On the other hand, Phaleas, who is known to us from a short passage in book 2 of Aristotle's *Politics*, is sometimes considered a contemporary of Plato, although there is little evidence to support this view. According to some scholars there are certain parallels between Phaleas's and Plato's theories suggesting that Phaleas must have been active around 400 BC.[7] However, there are also some parallels between Phaleas and Hippodamus, who was active in the first half of the fifth century BC, as argued above.[8] Judging from book 2 of Aristotle's *Politics*, it actually seems likely that Phaleas was a contemporary of Hippodamus, or even older than him. For after dealing in length with Plato's *Republic* and the *Laws*, Aristotle mentions that there are also other constitutions, some designed by "amateurs," some by philosophers and politicians (1266a). He discusses two of them – Phaleas and Hippodamus – before turning to the traditional constitutions of Sparta and Crete. According to Aristotle, Phaleas was the *first* to address the question of equal property in the polis, whereas Hippodamus was "the first man not engaged in politics who attempted to speak on the subject of the best form of constitution."[9] The two philosophers are presented here as first inventors (of the idea of equal property in the case of Phaleas, of political theory as distinct from political practice in the case of Hippodamus), which suggests that Aristotle discusses them in chronological order. This is likely for yet another reason: Aristotle's knowledge of Phaleas's theories is even more cursory than his knowledge of Hippodamus. If Phaleas had been a contemporary of Plato, one would expect Aristotle to have much more detailed information. Therefore Phaleas was probably a predecessor or a contemporary of Hippodamus; he certainly was not a contemporary of Plato. At the same time, Aristotle (Pol. 1266b) makes a clear distinction between Phaleas on the one hand and Solon and other politicians of the "old times" who discussed property issues on the other. It is therefore likely that Phaleas lived considerably

---

[6]   Hoepfner, Schwandner 1994: 302.
[7]   Canfora 2011: 454–455.
[8]   Szidat 1980.
[9]   Pol. 1267b (transl. H. Rackham, 1944).

later than Solon and earlier than Plato, in other words between the second half of the sixth and the first half of the fifth century BC.

Joachim Szidat (1980) has argued, quite convincingly I believe, that in his discussion of Hippodamus, Aristotle drew on Athenian archives and traditions. This may explain why Aristotle presents Hippodamus as an inventor, although his alleged inventions – orthogonal grids and the division of the urban area into public and private zones – are archaeologically attested much earlier, in the seventh century BC.[10] The idea that Hippodamus invented all this when planning the Piraeus only makes sense from a local Athenian viewpoint.[11] By analogy, one of Aristotle's main sources about Phaleas may have been the *politeia* (constitution) of Phaleas's home town Chalcedon, which Aristotle studied for his collection of constitutions. During his stay at Plato's Academy, Aristotle met Xenocrates of Chalcedon with whom he is said to have gone on a trip to Assos;[12] Aristotle could have learned all he wanted about the history of Chalcedon from Xenocrates. If Aristotle obtained his information about Phaleas and Hippodamus from the study of local archives and traditions, this would explain why later authors (Strabo, Vitruvius, Pliny, etc.) who addressed similar issues but had no access to these sources mention little or nothing about Phaleas and Hippodamus.

PHALEAS

The starting point of Phaleas's political theory is equality. This has attracted the attention of modern writers, especially those with Marxist and left-wing approaches, such as Max Weber, Max Beer, Gérard Walter, Max Hamburger, and Giovanni Agnoli.[13] However, the relevant passage in Aristotle's *Politics* is not entirely clear:

> In the opinion of some, the regulation of property is the chief point of all, that being the question upon which all revolutions turn. This danger was recognized by Phaleas of Chalcedon, who was the first to affirm (*eisénenke*: literally 'introduced') that the citizens of a state ought to have equal possessions. He thought that in a new colony the equalization might be accomplished without difficulty, not so easily when a state was already established ...
>
> (Aristotle, Pol. 1266a; transl. H. Rackham, 1944)

Scholars continue to debate how the word *eispherein* (to introduce) is to be understood: Did Phaleas bring up the topic of economic equality in a merely

---

[10]   Mertens 2006: 63–89.
[11]   Szidat 1980: 39; see also Gill 2006.
[12]   Strabo XIII 1,57.
[13]   On the reception of Phaleas see Balot 2001; Canfora 2011: 454–456.

theoretical manner or was he an active politician who introduced egalitarian laws?[14] If Aristotle drew his knowledge of Phaleas from the constitution
of Chalcedon, the latter hypothesis is more likely, for someone only occupied with theory would hardly have been included in the political history
of Chalcedon or any other city. Of course, Aristotle might have used other
sources of which we are unaware. Whatever the case, in the history of Late
Archaic Chalcedon (the period in which Phaleas probably lived), there were
several occasions when new laws and a redistribution of land (Phaleas was concerned primarily with landownership: Pol. 1267b) may have been introduced.
When the Persian king Darius returned from his Scythian expedition in 512
BC, he destroyed the city, since the citizens of Calchedon were suspected of
having plotted to demolish the bridge over the Bosporus.[15] Several years later,
the Persian satrap Otanes captured the city (Hdt. V 26). Later, Calchedon participated in the Ionian revolt and was attacked by a Persian fleet in 493 BC. On
this occasion, some citizens fled to Mesambria on the Black Sea, a city founded
jointly by Calchedon and its own mother-city Megara about twenty years earlier (this is where Phaleas might have gotten his insights into colonization).[16]
It is not entirely clear whether Calchedon was recaptured by the Persians. In
any case, a military campaign under the Spartan general Pausanias (Thuc. I 94)
in 478 BC would have put an end to Persian dominance. In the fifth century
BC, Calchedon became a member of the Delian League.

Like Hippodamus of Miletus, Phaleas of Chalcedon was probably first and
foremost a philosopher in the Ionian tradition who offered practical advice
to his city or to other cities during and/or after the Persian wars. Apart from
the introduction of egalitarian laws, maybe through a redistribution of land,
Phaleas developed several political ideas that were purely theoretical such as
equality in education (Aristotle criticizes him for not specifying what he meant
by education: Pol. 1266b). Phaleas also commented on the role of artisans in
the polis, where he put forward an audacious idea (Aristotle, Pol. 1267b). Since
the correct translation of some terms is still the subject of debate, I quote here
from the original Greek:

> φαίνεται δ' ἐκ τῆς νομοθεσίας κατασκευάζων τὴν πόλιν μικράν, εἴ γ' οἱ
> τεχνῖται πάντες δημόσιοι ἔσονται καὶ μὴ πλήρωμά τι παρέξονται τῆς
> πόλεως. ἀλλ' εἴπερ δεῖ δημοσίους εἶναι τοὺς τὰ κοινὰ ἐργαζομένους,
> δεῖ καθάπερ ἐν Ἐπιδάμνῳ τε καὶ ὡς Διόφαντός ποτε κατεσκεύαζεν
> Ἀθήνησι τοῦτον ἔχειν τὸν τρόπον.

And it is clear from Phaleas's legislation that he makes the citizen-
population a small one, inasmuch as all the artisans are to be publicly

---

[14] Canfora 2011: 454–455.
[15] See Avram 2004: 979.
[16] Avram 2004: 980.

owned slaves and are not to furnish any complement of the citizen-body. But if it is proper to have public slaves, the laborers employed upon the public works ought to be of that status as is the case at Epidamnos and as Diophantos once tried to institute at Athens.

(transl. H. Rackham, 1944, slightly altered)

The word *demosioi* is often translated as "publicly owned slaves" or "public slaves." They could not of course have been part of the citizen-body. However, Gérard Walter (1931: 316–317) and others have objected that *demosios* might also indicate some kind of public appointee.[17] According to this view, Phaleas aimed to bring craft production completely under the control of the state, though not by using public slaves (unfortunately, we are unfamiliar with the cases of Epidamnos and Athens alluded to in the text). Much depends on the interpretation of the word *pleroma*. The text implies that the alternative to artisans being *demosioi* is their being a "complement" *(pleroma)* of the city. In the view of those who interpret *demosioi* as public slaves, this means that artisans are either public slaves or a supplementary part *(pleroma)* of the citizen-body. Those who interpret *demosioi* as public appointees view this differently. Luciano Canfora (2011: 455), for example, argues (following Walter) that what is actually intended here is that either the artisans were a mere "complement" of the city in the sense that they were completely excluded from the polis, or they were an integral part of the polis insofar as they were *demosioi* or public appointees.

In my opinion, the first interpretation is far more convincing. It is indeed likely that Phaleas advocated the use of public slaves in the field of craft production, thus placing himself in an aristocratic tradition inspired by the model of Sparta.[18] When applied to a person, *demosios* normally has the meaning public slave/servant.[19] Moreover, the word *pleroma* is little more than an objective description of the status of artisans in most Greek cities: The importance of craft production was generally acknowledged, but artisans were despised and marginalized by the ruling classes. In this context, artisans actually appear to be some sort of complement. They were needed to form a fully autarchic polis, but they were not admitted to the elite group of landowners and active citizens who formed the polis in the narrow sense of the term.

Phaleas had various opportunities to engage with colonization and land redistribution during his lifetime. Furthermore, colonization was actually one of the very premises of his thinking, as becomes clear from the *Politics* (1266b) where Aristotle says that Phaleas "thought that this [ensuring equality among

---

[17] Walter 1931: 316–317; Canfora 2011: 455.
[18] Henkel 1872: 165; Newman 1887, II: 293; Pöhlmann 1893: 266–267; Guthrie 1969: 152.
[19] Liddell, H.G., Scott, R., Jones, H.S. 1996. *A Greek-English Lexicon, 9th edition: With a revised supplement*, s.v. *demosios*. Oxford: Oxford University Press.

all citizens] would not be difficult to secure at the outset for cities in the process of foundation."

In a historical context of colonization and resettlement, Phaleas came up with the idea of a class of equal citizens. He added a subaltern class of craftsmen to the class of citizens to ensure the survival and economic independence of the community. However one interprets the term *demosioi* in Aristotle's text, Phaleas's ideal state consisted of an egalitarian class of landowners and a class of *technitai* owned and/or controlled by the landowners who *constituted* the polis. Given the series of dramatic events that took place in Phaleas's hometown Calchedon during the late Archaic and early Classical periods, his class model may be considered a reaction to instability and social change.

HIPPODAMUS

Class models remained *en vogue* throughout the fifth century BC. Like Phaleas, Hippodamus imagined a class of artisans for his ideal state. In addition, he divided farmers and warriors (who were not distinguished by Phaleas) into two separate classes, thus arriving at a total number of three classes. Our main source is once again Aristotle (Pol. 1267b–1269a):

> His system was for a city with a population of ten thousand, divided into three classes; for he made one class of artisans, one of farmers, and the third the class that fought for the state in war and was the armed class. He divided the land into three parts, one sacred, one public and one private: sacred land to supply the customary offerings to the gods, common land to provide the warrior class with food, and private land to be owned by the farmers.
>
> (Pol. 1267b, transl. H. Rackham, 1944)

According to Aristotle, in Hippodamus's ideal state the warriors practically own the public land and dominate the two other classes. The farmers have no weapons, the artisans neither weapons nor land. In theory all classes are part of the citizen-body and eligible for political office. Aristotle criticizes the fact that it remains unclear who works the fields of the warrior class and to whom the farmers sell/give their surplus (to the artisans and/or to the warriors, although the latter had land of their own).

In modern scholarship, Hippodamus is often seen primarily as an urban planner and architect,[20] but the evidence does not support such views. Hippodamus was primarily occupied with political philosophy and physics.[21] He contributed to the reconstruction of the Piraeus after 479 BC, but his contribution may have been limited to the measurement and the allotment

---

[20] Ehrenberg 1973: 239–240; Bengtson 1977: 205–206; Hoepfner, Schwandner 1994: 302.
[21] Szidat 1980: 44.

of the land.[22] Aristotle's statement that Hippodamus "invented the division of cities and parceled the Piraeus" (τὴν τῶν πόλεων διαίρεσιν εὗρε καὶ τὸν Πειραιᾶ κατέτεμεν) might be understood in the sense that he was the first who proposed a division of the citizens into various classes.[23] We have seen that Phaleas had excluded the artisans from the polis, which thus remained a totally homogeneous community of citizens/landowners. The real invention of Hippodamus might not have been the orthogonal street system (this perhaps was a later misunderstanding), but the division of the citizen-body into three classes based on the division of labor (rather than on tax classes as advocated by Solon and others). Hippodamus's activity in Piraeus is mentioned by Aristotle in a list of other activities linked by a series of καὶ (and).[24] This suggests that land measurement and urban planning were not Hippodamus's main occupation, but only one of his activities.

THE CULTURAL BACKGROUND OF CLASS THEORY

The Greeks of the fifth century BC did not consider class theory as something genuinely Greek. Rather, they thought of it as something that had been developed in other regions, namely in Egypt and Mesopotamia, and had only been adopted in Greece in relatively recent times. Apart from Plato, this becomes clear from book 2 of Herodotus's *Histories* (II 164–8):

> The Egyptians are divided into seven classes: priests, warriors, cowherds, swineherds, merchants, interpreters, and pilots. There are this many classes, each named after its occupation. The warriors are divided into Kalasiries and Hermotubies, and they belong to the following districts (for all divisions in Egypt are made according to districts). The Hermotubies are from the districts of Busiris, Saïs, Khemmis, and Papremis, the island called Prosopitis, and half of Natho – from all of these; their number, at its greatest, attained to a hundred and sixty thousand. None of these has learned any common trade; they are free to follow the profession of arms

---

[22] Szidat 1980: 33.

[23] Gorman 1995.

[24] Cf. Gehrke 1989: 58. The whole phrase reads: "Ἱππόδαμος δὲ Εὐρυφῶντος Μιλήσιος (ὃς καὶ τὴν τῶν πόλεων διαίρεσιν εὗρε καὶ τὸν Πειραιᾶ κατέτεμεν, γενόμενος καὶ περὶ τὸν ἄλλον βίον περιττότερος διὰ φιλοτιμίαν οὕτως ὥστε δοκεῖν ἐνίοις ζῆν περιεργότερον τριχῶν τε πλήθει καὶ κόσμῳ πολυτελεῖ, ἔτι δὲ ἐσθῆτος εὐτελοῦς μὲν ἀλεεινῆς δέ, οὐκ ἐν τῷ χειμῶνι μόνον ἀλλὰ καὶ περὶ τοὺς θερινοὺς χρόνους, λόγιος δὲ καὶ περὶ τὴν ὅλην φύσιν εἶναι βουλόμενος) πρῶτος τῶν μὴ πολιτευομένων ἐνεχείρησέ τι περὶ πολιτείας εἰπεῖν τῆς ἀρίστης." Transl. H. Rackham, 1944, slightly altered: "Hippodamus son of Euryphon, a Milesian (who invented the division of cities and cut up the Piraeus, and who also became somewhat eccentric in his general mode of life owing to a desire for distinction, so that some people thought that he lived too fussily, with a quantity of hair and expensive ornaments, and also a quantity of cheap yet warm clothes not only in winter but also in the summer periods, and who wished to be a man of learning in natural science generally), was the first man not engaged in politics who attempted to speak on the subject of the best form of constitution."

alone. The Kalasiries are from the districts of Thebes, Bubastis, Aphthis, Tanis, Mendes, Sebennys, Athribis, Pharbaïthis, Thmuis, Onuphis, Anytis, Myecphoris (this last is in an island opposite the city of Bubastis) – from all of these; their number, at its greatest, attained to two hundred and fifty thousand men. These too may practise no trade but war, which is their hereditary calling. Now whether this, too, the Greeks have learned from the Egyptians, I cannot confidently judge. I know that in Thrace and Scythia and Persia and Lydia and nearly all foreign countries, those who learn trades are held in less esteem than the rest of the people, and those who have least to do with artisans' work, especially men who are free to practise the art of war, are highly honored. This much is certain: that this opinion, which is held by all Greeks and particularly by the Lacedaemonians, is of foreign origin. It is in Corinth that artisans are held in least contempt. The warriors were the only Egyptians, except the priests, who had special privileges: for each of them an untaxed plot of twelve acres was set apart. This acre is a square of a hundred Egyptian cubits each way, the Egyptian cubit being equal to the Samian. These lands were set apart for all; it was never the same men who cultivated them, but each in turn.

(transl. A.D. Godley, 1920)

It is of course unclear where Herodotus got his information from and how accurate it is. Moreover, we know very little about the economic and social structure of Egyptian society during the twenty-sixth and twenty-seventh dynasties (672–404 BC). The two groups of warriors mentioned by Herodotus (Kalasiries and Hermotubies) actually appear in some demotic papyri. There are also some papyrus fragments mentioning the apportionment of land to soldiers belonging to these groups. An Aramaic papyrus in Munich from 515 BC mentions a foreign soldier leasing land to an Egyptian farmer.[25]

The Persians, who ruled Egypt during the First Achaemenid Period (twenty-seventh dynasty, 525–404 BC), may have modified the traditional social order of Egypt, possibly by introducing a new class system. Ancient sources suggest that the Persians originally distinguished between four classes: priests, warriors, farmers, and artisans. Here, too, there are parallels with Hippodamus and Phaleas.[26]

However, the number of classes that existed in Egypt and Persia and how they were structured is perhaps not particularly significant here; the important thing is that the Greeks ascribed the idea of class society to other peoples, as clearly indicated by Herodotus. With regard to Egypt, Plato refers to six classes: priests, artisans, warriors, herdsmen, hunters, farmers, and further opinions on the number and function of Egyptian classes can be found in authors

[25] Schütze, forthcoming.
[26] Ehtécham 1946: 29–32; Gehrke 1989: 63.

from the fourth century BC onward.[27] Greek philosophers and historians who lived in a world of instability and continuous social struggle seem to have been fascinated by the presumed immutability of the Egyptian class system.[28] Social theorists of the fifth century BC aimed to adopt similar systems and to concentrate political power in the hands of the warriors and landowners who formed the ruling class (as there was no priestly class in Greece). In the eyes of Herodotus and his contemporaries, Sparta was the polis that came closest to this ideal, and there was even a tradition of viewing the Egyptian *machimoi* (warrior class) as prototypes for the Spartan *homoioi*.[29]

PLATO ABANDONS CLASS THEORY

Greek class theory culminated in Plato's *Republic*, the first drafts of which circulated as early as the 390s BC.[30] Here, the polis is divided into three classes: farmers and artisans, warriors, and the "guardians." The latter are not really a distinct class but rather elderly wise warriors in charge of ruling the state. Plato further envisaged the emancipation of women and their inclusion within the class system of the polis.[31]

In the *Laws*, however, Plato dismisses the idea of dividing the citizens into classes of specialists for craft production and agriculture, warfare, and government. He returns to the idea that artisans and merchants should be excluded from the citizen-body as advocated by Phaleas. Dividing the polis into classes of farmers, artisans, and warriors had been a means of guaranteeing economic autarky, at least in theory. Interestingly, when Plato abandons the idea of citizen classes, he does not come up with any consistent alternative (nor does Aristotle, as we shall see). Thus, in terms of economic theory, the problem of autarky remains unresolved. In the *Republic*, Plato broaches the question of the best state by asking what is meant by justice. He then goes on to ask what professions are required to supply all essential needs, starting with shelter, food, and clothing (368b–c). In this case, Plato views the origin of the state as a community of different specialists. As he states in book 2 (*Rep.* 369d–e), the "indispensable minimum of a city would consist of four or five men," namely a farmer, a builder, a weaver, a cobbler and "some other purveyor for the needs of the body." The division of labor lies at the very origin of the *Republic*. In the *Laws*, on the other hand, the same question of how to divide labor (agriculture, craft production, trade, etc.) is discussed at a much later point in two short passages in the middle of the work. The starting point is not justice, but laws (hence the

---

[27] Lloyd 1993: 182.
[28] Lloyd 1993: 183.
[29] *Ibid*, Cf. Janni 1984.
[30] Canfora 2014: 16–32.
[31] Samaras 2010; Canfora 2014: 40–41.

title) and rights; not essential needs and their fulfillment as a sort of dialectic origin of political communities, as in the *Republic*, but the question of what rights correspond to the ethical purpose of the state. Following the logic of ethics (and not of economics as in the *Republic*), Plato reaches the conclusion that the best state should consist of a citizen-body of landowners. The citizens could be divided into several census classes (*timemata* in contrast to social classes, or *mere*, the term used by earlier theorists), though only within a certain range: the wealthiest must not possess more than four times the original land-lot, which is the inalienable minimum possession of each citizen. The *Laws* continue to focus on this class of (male) citizens and landowners. It is no coincidence that the text states practically nothing about the role of women. The discussion of the role of women in book 6 (781a–d) sounds almost like an excuse for the revolutionary positions held in the *Republic*.[32] It is also no coincidence that the first social group to be defined in the *Laws* are free male citizens, where Plato argues that all of them should be landowners (744a–745e). The role of other groups, namely artisans and merchants, is discussed much later, in book 8 (846d–848b). Plato stresses that neither locals (citizens) nor their slaves shall be numbered among those who engage in artisanal production and crafts (846d). All artisans are therefore foreigners/strangers *(xenoi:* cf. 848a) in other words people that do not technically belong to the polis.[33]

ARISTOTLE'S BEST STATE

Aristotle's best state as described in book 7 of the *Politics* owes much to Plato's *Laws*, as becomes evident from various aspects: citizenship is confined to an elite of warriors and landowners; each citizen shall own two land-lots, one near the city and one near the border of the territory; and artisans and merchants are excluded from citizenship. Yet, the *Politics* go further.

What is new in the light of Classical political theory is the fact that Aristotle does not even raise the question of what social and economic position artisans and other nonelite groups should have in the state and what their living conditions should be. While Plato spent some energy on this (elaborating on the problem of money which he attempted to avoid as far as possible), Aristotle systematically defers economic issues in his discussion of the best state. The following passage is the most detailed statement about the role of subaltern groups in Aristotle's *Politics*, and yet it is full of opaque allusions and presuppositions:

> Since the state also contains the military class and the class that deliberates about matters of policy and judges questions of justice, and these

---

[32] Cf. Canfora 2014: 287–293.
[33] On the development of Plato's political theory, see Morrow 1960; Klasko 2006.

are manifestly in a special sense parts of the state, are these classes also to be set down as distinct or are both functions to be assigned to the same persons? But here also the answer is clear, because in a certain sense they should be assigned to the same persons, but in a certain sense to different ones. Inasmuch as each of these two functions belongs to a different prime of life, and one requires wisdom, the other strength, they are to be assigned to different people; but inasmuch as it is a thing impossible that when a set of men are able to employ force and to resist control, these should submit always to be ruled, from this point of view both functions must be assigned to the same people; for those who have the power of arms have the power to decide whether the constitution shall stand or fall. The only course left them is to assign this constitutional function to both sets of men without distinction, yet not simultaneously, but, as in the natural order of things strength is found in the younger men and wisdom in the elder, it seems to be expedient and just for their functions to be allotted to both in this way, for this mode of division possesses conformity with merit. Moreover the ownership of properties also must be centered round these classes, for the citizens must necessarily possess plentiful means, and these are the citizens. For the artisan class has no share in the state, nor has any other class that is not 'an artificer of virtue.' And this is clear from our basic principle; for in conjunction with virtue happiness is bound to be forthcoming, but we should pronounce a state happy having regard not to a particular section of it but to all its citizens. And it is also manifest that the properties must belong to these classes, inasmuch as it is necessary for the tillers of the soil to be slaves or barbarians living in the area. There remains of the list enumerated the class of priests; and the position of this class also is manifest. Priests must be appointed neither from the tillers of the soil nor from the artisans, for it is seemly that the gods should be worshipped by citizens; and since the citizen body is divided into two parts, the military class and the councilor class, and as it is seemly that those who have relinquished these duties owing to age should render to the gods their due worship and should spend their retirement in their service, it is to these that the priestly offices should be assigned.

We have therefore stated the things indispensable for the constitution of a state, and the things that are parts of a state: tillers of the soil, craftsmen and the laboring class generally are a necessary appurtenance of states, but the military and deliberative classes are parts of the state; and moreover each of these divisions is separate from the others, either permanently or by turn.

And that it is proper for the state to be divided up into classes and for the military class to be distinct from that of the tillers of the soil does not seem to be a discovery of political philosophers of today or one made recently. In Egypt this arrangement still exists even now, as also in Crete; it is said to have been established in Egypt by the legislation of Sesostris and in Crete by that of Minos. Common meals also seem to be an ancient institution, those in Crete having begun in the reign of Minos, while those in Italy are much older than these. According to the historians one of the settlers there, a certain Italus, became king of Oenotria, and from him they took the name of Italians instead of that of Oenotrians, and the name of Italy was given to all that promontory of Europe lying between the Gulfs of Scylletium and of Lametus, which are half a day's journey apart.

[There follows an excursus on Italy and Egypt.]

It has been stated before that the land ought to be owned by those who possess arms and those who share the rights of the constitution, and why the cultivators ought to be a different class from these, and what is the proper extent and conformation of the country. We have now to discuss first the allotment of the land, and the proper class and character of its cultivators; since we advocate not common ownership of land, as some have done, but community in it brought about in a friendly way by the use of it, and we hold that no citizen should be ill supplied with means of subsistence. As to common meals, all agree that this is an institution advantageous for well-organized states to possess; our own reasons for sharing this view we will state later. But the common meals must be shared by all the citizens, and it is not easy for the poor to contribute their assessed share from their private means and also to maintain their household as well. And moreover the expenses connected with religion are the common concern of the whole state. It is necessary therefore for the land to be divided into two parts, of which one must be common and the other the private property of individuals; and each of these two divisions must again be divided in two.

[There follow some thoughts about the right way to divide the land.]

Those who are to cultivate the soil should best of all, if the ideal system is to be stated, be slaves, not drawn from people all of one tribe nor of a spirited character (for thus they would be both serviceable for their work and safe to abstain from insurrection), but as a second best they should be neighboring barbarians *(barbaroi perioikoi)* of a similar nature. Of these laborers those in private employment must be among the private possessions of the owners of the estates, and those working on the common land common property. How slaves should be employed, and why it is advantageous that all slaves should have their freedom set before them as a reward, we will say later.

(Aristotle, Pol. 1329a-1330a, transl. H. Rackham, 1944, slightly altered. Note that the promise in the last phrase is not fulfilled in the preserved text.)

With regard to the questions discussed here, three points are particularly important:

- Aristotle speaks of classes *(mere)* but he does not specify how these classes are to be created. He claims that neither "tillers of the soil" nor artisans and merchants shall be citizens. The citizen-body of Aristotle's best state consists of warriors who own all the land and who alone are worthy to serve as priests.

- Unlike Plato, Aristotle says almost nothing about the role of women in the state; in the *Politics*, women are practically absent.[34]

- The position and living conditions of peasants and barbarians in the best state remain obscure. Unlike Plato, Aristotle says nothing about how and where they should live, whether they may become citizens, whether they shall be obliged to do military service, and so forth. Likewise, it remains completely unclear what status the *barbaroi perioikoi* have within the polis. Are they included in the social hierarchy as subaltern serfs, or do they belong to separate communities of non-Greeks?

It might appear paradoxical, but Plato the "idealist" says a lot more about the living conditions of women, slaves, artisans, and merchants than his pupil Aristotle. This does not mean that the exploitative and discriminating attitude towards nonelite groups changed significantly from the fifth to the fourth centuries BC. Only Epicurus would break with this tradition by admitting women and slaves to his circle, but this took place in the context of a radically anti-political philosophy. Epicurus did not argue against Plato or against Aristotle's *Politics*, but against politics in general. For obvious reasons, he is not considered a political philosopher.

By elaborating on Plato's *Laws*, Aristotle radically revises the relationship between politics (especially citizenship) and economics. Aristotle's main concern is the question of how the citizens can achieve a good life. He deliberately separates this question from economic issues such as subsistence and the division of labor, and thus separates two fields that belonged together in Plato's *Republic*. As Jean-Pierre Vernant has observed, fifth century BC class theory did make some attempts to separate the military sphere from that of economics. Vernant (1978: 226) states: "*Il s'aggissait pour Hippodame, en isolant la fonction militaire, proche par sa nature du politique, de la purifier de tout contact avec la vie économique, avec cette sphère d'intérêts privés qui apparaît maintenant comme un facteur de division et d'opposition entre les citoyens.*"[35] In the *Laws* and in Aristotle's *Politics*, this idea is developed further: the political sphere as a whole is now purified from the economic sphere. This process has been labeled in various ways: from the "discovery of the economy" (K. Polanyi 1957) to the "genesis of the economic space" (L. Ruggiu 1982). More recent studies have put the idea of a "Great Divide" in the fourth century BC into perspective by pointing out that the origins of economic theory actually date back to the fifth

---

[34] See Deslauriers 2015.

[35] "For Hippodamus, it was about isolating the military sphere, which by its nature was associated with politics, and purifying it from any contact with economic life as a sphere of private interest that now appeared as a factor of division and opposition between the citizens."

century BC.[36] Yet fourth-century political theory accelerated a process that had begun earlier. What is still lacking is a reading that relates these developments to Greek colonization.

POLITICAL PHILOSOPHY AND CLASSICAL COLONIZATION

I argue here that Aristotle's conceptualization of citizenship and subalternity should be seen against the backdrop of colonial practices in Classical Greece. As arbitrary and enigmatic as his statements about peasants and barbarians may appear in the context of "pure" philosophy, they are coherent and understandable within the historical context of Classical colonization.[37]

Aristotle did not find significant empirical data on class systems as formulated by Phaleas, Hippodamus, and the young Plato. He could not think of any polis where all artisans were public slaves, as advocated by Phaleas.[38] Nor did he come across Greek cities where the citizens were formally divided into classes of warriors and/or landowners, farmers, and artisans. At this point, Aristotle returns to the ideal of a citizen-class of landowners and warriors, just like Plato in the *Laws*, but he avoids discussing the economic implications of this model. Aristotle's 'best state' does not include any kind of redistribution system, such as Plato's Cretan colony, nor is the status of noncitizens clearly defined. It remains totally unclear who the *georgoi, banausoi,* and *barbaroi* in Aristotle's text are, where they come from, and how they relate to the polis.

In this context, the fact that Aristotle develops a theory of money should not be underestimated. Throughout his philosophical work, Plato aimed to restrict the use of money to a minimum. By contrast, Aristotle emphasizes the usefulness of money.[39] What is important here is that Aristotle's positive view of money allows him to defer the problem of subalternity and subsistence to the field of economics. Put shortly, the life of the citizens is determined by ethics, the life of all the others by the market. It is not some group or class of people that have to provide the necessary goods for the citizens, but the market. The question of how and by whom these goods were produced vanishes behind the efficiency of a monetized economy.

It is at this point that Aristotle's political thought reveals its colonial background. As we have seen, most Classical colonies were created as agricultural

---

[36]   Descat 2010; Pébarthe 2012.

[37]   Purely philosophical approaches aimed at offering a practical critique and reevaluation of Aristotle (e.g., Nussbaum 1990; Butler 2010) tend to see his statements on slaves and women as rather arbitrary, marginal, or even "stupid" accessories that do not really affect the core concepts of his thinking. Cf. Knoll 2009.

[38]   Aristotle's observations in Pol. II 1267b suggest that the closest example he could think of was Epidamnus, maybe because public works were carried out by public slaves there: Canfora 2011: 454.

[39]   von Reden 1995: 184–187; Peacock 2013: 134–135.

communities. The citizen-body in most Greek colonies of the fifth and fourth centuries BC consisted of a class of landowners and warriors – Ackerbürger poleis in the terminology of Max Weber. The model of the Ackerbürger polis entailed significant economic shortcomings: It could only survive with the help of subaltern groups and wider economic networks.

If Aristotle omitted issues like labor and subsistence in his discussion of the best state, he probably did so not because he did not know better, but because colonial experience suggested that this was a reasonable approach. In terms of ideology, the colonies were independent communities of landowners and warriors. The fact that they depended *de facto* on the work of subaltern groups and trade was hidden below the surface. The foundation process and the official political structure of Classical colonies suggested that a polis could be created out of a community of citizens/landowners, and that everything else would somehow work out. For the official image of the colony was that of an independent Ackerbürger polis, while the intrinsic interdependence of the colony, linked to subaltern groups and interregional networks, remained largely invisible. In other words, if someone like Aristotle had no problem in separating the spheres of politics and economics, he was encouraged to do so by the illusion that an independent Ackerbürger polis could exist. This illusion was fostered by colonial ideology and practice.

Colonial practice	Political theory
De iure, independent communities of landowners and warriors	Discussion of the best state limited to status of male citizens as landowners and warriors
De facto, agricultural economies that depended heavily on larger economic networks and support from outside	The living conditions of other groups are located within economic discourse

Through law, urban planning, and culture, the colony was identified with the elite of male citizens. Women, slaves, barbarians, children, artisans, and peasants are not mentioned in any foundation decree or official account of a colony from the Classical period. The foundation decree of Korkyra Melaina mentions the settlers and the local ruler Pyllos and his son. There is not the slightest hint of other locals, specialist laborers or women in the text. If Aristotle treats noncitizens so superficially, this has a background in colonial practice. Aristotle was aware that despite the limitations of the Ackerbürger polis, most colonies managed to survive somehow – some of them even developed into regional centers. In the colonies, the role of women, artisans, barbarians, slaves, and peasants was not formerly defined and fixed. These groups eventually emerged and contributed to the survival of the community, but they remained marginal and voiceless. Aristotle's statements on agricultural laborers are particularly revealing in this regard. In the text passage quoted earlier in the chapter, the organization of agricultural labor in the best state is addressed in two short passages. There is no further reference to the subject in any other passage of the work (at least not in its preserved state).[40] First, Aristotle states that "it is necessary for the tillers of the soil to be slaves or neighboring barbarians" (1329a). Then, in 1330a, he points out that "those who are to cultivate the soil should best of all, if the ideal system is to be stated, be slaves, not drawn from people all of one tribe nor of a spirited character (...), but as a second best they should be neighboring barbarians *(barbaroi perioikoi)* of a similar nature." The text remains enigmatic for a series of reasons: If the second best solution is using barbarians, does this mean that the agricultural slaves mentioned before are Greeks? Or should agricultural slaves be barbarians, while the *barbaroi perioikoi* would be formally free dependent laborers from non-Greek communities in the vicinity? What juridical, economic, or cultural relations exist between the *barbaroi perioikoi* and the polis? Furthermore, how could the polis control the ethnic structure of the agricultural slaves, if the land and the slaves in the best state are private rather common property (cf. Pol. 1263a)?

These are some of the questions that find no answers in the text and may be understood only within the historical context of Classical colonization. The idea that the land should be worked by slaves is clearly inspired by the model of Sparta, only that unlike the Helots, the slaves in the best state are supposed to be of heterogeneous ethnic origin. We have seen that most colonies of the fifth and fourth centuries BC originated in rather primitive agricultural settlements that did not permit any formal division of the population into warriors/landowners and farmers. This may explain why Aristotle comes up with a second best solution. In this context he refers to *barbaroi perioikoi*, thereby revealing that he has some colonial setting in mind (in mainland Greece it would make little sense to draw on such groups). Aristotle might have thought of barbarized Greek farmers who lived in the countryside or of rural dwellers from neighboring communities that entertained economic relations with Greek colonies.

In Chapter 6, I tried to show how these groups were united by hybrid identities and economic interests that opposed them to the central-place. The fact that Aristotle indirectly compares their status to that of slaves is hardly surprising in the context of colonization, given that rural populations were not only perceived as less Greek and more barbarian, but also as politically declassed members of the community. In a sense, the vagueness of Aristotle's statements about agricultural slaves and barbarians corresponds to the hybrid and marginal status of rural dwellers in many Greek colonies.

---

[40] On the unity and structure of the text, see the summary and bibliography in Deslauriers, Destrée 2013: 7–8.

There is another important reason why Aristotle may have chosen not to define the economic and juridical relations between agricultural laborers (slaves/barbarians), artisans, and citizens: his belief in money and the workings of the market. In a monetized economy, the juridical and ethnic status of the producers of necessary goods may indeed appear to be a secondary matter. As long as these goods are supplied, the political role of their producers appears of negligible importance. Note the difference with Phaleas and Plato, for whom agricultural and craft production were highly political issues.

The separation of politics and economics that emerges in Plato's *Laws* and even more clearly in Aristotle's works, was a new feature in terms of political theory, but it was prefigured in colonial practices. We have seen that the Ackerbürger model was widely diffused. From an economic viewpoint, this model was clearly a failure, since it stifled economic development and autarky, and made the colonies reliant on their mother-cities and larger regional networks. At the same time, the shortcomings of the Ackerbürger polis were relocated in the emerging field of economics which was separated from ethics and politics. Politically, the colonies were egalitarian communities of landowners. The fact that they were economically dependent on the labor of subaltern groups whose hybrid identities undermined Classical concepts of citizenship and Greekness could be screened out thanks to monetization and interregional trade. Thus, the topographical layout of colonial settlements (their "geometry" as seemingly egalitarian, nucleated settlements of urban farmers) diverges drastically from the complex and far-reaching economic geography of the communities that lived in these settlements. As in the globalized world of today, though on a much smaller scale, monetization and interregional trade allowed the physical and political separation of citizen communities from subaltern groups whose labor force guaranteed the survival of these communities – a separation that fostered the illusion that the polis could be organized entirely around a class of male citizens.

What remains hidden is that it was interregional networks, trade, and monetization that made it possible to establish communities of equal male citizens without defining the role and status of subaltern groups. This may have been different in the Archaic period, when the colonies had to produce all necessary goods locally. In the Classical period, the economic shortcomings of colonial communities could be overcome by support from larger networks. This is clear in many colonial settlements, but also in some fourth century BC foundations in Caria.[41] If the question of what role barbarians, children, women, slaves, and peasants should play in a Greek polis was no longer seen as a political question (i.e., as one regarding citizenship), these settlements confirmed such an approach. This does not mean that subaltern groups were now ignored in

---

[41] Caliò 2012: 379–388.

Greek philosophy. But the life and work of subaltern groups was no longer a matter of politics in the strict sense. Instead, it became a matter of economics and ethics. One generation after Aristotle, Epicurus admitted women and slaves to his circle without this becoming a political issue. But this happened at a time when the question of who produced food, wove fabrics, built houses, and made shoes was no longer seen as a political problem.

If the discussion of minimum wages and social welfare in Europe and North America is separated from the discussion of working and living conditions in Third World countries (conditions that heavily influence prices and living standards in the West), this kind of discursive separation belongs to the tradition of Plato's *Laws* and Aristotle.[42] As Bernard Williams (1993) has pointed out, the way in which modern Western democracies view the conditions of subaltern groups in other parts of the world as some sort of natural state of affairs or necessity may be compared to attitudes towards slavery and subalternity in ancient authors such as Plato and Aristotle.

As I have tried to demonstrate, colonization and subalternity in the colonies indirectly contributed to the relocation of political theory into an abstract, ideal space, while the places of daily life and work were obscured by the shadows of money and trade – two highly suspect fields in the eyes of Classical philosophers and their successors. From the Classical period onward, the economy has become an epistemological tool for referring to production and consumption, and the necessities of life in general – without interfering with the abstract space of the political sphere. If equality and justice (in terms of rights, education, access to resources, etc.) are located today not in a globalized economic space but in political spaces defined by national territories, this has its roots in the colonial practices and ideologies of Classical Greece. In practice and theory, Classical colonization has laid the foundations for the systematic concealment of exploitation and subalternity through the abstract space of the political.

[42] On the impact of Aristotle on Medieval and Modern economic theories, see Meikle 1995.

BIBLIOGRAPHY

Achebe, C. 1977. An Image of Africa. *The Massachusetts Review* 18.4: 782–794.

Adamesteanu, D. 1969. Siris-Heraclea. Scavi, ricerche e considerazioni storico-topografiche. In *Policoro 1959–1969: dieci anni di autonomia comunale*, 189–224. Lecce: Matino.

Adamesteanu, D. 1970. L'attività archeologica in Basilicata. In *Atti del 10° Convegno di Studi sulla Magna Grecia*, 467–485. Taranto: Istituto per la Storia e l'Archeologia della Magna Grecia.

Adamesteanu, D. 1972. Greci e indigeni nell'agro di Heraclea (Policoro). *Atti dell'Accademia nazionale dei Lincei, Classe di scienze morali, storiche e filologiche: Memorie* 26: 643–651.

Adamesteanu, D. 1973. Le suddivisioni di terra nel Metapontino. In Finley, M.I. (ed.). *Problèmes de la terre en Gréce ancienne*, 49–61. Paris: Mouton.

Adamesteanu, D. (ed.) 1974. *La Basilicata antica*. Cava de'Tirreni: Di Mauro.

Adamesteanu, D., Dilthey, H. 1978. Siris. Nuovi contributi archeologici. *Mélanges de l'École française de Rome – Antiquité* 90: 515–565.

Adam-Veleni, P., Poulaki, E., Tzanavari, K. (eds.) 2003. *Ancient Country Houses on Modern Roads: Central Macedonia*. Athens: The Archaeological Receipts Fund.

Alcock, S.E., Cherry, J.F., Davis, J.L. 1994. Intensive Survey, Agricultural Practice and the Classical Landscape of Greece. In Morris, I. (ed.). *Classical Greece: Ancient Histories and Modern Archaeologies*, 137–170. Cambridge/ New York: Cambridge University Press.

Alcock, S.E., Cherry, J.F. (eds.) 2004. *Side-by-Side Survey. Comparative Regional Studies in the Mediterranean World*. Oxford: Oxbow.

Alexander, J.A. 1963. *Potidaea. Its History and Remains*. Athens: University of Georgia Press.

Allegro, N. (ed.) 2008. *Himera, vol. V. L'abitato: isolato II. I blocchi 1–4 della zona 1*. Palermo: Università di Palermo.

Allegro, N., Belvedere, O., Bonacasa, N., Bonacasa Carra, R.M., Di Stefano, C.A., Epifanio, E., Joly, E., Manni Piratino, M.T., Tullio, A., Tusa Cutroni, A. 1976. *Himera, vol. II. Campagne di scavo 1966–1973*. Rome: 'L'Erma' di Bretschneider.

Alliata, V., Belvedere, O., Cantoni, A., Cusimano, G., Marescalchi, P., Vassallo, S. 1988. *Himera, vol. III, 1. Prospezione archeologica nel territorio*. Rome: 'L'Erma' di Bretschneider.

Amati, M. 2010. Meton's Star-City: Geometry and Utopia in Aristophanes' Birds. *Classical Journal* 105.3: 213–227.

Arcelin, P. 1986. Le territoire de Marseille grecque dans son contexte indigène. *Études Massaliotes* 1: 43–104.

Archibald, Z.H. 1998. *The Odrysian Kingdom of Thrace: Orpheus Unmasked*. Oxford: Clarendon.

Archibald, Z.H., Davies, J., Gabrielsen, V. (eds.) 2011. *The Economies of Hellenistic Societies, Third to First Centuries BC*. Oxford: Oxford University Press.

Arendt, H. 1958. *The Human Condition*. Chicago: University of Chicago Press.

Asheri, D. 1966. *Distribuzioni di terre nell'antica Grecia*. Torino: Accademia delle Scienze.

Asheri, D. 1967. Studio sulla storia della colonizzazione di Anfipoli sino alla conquista macedone. *Rivista di Filologia e di Istruzione Classica* 95: 5–30.

Asheri, D. 1999. Processi di "decolonizzazione" in Magna Grecia: il caso di Poseidonia Lucana. In *La Colonisation grecque en Méditerranée occidentale*, 361–370. Rome: École française de Rome.

Attema, P. 2008. Conflict or Coexistence? Remarks on Indigenous Settlement and Greek Colonization in the Foothills and Hinterland of the Sibaritide (Northern Calabria, Italy). In Guldager Bilde, P., Hjarl Petersen, J. (eds.). *Meeting of Cultures – Between Conflicts and Coexistence*, 67–100. Aarhus: Aarhus University Press.

Attema, P., Burgers, G.-J., van Leusen, P.M. (eds.) 2010. *Regional Pathways to Complexity: settlement and land-use dynamics in early Italy from the Bronze Age to the Republican period*. Amsterdam: University Press.

Ault, B.A. 1994. *Classical Houses and Households. An architectural and artifactual case from Halieis, Greece*. Microfiche Ann Arbor.

Ault, B.A. 1999. Koprones and Oil Presses at Halieis. Interactions of town and country and the integration of domestic and regional economies. *Hesperia* 68: 549–573.

Ault, B.A. 2005. *The Excavations at Ancient Halieis, vol. II. The Houses: Organisation and Use of Domestic Space*. Indianapolis: Indiana University Press.

Ault, B.A., Nevett, L. 1999. Digging houses. Archaeologies of Classical and Hellenistic Greek domestic assemblages. In Allison, P.M. (ed.). *The Archaeology of Household Activities*, 43–56. London/New York: Routledge.

Avram, A. 2004. The Propontic Coast of Asia Minor. In Hansen, M.H., Nielsen, T.H. (eds.) 2004. *An Inventory of Archaic and Classical Poleis. An Investigation Conducted by the Copenhagen Polis Centre for the Danish National Research Foundation*, 974–999. Oxford: Oxford University Press.

Balot, R.K. 2001. Aristotle's Critique of Phaleas: Justice, Equality, and Pleonexia. *Hermes* 129.1: 32–44.

Balot, R.K. 2006. *Greek Political Thought*. Malden, MA/Oxford/Victoria: Blackwell.

Barberis, V. 1999. I siti tra Sinni e Bradano tra l'età arcaica e l'età ellenistica: schede. In Barra Bagnasco, M., de Miro, E., Pinzone, A. (eds.). *Origini e incontri di culture nell'antichità. Magna Grecia e Sicilia. Stato degli studi e prospettive di ricerca (Atti dell'Incontro di Studio, Messina 1996)*, 59–105. Catanzaro: Di.Sc.A.M.

Barile, M.D. 1983/4. *Matrici fittili ellenistiche con figure atletiche da Eraclea. Tesi di Laurea in Archeologia e Storia dell'Arte Greca*. Università degli Studi di Bari (unpublished).

Bats, M. 1990. Antibes. In *Voyage en Massalie: 100 ans d'archéologie en Gaule du Sud* (Catalog of the Exhibition, Marseilles), 220–221. Marseille: Musée de Marseille.

Bats, M. 1992. Marseille, les colonies massaliètes et les relais indigènes dans le traffic le long du littoral méditerréen gaulois (VIe – Ier s. av. J.C.). *Études Massaliotes* 3: 263–278.

Bats, M., Dewailly, M., Cavassa, L. 2010. Moio della Civitella. In Tréziny, H. (ed.). *Grecs et indigènes de la Catalogne à la Mer Noire: actes des rencontres du programme européen Ramses², 2006–2008*, 171–185. Paris: Errance.

Bats, M., Legouilloux, M., Brien-Poitevin, F. 1995. La tour d'angle sud-est d'Olbia et son dépotoir (v. 225-150 av. J.-C.). *Études Massaliotes* 4: 371–392.

Battiloro, I., Bruscella, A., Osanna, M. 2010. Ninfe ad Heraklea Lucana? Il santuario extra-urbano di Masseria Petrulla nella Valle del Sinni (Policoro – MT). *Kernos* 23: 239–270.

Battiloro, I., Osanna, M., forthcoming. I santuari della Lucania antica: articolazione degli spazi e regime delle offerte (IV-III sec. a.C.). In Lippolis, E. (ed.). *Il ruolo del culto nello sviluppo delle comunità dell'Italia antica tra IV e I sec. a.C.: strutture, funzioni e interazioni culturali (Atti del senimanrio conclusivo del PRIN 2008, Roma 5 ottobre 2012)*.

Baudy, G. 1999. Der kannibalische Hirte. Ein Topos der antiken Ethnographie in kulturanthropologischer Deutung. In Keck, A., Kording, I., Porchaska, A. (eds.). *Verschlungene Grenzen. Anthropophagie in Literatur und Kulturwissenschaften*, 221–242. Tübingen: G. Narr.

Beazley, J.D. 1968. *Attic Red-Figure Vase Painters, 2nd edition, vol. 1 & 2*. London: Clarendon.

Belov, G.D. 1950. Nekropol' Chersonesa klassičeskoj épochi. *Sovetskaya archeologiya* 13: 272–284.

Belov, G.D. 1981. The Chersonese necropolis of the classical period (Russian with English abstract). *Sovetskaya archeologiya* 1981.3: 163–180.

Belvedere, O., Bestini, A., Boschian, G., Burgo, A., Contino, A., Cucco, R.M., Lauro, D. 2002. *Himera, vol. III, 2. Prospezione archeologica nel territorio*. Rome: 'L'Erma' di Bretschneider.

Benac, A., Čović, B. 1957. *Glasinac, vol. II. Eisenzeit/Željenno Doba* (German/Croatian). Sarajevo: National Museum.

Bencivenga Trillmich, C. 1988. Pyxous-Buxentum. *Mélanges de l'École française de Rome – Antiquité* 100: 701–729.

Bengtson, H. 1975. *Staatsverträge des Altertums, vol. II. Die Verträge der griechisch-römischen Welt 700–338 v. Chr.* Munich: C.H. Beck.

Bengtson, H. 1977. *Griechische Geschichte, 5th edition.* Munich: C.H. Beck.

Benoit, J. 1985. L'étude des cadastres antiques: à propos d'Olbia de Provence. *Documents d'Archéologie Méridionale* 8: 25–48.

Bentz, M., Adorno, L., Albers, J., Müller, J.-M., Zuchtriegel, G. 2013. Das Handwerkerviertel von Selinunt. Die Töpferwerkstatt in der Insula S 16/17-E. Vorbericht zu den Kampagnen 2010–2012. *Mitteilungen des Deutschen Archäologischen Instituts, Römische Abteilung* 119: 69–98.

Béquignon, Y. 1937. *La Vallée du Spercheios des origines au IVe siècle.* Paris: Boccard.

Berlingò, I. 1986. La necropoli arcaica di Policoro in contrada Madonnelle. In De Siena, A., Tagliente, M. (eds.). *Siris-Polieion. Fonti letterarie e nuova documentazione archeologica (Incontro di Studi, Policoro 8–10 giugno 1984)*, 117–125. Galatina: Congedo.

Berlingò, I. 1993. Le necropoli di Siris. *Bollettino di Archeologia* 22: 1–21.

Berlingò, I. 1994. Piano Sollazzo. *Bibliografia topografica della Colonizzazione Greca in Italia* 13, 533–534.

Berlingò, I. 2005. La necropoli arcaica sud-occidentale di Siris (in proprietà Schirone). *Notizie degli Scavi* 2004/5: 329–382.

Berlingò, I. 2010. La nécropole archaïque de Siris (Policoro). In Tréziny, H. (ed.). *Grecs et indigènes de la Catalogne à la Mer Noire: actes des rencontres du programme européen Ramses², 2006–2008*, 529–535. Paris: Errance.

Bernbeck, R. 2010. 'La Jalousie' und Archäologie: Plädoyer für subjektloses Erzählen. *Ethnologisch-Archäologische Zeitschrift* 51: 64–86.

Berthelot, H. 2012. La 'stele des céréals' de Cyrène. *Camenulae* 8: 1–12.

Bettelli, M., De Faveri, C., Osanna, M. (eds.) 2008. *Prima delle colonie. Organizzazione territoriale e produzioni ceramiche specializzate in Basilicata e in Calabria settentrionale ionica nella prima età del Ferro.* Venosa: Osanna.

Bhabha, H.K. 1994. *The Location of Culture.* London/New York: Routledge.

Bianco, S. (ed.) 1996. *I Greci in Occidente. Greci, Enotri e Lucani nella Basilicata meridionale* (Catalog of the Exhibition, Policoro). Milan: Electa.

Bianco, S. 1996. Siris-Herakleia: il territorio, la chora. In Otto, B. (ed.) 1996. *Herakleia in Lukanien und das Quellheiligtum der Demeter*, 15–22. Innsbruck: Leopold-Franzens-Universität.

Bianco, S. (ed.) 1999. *Il Museo Nazionale della Siritide di Policoro.* Bari: Edipuglia.

Bianco, S. 2000. La chora di Siris-Herakleia. In *Atti del 40° Convegno di Studi sulla Magna Grecia*, 807–818. Taranto: Istituto per la Storia e l'Archeologia della Magna Grecia.

Bianco, S. 2010. Santa Maria d'Anglona. *Bibliografia topografica della Colonizzazione Greca in Italia* 18: 290–292.

Bianco, S. 2012. Policoro: presenze insediative indigene e 'proto coloniali' nell'area del Presidio Ospedaliero. Nota preliminare. In Osanna, M., Zuchtriegel, G. (eds.). *ΑΜΦΙ ΣΙΡΙΟΣ ΡΟΑΣ. Nuove ricerche su Eraclea e la Siritide*, 45–67. Venosa: Osanna.

Bianco, S., Crupi, G.S., Pasquino, M.D. 2012. Il deposito votivo di proprietà Favale: la coroplastica. In Osanna, M., Zuchtriegel, G. (eds.). *ΑΜΦΙ ΣΙΡΙΟΣ ΡΟΑΣ. Nuove ricerche su Eraclea e la Siritide*, 161–180. Venosa: Osanna.

Bianco, S., Giardino, L. 2010. Forme e processi di urbanizzazione e di territorializzazione nella fascia costiera ionica tra i fiumi Sinni e Basento. In *Atti del 50° Convegno di Studi sulla Magna Grecia*, 609–641. Taranto: Istituto per la Storia e l'Archeologia della Magna Grecia.

Bini, M.P. 1989. Il territorio di Eraclea nel IV e III sec. a.C. In *Studi su Siris-Eraclea* (Archaeologia Perusiana 8), 15–21. Rome: G. Bretschneider.

Bintliff, J. 2014. Spatial Analysis of Past Built Environments: houses and society in the Aegean from the Early Iron Age to the impact of Rome. In Paliou, E., Lieberwirth U., Polla, S. (eds.). *Spatial Analysis and Social Spaces*, 263–276. Berlin: W. de Gruyter.

Bintliff, J., Gaffney, V. 1988. *The Ager Pharensis/Hvar Project 1987.* In Chapman, J.C., Bintliff, J., Gaffney, V., Slapšak, B. (eds.). *Recent Developments in Yugoslav Archaeology*, 151–176. Oxford: BAR.

Bintliff, J., Howard, P., Snodgrass, A. 2007. *Testing the Hinterland. The Work of the Boeotia Survey (1989–1991) in the Southern Approaches to the City of Thespiai.* Cambridge: McDonald Institute for Archaeological Research.

Blösel, W. 2004. *Themistokles bei Herodot. Spiegel Athens im 5. Jahrhundert. Studien zur Geschichte und historiographischen Konstruktion des griechischen Freiheitskampfes 480 v. Chr.* Stuttgart: F. Steiner.

Boehringer, Chr. 2008. Über die Münzen von Katane im letzten Jahrzehnt des V. Jahrhunderts v. Chr. *Schweizerische Numismatische Rundschau* 87: 5–21.

Bonačić Mandinić, M., Visona, P. 2002. Monetary Circulation on the Island of Vis (Issa), c. 350 B.C. to A.D. 600. In Cambi, N., Kirigin, B., Čače, S. (eds.). *Grčki utjecaj na istočnoj obali Jadrana. Greek Influence along the East Adriatic Coast. Zbornik radova sa znanstvenog skupa održanog 24. do 26. rujna 1998. godine u Splitu = Proceedings of the International Conference held in Split from September 24th to 26th 1998,* 319–374. Split: s.n.

Bonanno Aravantinos, M., Pisani, M. (eds.) 2014. *Camarina: ricerche in corso. Atti della giornata di studio, Roma 12 marzo 2013.* Tivoli: Tored.

Bottini, A. 1992. *Archeologia della salvezza. L'escatologia greca nelle testimonianze archeologiche.* Milan: Longanesi.

Bottini, A. 1999. Gli indigeni nel V secolo a.C. In Adamesteanu, D. (ed.). *Storia della Basilicata, vol. 1. L'antichità,* 419–453. Bari: Laterza.

Bottini, A. 2001. Il pittore di Dolone all'opera: il caso di un'olla da Ruvo di Puglia. *Ostraka* 20: 7–11.

Bottini, A. 2013. La panoplia oplitica della tomba 672 di Chiaromonte (PZ). *SIRIS* 13: 33–40.

Bottini, A., Lecce, L. 2013. La mesogaia lucana e il caso di Pisticci. In Todisco, L. (ed.). *La comunicazione verbale tra Greci e indigeni in Apulia nel V-IV secolo a.C.: quali elementi? Atti del Seminario di studi linguistici, archeologici e storici (Bari, Università degli Studi Aldo Moro, 30 ottobre 2012),* 45–60. Napoli: Loffredo.

Bottini, A., Lecce, L., 2015. Una tomba di armato a Herakleia di Lucania. *SIRIS* 15: 9–20.

Bottini, A., Graells, R., Vullo, M., forthcoming. Tombe arcaiche da Metaponto. In *Atti del 56° Convegno di Studi sulla Magna Grecia.* Taranto: Istituto per la Storia e l'Archeologia della Magna Grecia.

Braccesi, L. 1973/4. Ancora su IG I² 53. *Archeologia Classica* 25/6: 68–73.

Braccesi, L. (ed.) 2004. *Studi sulla grecità d'occidente. I greci in Adriatico, vol. 2* (Hesperia 18). Rome: "L'Erma" di Bretschneider.

Bradley, G., Wilson, J.P. (eds.) 2006. *Greek and Roman Colonization: Origins, Ideologies and Interactions.* Swansea: Classical Press of Wales.

Briant, P. 1978. Colonisation hellénistique et populations indigènes. La phase d'installation. *Klio* 60: 57–93.

Briant, P. 1994. Prélèvements tributaires et échanges en Asie Mineure achéménide et hellénistique. In *Économie antique. Les échanges dans l'Antiquité: le rôle de l'Etat,* 69–81. Saint-Bertrand-de-Comminges: Musée Archéologique Départemental.

Brugsch, H., Erman, A. 1894. Die Pithom-Stele. *Zeitschrift für ägyptische Sprache und Altertumskunde* 32: 74–87.

Bruins, E.M. 1964. *Codex Constantinopolitanus Palatii Veteris no. 1, vol. 3: commentary and translation.* Leiden: Brill.

Brun, J.-P. 2010. Viticulture et oléiculture grecques et indigènes en Grande Grèce et en Sicile. In Tréziny, H. (ed.). *Grecs et indigènes de la Catalogne à la Mer Noire: actes des rencontres du programme européen Ramses², 2006–2008,* 425–431. Paris: Errance.

Bugno, M. 1999. *Da Sibari a Thurii. La fine di un impero.* Naples: Centre Jean Bérard.

Bujskich, A. 2006. Die Chora des pontischen Olbia: die Hauptetappen der räumlich-strukturellen Entwicklung. In Bilde, P.G., Stolba, V.F. (eds.). *Surveying the Greek chora: The Black Sea region in a comparative perspective,* 115–139. Aarhus: Aarhus University Press.

Burford, A. 1972. *Craftsmen in Greek and Roman Society.* London: Thames & Hudson.

Burford, A. 1993. *Land and Labor in the Greek World.* Baltimore/London: Johns Hopkins University Press.

Burgers, G.-J., Crielaard, J.P. (eds.) 2011. *Greci e indigeni a L'Amastuola.* Mottola: Stampa Sud.

Butler, S.A. 2010. Arendt and Aristotle on Equality, Leisure, and Solidarity. *Journal of Social Philosophy* 41: 470–490.

Cabanes, P. 2008. Greek Colonisation in the Adriatic. In Tsetskhladze, G.R. (ed.). *An Account of Greek Colonies and Other Settlements Overseas, vol. 2*, 155–185. Leiden/Boston: Brill.

Cahill, N. 2002. *Household and City Organization at Olynthus*. New Haven: Yale University Press.

Caliò, L. 2012. *Asty. Studi sulla città greca*. Rome: Quasar.

Calvaruso, O.T. 2012. Eraclea di Lucania. Proposta di classificazione delle ceramiche di III secolo a.C. dalle fornaci della terrazza meridionale. In Osanna, M., Zuchtriegel, G. (eds.). *ΑΜΦΙ ΣΙΡΙΟΣ ΡΟΑΣ. Nuove ricerche su Eraclea e la Siritide*, 241–257. Venosa: Osanna.

Canfora, L. 2011. *Il mondo di Atene*. Bari: Laterza.

Canfora, L. 2014. *La crisi dell'utopia. Aristofane contro Platone*. Bari: Laterza.

Cantilena, R., Munzi, P. 2001. La casa della zecca a Laos (Marcellina, Santa Maria del Cedro). In *I luoghi della moneta. Le sedi delle zecche dall'antichità all'età moderna. Atti del convegno internazionale. Milano 22–23 ottobre 1999*, 175–181. Milan: Comune di Milano.

Cappers, R.T.J., Neef, R. 2012. *Handbook of Plant Palaeoecology*. Groningen: Groningen University Library.

Carafa, P., Luppino, S. 2011. Il paesaggio agrario della Calabria settentrionale tra IV e III secolo a.C. In De Sensi Sestito, G., Mancuso, S. (eds.). *Enotri e Brettii in Magna Grecia: modi e forme di interazione culturale*, 175–189. Soveria Mannelli: Rubbettino.

Carpenter, Th.H., Lynch, K.M., Robinson, E.S.G. (eds.) 2014. *The Italic People of Ancient Apulia: New Evidence From Pottery for Workshops, Markets, and Customs*. Cambridge/New York: Cambridge University Press.

Carter, J.C. (ed.) 1998. *The Chora of Metaponto: The Necropoleis*. Austin: University of Texas Press.

Carter, J.C. 2003. *Crimean Chersonesos. City, Chora, Museum and Environs*. Austin: Institute of Classical Archaeology.

Carter, J.C. 2008. *La scoperta del territorio rurale di Metaponto*. Venosa: Osanna.

Carter, J.C., Prieto, A. (eds.) 2011. *The Chora of Metaponto, vol. 3. Archaeological Field Survey Bradano to Basento*. Austin: University of Texas Press.

Cartledge, P. 2009. *Ancient Greek Political Thought in Practice*. Cambridge/New York: Cambridge University Press.

Cartledge, P., Cohen, E. Foxhall, L. (eds.) 2002. *Money, Labour and Land. Approaches to the Economies of Ancient Greece*. London/New York: Routledge.

Casevitz, M. 1985. *Le vocabulaire de la colonisation en grec ancien: étude lexicologique: les familles de ktizō et de oikeō-oikizō*. Paris: Klincksieck.

Castanyer, P., Santos, M., Tremoleda, J. 2015. Nuevos datos arqueológicos sobre la evolución urbana de Emporion. *Bibliotèque d'Archéologie Méditerannéenne et Africaine* 15: 121–130.

Cataldi, S. 1990. *Prospettive occidentali allo scoppio della guerra del Peloponneso*. Pisa: ETS.

de Cazanove, O. 2008. *Cività di Tricarico, vol. 1. Le quartiere de la maison du monolithe et l'enceinte intermédiaire*. Rome: École française de Rome.

de Cazanove, O., Féret, S., Caravelli, A.M. (eds.) 2014. *Civita di Tricarico, vol. 2. Habitat et artisanat au centre du plateau*. Rome: École française de Rome.

Ceccatelli, G. 1975/6. *Matrici di figure fittili femminili del IV-III sec. a.C. da Eraclea di Lucania*. Tesi di Laurea in Lettere e Filosofia. Università degli Studi di Milano (unpublished).

Chatzopoulos, M.V. 1991. *Actes de vente d'Amphipolis*. Athens: Centre de recherches de l'antiquité grecque et romaine.

Cipriani, M. 2000. Italici a Poseidonia nella seconda metà del V sec. a.C. Nuove ricerche nella necropoli del Gaudo. In Greco, E., Longo, F. (eds.). *Paestum. Scavi, studi, ricerche. Bilancio di un decennio (1988-1998)*, 197–212. Paestum: Pandemos.

Cipriani, M., Longo, F., Viscione, M. (eds.) 1996. *Poseidonia e i Lucani* (Catalog of the Exhibition, Paestum). Naples: Electa.

Clavel-Lévêque, M. 1982. Un cadastre grec en Gaule: la chora d'Agde (Hérault). *Klio* 64: 21–28.

Closterman, W.E. 2013. Family Groupings in Classical Attic Peribolos Tombs. In Sporn, K. (ed.). *Griechische Grabbezirke klassischer Zeit: Normen und Regionalismen. Akten des Internationalen Kolloquiums am Deutschen Archäologischen Institut, Abteilung Athen, 20.-21. November 2009*, 45–53. Munich: Hirmer.

Coarelli, F. 1998. Problemi e ipotesi sulle tavole greche di Eraclea. In *Siritide e Metapontino. Storie di due territori coloniali. Atti dell'incontro di studio di Policoro, 31 ottobre – 2 novembre 1991*, 281–289. Naples: Centre Jean Bérard.

Cohen, B. (ed.) 2000. *Not the Classical Ideal. Athens and the Construction of the Other in Greek Art.* Leiden: Brill.

Cohen, G.M. 1978. *The Seleucid Colonies: Studies in Founding, Administration, and Organisation.* Wiesbaden: Steiner.

Cohen, G.M. 1995. *The Hellenistic Settlements in Europe, the Islands, and Asia Minor.* Berkeley: University of California Press.

Cohen, G.M. 2006. *The Hellenistic Settlements in Syria, the Red Sea Basin, and North Africa.* Berkeley: University of California Press.

Comaroff, J.L., Comaroff, J. 2009. *Ethnicity Inc.* Chicago: University of Chicago Press.

Consolo Langher, S.N. 1977. Vita economica di Tindari. *Archivio storico messinese* 2: 161–168.

Cordano, F. 2007. Da Atene a Thurii: ecisti, legislatori, storici e altro. In *Atti del 47° Convegno di Studi sulla Magna Grecia*, 197–206. Taranto: Istituto per la Storia e l'Archeologia della Magna Grecia.

Cordano, F. 2014. I cittadini di Camarina del V secolo a.C. In Bonanno Aravantinos, M., Pisani, M. (eds.) 2014. *Camarina: ricerche in corso. Atti della giornata di studio, Roma 12 marzo 2013*, 9–23. Tivoli: Tored.

Cordova, C.E., Lehman, P.H. 2006. Mediterranean agriculture in southwestern Crimea: paleoenvironments and early adapations. In Peterson, D.L, Popova, L.M., Smith, A.T. (eds.). *Beyond the Steppe and the Sown. Proceedings of the 2002 University of Chicago Conference on Eurasian Archaeology*, 425–447. Leiden/Boston: Brill.

Corvisier, J.-N., Suder, W. 2000. *La population de l'antiquité classique.* Paris: Puf.

Coscia, A. 2012. I Tumuli sacri di Thurii. *Fenix* 39.1: 64–70.

Costabile, F. 1987. Finanze pubbliche. L'amministrazione finanziaria templare. In Pugliese Carratelli, G. (ed.). *Magna Grecia. Lo sviluppo politico, sociale ed economico*, 103–114. Milan: Electa.

Crawford, M.H. 2006. From Poseidonia to Paestum via the Lucanians. In Bradley, G., Wilson, J.P. (eds.). *Greek and Roman Colonization: Origins, Ideologies and Interactions*, 59–72. Swansea: Classical Press of Wales.

Crelier, M.-C. 2008. *Kinder in Athen im gesellschaftlichen Wandel im 5. Jahrhundert v. Chr. Eine archäologische Annäherung.* Remshalden: Greiner.

de Ste Croix, G.E.M. 1981. *The Class Struggle in the Ancient Greek World: From the Archaic Age to the Arab Conquests.* Ithaca, NY: Cornell University Press.

Crupi, G.S., Pasquino, M.D. 2012. L'area sacra di Piano Sollazzo (Rotondella – Mt), con una appendice di A. Casalicchio. In Osanna, M., Zuchtriegel, G. (eds.). *ΑΜΦΙ ΣΙΡΙΟΣ ΡΟΑΣ. Nuove ricerche su Eraclea e la Siritide*, 305–338. Venosa: Osanna.

Crupi, S., Pasquino, M.D. 2015. La necropoli meridionale di Herakleia. Note preliminari della campagna di scavo 2009. In Meo, F., Zuchtriegel, G. (eds.). *Siris Herakleia Polychoron: città e campagna tra antichità e medioevo. Atti del convegno Policoro, 12 luglio 2013 (SIRIS 14)*, 101–118. Bari: Edipuglia.

Culasso Gastaldi, E., Marchiandi, D. (eds.) 2012. *Gli Ateniesi fuori dall'Attica: modi d'intervento e di controllo del territorio (Torino, 8–9 aprile 2010). Annuario della Scuola Archeologica di Atene e delle Missioni Italiane in Oriente* 88: 209–508.

Curti, E. 1989. Il culto d'Artemis Bendis ad Eraclea. In *Studi su Siris-Eraclea* (Archaeologia Perusiana 8), 23–30. Rome: G. Bretschneider.

Curtius, E. 1883. *Die Griechen als Meister der Colonisation. Rede zum Geburtsfeste Seiner Majestät des Kaisers und Königs.* Berlin: Königliche Akademie der Wissenschaften.

D'Andria, F., Roubis, D. 1999. L'insediamento indigeno di Difesa San Biagio a Montescaglioso. Seconda campagna di scavo 1996. *SIRIS* 1: 125–155.

D'Esposito, L., Galioto, G. 2012. L'area sacra del 'Vallo' ad Eraclea. In Osanna, M., Zuchtriegel, G. (eds.). *ΑΜΦΙ ΣΙΡΙΟΣ ΡΟΑΣ.*

Nuove ricerche su Eraclea e la Siritide, 143–160. Venosa: Osanna.

Dakaris, S.I. 1986. Το Όρραον. Το σπίτι στην αρχαία Ήπειρο. *Archaiologike Ephemeris* 125: 108–146.

Dasen, V. (ed.) 2004. *Naissance et petite enfance dans l'Antiquité. Actes du colloque de Fribourg, 28 novembre – 1er décembre 2001.* Fribourg: Academic Press.

Daubner, F. (ed.) 2010. *Militärsiedlungen und Territorialherrschaft in der Antike.* Berlin/New York: W. de Gruyter.

Davies, J.K. 2007. The Legacy of Xerxes: The Growth of Athenian Naval Power. In Greco, E., Lombardo, M. (eds.). *Atene e l'Occidente, i grandi temi: le premesse, i protagonisti, le forme della comunicazione e dell'interazione, i modi dell'intervento ateniese in Occidente. Atti del Convegno Internazionale, Atene 25–27 maggio 2006*, 71–98. Athens: Scuola Archeologica Italiana di Atene.

De Gennaro, R. 2005. *I circuiti murari della Lucania antica (IV-III sec. a.C.).* Paestum: Fondazione Paestum.

de Haas, T. 2012. Beyond Dots on the Map: intensive survey data and the interpretation of small sites and off-site distributions. In Attema, P., Schörner, G. (eds.). *Comparative Issues in the Archaeology of the Roman Rural Landscape. Site classification between survey, excavation and historical categories*, 55–79. Portsmouth: Journal of Roman Archaeology.

De Siena, A. 1999. La colonizzazione achea del Metapontino. In Adamesteanu, D. (ed.). *Storia della Basilicata, vol. 1. L'antichità*, 211–245. Bari: Laterza.

De Siena, A., Giardino, L. 1994. Heraclea e Metaponto. Trasformazioni urbanistiche e produzione agricola tra tarda repubblica e primo impero: nuovi dati archeologici. In *Le ravitaillement en blé de Rome et des centres urbains des débuts de la République jusqu'au Haut Empire (Actes du colloque international de Naples 1991)*, 197–211. Naples: Centre Jean Bérard.

De Siena, A., Giardino, L. 2001. Trasformazioni delle aree urbane e del paesaggio agrario in età romana nella Basilicata sudorientale. In Lo Cascio, E., Storchi Marino, A. (eds.). *Modalità insediative e strutture agrarie nell'Italia meridionale in età romana*, 129–167. Bari: Edipuglia.

Degrassi, N. 1967. Meisterwerke frühitaliotischer Vasenmalerei aus einem Grab in Policoro. In Neutsch, B. (ed.). *Herakleiastudien* (Archäologische Forschungen in Lukanien 2), 193–231. Heidelberg: F.H. Kerle.

Dell'Aglio, A. 2015. Taranto fra V e IV secolo a.C. In Meo, F., Zuchtriegel, G. (eds.). *Siris Herakleia Polychoron: città e campagna tra antichità e medioevo. Atti del convegno Policoro, 12 luglio 2013 (SIRIS 14)*, 63–71. Bari: Edipuglia.

Delorme, J. 1960. *Gymnasion: étude sur les monuments consacrés à l'éducation en Grèce (des origines à l'Empire Romain).* Paris: E de Boccard.

Denoyelle, M. 2007. La ceramica: appunti sulla nascita delle produzioni italiote. In *Atti del 47° Convegno di Studi sulla Magna Grecia*, 339–350. Taranto: Istituto per la Storia e l'Archeologia della Magna Grecia.

Descat, J.A.R. 2010. Thucydide e l'économie: aux origines du logos oikonomikos. In Fromentin, V., Gottelard, S., Payen, P. (eds.). *Ombres de Thucydide: la réception de l'historien depuis l'Antiquité jusqu'au début du XXe siècle*, 403–409. Bordeaux: Ausonius.

Deslauriers, M. 2015. Political Rule over Women in Politics I. In Lockwood, Th., Samaras, Th. (eds.). *Aristotle's Politics: A Critical Guide*, 27–45. Cambridge/New York: Cambridge University Press.

Deslauriers, M., Destrée, P. (eds.) 2013. *The Cambridge Companion to Aristotle's Politics.* Cambridge: Cambridge University Press.

Di Stefano, G. 1993/4. Scavi e ricerche a Camarina e nel Ragusano (1988–1992). *Kokalos* 39/40: 1367–1421.

Di Stefano, G. 1996. Insediamenti rurali nella chora di Camarina. *Aitna* 2: 25–34.

Di Stefano, G. 2000. Sacelli e altari nell'agorà di Camarina. In *Damarato: studi di antichità classica offerti a Paola Pelagatti*, 276–287. Milan: Electa.

Di Stefano, G. 2012. Camarina (Sicilia). Le aree artigianali e produttive di età classica. Un esempio di organizzazione dello spazio produttivo della Grecia d'Occidente. In Esposito, A., Sanidas, G.M. (eds.). *'Quartiers' artisanaux en Grèce ancienne: une perspective méditerranéenne*, 301–310. Lille: Presses Universitaires du Septentrion.

Di Stefano, G. 2014. Camarina: una città di seconda generazione. Gli spazi urbani e della chora. In Bonanno Aravantinos, M., Pisani, M. (eds.) 2014. *Camarina: ricerche in corso. Atti della giornata di studio, Roma 12 marzo 2013*, 55–64. Tivoli: Tored.

Díaz-Andreu García, M. 2005 *The Archaeology of Identity: Approaches to Gender, Age, Status, Ethnicity and Religion*. London/New York: Routledge.

Dietler, M. 2005. The Archaeology of Colonization and the Colonization of Archaeology: Theoretical Challenges from an Ancient Mediterranean Colonial Encounter. In Stein, G.J. (ed.). *The Archaeology of Colonial Encounters: Comparative Perspectives*, 33–68. Santa Fe: School of American Research Press.

Dietler, M. 2010. *Archaeologies of Colonialism. Consumption, Entanglement, and Violence in Ancient Mediterranean France*. Berkeley: University of California Press.

Dillon, J., Hershbell, J. 1991. *Iamblichus: On the Pythagorean Way of Life. Text, Translation, and Notes*. Atlanta: Scholars Press.

Ditaranto, I. 2010. Herakleia: un contributo per la ricostruzione dell'antica colonia greca e del suo territorio attraverso la fotografia aerea. In Ceraudo, G. (ed.). *100 anni di Archeologia Aerea in Italia*, 357–359. Foggia: Grenzi.

Domínguez, A.J. 2013. Los primeros griegos en la Península Ibérica (s. IX-VI a. C.): mitos, probabilidades, certezas. In Paz de Hoz, M., Mora, G. (eds.). *El oriente griego en la Península Ibérica: epigrafía e historia*, 11–42. Madrid: Real Academia de la Historia.

van Dommelen, P. 1996/7. Colonial Constructs. Colonialism and Archaeology in the Mediterranean. *World Archaeology* 28: 305–323.

van Dommelen, P. 1998. *On Colonial Grounds. A comparative study of colonialism and rural settlement in first millennium BC west central Sardinia* (Archaeological Studies University of Leiden 2). Leiden: Leiden University Press.

van Dommelen, P. 2002. Ambiguous Matters: Colonialism and local identities in Punic Sardinia. In Lyons, C. L., Papadopoulos, J.K. (eds.). *The Archaeology of Colonialism*, 121–147. Los Angeles: Getty Research Institute.

van Dommelen, P. 2005. Colonial Interactions and Hybrid Practices. In Stein, G.J. (ed.). *The Archaeology of Colonial Encounters*, 109–142. Santa Fe: School of American Research Press.

van Dommelen, P. 2006. Colonial Matters. Material Culture and Postcolonial Theory in Colonial Situations. In Tilley, C., Keane, W., Kuechler, S., Rowlands, M., Spyer, P. (eds.). *Handbook of Material Culture*, 267–308. London: Sage.

van Dommelen, P. 2014. Subaltern Archaeologies. In Ferris, N., Harrison, R., Wilcox, M. (eds.) 2014. *Rethinking Colonial Pasts through Archaeology*, 469–475. Oxford: Oxford University Press.

van Dommelen, P., Gómez Bellard, C., 2008. *Rural Landscapes of the Punic World*. London: Equinox.

van Dommelen, P., Terrenato, N. (eds.) 2007. *Articulating Local Cultures: Power and Identity Under the Expanding Roman Republic (International Roman Archaeology Conference 2001, Glasgow, Scotland)*. Portsmouth: Journal of Roman Archaeology.

Dörpfeld, H. (ed.) 1901. *Antike Denkmäler, vol. II,4*. Berlin: W. de Gruyter.

Dougherty, C. 1993. *The Poetics of Greek Colonization: From City to Text in Archaic Greece*. Oxford: Oxford University Press.

Eder, B., Mitsopoulos-Leon, V. 1999. Zur Geschichte der Stadt Elis vor dem Synoikismos von 471 v. Chr. *Jahrbuch des Österreichischen Archäologischen Instituts* 68, Beiblatt: 2–40.

Ehrenberg, V. 1973. *From Solon to Socrates: Greek History and Civilization during the 6th and 5th centuries BC, 2nd edition*. London: Methuen.

Ehtécham, M. 1946. *L'Iran sous les Achéménides. Contribution à l'étude de l'organisation sociale et politique du premier Empire des Perses*. Fribourg: St. Paul.

Esposito, A., Pollini, A. 2013. La visibilité des classes subalternes dans les sources archéologiques. Considérations sur quelques cas d'étude en Grande Grèce. *Ktema* 38: 117–134.

Faure, P. 1981. *Die griechische Welt im Zeitalter der Kolonisation*. Stuttgart: Reclam.

Ferris, N., Harrison, R., Wilcox, M. (eds.) 2014. *Rethinking Colonial Pasts Through Archaeology*. Oxford: Oxford University Press.

Ferro, M. 1997. *Colonization: A Global History*. London/New York: Routledge.

Figueira, T.J. 1991. *Athens and Aegina in the Age of Imperial Colonization*. Baltimore: Johns Hopkins University Press.

Figueira, T.J. 2008. Colonisation in the Classical Period. In Tsetskhladze, G.R. (ed.). *An Account of Greek Colonies and Other Settlements Overseas, vol. 2*, 427–523. Leiden/Boston: Brill.

Finley, M.I. 1973. *The Ancient Economy*. London: Chatto & Windus.

Finocchietti, L. 2009. Il distretto tarantino in età greca. *Workshop di Archeologia Classica* 6: 65–112.

Forbes, H. 1976. The 'three-ploughed field'. Cultivation techniques in ancient and modern Greece. *Expedition* 19.1: 5–11.

Forbes, H. 2000. The Agrarian Economy of the Ermionidha Around 1700. An ethno-historical reconstruction. In Buck Sutton, S. (ed.). *Contingent Countryside. Settlement, Economy, and Land Use in the Southern Argolid Since 1700*, 41–70. Standford: Standford University Press.

Forbes, H. 2007. *Meaning and Identity in a Greek Landscape: An Archeological Ethnography*. Cambridge: Cambridge University Press.

Forbes, H. 2013. Off-site Scatters and the Manuring Hypothesis in Greek Survey Archaeology. *Hesperia* 82.4: 551–594.

Fortunato, A. 1997. Contributo sulle Tavole di Eraclea. Gli epoíkia nei terreni di Dioniso. *Studi di Antichità* 10: 303–312.

Foxhall, L. 1990. The Dependent Tenant. Land Leasing and Labor in Italy and Greece. *Journal of Roman Studies* 80: 97–114.

Foxhall, L. 1993. Farming and fighting in ancient Greece. In Rich, J., Shipley, G. (eds.). *War and Society in the Greek World*, 134–145. London/New York: Routledge.

Foxhall, L. 1999. *Olive Cultivation in Ancient Greece. Seeking the Ancient Economy*. Oxford: Oxford University Press.

Foxhall, L. 2002. Access to Resources in Classical Greece. The egalitarianism of the polis in practice. In Cartledge, P., Cohen, E. Foxhall, L. (eds.). *Money, Labour and Land. Approaches to the economies of ancient Greece*, 209–220. London/New York: Routledge.

Foxhall, L. 2003. Cultures, Landscapes, and Identities in the Mediterranean World. *Mediterranean Historical Review* 18.2: 75–92.

Foxhall, L. 2009. Produzione e commercio del vino in Grecia. In *Atti del 49° Convegno di Studi sulla Magna Grecia*, 33–52. Taranto: Istituto per la Storia e l'Archeologia della Magna Grecia.

Foxhall, L., Michelaki, K., Lazrus, P. 2007. The Changing Landscapes of Bova Marina, Calabria. In Fitzjohn, M. (ed.). *Uplands of Ancient Sicily and Calabria: The Archaeology of Landscape Revisited*, 19–34. London: Accordia.

Fraguna, M. 2000. A proposito degli archivi nel mondo greco: terra e registrazioni fondiarie. *Chiron* 30: 64–115.

Franz, J. 1853. *Corpus Inscriptionum Graecarum, vol. 3*. Berlin: Akademie-Verlag.

Frasca, M. 2000. Sull'urbanistica di Catania in età greca. In *Damarato: studi di antichità classica offerti a Paola Pelagatti*, 119–125. Milan: Electa.

Frisone, F. 2007. Tra reazione e integrazione: Thurii nel contesto magnogreco. In *Atti del 47° Convegno di Studi sulla Magna Grecia*, 233–276. Taranto: Istituto per la Storia e l'Archeologia della Magna Grecia.

Frisone, F. 2009. Strategie territoriali ed esperienze sub-coloniali in Magna Grecia. In Lombardo, M., Frisone, F. (eds.). *Colonie di colonie: le fondazioni sub-coloniali greche tra colonizzazione e colonialismo. Atti del Convegno, Lecce 22–24 Giugno 2006*, 99–122. Galatina: Congedo.

Furtwängler, A. 1893. *Meisterwerke der griechischen Plastik*. Leipzig/Berlin: Gieseke & Devrient.

Gabba, E. 2006. Sui fondamenti e i valori d'estimo nelle tavole eracleensi. *Aestimum* 48: 99–103.

Gaffney, V., Kirigin, B., Petric, M., Vujnovic, N. 1997. *The Adriatic Islands Project: Contact, commerce and colonisation 6000 BC – AD 600, vol. 1. The Archaeological Heritage of Hvar, Croatia*. Oxford: BAR.

Gaffney, V., Kirigin, B. (eds.) 2006. *The Adriatic Island Project, vol. 3. The Archaeological Heritage of Vis, Biševo, Svetac, Palagruža and Šolta*. Oxford: BAR.

Gaffney, V., Stančič, Z. 1991. *GIS Approaches to Regional Analysis: A Case Study of the Island of Hvar*. Ljubjana: s.n.

Gallant, T.W. 1991. *Risk and Survival in Ancient Greece. Reconstructing the Rural Domestic Economy*. Cambridge: Polity Press.

Gallo, L. 2009. L'isomoiria: realtà o mito? In Antonientti, C., De Vido, S. (eds.). *Temi selinuntini*, 129–136. Pisa: ETS.

Gallotta, S. 2010. Atene e il Chersoneso tracico. *Annuario della Scuola Archeologica di Atene e delle Missioni Italiane in Oriente* 88: 415–418.

Galt, A.H. 1992. *Town and Country in Locorotondo*. Fort Worth: Harcourt-Brace-Jovanovich College Publishers.

Garland, R. 2014. *Wandering Greeks: The Ancient Greek Diaspora from the Age of Homer to the Death of Alexander the Great*. Princeton/ Oxford: Princeton University Press.

Garnsey, P. 1998. *Cities, Peasants and Food in Classical Antiquity. Essays in Social and Economic History*, edited by W. Scheidel. Cambridge: Cambridge University Press.

Gavriljuk, N.A. 2003. The Graeco-Scythian slave-trade in the 6th and 5th centuries BC. In Bilde, P.G., Højte, J.M., Stolba, V.F. (eds.). *The Cauldron of Ariantas. Studies presented to A.N. Šceglov on the occasion of his 70th birthday*, 75–86. Aarhus: Aarhus University Press.

Gehrke, H.-J. 1985. *Stasis. Untersuchungen zu den inneren Kriegen in den griechischen Staaten des 5. und 4. Jahrhunderts v. Chr.* Munich: C.H. Beck.

Gehrke, H.-J. 1989. Bemerkungen zu Hippodamos von Milet. In Schuller, W., Hoepfner, W., Schwandner, E.L. (eds.). *Demokratie und Architektur. Der hippodamische Städtebau und die Entstehung der Demokratie, Konstanzer Symposion vom 17. bis 19. Juli 1987*, 58–63. Munich: Deutscher Kunstverlag.

Geitl, R., Doneus, M., Fera, M. 2008. Cost Distance Analysis in an Alpine Environment: comparison of different cost surface modules. In Posluschny, A., Lambers, K., Herzog, I. (eds). *Layers of Perception. Proceedings of the 35th International Conference on Computer Applications and Quantitative Methods in Archaeology (Berlin, Germany, April 2–6, 2007)*, 342–350. Bonn: Habelt.

Gertl, V. 2012. Il santuario di Demetra ad Eraclea: offerte votive e aspetti cultuali. In Osanna, M., Zuchtriegel, G. (eds.). *ΑΜΦΙ ΣΙΡΙΟΣ ΡΟΑΣ. Nuove ricerche su Eraclea e la Siritide*, 119–142. Venosa: Osanna.

Ghinatti, F. 1980. Nuovi efori in epigrafi di Eraclea lucana. In *Forschungen und Funde. Festschrift für Bernhard Neutsch*, 137–143. Innsbruck: Verlag des Institutes für Sprachwissenschaft der Universität Innsbruck.

Ghisellini, E. 2010. Stele funerarie di età classica dalla Sicilia sud-orientale. In Adornato, G. (ed.). *Scolpire il marmo: importazioni, artisti itineranti, scuole artistiche nel Mediterraneo antico. Atti del Convegno di studio tenuto a Pisa, Scuola Normale Superiore, 9–11 novembre 2009*, 279–308. Milan: LED.

Giardino, L. 1996. Herakleia. In Lippolis, E. (ed.). *Arte e artigianato in Magna Grecia* (Catalog of the Exhibition, Taranto), 35–43. Naples: Electa.

Giardino, L. 1998. Aspetti e problemi dell'urbanistica di Herakleia. In *Siritide e Metapontino. Storie di due territori coloniali. Atti dell'incontro di studio di Policoro, 31 ottobre – 2 novembre 1991*, 171–220. Naples: Centre Jean Bérard.

Giardino, L. 2003. Gli insediamenti della foce del Sinni in rapporto alle attività portuali delle colonie di Siris e di Herakleia. In Quilici, L., Quilici Gigli, S. (eds.). *Carta archeologica della Valle del Sinni, Fasciolo 1* (Atlante Tematico di Topografia Antica 10, suppl.), 179–206. Rome: 'L'Erma' di Bretschneider.

Giardino, L. 2004. Herakleia e Metaponto: dalla polis italiota all'abitato protoimperiale. In *Atti del 44° Convegno di Studi sulla Magna Grecia*, 387–432. Taranto: Istituto per la Storia e l'Archeologia della Magna Grecia.

Giardino, L. 2010. Forme abitative indigene alla periferia delle colonie greche. Il caso di Policoro. In Tréziny, H. (ed.). *Grecs et indigènes de la Catalogne à la Mer Noire: actes des rencontres du programme européen Ramses², 2006–2008*, 349–369. Paris: Errance.

Giardino, L. 2012. Il ruolo del sacro nella fondazione di Eraclea di Lucania e nella definizione del suo impianto urbano. Alcuni spunti di riflessione. In Osanna, M., Zuchtriegel, G. (eds.). *ΑΜΦΙ ΣΙΡΙΟΣ ΡΟΑΣ. Nuove ricerche su Eraclea e la Siritide*, 89–118. Venosa: Osanna.

Giardino, L., Calvaruso, O.T. 2015. Sistema di classificazione delle forme ceramiche prodotte a Herakleia lucana nel III secolo a.C.: nuove applicazioni. In Meo, F., Zuchtriegel, G. (eds.). *Siris Herakleia Polychoron: città e campagna tra* antichità e medioevo. Atti del convegno Policoro, 12 luglio 2013 (SIRIS 14), 119–136. Bari: Edipuglia.

Gill, D.W.J. 2006. Hippodamus and the Piraeus. Historia 55: 1–15.

Gill, D.W.J., Vickers, M. 1990. Reflected Glory. Pottery and Precious Metal in Classical Greece. Jahrbuch des Deutschen Archäologischen Instituts 105: 1–30.

Given, M. 2004. The Archaeology of the Colonized. London/New York: Routledge.

Goldberg, M.Y. 1999. Spatial and Behavioural Negotiation in Classical Athenian City Houses. In Allison, P.M. (ed.). The Archaeology of Household Activities, 142–161. London/New York: Routledge.

Gorman, V.B. 1995. Aristotle's Hippodamos (Politics 2.1267b 22–30). Historia 44: 385–395

Gow, A.S.F. 1914. The Ancient Plough. Journal of Hellenic Studies 34: 249–275.

Graham, A.J. 1964. Colony and Mother City in Ancient Greece. New York: Barnes & Noble.

Gramegna, G. 2015/16. Eraclea di Lucania. Contesti di età classical nell'Insula I del quartiere centrale, Tesi di Specializzazione in Etruscologia e Antichità italiche. University of Basilicata, Italy (unpublished).

Gramsci, A. [2007]. La quistione meridionale, a cura di Marcello Montanari. Bari: Palomar.

Grandjean, Y. 1988. Recherches sur l'habitat thasien à l'epoque grecque (Études thasiennes 12). Athens/Paris: École Française d'Athènes.

Gras, M. 2003. Antipolis et Nikaia: Les ambiguïtés de la frontère entre la Massalie et l'Italie. In Peuples et territoires en Gaule méditerranéenne. Hommage à Guy Barruol, 241–246. Montpellier: Université Paul Valéry.

Greco, E. 1981. Dal territorio alla città: lo sviluppo urbano di Taranto. Annali dell'Istituto Universitario Orientale di Napoli. Dipartimento di Studi del mondo classico e del Mediterraneo antico. Sezione di archeologia e storia antica 3: 139–157.

Greco, E. 1982. Considerazioni su alcuni modelli di organizzazione dello spazio agrario nelle città dell'Italia meridionale. Archaeologia Warszawa 33: 47–58.

Greco, E. (ed.) 1999. La città greca antica: istituzioni, società e forme urbane. Rome: Donzelli.

Greco, E. 2008. Ippodamo e l'urbanistica di Thurii. In Atti del 48° Convegno di Studi sulla Magna Grecia, 281–286. Taranto: Istituto per la Storia e l'Archeologia della Magna Grecia.

Greco, E. 2009. The Urban Plan of Thurii. Literary sources and archaeological evidence for a Hippodamean city. In Owen, S., Preston, L. (eds.). Inside the City in the Greek World: Studies of Urbanism From the Bronze Age to the Hellenistic Period, 108–117. Oxford/Oakville, CT: Oxbow.

Greco, E. 2014. La tomba del fondatore e le origini di Poseidonia. Paestum: Pandemos.

Greco, E., Ficuciello, L. 2012. Cesure e continuità: Lemno dai 'Tirreni' agli Ateniesi. In Culasso Gastaldi, E., Marchiandi, D. (eds.). Gli Ateniesi fuori dall'Attica: modi d'intervento e di controllo del territorio (Torino, 8–9 aprile 2010). Annuario della Scuola Archeologica di Atene e delle Missioni Italiane in Oriente 88: 149–168.

Greco, E., Lombardo, M. 2010. La colonizzazione greca: modelli interpretativi nel dibattito attuale. In Atti del 50° Convegno di Studi sulla Magna Grecia, 37–60. Taranto: Istituto per la Storia e l'Archeologia della Magna Grecia.

Greco, E., Theodorescu, D. (eds.) 1983. Poseidonia-Paestum, vol. 2. L'agorà. Rome: École française de Rome.

Groot, M., Lentjes, D., Zeiler, J. (eds.) 2013. Barely Surviving or More Than Enough? The Environmental Archaeology of Subsistence, Specialisation and Surplus Food Production. Leiden: Sidestone Press.

Gualtieri, M. 2003. La Lucania romana: cultura e società nella documentazione archeologica. Naples: Loffredo.

Guthrie, W.K.C. 1969. A History of Greek Philosophy, vol. 3. Cambridge: Cambridge University Press.

Gutschker, T. 2002. Aristotelische Diskurse. Aristoteles und die politische Philosophie des 20. Jahrhunderts. Stuttgart/Weimar: Metzler.

Guy, M. 1995. Cadastres en bandes de Métaponte à Agde: Questions et méthods. Études Massaliètes 4: 427–444.

Guy, M. 1998. La topographie des territoires décrits dans les tables d'Héraclée. In Siritide e Metapontino. Storie di due territori coloniali. Atti dell'incontro di studio di Policoro, 31 ottobre – 2 novembre 1991, 261–280. Naples: Centre Jean Bérard.

Guzzo, P.G. 1997. Thurii e la Sibaritide. *Ostraka* 6: 379–387.

Guzzo, P.G. 2005. Ricerche intorno a Sibari: da Cavallari a Zanotti Bianco. In Settis, S., Parra, M.C. (eds.). Magna Graecia. *Archeologia di un sapere* (Catalog of the Exhibition, Catanzaro), 133–135. Milan: Electa

Guzzo, P.G. 2013. Caronda e coloro che si nutrono dallo stesso granaio. Ipotesi sulle strutture circolari di Megara Hyblea, Selinunte e Himera. *Mitteilungen des Deutschen Archäologischen Instituts, Römische Abteilung* 119: 33–42.

Hall, J. 2002. *Hellenicity. Between Ethnicity and Culture.* Chicago/London: University of Chicago Press.

Hallof, K. 2003. Zur Gerichtsbarkeit in attischen Kleruchien des 4. Jahrhunderts. In *Symposion 1999. Vorträge zur griechischen und hellenistischen Rechtsgeschichte (Akten der Gesellschaft für griechische und hellenistische Rechtsgeschichte, vol. 14),* 229–234. Köln/Weimar/Wien: Böhlau.

Hallof, K., Habicht, Chr. 1995. Buleuten und Beamte der athenischen Kleruchie in Samos. *Mitteilungen des Deutschen Archäologischen Instituts, Abteilung Athen* 110: 273–304.

Hamilakis, Y. 2012. Are We Postcolonial Yet? Tales From the Battlefield. *Archaeologies: Journal of the World Archaeological Congress* 8.1: 67–76.

Hänsel, B. 1973. Policoro (Matera). Scavi eseguiti nell'area dell'acropoli di Eraclea negli anni 1965–1967. *Notizie degli Scavi* 1973: 400–492.

Hansen, M.H. 2004. The Concept of the Consumption City Applied to the Greek Polis. In Nielsen, T.H. (ed.). *Once Again: Studies in the Ancient Greek Polis,* 9–47. Stuttgart: F. Steiner.

Hansen, M.H. 2006. *The Shotgun Method. The Demography of the Ancient Greek City State Culture.* Columbia/London: University of Missouri Press.

Hansen, M.H., Nielsen, T.H. (eds.) 2004. *An Inventory of Archaic and Classical Poleis. An Investigation Conducted by the Copenhagen Polis Centre for the Danish National Research Foundation.* Oxford: Oxford University Press.

Hanson, V. 1995. *The Other Greeks: The Family Farm and the Agrarian Roots of Western Civilization.* New York: The Free Press.

Henkel, H. 1872. *Studien zur Geschichte der griechischen Lehre vom Staat.* Leipzig: Teubner.

Hennig, D. 1989. Besitzgleichheit und Demokratie. In Schuller, W., Hoepfner, W., Schwandner, E.L. (eds.). *Demokratie und Architektur. Der hippodamische Städtebau und die Entstehung der Demokratie, Konstanzer Symposion vom 17. bis 19. Juli 1987, 25–35.* Munich: Deutscher Kunstverlag.

Henning, A. 2011. Due siti fortificati in Lucania. La campagna di ricognizione 2011 a Monte Croccia e Monte Torretta. *SIRIS* 11: 79–100.

Hiller von Gaertringen, F. 1906. *Inschriften von Priene.* Berlin: G. Reimer.

Hiller von Gaertringen, F., Wilski, P. 1904. *Thera, vol. 3. Die Stadtgeschichte von Thera.* Berlin: Reimer.

Himmelmann, N. 1971. Archäologisches zum Problem der griechischen Sklaverei. *Mainzer Akademie der Wissenschaften und der Literatur. Abhandlungen der Geistes- und Sozialwissenschaftlichen Klasse* 1971.13: 615–659.

Hind, J. 1998. Megarian Colonisation in the Western Half of the Black Sea. In Tsetskhladze, G.R. (ed.). *The Greek Colonisation of the Black Sea Area. Historical Interpretation of Archaeology,* 131–152. Stuttgart: F. Steiner.

Hodkinson, S. 2000. *Property and Wealth in Classical Sparta.* London: Duckworth.

Hodkinson, S. 2002. Spartiate Landownership and Inheritance. In Whitby, M. (ed.). *Sparta,* 86–89. Edinburgh: Edinburgh University Press.

Hodos, T. 2006. *Local Responses to Colonisation in the Iron Age Mediterranean.* London/New York: Routledge.

Hoepfner, W. 1989. Die frühen Demokratien und die Architekturforschung. In Schuller, W., Hoepfner, W., Schwandner, E.L. (eds.) 1989. *Demokratie und Architektur. Der hippodamische Städtebau und die Entstehung der Demokratie, Konstanzer Symposion vom 17. bis 19. Juli 1987,* 9–13. Munich: Deutscher Kunstverlag.

Hoepfner, W. (ed.) 1999. *Geschichte des Wohnens, vol. 1. 5000 v. Chr. – 500 n. Chr.* Stuttgart: Deutsche Verlags-Anstalt.

Hoepfner, W., Schwandner, E.-L. 1994. *Haus und Stadt im klassischen Griechenland.* Munich: Deutscher Kunstverlag.

Horden, P., Purcell, N. 2000. *The Corrupting Sea. A Study of Mediterranean History*. Oxford: Blackwell.

Horky, P.S. 2013. *Plato and Pythagoreanism*. Oxford/New York: Oxford University Press.

Hornblower, S. 1982. *Mausolus*. Oxford: Clarendon.

Horsnaes, H.W. 2002. *The Cultural Development in North-Western Lucania c. 600–273 BC*. Rome: "L'Erma" di Bretschneider.

Houby-Nielsen, S. 1996. The Archaeology of Ideology in the Kerameikos. New Interpretations of the Opferrinnen. In Hägg, R. (ed.). *The Role of Religion in the Early Greek Polis: Proceedings of the Third International Seminar on Ancient Greek Cult Organized by the Swedish Institute at Athens, 16–18 October 1992*, 41–54. Stockholm: Svenska Institutet i Athen.

Hout, J.-L. (ed.) 1988. *La ville neuve: une idée de l'Antiquité?* Paris: Éditions Errance.

Hoxha, G., Oettel, A. 2011. Lissos 2011. *Iliria* 36: 435–437.

Hultsch, F. 1854. *Metrologicorum Scriptorum Reliquae, vol. 1*. Leipzig: Teubner.

Hultsch, F. 1862. *Griechische und römische Metrologie*. Berlin: Weidmannsche Buchhandlung.

Hurst, H., Owen, S. (eds.) 2005. *Ancient Colonizations: Analogy, Similarity and Difference*. London: Duckworth.

Isaac, B. 2004. *The Invention of Racism in Classical Antiquity*. Princeton: Princeton University Press.

Isager, S., Skydsgaard, J.E. 1995. *Greek Agriculture. An Introduction*. London/New York: Routledge.

Isayev, E. 2007. *Inside Ancient Lucania: Dialogues in History & Archaeology*. London: Institute of Classical Studies.

Ivantchik, A.I. 2008. Greeks and Iranians in the Cimmerian Bosporus in the Second and First Centuries BC. New epigraphic data from Tanais. In Darbandi, S.M.R., Zournatzi, A. (eds.). *Ancient Greece and Ancient Iran: Cross-Cultural Encounters, 1st International Conference (Athens, 11–13 November 2006)*, 93–107. Athens: National Hellenic Research Foundation.

Jameson, M.H. 1977/8. Agriculture and Slavery in Classical Athens. *Classical Journal* 73: 122–125.

Jameson, M.H., Jordan, D.R., Kotansky, R.D. 1993. *A Lex Sacra From Selinous*. Durham, North Carolina: Duke University.

Jameson, M.H., Runnels, C.N., van Andel, T.H. 1994. *A Greek Countryside. The Southern Argolid from Prehistory to the Present Day*. Standford: Stanford University Press.

Janni, P. 1984. Sparta 'ritrovata'. Il modello spartano nell'etnografia antica. In Lanzilotto, E. (ed.). *Problemi di storia e cultura spartane*, 29–58. Rome: G. Bretschneider.

Johannowsky, W. 1992. Appunti su Pyxous-Buxentum. *Atti e Memorie della Società Magna Grecia* 13: 173–183.

Joshel, S.R., Hackworth Peterson, L. 2014. *The Material Life of Roman Slaves*. Cambridge/New York: Cambridge University Press.

Kamps, W. 1938. L'emphytéose en droit grec et sa réception en droit roman. In *Recueils de la Société J. Bodin, vol. 3: la tenure*, 67–121. Bruxelles: Dessain & Tolra.

Katz, B. 1976. The Birds of Aristophanes and Politics. *Athenaeum* 53: 353–381.

Katz, M.A. 1995. Ideology and the 'Status of Women' in Ancient Greece. In Golden, M., Toohey, P. (eds.). *Sex and Difference in Ancient Greece and Rome*, 30–43. Edinburgh: Edinburgh University Press.

Kelso, W.M. 2005. *Jamestown: The Buried Truth*, Charlottesville: University of Virginia Press.

Kelso, W.M., Straube, B., Schmidt, D. (eds.) 2012. *2007–2010 Interim Report on the Preservation Virginia Excavations at Jamestown, Virginia* (online) http://historicjamestowne.org/download/field-reports-3/

van Keuren, F.D. 1994. *The Coinage of Heraclea Lucaniae*. Rome: G. Bretschneider.

Kiderlen, M. 1995. *Megale Oikia: Untersuchungen zur Entwicklung aufwendiger griechischer Stadthausarchitektur von der Früharchaik bis ins 3. Jh. v. Chr.* Hürth: Lange.

Kilmer, M.F. 1993. *Greek Erotica on Attic Red-Figure Vases*. London: Duckworth.

Kindberg Jacobsen, J., Handberg, S. 2010. A Greek Enclave at the Iron Age Settlement of Timpone della Motta. In *Atti del 50° Convegno di Studi sulla Magna Grecia*, 685–718. Taranto: Istituto per la Storia e l'Archeologia della Magna Grecia.

Kirigin, B. 2006. *Pharos: The Parian Settlement. A Study of a Greek Colony in the Adriatic.* Oxford: BAR.

Kirigin, B., Popovič, P. 1988. Maslinovik: A Greek Watchtower in the Chora of Pharos. A preliminary report. In Chapman, J.C., Bintliff, J., Gaffney, V., Slapšak, B. (eds.). *Recent Developments in Yugoslav Archaeology*, 177–190. Oxford: BAR.

Kirsten, E., Opelt, I. 1989. Eine Urkunde der Gründung von Arsinoe in Kilikien. *Zeitschrift für Papyrologie und Epigraphik* 77: 55–66.

Klasko, G. 2006. *The Development of Plato's Political Theory, 2nd edition.* Oxford: Oxford University Press.

Knigge, U. 1976. *Kerameikos, vol. 9. Der Südhügel.* Berlin: W. de Gruyter.

Knigge, U. 1988. *Der Kerameikos von Athen. Führung durch Ausgrabungen und Geschichte.* Athens: Krene.

Knoll, M. 2009. *Aristokratische oder demokratische Gerechtigkeit? Die politische Philosophie des Aristoteles und Martha Nussbaums egalitaristische Rezeption.* Munich: Fink.

Kolb, F. 1984. *Die Stadt im Altertum.* Munich: C.H. Beck.

Kolb, F. (ed.) 2004. *Chora und Polis.* Munich: Oldenbourg.

Koukouli-Chrysanthaki, C. 2002. Classical Amphipolis. In Stamatopoulou, M., Yeroulanou, M. (eds.). *Excavating Classical Culture: Recent Discoveries in Greece*, 57–73. Oxford: Archaeopress.

Krause, K.-J. 1998. *Raumplanung im griechischen Altertum.* Dortmund: Informationskreis Raumplanung.

Krinzinger, F. 1994. Intorno alla pianta di Velia. In Greco, G., Krinzinger, F. (eds.). *Velia. Studi e ricerche*, 19–54. Modena: Panini.

Kron, U. 1971. Zum Hypogäum von Paestum. *Jahrbuch des Deutschen Archäologischen Instituts* 86: 117–148.

Kunze-Götte, E., Trancke, K., Vierneisel, K. 1999. *Kerameikos, vol. 7.2: Die Nekropole von der Mitte des 6. bis zum Ende des 5. Jahrhunderts. Die Beigaben.* München: Hirmer.

Kurtz, D.C., Boardman, J. 1971. *Greek Burial Customs.* London: Thames & Hudson.

Kuznecov, V.D. 1999. Early Types of Greek Dwelling Houses in the North Black Sea. In Tsetskhladze, G. (ed.). *Ancient Greeks West and East*, 531–564. Leiden: Brill.

La Rocca, E. 1972/3. Una testa femminile nel Museo dei Conservatori e l'Afrodite Louvre Napoli. *Annuario della Scuola Archeologica di Atene* 50/51: 419–450.

La Torre, G.F. 2004. Il processo di romanizzazione della Sicilia. Il caso di Tindari. *Sicilia Antiqua* 1: 111–146.

Lachenal, L. (ed.) 1993. *Da Leukania a Lucania. La Lucania centro-orientale fra Pirro e i Giulio-Claudii* (Catalogue of the Exhibition, Venosa). Rome: Istituto poligrafico e Zecca dello Stato.

Lane, M. 2014. *Greek and Roman Political Ideas.* London/New York: Penguin.

Lanza, M. 2012. La necropoli meridionale di Eraclea: le tombe di via Umbria. In Osanna, M., Zuchtriegel, G. (eds.). *ΑΜΦΙ ΣΙΡΙΟΣ ΡΟΑΣ. Nuove ricerche su Eraclea e la Siritide*, 181–203. Venosa: Osanna.

Lanza, M. 2015. Topografia e sviluppo della necropoli meridionale di Herakleia. In Meo, F., Zuchtriegel, G. (eds.). *Siris Herakleia Polychoron: città e campagna tra antichità e medioevo. Atti del convegno Policoro, 12 luglio 2013* (SIRIS 14), 89–99. Bari: Edipuglia.

Lanza, M.T. (ed.) 1990. *Paolo Orsi, La Necropoli di Passo Marinaro a Camarina: campagne di scavo 1904–1909.* Rome: Accademia Nazionale dei Lincei.

Lauter, H. 1980. Zu Heimstätten und Gutshäusern im klassischen Attika. In *Forschungen und Funde. Festschrift für Bernhard Neutsch*, 279–286. Innsbruck: Verlag des Institutes für Sprachwissenschaft der Universität Innsbruck.

Lauter, H. 1986. *Die Architektur des Hellenismus.* Darmstadt: Wissenschaftliche Buchgesellschaft.

Lazaridis, D. 1972. *Ἀμφίπολις καὶ Ἄργιλος.* Athens: Athēnaïkos Technologikos Homilos.

Lazaridis, D. 1983. Ανασκαφές και έρευνες στην Αμφίπολη. *Praktika* 139: 35–41.

Lazaridis, D. 1984. Ανασκαφές και έρευνες στην Αμφίπολη. *Praktika* 140: 33–39.

Lazaridis, D. 1997. *Amphipolis.* Athens: Ministery of Culture.

Lear, A. 2015. Was Pederasty Problemized? In Masterson, M., Sorkin Rabinowitz, N., Robson, J. (eds.). *Sex in Antiquity: Exploring Gender and Sexuality in the Ancient World*, 115–136. London/New York: Routledge.

Lentini, M.C. (ed.) 1998. *Naxos a quarant'anni dall'inizio degli scavi*. Messina: Museo Archeologico di Naxos.

Lentini, M.C., Garaffo, S. 1995. *Il tesoretto di Naxos (1985) dall'isolato urbano C4, casa 1–2*. Roma: Istituto Italiano di Numismatica.

Lentjes, D. 2013. From Subsistence to Market Exchange: The Development of an Agricultural Economy in 1st Millenium BC Southeast Italy. In Groot, M., Lentjes, D., Zeiler, J. (eds.). *Barely Surviving or More Than Enough? The Environmental Archaeology of Subsistence, Specialisation and Surplus Food Production*, 101–130. Leiden: Sidestone Press.

Lepsius, R. 1855. Über eine Hieroglyphische Inschrift am Tempel von Edfu (Appollinopolis Magna) in welcher der Besitz dieses Tempels an Ländereien unter der Regierung Ptolemaeus IX Alexander I verzeichnet ist. *Abhandlungen der Königlichen Akademie der Wissenschaften zu Berlin, phil.-hist. Klasse 1855*: 69–113.

Leyden, W. 1994. *Aristotle on Equality and Justice: His Political Argument*. Handmills: Macmillan.

Liebmann, M., Rizvi, U. (eds.) 2008. *Archaeology and the Postcolonial Critique*. Lanham, Maryland: Altamira Press.

Lippolis, E. (ed.) 1994. *Catalogo del Museo Nazionale Archeologico di Taranto, vol. 3.1. Taranto e la necropoli: aspetti e problemi della documentazione archeologica dal VII al I sec. a.C.* Taranto: La Colomba.

Lippolis, E. (ed.) 1996. *Arte e artigianato in Magna Grecia* (Catalog of the Exhibition, Taranto). Naples: Electa.

Lippolis, E. 1997. Taranto e la politica di Atene in Occidente. *Ostraka* 6: 359–378.

Lippolis, E. 2001. Taranto: forma e sviluppo della topografia urbana. In *Atti del 41° Convegno di Studi sulla Magna Grecia*, 119–169. Taranto: Istituto per la Storia e l'Archeologia della Magna Grecia.

Lippolis, E. 2011. Taranto nel IV secolo a.C. In Neudecker, R. (ed.). *Krise und Wandel. Süditalien im 4. und 3. Jahrhundert v. Chr. Internationaler Kongress anlässlich des 65. Geburtstages von Dieter Mertens, Rom 26. bis 28. Juni 2006*, 121–145. Wiesbaden: Reichert.

Lippolis, E., Garraffo, S., Nafissi, M. 1995. *Taranto (Culti greci in Occidente 1)*. Taranto: Istituto per la Storia e l'Archeologia della Magna Grecia.

Lloyd, A.B. 1993. *Herodotus, Book II. Commentary 99–182, Second Impression*. Leiden/New York: Brill.

Lo Cascio, E., Storchi Marino, A. (eds.) 2001. *Modalità insediative e strutture agrarie nell'Italia meridionale in età romana*. Bari: Edipuglia.

Lo Porto, F.G. 1961. Ricerche archeologiche in Heraclea di Lucania. *Bollettino d'Arte* 46: 133–150.

Lo Porto, F.G. 1992. Ricerche sulle antiche mura di Taranto. Gli scavi di Masseria del Carmine. *Taras* 12.1: 7–27.

Lohmann, H. 1993. *Atene. Forschungen zu Siedlungs- und Wirtschaftsstruktur des klassischen Attika*. Köln: Böhlau.

Lomas, K. 1996. Greeks, Romans, and Others: Problems of Colonialism and Ethnicity in Southern Italy. In Webster, J., Cooper N. (eds.). *Roman Imperialism: Post-Colonial Perspectives (A collection of papers originally presented to a symposium held at Leicester University in November 1994)*, 135–144. Leicester: University of Leicester.

Lombardo, M. 1982. Antileon tirannicida nelle tradizioni metapontina ed eracleota. *Studi di Antichità* 3: 189–205.

Lombardo, M. 1992. Lo psephisma di Lumbarda: note critiche e questioni esegetiche. *Hesperìa* 3: 161–188.

Lombardo, M. 1996. Greci, Enotri e Lucani nella Basilicata meridionale tra l'VIII e il III secolo a.C.: aspetti e momenti dei processi storici. In Bianco, S. (ed.). *I Greci in Occidente. Greci, Enotri e Lucani nella Basilicata meridionale* (Catalog of the Exhibition, Policoro), 15–26. Milan: Electa.

Lombardo, M. 2005. The psephisma of Lumbarda: a new fragment. In *Illyrica antiqua: ob honorem Duje Rendić-Miočević. Radovi s međunarodnoga skupa o problemima antičke arheologije, Zagreb, 6.-8.XI.2003*, 353–360. Zagreb: Filozofski fakultet, Odsjek za arheologiju.

Lombardo, M. 2009. Modelli e dinamiche coloniali nell'area ionico-adriatica. In Lombardo, M. and Frisone, F. (eds.). *Colonie di colonie: le fondazioni sub-coloniali greche tra colonizzazione e colonialismo (Atti del convegno internazionale di Lecce, 22–26 giugno 2009)*, 133–144. Galatina: Congedo.

Lorber, C.C. 1990. *Amphipolis: The Civic Coinage in Silver and Gold*. Los Angeles: Numismatic Fine Arts.

Lorentzen, J., Pirson, F., Schneider, P., Wulf-Rheidt, U. (eds.) 2010. *Aktuelle Forschungen zur Konstruktion, Funktion und Semantik antiker Stadtbefestigungen, Kolloquium 9./10. Februar 2007 in Istanbul* (Byzas 10). Istanbul: Ege Yayınları.

Luppino, S., Granese, T., Quondam, F., Vanzetti, A. 2010. Sibartide: riletture di alcuni contesti funerari tra VIII e VII sec. a.C. In *Atti del 50° Convegno di Studi sulla Magna Grecia*, 643–682. Taranto: Istituto per la Storia e l'Archeologia della Magna Grecia.

Luraghi, N. 1994. *Tirannidi arcaiche in Sicilia e Magna Grecia*. Firenze: Olschki.

Lyons, C. 1996. *Morgantina Studies, vol. 5: The Archaic Cemeteries*. Princeton: Princeton University Press.

Lyttkens, C.H. 2013. *Economic Analysis of Institutional Change in Ancient Greece*. London/New York: Routledge.

Maddoli, G. 1986. Manomissioni sacre in Eraclea Lucana (SEG XXX, 1162–1179). *Parola del Passato* 41: 99–107.

Maddoli, G. 2007. La politica occidentale di Atene: una questione ancora aperta. In *Atti del 47° Convegno di Studi sulla Magna Grecia*, 157–164. Taranto: Istituto per la Storia e l'Archeologia della Magna Grecia.

Malanima, P. 1999. Risorse, popolazioni, redditi: 1300–1861. In Ciocca, P., Toniolo, G. (eds.). *Storia economica d'Italia*, 43–124. Roma/Bari: Laterza.

Malkin, I. 1984. What were the sacred precincts of Brea? (IG³ 46). *Chiron* 14: 44–48.

Malkin, I. 1987. *Religion and Colonization in Ancient Greece*. Leiden/New York: Brill.

Malkin, I. 1994a. *Myth and Territory in the Spartan Mediterranean*. Cambridge: Cambridge University Press.

Malkin, I. 1994b. Inside and Outside: Colonization and the Formation of the Mother City. *Annali dell'Istituto Universitario Orientale di Napoli. Dipartimento di Studi del mondo classico e del Mediterraneo antico. Sezione di archeologia e storia antica, n.s.*, 1: 1–9.

Malkin, I. 2004. Postcolonial Concepts and Ancient Greek Colonisation. *Modern Language Quarterly* 65.3: 341–364.

Malkin, I. 2008. Review of Henry Hurst, Sara Owen (ed.). Ancient Colonizations. Analogy, Similarity & Difference. London: Duckworth, 2005. *Bryn Mawr Classical Review* 2008.11.08 (online) http://bmcr.brynmawr.edu/2008/2008-11-08.html

Malkin, I. 2013. *A Small Greek World. Networks in the Ancient Mediterranean*. Oxford/New York: Oxford University Press.

Mandić, J., Vita, C. 2015. Le comunità dell'entroterra: il caso di San Brancato di Sant'Arcangelo (PZ). La necropoli lucana. In Meo, F., Zuchtriegel, G. (eds.). *Siris Herakleia Polychoron: città e campagna tra antichità e medioevo. Atti del convegno Policoro, 12 luglio 2013 (SIRIS 14)*, 173–201. Bari: Edipuglia.

Mannino, K. 1996. Gli ateliers attici e la nascita della produzione figurata. In Lippolis, E. (ed.). *Arte e artigianato in Magna Grecia* (Catalog of the Exhibition, Taranto), 363–370. Naples: Electa.

Mari, M. 2010. Atene, l'impero e le apoikiai. Riflessioni sulla breve vita di Anfipoli 'ateniese'. *Annuario della Scuola Archeologica di Atene e delle Missioni Italiane in Oriente* 88: 391–413.

Martin, R. 1957. Sur deux expressions techniques de l'architecture grecque. *Revue Philologique* 31: 66–81.

McClintock, A. 1992. The Angel of Progress: Pitfalls of the Term 'Post-Colonialism'. *Social Text* 31/2: 84–98.

McGuire, R.H., Paynter, R. (eds.) 1991. *The Archaeology of Inequality*. Oxford: Blackwell.

Medovoi, L., Raman, S., Robinson, B. 1990. Can the Subaltern Vote? *Socialist Review* 20.3: 133–149.

Mee, C., Forbes, H. (eds.) 1997. *A Rough and Rocky Place: The Landscape and Settlement History of the Methana Peninsula, Greece. Results of the Methana Survey Project sponsored by the British*

School at Athens and the University of Liverpool. Liverpool: Liverpool University Press.

Meikle, S. 1995. *Aristotle's Economic Thought.* Oxford: Clarendon Press.

Mele, A. 1997. Allevamento ovino nell'antica Apulia e lavorazione della lana a Taranto. In *Schiavi e dipendenti nell'ambito dell'oikos e della familia.Atti del 22° Colloquio GIREA, Pontignano, 19-20 novembre 1995*, 97–104. Pisa: ETS.

Meo, F. 2011. Rediscovering Ancient Activities: Textile Tools in a 3rd – 2nd Century B.C. Context from Herakleia (Southern Basilicata, Italy). *Archaeological Textile Newsletter* 53: 2–11.

Meo, F. 2012. Attestazioni archeologiche di attività laniera a Eraclea di Lucania tra III e II secolo a.C. Nota preliminare. In Osanna, M., Zuchtriegel, G. (eds.). *ΑΜΦΙ ΣΙΡΙΟΣ ΡΟΑΣ. Nuove ricerche su Eraclea e la Siritide*, 259–271.Venosa: Osanna.

Meo, F. 2015. L'industria tessile a Herakleia di Lucania e nel territorio tra III e I secolo a.C. In Meo, F., Zuchtriegel, G. (eds.). *Siris Herakleia Polychoron: città e campagna tra antichità e medioevo. Atti del convegno Policoro, 12 luglio 2013 (SIRIS 14)*, 137–151. Bari: Edipuglia.

Meo, F., Zuchtriegel, G. (eds.) 2015. *Siris Herakleia Polychoron: città e campagna tra antichità e medioevo. Atti del convegno Policoro, 12 luglio 2013 (SIRIS 14).* Bari: Edipuglia.

Mercuri, A.M., Florenzano, A., Massamba N'Siala, I., Olmi, L., Roubis, D., Sogliani, F. 2012. Pollen from archaeological layers and cultural landscape reconstruction: Case studies form the Bradano valley (Basilicata, southern Italy). *Plant Biosystems* 144.4: 888–901.

Mertens, D. 2006. *Städte und Bauten der Westgriechen.* Munich: Hirmer.

Mertens, D., Hoesch, N., Dehl-von Kaenel, Chr. 2003. Die Agora von Selinunt. Neue Grabungsergebnisse zur Frühzeit der griechischen Kolonialstadt. Ein Vorbericht. *Mitteilungen des Deutschen Archäologischen Instituts, Römische Abteilung* 110: 289–445.

Mertens-Horn, M. 1992. Die archaischen Baufriese von Metapont. *Mitteilungen des Deutschen Archäologischen Instituts, Römische Abteilung* 99: 225–248.

Milićević Bradač, M. 2007. Die Griechen in Kroatien. In Sanader, M. (ed.). *Kroatien in der Antike*, 37–60. Mainz: Zabern.

Miller, M.C. 1997. *Athens and Persia in the Fifth Century B.C.: A Study in Cultural Receptivity.* Cambridge: Cambridge University Press.

Miller, T. 1997. *Die griechische Kolonisation im Spiegel literarischer Zeugnisse.* Tübingen: G. Narr.

Minar, E.L. 1942. *Early Pythagorean Politics in Practice and Theory.* Baltimore: Waverly.

Moggi, M. 1995. Proprietà della terra e cambiamenti costituzionali. In *L'incidenza dell'antico. Studi in memoria di Ettore Lepore, vol. 1*, 389–403. Naples: Luciano.

Moggi, M. 2001. Taranto fino al V secolo a.C. In *Atti del 41° Convegno di Studi sulla Magna Grecia*, 45–78. Taranto: Istituto per la Storia e l'Archeologia della Magna Grecia.

Möller, A. 2007. Classical Greece: distribution. In Scheidel, W., Morris, I., Saller, R. (eds.). *The Cambridge Economic History of the Graeco-Roman World*, 362–384. Cambridge/ New York: Cambridge University Press.

Monod, S., Coquery-Vidrovitch, C., Halen, P. Balandier, G. Omasombo-Tschonda, J., M'Bokolo, E. 2007. Joseph Conrad and the 'Darkness' of Central Africa – a record of a discussion. *Konteksty* 2007 3/4: 113–120.

Moore, K.R. 2012. *Plato, Politics and a Practical Utopia. Social Constructivism and Civic Planning in the Laws.* New York: Bloomsbury.

Morel, J.-P. 1978. La laine de Tarante (De l'usage des textes anciens en histoire économique). *Ktema* 3: 94–110.

Morel, J.-P. 1981. *Céramique Campanienne: les formes.* Rome: École française de Rome.

Moreno, A. 2007. *Feeding the Democracy: The Athenian Grain Supply in the Fifth and Fourth Centuries BC.* Oxford: Oxford University Press.

Morris, I. 1998. Remaining Invisible: The Archaeology of the Excluded in Classical Athens. In Joshel, S.R., Murnaghan, S. (eds.). *Women and Slaves in Greco-Roman Culture: Differential Equations*, 193–220. London/ New York: Routledge.

Morris, I. 2003. Mediterraneanization. *Mediterranean Historical Review* 18.2: 30–55.

Morris, S.P., Papadopoulos, J.K. 2005. Greek Towers and Slaves: an Archaeology of Exploitation. *American Journal of Archaeology* 109.2: 155–225.

Morrow, G.R. 1960. *Plato's Cretan City: A Historical commentary on the Laws*. Princeton: Princeton University Press.

Mossé, C. 1993. *Le citoyen dans la Grèce antique*. Paris: Nathan.

Mueller, K. 2006. *Settlements of the Ptolemies. City Foundations and New Settlement in the Hellenistic World*. Dudley, MA: Peeters.

Müller, C. 2010. *D'Olbia à Tanaïs. Territoires et réseaux d'échanges dans la mer Noire septentrionale aux époques classique et hellénistique*. Paris: De Boccard.

Müller, H.H. 1967. *Märkische Landwirtschaft vor der Agrarreform von 1807. Entwicklungstendenzen des Ackerbaus in der zweiten Hälfte des 18. Jahrhunderts*. Potsdam: Bezirksheimatmuseum.

Musti, D. 2005. *Magna Grecia. Il quadro storico*. Bari: Laterza.

Mylonas, G. 1943. Excavations at Mecyberna 1934–1938. *American Journal of Archaeology* 47: 78–87.

Nafissi, M. 2007. Sibariti, Ateniesi e Peloponnesiaci. Problemi storici e storiografici nel racconto di Diodoro sulla fondazione di Thurii. In Greco, E., Lombardo, M. (eds.). *Atene e l'Occidente, i grandi temi: le premesse, i protagonisti, le forme della comunicazione e dell'interazione, i modi dell'intervento ateniese in Occidente. Atti del Convegno Internazionale, Atene, 25–27 maggio 2006*, 385–413. Athens: Scuola Archeologica Italiana di Atene.

Nava, M.L., Osanna, M., De Faveri, C. (eds.) 2007. *Antica Flora Lucana. Dizionario archeologico*. Venosa: Osanna.

Neubauer, J. 2011. *Türkische Deutsche, Kanakster und Deutschländer: Identität und Fremdwahrnehmung in Film und Literatur: Fatih Akin, Thomas Arslan, Emine Sevgi Özdamar, Zafer Şenocak und Feridun Zaimoğlu*. Würzburg: Königshausen & Neumann.

Neutsch, B. 1967. Archäologische Studien und Bodensondierungen bei Policoro in den Jahren 1959–1964. In Neutsch, B. (ed.). *Herakleiastudien* (Archäologische Forschungen in Lukanien 2), 100–180. Heidelberg: F.H. Kerle.

Neutsch, B. 1968. Neue archäologische Forschungen in Siris und Herakleia am Golf von Tarent. *Archäologischer Anzeiger* 1968: 753–794.

Nevett, L. 1999. *House and Society in the Ancient Greek World*. Cambridge/New York: Cambridge University Press.

Newman, W.L. 1887. *The Politics of Aristotle, vol. 1 & 2*. Oxford: Clarendon.

Newman, W.L. 1902. *The Politics of Aristotle, vol. 3 & 4*. Oxford: Clarendon

Nicholas, G., Hollowell, J. 2007. Ethical Challenges to a Postcolonial Archaeology: The Legacy of Scientific Colonialism. In Hamilakis, Y., Duke, P. (eds.). *Archaeology and Capitalism. From Ethics to Politics*, 59–82. Walnut Creek: Left Coast Press.

Nickels, A. 1995. Les sondages de la rue Perben à Agde (Hérault). *Études Massaliotes* 4: 59–98.

Nikolaenko, G.M. 2006. The Chora of Tauric Chersonesos and the Cadastre of the 4th – 2nd Century BC. In *Surveying the Greek Chora. The Black Sea Region in a Comparative Perspective*, 151–174. Aarhus: Aarhus University Press.

Nowak, C. 2009. La spiegazione etnica come modello interpretativo dei processi di trasformazione nei rituali funerari – Il caso di Poseidonia. *Bollettino quadrimestrale dell'Associazione Internazionale di Archeologia Classica* 5.1/2, 13–14.

Nowak, C. 2014. *Bestattungsrituale in Unteritalien vom 5. bis 4. Jh. v. Chr. Überlegungen zur sog. Samnitisierung Kampaniens*. Wiesbaden: Reichert.

Nussbaum, M. 1990. Aristotelian Social Democracy. In Douglas, R.B., Mara, G., Richardson, H. (eds.). *Liberalism and the Good*, 203–252. London/New York: Routledge.

Ober, J. 1991. Aristotle's Political Sociology: Class, Status, and Order in the Politics. In Lord, C., O'Connor, D.K. (eds.). *Essays on the Foundations of Aristotelian Political Science*, 112–135. Berkeley: University of California Press.

Oller Guzmán, M. 2013. Griegos e indígenas en Empórion (s. vi–iv a.C.): un estado de la cuestión. In Santiago Álvarez, R.-A., Oller Guzmán, M. (eds.). *Contacto de poblaciones y extranjería en el mundo griego antiguo: estudio de fuentes*, 187–202. Barcelona: Universitat Autònoma.

Orlandini, P. 1983. Le arti figurative. In Pugliese Caratelli, G. (ed.). *Megale Hellas: storia e civiltà della Magna Grecia*, 329–554. Milan: Scheiwiller.

Orsini, M. 2008. *Memoria storica del nostro '900.* Mottola: Stampa Sud.

Osanna, M. 1992. *Chorai coloniali da Taranto a Locri. Documentazione archeologica e ricostruzione storica.* Roma: Quasar.

Osanna, M. 2000. Fattorie e villaggi in Magna Grecia. In *Atti del 40° Convegno di Studi sulla Magna Grecia,* 203–220. Taranto: Istituto per la Storia e l'Archeologia della Magna Grecia.

Osanna, M. 2008. La documentazione archeologica. In Osanna, M., Prandi, L., Siciliano, A. *Eraclea* (Culti greci in occidente 2), 21–67. Taranto: Istituto per la Storia e l'Archeologia della Magna Grecia.

Osanna, M. (ed.) 2009. *Verso la città. Forme insediative in Lucania e nel mondo italico fra IV e III sec. a. C.* Venosa: Osanna.

Osanna, M. 2010a. Greci ed indigeni nei santuari della Magna Grecia: i casi di Timmari e Garaguso. In Tréziny, H. (ed.). *Grecs et indigènes de la Catalogne à la Mer Noire: actes des rencontres du programme européen Ramses², 2006–2008,* 605–611. Paris: Errance.

Osanna, M. 2010b. Paesaggi agrari e organizzazione del territorio in Lucania tra IV e III sec. a.C. *Bollettino di Archeologia Online, Volume Speciale* (online) www.bollettinodiarcheologiaonline.beniculturali.it/documenti/generale/4_Osanna_paper.pdf

Osanna, M. 2012a. Prima di Eraclea: l'insediamento di età arcaica tra il Sinni e l'Agri. In Osanna, M., Zuchtriegel, G. (eds.). *AMΦI ΣIPIOΣ POAΣ. Nuove ricerche su Eraclea e la Siritide,* 17–43. Venosa: Osanna.

Osanna, M. 2012b. L'entroterra lucano tra Bradano e Sinni nel III sec. a.C. In *Atti del 52° Convegno di Studi sulla Magna Grecia,* 431–467. Taranto: Istituto per la Storia e l'Archeologia della Magna Grecia.

Osanna, M. 2013. Un palazzo come un tempio: l'anaktoron di Torre di Satriano. In Osanna, M., Vullo, M. (eds.). *Segni del potere. Oggeti di lusso dal Mediterraneo nell'Appennino lucano di età arcaica* (Catalog of the Exhibition, Potenza), 45–68. Venosa: Osanna.

Osanna, M., Capozzoli, V. (eds.) 2012. *Lo spazio del potere, vol. II: nuove ricerche nell'area dell'anaktoron di Torre di Satriano (Atti del terzo e quarto convegno di studi su Torre di Satriano, Tito, 16–17 ottobre 2009, 29–30 settembre 2010).* Venosa: Osanna.

Osanna, M., Prandi, L., Siciliano, A. 2008. *Eraclea* (Culti greci in Occidente 2). Taranto: Istituto per la Storia e l'Archeologia della Magna Grecia.

Osanna, M., Roubis, D., Sogliani, F. 2007. Ricerche archeologiche ad Altojanni (Grottole – Mt) e nel suo territorio. Rapporto preliminare (2005–2007). *SIRIS* 8: 137–156.

Osanna, M. Sica, M.M. (eds.) 2005. *Torre di Satriano, vol. 1. Il santuario lucano.* Venosa: Osanna.

Osanna, M., Verger, S., Pace, R., Zuchtriegel, G., Silvestrelli, F. 2015. Première campagne des fouilles franco-italienne à Policoro (Basilicate). Compte rendu preliminaire. *SIRIS* 15: 153–162.

Osanna, M., Vullo, M. (eds.) 2013. *Segni del potere. Oggeti di lusso dal Mediterraneo nell'Appennino lucano di età arcaica* (Catalog of the Exhibition, Potenza). Venosa: Osanna.

Osanna, M., Zuchtriegel, G. (eds.) 2012. *AMΦI ΣIPIOΣ POAΣ. Nuove ricerche su Eraclea e la Siritide.* Venosa: Osanna.

Osborne, R. 1985. Buildings and Residence on the Land in Classical and Hellenistic Greece: the contribution of epigraphy. *Annual of the British School at Athens* 80: 119–128.

Osborne, R. 1987. *Classical Landscape with Figures. The Ancient Greek City and its Countryside.* London: G. Philip.

Osborne, R. 1998. Early Greek colonization? The nature of Greek settlement in the West. In Fisher, N., van Wees, H. (eds.). *Archaic Greece: New Approaches and New Perspectives,* 251–269. London: Duckworth with The Classical Press of Wales.

Osborne, R. 2000. An Other View. An Essay in Political History. In Cohen, B. (ed.). *Not the Classical Ideal. Athens and the Construction of the Other in Greek Art,* 1–42. Leiden/Boston: Brill.

Osborne, R. 2009. *Greece in the Making 1200–479 BC, 2nd edition.* London/New York: Routledge.

Otto, B. 2008. Il santuario di Demetra a Policoro. In Osanna, M., Prandi, L., Siciliano, A. *Eraclea* (Culti greci in Occidente 2), 69–94. Taranto: Istituto per la Storia e l'Archeologia della Magna Grecia.

Owens, E. 2011. Documentary Sources for Latrines, Waste and Waste Removal in the

Greek World. In Jansen, G.C.M., Koloski-Ostrow, A.O., Moormann, E. (eds.). *Roman Toilets. Their Archaeology and Cultural History*, 25–29. Leuven: BABesch.

Pace, B. 1927. *Camarina. Topografia, storia, archeologia*, Catania: Guaitolini.

Paliou, E., Lieberwirth, U., Polla, S. (eds.) 2014. *Spatial Analysis and Social Spaces: Interdisciplinary Approaches to the Interpretation of Prehistoric and Historic Built Environments*. Berlin: W. de Gruyter.

Pappa, E. 2013. Postcolonial Baggage at the End of the Road: How to Put the Genie Back into its Bottle and Where to Go from There. In van Pelt, P. (ed.), *Archaeology and Cultural Mixture. Archaeological Review from Cambridge* 28.1: 19–42.

Parente, A.R. 2009. Per un'economia del territorio in Lucania di IV e III sec. a.C.: la documentazione numismatica. In Osanna, M. (ed.). *Verso la città. Forme insediative in Lucania e nel mondo italico fra IV e III sec. a.C.*, 45–67. Venosa: Osanna.

Pazdera, M. 2006. *Getreide für Griechenland. Untersuchungen zu den Ursachen der Versorgungskrisen im Zeitalter Alexanders des Großen und der Diadochen*. Münster: LIT.

Peacock, M. 2013. *Introducing Money*. London/New York: Routledge.

Pébarthe, C. 2012. La chose et le mot. De la possibilité du marché en Grèce ancienne. In Konuk, K. (ed.). *Stephanèphoros de l'économie antique à l'Asie Mineure: hommages à Raymond Descat*, 125–138. Bordeaux: Ausonius.

Pelagatti, P. 1976/7. L'attività della Soprintendenza alle antichità della Sicilia orientale. *Kokalos* 22: 519–550.

Pelgrom, J. 2012. *Colonial Landscapes. Demography, Settlement Organization and Impact of Colonies Founded by Rome (4th-2nd centuries BC)*. PhD Thesis Leiden.

Peristeri, K., Zographou, E., Darakis, K. 2006. Αμφίπολη 2006: πρώτες ενδείξεις μιας συνοικίας ελληνιστικών χρόνων. *Archaiologikó Érgo sti Makedonía kai Thráki* 20: 165–174.

Perlman, P. 2010. The People of the Citadel Necropolis. In Posamentir, R. *The Polychrome Grave Stelai from the Early Hellenistic Necropolis* (Chersonesan Studies 1), 383–408. Austin/Texas: University of Texas Press.

Pharos, antički Stari Grad (Catalog of the Exhibition, Zagreb). Zagreb: National Museum, 1995.

Pianu, G. 1989. Riflessioni sulla c.d. Tomba del Pittore di Policoro. In *Studi su Siris-Eraclea* (Archaeologia Perusiana 8), 85–94. Rome: G. Bretschneider.

Pianu, G. 1990. *La necropoli meridionale di Heraclea, vol. 1. Le tombe di secolo IV e III a.C.* Rome: Quasar.

Pianu, G. 1997. Eraclea Lucana. *Ostraka* 6: 161–165.

Pianu, G. 2002. *L'agorà di Eraclea Lucana*. Rome: Carocci.

Piranomonte, M. (ed.) 2001. *Genti in arme: aristocrazie guerriere della Basilicata antica* (Catalog of the Exhibition, Rome). Rome: De Luca.

Pisani, M. 2008. *Camarina. Le terrecotte figurate e la ceramica da una fornace di V e IV secolo a.C.* Rome: 'L'Erma' di Bretschneider.

Plana, R. 1994. *La Chora d'Emporion: paysage et structures agraires dans le nord-est catalan à la période pre-rómaine*. Paris: Université de Besançon.

Poccetti, P. 1989. Le popolazioni anelleniche d'Italia tra Sicilia e Magna Grecia nel IV secolo a.C. Forme di contatto linguistico e di interazione culturale. *Annali dell'Istituto Universitario Orientale di Napoli. Dipartimento di studi del mondo classico e del Mediterraneo antico. Sezione filologico-letteraria* 11: 97–135.

Podlecki, A.J. 1998. *Pericles and His Circle*. London/New York: Routledge.

Pöhlmann, R. 1893. *Geschichte des antiken Kommunismus und Sozialismus*. Munich: C.H. Beck.

Polanyi, K. 1957. Aristotle Discovers the Economy. In Polanyi, K., Arensberg, C.M., Pearson, H.W. (eds.). *Trade and Market in Early Empires: Economies in History and Theory*, 64–96. New York: Free Press.

Poli, N. 2010a. *Collezione Tarentina del Civico Museo di Storia e Arte di Trieste. Coroplastica arcaica e classica*. Trieste: Edizioni Comune di Trieste.

Poli, N. 2010b. Terrecotte di cavalieri dal deposito del Pizzone (Taranto): iconografia e interpretazione del soggetto. *Archeologia Classica* 59: 41–73.

Pontrandolfo, A. 1982. *I Lucani: etnografia e archeologia di una regione antica*. Milan: Longanesi.

Posamentir, R. 2005. Spätklassische Grabstelen und die griechische Besiedlung von Chersonesos. In Fless, F., Treister, M. (eds.). *Bilder und Objekte als Träger kultureller Identität und interkultureller Kommunikation im Schwarzmeergebiet, Kolloquium in Zschortau/ Sachsen vom 13.2-15.2.2003*, 105–110. Rahden: M. Leidorf.

Posamentir, R. 2007. Colonisation and Acculturation in the Early Necropolis of Chersonesos. In Erkut, G., Mitchel, S. (eds.). *The Black Sea. Past, Present and Future*, 45–55. London: British Institute at Ankara.

Posamentir, R. 2011. *The Polychrome Grave Stelai from the Early Hellenistic Necropolis* (Chersonesan Studies 1). Austin/Texas: University of Texas Press.

Prag, J.R.W., Crawley Quinn, J. (eds.) 2013. *The Hellenistic West. Rethinking the Ancient Mediterranean*. Cambridge/New York: Cambridge University Press.

Prandi, L. 2008. Eracela: il quadro storico. In Osanna, M., Prandi, L., Siciliano, A. *Eraclea* (Culti greci in Occidente 2), 9–17. Taranto: Istituto per la Storia e l'Archeologia della Magna Grecia.

Prieto, A. 2005. *Landscape Organization in Magna Graecia*. Dissertation Presented to the Faculty of the Graduate School of the University of Texas at Austin.

Prieto, A., Polleichtner, W. 2007. Erodoto e Siris. In *Atti del 47° Convegno di Studi sulla Magna Grecia*, 181–195. Taranto: Istituto per la Storia e l'Archeologia della Magna Grecia.

Pritchard, D.M. 2013. *Sport, Democracy and War in Classical Athens*. Cambridge/ New York: Cambrdige University Press.

Pritchett, W.K. 1980. Amphipolis Restudied. In *Studies in Ancient Greek Topography, vol. 3*, 298-246. Berkley: University of California Press.

Puig Griessenberger, A.M. 2010. Rhodé (c. 375-195 av. J.-C.). In Tréziny, H. (ed.). *Grecs et indigènes de la Catalogne à la Mer Noire: actes des rencontres du programme européen Ramses², 2006–2008*, 79–88. Paris: Errance.

Puig Griessenberger, A.M. 2015. Caractérisation des ateliers céramiques de Rhodè (Roses, Catalogne). In Roure, R. (ed.). *Contacts et acculturations en Méditerranée occidentale: hommages à Michel Bats: actes du colloque de Hyères, 15–18 septembre 2011*, 395–414. Aix-en-Provence: Maison Méditeranéenne des Sciences de l'Homme.

Quilici, L. 1967. *Siris-Heraclea* (Forma Italiae, vol. 3.1). Rome: De Luca.

Quilici, L. 1997. Valsinni. La guardia del passo tra alto e basso corso del fiume. *Atlante Tematico di Topografia Antica* 6: 241–260.

Quilici, L., Pala, C., De Rossi, G.M. 1968/9. Carta archeologica della piana di Sibari. *Atti e memorie della Società Magna Grecia* 9/10: 91–155.

Quilici, L., Quilici Gigli, S. (eds.) 2001. *Carta archeologica della Valle del Sinni, Fascicolo 3: Dalle colline di Noepoli ai Monti di Colobraro* (Atlante Tematico di Topografia Antica 10, suppl.). Rome: 'L'Erma' di Bretschneider.

Quilici, L., Quilici Gigli, S. (eds.) 2002. *Carta archeologica della Valle del Sinni, Fascicolo 2: Da Valsinni a San Giorgio Lucano e Cresosimo* (Atlante Tematico di Topografia Antica 10, suppl.). Rome: 'L'Erma' di Bretschneider.

Quilici, L., Quilici Gigli, S. (eds.) 2003. *Carta archeologica della Valle del Sinni, Fasciolo 1* (Atlante Tematico di Topografia Antica 10, suppl.). Rome: 'L'Erma' di Bretschneider.

Räuchle, V. 2014. Das ewige Mädchen. Zum Bild der Sklavin im Athen klassischer Zeit. In Kieburg, A., Moraw, S. (eds.). *Mädchen im Altertum / Girls in Antiquity, 7th – 10th October 2010. Berlin*, 221–235. Münster: Waxmann.

Rausch, M. 2000. Das Hypogäum auf der Agora von Poseidonia: ein Kultort der Tritopatores? *Kernos* 13: 107–116.

Raviola, F. 2007. Temistocle, la Siritide e l'Italia. In *Atti del 47° Convegno di Studi sulla Magna Grecia*, 165–180. Taranto: Istituto per la Storia e l'Archeologia della Magna Grecia.

Reber, K. 1998. *Eretria, vol. 10. Die klassischen und hellenistischen Wohnhäuser im Westquartier*. Lausanne: Payot.

von Reden, S. 1995. *Exchange in Ancient Greece*. London: Duckworth.

Rescigno, C. 2012a. Frammenti archetottinici in pietra dall'insula I di Eraclea. In Osanna, M., Zuchtriegel, G. (eds.). *ΑΜΦΙ ΣΙΡΙΟΣ ΡΟΑΣ. Nuove ricerche su Eraclea e la Siritide*, 221–240. Venosa: Osanna.

Rescigno, C. 2012b. Note sul sacello acheo metapontino dal pianoro dell'Incoronata. *SIRIS* 12: 9–22.

Robinson, D.M. 1942. *Excavations at Olynthus, vol. 11. Necrolynthia: a study in Greek burial customs and anthropology.* Baltimore: Johns Hopkins University Press.

Robinson, D.M. 1946. *Excavations at Olynthus, vol. 12. Domestic and Public Architecture.* Baltimore: Johns Hopkins University Press.

Robinson, D.M. 1950. *Excavations at Olynthus, vol. 13. Vases found in 1934 and 1938.* Baltimore: Johns Hopkins University Press.

Robinson, D.M., Graham, J.W. 1938. *Excavations at Olynthus, vol. 8. The Hellenic House.* Baltimore: Johns Hopkins University Press.

Robinson, E. 1997. *The First Democracies. Early Popular Government Outside Athens.* Stuttgart: F. Steiner.

Romito, M. 1995. *I cinturoni sannitici.* Naples: Electa.

Rösener, W. 1985. *Bauern im Mittelalter.* Munich: C.H. Beck.

Roubis, D. 2012. Ricognizioni infrasito a Santa Maria d'Anglona (Tursi – Mt): primi dati. In Osanna, M., Zuchtriegel, G. (eds.). *ΑΜΦΙ ΣΙΡΙΟΣ ΡΟΑΣ. Nuove ricerche su Eraclea e la Siritide,* 291–304. Venosa: Osanna.

Roubis, D. 2015. Archeologia dei paesaggi a Pandosia: una prospettiva dalla chora di Herakleia verso l'eschatià. *SIRIS* 15: 163–176.

Roubis, D., Sogliani, F., Masini, N., Vitale, V., Leucci, G., Rizzo, E. 2015. Archeologia dei paesaggi montani in Basilicata: una ricerca integata nel territorio di Calvello, PZ (Basilicata). *Capitale Culturale* 12: 385–419.

Roure, R. (ed.) 2015. *Contacts et acculturations en Méditerranée occidentale: hommages à Michel Bats. Actes du colloque de Hyères, 15–18 septembre 2011.* Aix-en-Provence: Maison Méditeranéenne des Sciences de l'Homme.

Rüdiger, U. 1969. Santa Maria d'Anglona (Tursi, Mt). – Scavi nell'anno 1967. *Notizie degli Scavi* 1969: 171–197.

Rüdiger, U., Schläger, H. 1967. Santa Maria d'Anglona (Tursi, Mt). – Rapporto preliminare sulle due campagne di scavi negli anni 1965 e 1966. *Notizie degli Scavi* 1967: 331–353.

Ruffing, K. 1999. *Weinbau im römischen Ägypten.* St. Katharinen: Scripta Mercaturae.

Ruggiu, L. 1982. Aristotele e la genesi dello spazio economico. In Ruggiu, L. (ed.). *Genesi dello spazio economico,* 49–117. Naples: Guida Editori.

Ruhl, B. 2012. Gli Ateniesi sull'isola di Imbros. In Culasso Gastaldi, E., Marchiandi, D. (eds.). *Gli Ateniesi fuori dall'Attica: modi d'intervento e di controllo del territorio (Torino, 8–9 aprile 2010). Annuario della Scuola Archeologica di Atene e delle Missioni Italiane in Oriente* 88: 455–468

Rumscheid, F. 2014. Die hellenistischen Wohnhäuser von Priene. Befunde, Funde und Raumfunktionen. In Haug, A., Steuernagel, D. (eds.). *Hellenistische Häuser und ihre Funktionen. Internationale Tagung Kiel, 4. bis 6. April 2013,* 143–160. Bonn: Habelt.

Ruschenbusch, E. 1978. *Untersuchungen zu Staat und Politik in Griechenland vom 7.-4. Jahrhundert.* Bamberg: AKU.

Russo, A. (ed.) 2006. *Con il fuso e la conocchia. La fattoria lucana di Montemurro e l'edilizia domestica nel IV secolo a.C.* Lavello: Soprintendenza Archeologica della Basilicata.

Said, E.W. 1978. *Orientalism.* New York: Pantheon.

Salibra, R. 2014. L'incinerazione nella necropoli classica di Passo Marinaro a Camarina. Dagli scavi Orsi alle indagini di Paola Pelagatti negli anni '70 del '900. In Bonanno Aravantinos, M., Pisani, M. (eds.) 2014. *Camarina: ricerche in corso. Atti della giornata di studio, Roma 12 marzo 2013,* 151–184. Tivoli: Tored.

Sallares, R. 1991. *The Ecology of the Ancient Greek World.* London: Duckworth.

Salviat, F., Vatin, C. 1974. Le cadastre de Larissa. *Bulletin de Correspondance Hellénique* 98: 247–262.

Samaras, Th. 2010. Family and the Question of Women in the Laws. In Bobonich, C. (ed.). *Plato's Laws. A Critical Guide,* 172–196. Cambridge/ New York: Cambridge University Press.

Sanader, M. 2009. *Dalmatia. Eine römische Provinz an der Adria.* Mainz: Zabern.

Sanmartì, E. 1993. Els íbers a Emporion (segles VI-III a.C.). *Laietania* 8: 87–101.

Saprykin, S.J. 1994. *Ancient Farms and Land-Plots in the Khora of Khersonesos Taurike (Research in the Herakleian Peninsula 1974–1990).* Amsterdam: Gieben.

Sartori, F. 1967. Eraclea di Lucania: profilo storico. In Neutsch, B. (ed.). *Herakleiastudien* (Archäologische Forschungen in Lukanien 2), 16–95. Heidelberg: F.H. Kerle.

Sartori, F. 1992. Ancora sulle dediche a Demetra in Eraclea Lucana. In *Mélanges Pierre Lévêque, vol. 6. Réligion,* 269–277. Paris: Les Belles Lettres.

Ščeglov, A.N. 1986. Process i character territorial'noj ekspansii Chersonesa v IV v. do n.ė. In *Antičnaja graždanskaja obščina. Problemy social'no-političeskogo razvitija i ideologii,* 152–176. Leningrad: Academy of Sciences.

Schaefer, H. 1961. Polis myriandros. *Historia* 10: 292–317.

Schmiedt, G., Chevallier, R. 1959. *Caulonia e Metaponto: applicazioni della fotografia aerea in ricerche di topografia antica nella Magna Grecia.* Florence: I.G.M.

Schmitz, W. 2004. *Nachbarschaft und Dorfgemeinschaft im archaischen und klassischen Griechenland.* Berlin: Akademie-Verlag.

Schmitz-Berning, C. 1998. *Vokabular des Nationalsozialismus.* Berlin/New York: W. de Gruyter.

Schneiderwirth, H. 1897. *Zur Geschichte von Cherson (Sevastopol) in Taurien (Krim). – Theorkrit von Chios.* Berlin: Calvary.

Schofield, M. 2006. *Plato: Political Philosophy.* Oxford: Oxford University Press.

Schuller, W., Hoepfner, W., Schwandner, E.L. (eds.) 1989. *Demokratie und Architektur. Der hippodamische Städtebau und die Entstehung der Demokratie, Konstanzer Symposion vom 17. bis 19. Juli 1987.* Munich: Deutscher Kunstverlag.

Schütze, A. forthcoming. *Ägypten unter der Herrschaft der Achämeniden. Studien zur Verwaltung und Gesellschaft einer Provinz des Perserreiches.* Leipzig: PhD thesis.

Seifert, M. 2011. *Dazugehören: Kinder in Kulten und Festen von Oikos und Phratrie. Bildanalysen zu attischen Sozialisationsstufen des 6. bis 4. Jahrhunderts v. Chr.* Stuttgart: F. Steiner.

Settis, S., Parra, M.C. (eds.) 2005. *Magna Graecia. Archeologia di un sapere* (Catalog of the Exhibition, Catanzaro). Milan: Electa.

Shepherd, G. 1999. Fibulae and Females: Intermarriage in the Western Greek Colonies and the Evidence from the Cemeteries. In Tsetskhladze, G.R. (ed.). *Ancient Greeks West and East,* 267–300. Leiden: Brill.

Shepherd, G. 2007. Poor Little Rich Kids? Status and Selection in Archaic Western Greece. In Crawford, S., Shepherd, G. (eds.). *Children, Childhood and Society,* 93–106. Oxford: Archaeopress.

Shepherd, G. 2011. Hybridity and Hierarchy: Cultural Identity and Social Mobility in Archaic Sicily. In Gleba, M., Horsnaes, H.W. (eds.). *Communicating Identity in Italic Iron Age Communities,* 113–129. Oxford/Oakville, CT: Oxbow.

Shepherd, G. 2012. Women in Magna Graecia. In James, S.L., Dillon, S. (eds.). *A Companion to Women in the Ancient World,* 215–228. Oxford: Wiley-Blackwell.

Shepherd, G. 2013. Ancient Identities: Age, Gender, and Ethnicity in Ancient Greek Burials. In Tarlow, S., Nilsson Stutz, L. (eds.). *The Oxford Handbook of the Archaeology of Death and Burial,* 543–557. Oxford: Oxford University Press.

Shipley, G. 2005. Little Boxes on the Hillside: Greek Town Planning, Hippodamus, and Polis Ideology. In Hansen, M.H. (ed.). *The Imaginary Polis. Acts of the Copenhagen Polis Centre, vol. 7,* 335–403. Copenhagen: Kongelige Danske Videnskabernes Selskab.

Siciliano, A. 2008. La documentazione numismatica. In Osanna, M., Prandi, L., Siciliano, A. *Eraclea* (Culti greci in Occidente 2), 95–114. Taranto: Istituto per la Storia e l'Archeologia della Magna Grecia.

Silvestrelli, F. 2004. L'archeologia della produzione in Italia meridionale. Il caso di Metaponto. In Giannichedda, E. (ed.). *Metodi e pratica della cultura materiale. Produzione e consumo dei manufatti,* 107–116. Bordighera: Istituto Internazionale di Studi Liguri.

Silvestrelli, F. 2005. Le fasi iniziali della ceramica a figure rosse nel kerameikos di Metaponto. In Denoyelle, M., Lippolis, E., Mazzei, M. (eds.). *La céramique apulienne: bilan et perspectives, table ronde de Naples 2000,* 113–123. Naples: Centre Jean Bérard.

Silvestrelli, F. forthcoming. Potters at Metaponto. In *Zuschreibungen in der griechischen Vasenmalerei und die Organisation antiker Keramikproduktion. Kolloquium 29.–31. Oktober 2014, Bayerische Akademie der Wissenschaften.*

Siritide e Metapontino. Storie di due territori coloniali. Atti dell'incontro di studio di Policoro, 31 ottobre – 2 novembre 1991. Naples: *Centre Jean Bérard (1998).*

Slapšak, B. 1988. The 1982–1986 Ager Pharensis Survey. Potentials and limitations of 'wall survey' in Karstic environments. In Chapman, J.C., Bintliff, J., Gaffney, V., Slapšak, B. (eds.). *Recent Developments in Yugoslav Archaeology,* 145–149. Oxford: BAR.

Slapšak, B. (ed.) 2001. *On the Good Use of Geographic Information Systems in Archaeological Landscape Studies: Proceedings of the COST G2 WG2 Round Table, Ljubljana, 18 to 20 December 1998.* Luxembourg: European Commission Directorate-General for Research.

Sparkes, B.A. 1991. *Greek Pottery: An Introduction.* Manchester: Manchester University Press.

Spigo, U. 2005. Tindari: l'impianto urbano. In Minà, P. (ed.). *Urbanistica e architettura nella Sicilia greca,* 104–105. Palermo: Regione Sicilia.

Spivak, G.C. 1988. Can the Subaltern Speak? in Nelson, C., Grossberg, L. (eds.). *Marxism and the Interpretation of Culture,* 66–109. Chicago: University of Illinois Press.

Spivak, G.C. 1999. *A Critique of Postcolonial Reason.* Cambridge, MA/London: Harvard University Press.

Sporn, K. (ed.) 2013. *Griechische Grabbezirke klassischer Zeit: Normen und Regionalismen. Akten des Internationalen Kolloquiums am Deutschen Archäologischen Institut, Abteilung Athen, 20.-21. November 2009.* Munich: Hirmer.

Stančič, Z., Slapšak, B. 1988. A modular analysis of the field system of Pharos. In Chapman, J.C., Bintliff, J., Gaffney, V., Slapšak, B. (eds.). *Recent Developments in Yugoslav Archaeology,* 191–198. Oxford: BAR.

Steinhart, M. 2000. Athena Lemnia, Athen und Lemnos. *Archäologischer Anzeiger* 2000.3: 377–385.

Stockhammer, P.W. (ed.) 2012. *Conceptualizing Cultural Hybridization: A Transdisciplinary Approach. Papers of the Conference, Heidelberg, 21st – 22nd September 2009.* Berlin/Heidelberg: Springer.

Stockhammer, P.W. 2013. From Hybridity to Entanglement, from Essentialism to Practice. In van Pelt, P. (ed.). *Archaeology and Cultural Mixture. Archaeological Review from Cambridge* 28.1: 11–28.

Stolba, V. 2005a. *Hellenistic Chersonesos: Towards Establishing a Local Chronology.* In Stolba, V., Hannestad, L. (eds.). *Chronologies of the Black Sea Area in the Period c. 400–100 BC,* 153–177. Aarhus: Aarhus University Press.

Stolba, V. 2005b. The Oath of Chersonesos and the Chersonesean Economy in the Early Hellenistic Period. In Archibald, Z.H., Davies, J.K., Gabrielsen, V. (eds.). *Making, Moving and Managing. The New World of Ancient Economies, 323–31 BC,* 298–321. Oxford: Oxbow.

Stolba, V., Rugov, E.Y. 2012. *Panskoye 1, vol. 2: The Necropolis.* Aarhus: Aarhus University Press.

Sulosky Weaver, C.L. 2015. *The Bioarchaeology of Classical Kamarina. Life and Death in Greek Sicily.* Gainsville: University Press of Florida.

Szidat, J. 1980. Hippodamos von Milet. Seine Rolle in Theorie und Praxis der griechischen Stadtplanung. *Bonner Jahrbücher* 180: 31–44.

Tagliente, M. 1986a. Policoro: nuovi scavi nell'area di Siris. In De Siena, A., Tagliente, M. (eds.). *Siris-Polieion. Fonti letterarie e nuova documentazione archeologica (Incontro di Studi, Policoro 8–10 giugno 1984),* 129–133. Galatina: Congedo.

Tagliente, M. 1986b. Nuclei di abitato arcaico nel territorio di Policoro. In *I Greci sul Basento: mostra degli scavi archeologici all'Incoronata di Metaponto, 1971–1984* (Catalog of the Exhibition, Milano), 193–198. Como: New Press.

Taliano Grasso, A., D'Alessio, A. 2014. Il santuario in località 'Area delle Fate' a Rose. In Iannelli, S., Sabbione, C. (eds.). *Le spose e gli eroi. Offerte in bronzo e in ferro dai santuari e dalle necropoli della Calabria greca,* 95–99. Vibo Valentia: Adhoc.

Torelli, M. 1993. Da Leukania a Lucania. In Lachenal, L. (ed.) 1993. *Da Leukania a Lucania. La Lucania centro-orientale fra Pirro e i Giulio-Claudii* (Catalogue of the Exhibition, Venosa), p. XIII-XXVII. Rome: Istituto poligrafico e Zecca dello Stato.

Torelli, M. 2003. Un avo della domi nobilis Mineia M.F. in una nuova iscrizione lucana di Paestum. *Ostraka* 12: 103–106.

Trendall, A.D. 1989. *Red-Figure Vases of South Italy and Sicily*. London/New York: Thames & Hudson.

Trendall, A.D., Cambitoglou, A. 1978. *The Red-Figured Vases of Apulia, vol. 1. Early and Middle Apulian*. Oxford: Clarendon.

Trott, A.M. 2014. *Aristotle on the Nature of Community*. Cambridge/New York: Cambridge University Press.

Trümper, M. 2011. Space and Social Relationships in the Greek Oikos of the Classical and Hellenistic Periods. In Rawson, B. (ed.). *A Companion to Families in the Greek and Roman Worlds*, 32–52. Malden: Blackwell.

Tscherikower, V. 1927. *Die hellenistischen Städtegründungen von Alexander dem Großen bis auf die Römerzeit*. Leipzig: Dietrich'sche Verlagsbuchhandlung.

Tsetskhladze, G.R. (ed.) 1998. *The Greek Colonisation of the Black Sea Area. Historical Interpretation of Archaeology*. Stuttgart: F. Steiner.

Tsetskhladze, G.R. (ed.) 2008. *An Account of Greek Colonies and Other Settlements Overseas, vol. 2*. Leiden/Boston: Brill.

Uggeri, G. 1969. Kléroi arcaici e bonifica classica nella chora di Metaponto. *Parola del Passato* 124: 51–71.

Ugolini, D. 2012. D'Agde à Béziers: les Grecs en Languedoc occidental (de 600 à 300 av. J.-C.). In: Hermary, A., Tsetskhladze G.R. (eds.). *From the Pillars of Hercules to the Footsteps of the Argonauts*, 163–203. Leuven: Peeters.

Uguzzoni, A., Ghinatti, F. 1968. *Le tavole greche di Eraclea*. Rome: Erma.

Vasallo, S. 2005. *Himera città greca. Guida alla storia e ai monumenti*. Palermo: Regione Sicilia.

Veder greco. Le necropoli di Agrigento (Catalog of the Exhibition, Agrigento 1988), Rome: "L'Erma" di Bretschneider, 1988.

Verger, S. 2015. Kolophon e Polieion. À propos de quelques objets métalliques archaïques de Policoro. In Meo, F., Zuchtriegel, G. (eds.). *Siris Herakleia Polychoron: città e campagna tra antichità e medioevo. Atti del convegno Policoro, 12 luglio 2013 (SIRIS 14)*, 15–41. Bari: Edipuglia.

Verger, S., Pernet, L. 2013 (eds.). *Une Odyssée gauloise: parures de femmes à l'origine des premiers échanges entre la Grèce et la Gaule*. Arles: Édition Errance.

Vernant, J.-P. 1978. *Mythe et pensée chez les Grecs, vol. 1*. Paris: La Découverte.

Vickers, M.J. 2004. Was ist Material wert? Eine kleine Geschichte über den Stellenwert griechischer Keramik. *Antike Welt* 35.2: 63–69.

Visona, P. 1995. Colonization and Money Supply at Issa in the 4th Century B.C. *Chiron* 25: 55–62.

Visona, P. 2005. The Coinage of Corcyra Melaina. In *Zbornik radova 4. međunarodnog numizmatičkog kongresa u Hrvatskoj (INCC 2004)*, 243–252. Rijeka: Hrvatsko numizmatičko društvo.

Vlassopoulos, K. 2013. *Greeks and Barbarians*. Cambridge/New York: Cambridge University Press.

Vokotopoulou, J. 1991. Dodone et les villes de la Grande Grèce et de la Sicilie. In *Atti del 31° Convegno di Studi sulla Magna Grecia*, 63–90. Taranto: Istituto per la Storia e l'Archeologia della Magna Grecia.

Walter, G. 1931. *Histoire du communisme, vol. 1: les origines*. Paris: Payot.

Weber, M. 1909. Agrarverhältnisse im Altertum. In *Handwörterbuch der Staatswissenschaften, vol. 1.3. Gänzlich umgearbeitete Auflage*, 52–188. Jena: Fischer.

Weber, M. 1921. Die Stadt. Eine soziologische Untersuchung. *Archiv für Sozialwissenschaft und Sozialpolitik* 47: 621–772.

Williams, B. 1993. *Shame and Necessity*. Berkley: University of California Press.

Wilson, A.I. 2000. Drainage and Sanitation. In Wikander, O. (ed.). *Handbook of Ancient Water Technology*, 151–179. Leiden/Boston: Brill.

Witcher, R. 2006. Broken Pots and Meaningless Dots? Surveying the Rural Landscapes of Roman Italy. *Annual of the British School at Rome* 74: 39–72

Woodhead, G. 1970. The 'Adriatic Empire' of Dionysius I of Syracuse. *Klio* 52/53: 503–512.

Wörrle, M., Zanker, P. (eds.) 1995. *Stadtbild und Bürgerbild im Hellenismus*. Munich: C.H. Beck.

Yanuchevitch, Z.V., Nikolaenko, G., Kuzminova, N. 1985. La viticulture à Chersonèse de Taurique aux IVe-IIe siècles av. n.è. d'après les recherches archéologiques et paléoethnobotaniques. *Revue d'Archéologie* 1: 115–122.

Zahrnt, M. 1971. *Olynth und die Chalkidier. Untersuchungen zur Staatenbildung auf der Chalkidischen Halbinsel im 5. und 4. Jahrhundert v. Chr.* Munich: C.H. Beck.

Zaninović, M. 2004. Issa e Pharos. Paesaggio agrario e viticoltura. *Hesperìa* 18: 163–170.

Zedgenidze, A.A., Savelja, O.J. 1981. Nekropol' Chersonesa V–IV vv. do n.è. *Kratkie soobščenija* 168: 3–9.

Zuchtriegel, G. 2011a. Zur Bevölkerungszahl Selinunts im 5. Jh. v. Chr. *Historia* 60: 115–121.

Zuchtriegel, G. 2011b. Archaeological evidence of cesspits, sewers and latrines from the sixth to the fourth century B.C. In Jansen, G.C.M., Koloski-Ostrow, A.O., Moormann, E. (eds.). *Roman Toilets. Their Archaeology and Cultural History*, 29–33. Leuven: BABesch.

Zuchtriegel, G. 2012a. Potenzialità e sfruttamento agrario della chora di Eraclea. In Osanna, M., Zuchtriegel, G. (eds.). *ΑΜΦΙ ΣΙΡΙΟΣ ΡΟΑΣ. Nuove ricerche su Eraclea e la Siritide*, 273–289. Venosa: Osanna.

Zuchtriegel, G. 2012b. Nella chora. Un nuovo progetto di archeologia del paesaggio nel territorio di Eraclea. *SIRIS* 12: 141–156.

Zuchtriegel, G. 2015. Alle origini dell'ellenismo in Magna Grecia: agricoltura, investimento e stratificazione sociale secondo le 'Tavole di Eraclea' e l'archeologia del paesaggio. In Meo, F., Zuchtriegel, G. (eds.). *Siris Herakleia Polychoron: città e campagna tra antichità e medioevo. Atti del convegno Policoro, 12 luglio 2013 (SIRIS 14)*, 153–171. Bari: Edipuglia.

Zuchtriegel, G. 2016. Colonisation and hybridity in Herakleia and its hinterland (southern Italy), 5th to 3rd centuries BC. *Mélanges de l'École française de Rome – Antiquité* 128.1. URL: http://mefra.revues.org/3326;DOI:10.4000/mefra.3326.

Zuchtriegel, G. forthcoming. Siritide e Metapontino in epoca tardo-arcaica: nuovi dati e analisi cost-distance. In *Atti del 56° Convegno di Studi sulla Magna Grecia*. Taranto: Istituto per la Storia e l'Archeologia della Magna Grecia.

INDEX

Achaeans, 24, 168
  as colonists, 22, 26
Achebe, Chinua
  on racism, 11
  on slave trade, 165
Ackerbürger, 117–124
  in ancient Greek history, 118–120
  in the colonies, 122, 128, 132–134, 141, 154–155,
    160–163, 176, 195, 204,
    210–215, 216–217, 232–234
  as conceptualized by Max Weber, 118
Adamesteanu, Dinu
  on Heraclea Lucaniae, 49, 206
Adramyttion, 27, 39
Adriatic, 13, 28–30, 32, 51, 162, 211
Agathe, 30–31, 40
agora. 113, 118, 133, 157, 206
  as burial place of the city founder, 23, 61,
    84–86, 88
  at Heraclea Lucaniae, 58, 86, 119, 206
Agri (river), 38, 108, 147, 151
Agrigento, *see* Akragas
Aigina, 23 n71, 39
Aitna, 15, 34
Akiris, *see* Agri
Akragas, 15, 34, 64
  necropolis, 92, 204
Albania, 32
Aleander the Molossian, 184, 192
Alexander the Great, 45, 57
  and Hellenistic culture, 157
Alexandropolis, 45
Alianello, 168
Amphipolis, 19, 36–37
  Demeter sanctuary, 17
  early structures, 60–61
  economy, 206, 214–215
  foundation, 22–23, 86, 117, 164–165, 203
  necropolis, 75, 93–94
Ampurias, *see* Emporion
Amykos Painter, 197–198
  product exported to Heraclea
    Lucaniae, 79, 82
Anaxilaos of Rhegium, 15

Anchialos, 40
Ancona, 28, 43
andrapodismos, 23, 40, 44
andron, 47, 50, 54 n14
Andros, 35
Anglona, 38, 183, 187
  Demeter sanctuary, 72–73
  modern land use, 123
animal husbandry, 138, 185–189, 195
Antibes, *see* Antipolis
Antipolis, 30–31, 45
Aphrodite hoplismene, 101
Apulian red-figure, 197–199
  in Heraclea Lucaniae, 81, 86
archaism
  associated with Greek colonization, 5
archive, archives
  in Greek gymnasia, 193
  as sources for local histories, 220
Arendt, Hannah, 4 n7, 46
  on Plato, 218
Argilos, 214
Aristotle
  on the best state, 9, 227–231
  colonial background of his
    works, 231–235
  on equality, 137
  on the history of Megara, 138
  on the history of Thurii, 22
  on Phaleas and Hippodamus, 219–224
  on social order and subalternity, 132, 155, 157,
    159, 194–195, 218, 229–230
Aristoxenus of Tarentum, 172
Aristphanes, 1, 218
  criticism of imperialism and colonization,
    9–10, 130
Armi Sant'Angelo, 181–183
Arpi, 172
Artas of Messapia, 26
Artemis, 37, 38, 212
  Bendis, 72–74, 139, 200, 217
  and pastoralism, 188–189
Asheri, David, 3 n 4
  on land distribution, 115

assembly, 139, 155
  of Athens, 16, 155, 203
  in newly founded cities and colonies, 4, 29,
    133, 156
Astakos, 37
Astraia, 44
Athena
  at Heraclea Lucaniae, 38, 83, 87–88, 170–171
  lands of Athena at Heraclea Lucaniae, 136, 147–
    154, 190–192. *See also* Heraclea Tablets
  Lemnia, 19
Athena Lemnia, 19. *See also* Athena
Athenian red-figure
  in colonial areas, 83, 92–95, 174, 204–206, 213
  iconography of children, 103
  as model for southern Italian red-figure,
    197–199
Athens, Athenians, Athenian, 1–2, 82–83, 85, 88, 206.
    See also Athenian red-figure
  burial customs, 17, 99–101, 205
  colonization, 16–24, 31–32, 35–45, 86–87, 89–91,
    116, 197–199, 203, 210
  imperialism, 10, 22–27, 116, 214
  social order and subalternity, 33, 69, 72–73, 75,
    151, 155, 222
  urbanism, 63–65
Atria, 28, 43
Attica, *see* Athens
Azov Sea, 32

banqueting vessels, pottery, 77, 142, 177, 190
barbarian, barbarians
  in Aristotle, 228–231, 233–234
  in literary sources, 29, 30, 31, 117, 194
  as opposed to Greeks, 95 n67, 193–195, 217,
    232–234
barley, 150–154, 191
Basento (river), 108, 130
Bendis, *see* Artemis
Berezan, 202
Bernbeck, Reinhard, 11
Bhabha, Homi, 2
  on hybridity, 217
Bianco, Salvatore, 57, 112
Bintliff, John
  on architecture, 68
  on rural settlement and walking distances, 122
Birds (play), 1, 9–10
bloc
  according to A. Gramsci, 8
Boiotians, 26
Bosco Andriace, 146–147, 187
Bottini, Angelo
  on burial customs, 89–90, 170
Brasidas of Sparta
  at Amphipolis, 23, 61, 94, 214–215
Brea, 4 n7, 16–18, 24, 33, 36, 62, 114, 203, 210
Brettioi, 22, 168–169

Bronte, Charlotte, 68
bucolic, 162
Bulgaria, 32, 44
burial customs
  in colonial settlements, 17, 27, 70, 75–104, 132,
    142, 160, 198, 217
  in inland communities, 168–172, 177, 190–191
Burkert, Walter
  on Lampon, 91
Buxentum, *see* Pyxous

Cabanes, Pierre
  on Lissos, 30
Canfora, Luciano
  on rural dwellers in Attica, 155
  on Phaleas, 222
Caria, 234
carrying capacity, 120–122
Carter, Joseph C.
  on Chersonesus, 27, 136
  on land division in Metapontum, 130–132
Carthaginians, Carthage, 15, 59
case coloniche, 157–159
Cavone (river), 108, 130, 134, 147
Cazanove, Olivier de
  on Civita di Tricarico, 174
Cersosimo, 173, 182
Chalcedon
  hometown of Phaleas, 9, 219, 220–221
Chalchidike, 22
Charondas of Locri, 63
Chersonesus, *see* Chersonesus (Thracian),
    Chersonesus Taurike
Chersonesus (Thracian), 16, 18, 36
Chersonesus Taurike, 40, 165
  economy, 160–161, 190–191, 201–202, 214
  expansion to the so-called distant chora, 28, 44,
    159–160
  foundation, 27, 57
  land division and rural settlement,
    124–126, 128–129, 136–139, 159
  Oath of Chersonesus, 27, 194
  urban center and necropolis, 27, 56, 61, 70–71,
    75–76, 83, 92, 95–96
Chiaromonte, 134, 168–169
Cimon (Athenian general), 23
citizenship
  in the colonies, 130, 139, 195, 213, 216–217
  in political philosophy, 216, 227–235
class system, 218, 223–232
Cleandridas (Spartan general), 169
Cleon (Athenian politician and general)
  trying to recapture Amphipolis, 23, 61
cleruchy, cleruchies, 13, 16–19, 35, 36, 39, 115–116,
    130, 211
Clouds (play), 130
Coarelli, Filippo
  on rural settlement at Heraclea, 112, 141

coinage
  of Aitna, 34
  of Chersonesus, 27
  of Heraclea Lucaniae, 59, 206–208
  of Histiaia, 19
  of Laos, 176
colonialism
  comparison between modern and ancient
    colonization, 5–7, 9–10
  impact on Classical scholarship 4, 69
Comaroff, Jean, 2
Comaroff, John, 2
Conca d'Oro (ancient site), 71–74, 102, 111
Condrad, Joseph, 1, 10, 11 n30, 69
cooking ware, 3, 142, 145–146
Corcyra
  ally of Athens in 434/33 BC 25
Corinth
  as colonizer, 13, 37, 115–116
  in the Peloponesian War, 25
  urbanism and craft production, 64, 225
Corinthian War, 26
cost-distance analysis, 120–122, 134–135, 155–156
cremation, 76–77, 79, 83, 89–90, 92–95, 101, 170
Crimea, 27, 70
criminals (as colonists), 32–33
Croton, 20, 24, 133
Crupi, Giuseppina
  on burial clusters at Heraclea Lucaniae,
    98–99, 102
Cugno dei Vagni, 134
Cuma, see Kyme
Cyrene
  foundation, 33
  foundation decree, 116
  heroon, 86

Darius (king), 221
Daskyleion, 27, 39
Dazos, 114, 164
Degrassi, Nevio
  on the Tomb of the Policoro Painter, 81–83
Delian League, 221
Delos, Delians
  as colonists in Asia Minor and the Black Sea
    Region, 27, 39, 40
  expelled by the Athenians, 27
Delphi, 28, 71
  role of oracle for colonization, 13, 91
Demeter
  at Amphipolis, 17, 37
  at Heraclea Lucaniae, 38, 57, 70–73, 96, 102, 111,
    198, 199
  at Kamarina, 212
  at Thurii, 91
democracy, democratic
  in ancient written sources, 15, 18, 22, 27, 62, 77,
    125, 130, 155

legacy and impact on modern democracies, 235
  material and technological basis, 204
  in scholarly debate on Classical Greece, 3–4, 8,
    15 n44, 23, 26, 55, 88, 92, 105, 112–113, 126, 132,
    141–142, 154
demography, 31, 57–58, 76–77, 103–104, 129,
  133, 217
Demosthenes, 63
deportation, 11, 13, 15, 19, 26–27
Dietler, Micheal, 7, 11
digital elevation model, 120
Diodorus
  on Adriatic colonies, 28–30, 117, 164
  on Amphipolis, 23
  on Heraclea Lucaniae, 24–25, 88
  on Kamarina, 124, 213–214
  on Poteidaia, 19
  on Sicily, 15
  on Thurii, 20–22, 25, 91, 114, 115, 117, 136
Dionysus
  at Athens and Brea, 16
  lands of Dionysus at Heraclea Lucania, 136, 147,
    150–153
  mystery cult, 90
  sanctuary in Heraclea, 38
Dionysius II of Syracuse, 192
Dionysius the Elder, 28–29, 41–42, 43,
  44, 60, 168
dipolis, 31
Doberos, 44
Dodona
  oracle consulted by settlers, 51, 103 n94, 104
Dorian, Dorians
  as colonists, 15, 22
  ideology and propaganda, 87–88
Dorieus of Sparta 33
Drabeskos, 23, 165
Drin (river), 30
Dystos, 65

egalitarian
  burial customs, 94
  ideologies and policies, 3, 92, 137, 220–221, 223
  settlement and land distribution, 113, 115–116,
    117, 131, 134, 136, 137, 139, 141–142, 145, 148,
    156, 159, 199, 213, 234
  Spartan model, 203–204
Egypt, Egyptians
  as inventors of geometry, 129–130
  social order, 224–226, 228
Eion, 23, 35, 164, 218
ekklesia, 29. See also assembly
ekklesiasterion
  at Metapontum, 133
Elea, 62
Emporion, 30–31, 43
  mixed settlement, 164
Enneahodoi, 23, 33, 165. See also Amphipolis

enslavement, 13, 23, 32, 40, 196. *See also*
    andrapodismos
Epetion, 30, 31
ephoros
    at Heraclea Lucaniae, 207–208
Epicurus, 230, 235
Epidamnos
    aported colonization, 13, 33, 37, 115, 116, 203
    craft production, 202
    public serfs, 222, 231 n38
equality, 46, 105, 113–116, 117, 124, 130,
        137–139, 203–204, 216, 220–222, 235. *See also*
    egalitarian
Eretria
    colonization, 18, 23, 35
    urbanism, 67
eschatià, 137, 187, 194–195
ethnicity, 95–97, 157, 160, 168, 171, 193, 233–234
ethno-archaeology, ethno-archaeological, 12,
        120–123, 153
Etruria, Etruscans, 3, 165
Euesperides
    urbanism, 65, 67
Euripides
    Heracleidae, 88
    Hippolytus, 73
    Medea, 104
    vase-painting, 83 n16, 87
Europeans
    as colonizers, 5–6, 10, 62, 165
    and globalization, 235
exploitation
    of individuals and groups, 6–9, 13, 32, 74,
        230, 235
    of resources, 23, 137, 153, 194, 202, 214
expropriation, 13, 39

fabrics, 186–187, 206, 211, 235
family groups (tombs), 97–104
field measurement, 127, 129–130, 136,
        147–151, 203–204, 223–224
Figueira, Thomas
    on colonies and cleruchies, 12, 18
    on "criminals" as colonists, 32
    on imperialism in the Classical period, 211
figurines (statuettes)
    production, 176, 200, 212
    use, 72–73, 109, 110, 207
fortification, fortications, 116–117
    made of wood, 60–61
fortress
    border fortresses, 28, 30–31, 182–183
    wooden fortress north of Olbia, 193
foundation decree, 69, 232
    Brea, 4 n7, 16–17, 62, 203
    Cyrene, 116
    Korkyra Melaina, 113–115, 164, 232
Foxhall, Lin
    on Greekness and rural populations, 195

on land property and tenure, 139
France, 3, 30–31
frontier, frontier societies, 74, 139, 194, 217
Furtwängler, Adolf
    on southern Italian red-figure pottery, 197

Garaguso, 169
Gavriljuk, Nadežda A.
    on slave trade, 166
Gela
    role in the resettlement of Kamarina, 15, 35, 92,
        213–214
    trade, 204
Gelon, 15, 213
geometry
    land measurement in colonies, 130, 234
    original meaning and function, 129–130
geonomoi, 16, 62, 114, 203
georgos, georgoi, 155, 157, 163, 231
Giardino, Liliana
    on Heraclea Lucaniae, 53, 57, 112, 148
GIS analysis, 120, 127, 130, 142–145
Given, Michael, 2
globalization, 175, 234–235
Goldberg, Marilyn Y.
    on domestic architecture and gender, 69
Gómez Bellard, Carlos
    on rural populations, 3
grain, grain supply, 31, 123, 153, 161, 181, 190–192,
        194, 206. *See also* barley
Gramsci, Antonio, 8, 157
granaries, 63, 181, 191
Greco, Emanuele
    on Poseidonia/Paestum, 84–85
    on usefulness of postcolonial models in
        archaeology, 5–6 n14
Greekness, 70, 193–196, 216–217, 234
Guy, Max
    on the Heraclea Tablets, 148
gyas, 149–151
gynaikonitis, 47, 68–69

Hackworth Peterson, Lauren
    on visibility of subaltern classes in
        archaeology, 11
Hagnon, son of Nikias
    founder of Amphipolis, 22–23, 117
Halieis, 65
Hall, Jonathan
    on Greekness, 193, 194–195
Hansen, Mogens Herman
    on demography, 128
    on Max Weber and the ancient
        city, 118
harbor, 17, 62, 185
    Adramyttion, 27
    Chersonesus Taurike, 165
    Heraclea, 119, 187, 192, 208
    Issa, 29

Lissos, 30
Mekyberna, harbor of Olynthos, 54
Pharos, 29
Heart of Darkness (novel) 1, 10–11
hegemonic culture
    as conceptualized by A. Gramsci, 8
    in colonial areas, 6, 17, 136, 165, 175
hegemonic discourse, 8, 9, 11, 217
linked to urbanity, 162, 196, 216
Hellenism, 175
Hellenization, Hellenized, 27, 96 n67, 96
Helots, 233
Hephaistia, 17–18
Heraclea Lucaniae/in Lucania, 4, 33, 38, 133, 166
    economy and craft production, 138,
        197–202, 205–210, 213–215
    foundation, 24–26, 167
    necropolis, 76–89, 92, 95–104, 139, 170
    rural settlement and land use, 105–113, 118–123,
        141–163, 177–196
    sanctuaries and rituals, 18, 70–74
    urban center, 47–59, 61, 67–68
Heraclea Lynkestis, 44
Heraclea Pontica, 27, 40, 41, 70
Heraclea Sintike, 44
Heraclea Tablets, 136, 147–154, 190–192
Heraclea Trachinia/Trachis, 39
    foundation, 24, 26, 117
    Herakles, 30, 84, 88, 200
Herodotus, 3, 218
    on Egypt, 129, 224–226
    on Gelonus north of Olbia, 204
    on Siris and Thurii, 19 n61
    on Tarentum, 165
heroization, heroizing burials, 85, 89–90, 92
Heron of Alexandria
    on geometry and land measurement, 129
heroon, 85–88, 94
Hieron of Syracuse, 15, 34, 35
Himera, 15, 34, 63
Hippodamus, 3, 9, 54, 218, 219–220, 223–224, 230
Hippolytus (play), 73
Histiaia, 18–19, 36
Hoepfner, Wolfram
    on Classical settlements and type houses, 3–4, 10,
        13, 46, 53, 57
    on type burials, 76
Homer
    on Trachis, 26
homoioi, 115, 204, 226
Horden, Peregrine
    on mountain regions, 166–167
Hornblower, Simon
    on the refoundation of Priene, 57
house plots, 61, 63, 75, 119
    at Heraclea Lucaniae, 47, 49, 51
    at Kamarina, 35, 59
    at Korkyra Melaina, 114, 117
    at Olynthus and Mekyberna, 54, 113

Hume, David, 113
Hvar, see Pharos
hybridity, hybridization, hybrid identities
    in ancient Greek colonies and their hinterland,
        70–73, 96, 175, 195–196, 216–217, 233–234
    in postcolonial studies, 217 n1 and n2
hygiene, 64–65

Ibiza, 3, 161
Illyria, Illyrians, 29, 44, 164, 166, 211–212
Imbros, 18
imperialism
    ancient, 13, 24, 26, 32, 130, 212
    modern, 6–7
    Incoronata, 202
India
    orientalism, 218 n3
    postcolonial criticism and subaltern
        studies, 8
inhumation, 76–77, 89–90, 92–104, 170
Ionian Coast, Ionian Sea, 4, 19 n61, 20, 28, 142, 169,
    174, 197
Ionians
    as colonists, 22, 24, 26, 28, 109
Ischia, 202
Issa, 41
    economy and craft production, 202, 211
    foundation, 28–30
    as mother-city, 31, 45, 114, 164
    urban and rural settlement, 56, 61,
        124, 162, 214
iugerum, 149

James Fort, 62
Jamestown, 62
Jane Eyre (novel), 68
Jason (mythological figure), 82, 104
Jason of Pherai, 26
Joshel, Sandra R.
    on visibility of subaltern classes in
        archaeology, 11

Kabyle, 32, 45
Kallatis, 41
Kalos Limen, 28, 44, 125, 194
    rural settlement, 160
Kamarina, 35
    economy and craft production, 212–215
    foundation, 15
    necropolis, 75, 83, 92–93, 95
    rural settlement and land division, 124, 129,
        136–139
    urban center, 56, 59, 61
Karyai
    sanctuary of Artemis, 189
Karystos, 18, 35
Kassope
    chamber tomb, 86
Katane, 15, 34

Kerameikos
  necropolis of Athens, 84, 85, 89, 101
  potterys' quarter at Metapontum, 199
Kerkinitis, 28, 125, 160, 194
kiln, kilns, 146, 175, 198–201, 212–213
King's Peace, 29
kitchen ware, *see* cooking ware
kleros, 18, 39, 115, 116
kopron, koprones, 65–66
Korčula, *see* Korkyra Melaina
Korkyra Melaina, 31, 45
  foundation and first settlers, 30, 136, 164,
    203, 232
  settlement and land distribution, 113–115, 117,
    137–138, 176
  Krenides, 43
Kyme, 133

Laconia, Laconians, 26
Lampon of Athens
  at Thurri, 91
land division, redistribution, 15, 39, 40, 42, 105,
    113–116, 124–136, 138–139, 159, 203–204,
    221–222
land property, land ownership
  in colonial areas, 18, 22, 24, 33, 63, 105, 113–119,
    121–122, 124–130, 133–134, 137, 139–140, 155,
    162, 177, 194, 203–204, 216, 221–224, 226–227,
    231–234
  in mainland Greece, 151
  modern, 8, 157
landlot 15, 18, 24, 35, 113–116, 117, 124–130, 134,
    136–138, 159–161, 203, 213, 227
landscape archaeology, 2, 3 n6, 12
Lanza, Mariafrancesca
  on tomb clusters at Heraclea, 97–101
leather, 206, 214
  boots, 72
Lecce, Lucia
  on burial customs, 170
Lemnos, 17–18
Leonidas of Tarentum
  on olive oil, 190
Lepsius, Richard
  on ancient field measurement, 149–151
Lesbos
  Athenian cleruchy, 18, 24, 39, 115–116, 203
Levi, Carlo
  on southern Italian peasantry, 122
Lissos, 28–30, 41, 56, 57
Livy
  on Alexander the Molossian at
    Heraclea, 184
Locorotondo, 159
loom weights, 146, 186–189, 200
Lucania, Lucanian, Lucanians
  ancient people/region, 22, 167–170, 172
  burial customs, 96, 170

economy and craft production, 175–176,
    185–192
  settlement, 172–184
Lucanian red-figure, 197–199
Lumbarda, Lumbarda decree, *see* foundation
    decrees, Korkyra Melaina

Malkin, Irad
  on sacred precincts of Brea, 17
manumissio, 71
Massalia
  as mother-city, 30–31, 40, 43, 45
  role of priestess Aristarche during the
    foundation, 69 n73, 92
Masseria Petrulla, 112, 198
Massilia, *see* Massalia
Matera
  peasants in the 1950s, 123
Mauss, Lloyd de
  on childhood, 103
Medea
  play, 104
  vase painting, 82
medimnos, medimnoi, 151
Mefitis, 173
Megara Hyblaia
  granaries, 63
  urban grid, 204
Mekyberna, 54–55
Melos, 18, 23, 40
Meo, Francesco
  on weaving and wool trade, 186
mercenary, mercenaries, 170
  in Macedonia, 44
  in Sicily, 15, 28
Mesambria, 221
Mesopotamia, 224
Messapia, 26, 71, 170
Messenia, Messenians
  as colonists, 28, 41
Messina, 15, 28, 41
Metapontum, 24, 168
  Classical farmsteads, 59, 108, 113
  Late Archaic settlement and land division,
    130–136
  pottery workshops, 79, 175, 198–199, 202, 205
Mikythos of Rhegium, 15, 34
Miltiades the Elder, 16
mint
  at Heraclea Lucaniae, 206–207
money, monetized, 203–204, 218, 227, 231,
    234–235
Monte Coppolo, 166, 195
  hilltop settlement, 177–178
  loom weights and pastoralism, 184–187
  rural sites, 179–184
Moreno, Alfonso
  on colonial economy and trade, 211

multiple burial, 81, 86–87, 93, 101
mystai, mysteria, 90–91, 95

Naples, 136
Native Americans, 10
Naxos (in Sicily), 15, 34, 44
Naxos (island), 35
network, networks, 211–212, 215, 232, 234
nouveau roman, 11
Nymph, Nymphs, 112

Oath of Chersonesus, *see* Chersonesus Taurike
oikopedon, 117. *See also* house plot
oil press, 142, 190
Olbia (Black Sea), 193, 202
Olbia (southern France), 31, 45
oliganthropia, 57, 77, 119. *See also* demography
oligarchy, oligarchic
    Classical settlements, 22, 29, 55 n18, 112,
        132, 138
    political discourse, 132, 155
olives, olive oil, 31, 123, 151, 153, 161, 190
Olynthus
    necropolis, 94–95
    urbanism and architecture, 54–55, 57, 66–67
omphalos
    in field measurement, 127
Opferrinne, 84
oppidum, oppida, 172–174, 176, 195
Oreos, *see* Histiaia
Orientalism, 1, 218 n3
Orphic gold tablets, 89–91, 95
Orraon, 66
Orsini, Michele
    on southern Italian land reform, 157–158
Osanna, Massimo
    on Demeter sanctuary in Heraclea
        Lucaniae, 72
    on Lucanian sanctuaries, 177

Paestum, *see* Poseidonia
Palagiano, 157–158
Panevino, 146, 154
Pangaion, 23, 214
Pantikapaion, 202
parcels, *see* landlots
Paros, Parians
    mother-city of Pharos, 28–29, 42, 211
Pasquino, Mariadomenica
    on burial clusters at Heraclea Lucaniae,
        98–99, 102
Pausanias of Sparta, 221
Peisistratus, 16
Peloponnesian War, 18, 24–25, 27
Penelope, 68
pentakosiomedimnoi, 131
peristyle
    in Hellenistic houses, 50, 55, 199, 208

Perlman, Paula
    on non-Greek names in Chersonesus
        Taurike, 70
Persians, Perisa, 27, 39
    class system, 221, 225
Peucetians, 170
Phaleas of Chalcedon, 9, 137, 219–223, 225, 231, 234
    Pharos, 42
    economy, 211
    foundation, 28–29, 164
    land division, 126–127, 136–137, 138, 162
    settlement, 56, 117, 124
Philip II of Macedonia, 23, 32, 43, 44, 45
Philippi, 43
Philippopolis, 45
Philippoupolis, 44
Phocaea, Phocaeans, 62, 69 n73
Phrynon, 16
Piano Sollazzo, 108–111, 120, 181, 183, 187, 196, 208
Pianu, Giampiero
    on burials and demography, 57
    on the Tomb of the Policoro Painter, 83
pinax, pinakes, 110–111
Piraeus
    planned by Hippodamus, 219–220, 223–224
    urbanism, 3
Pisani, Marcella
    on craft production in Kamarina, 212
Pisticci, 134, 168
Pisticci Painter, 197–198
pithos ware, pithoi, 142, 146, 154, 179
Plato, 3
    on city foundations, 9, 137–138
    on division of labor and citizenship, 205, 218, 225
    on geometry, 129 n63
    on rural settlement and peasants, 155
    on women, 139–140
plethron, plethra, 114, 137, 151
Policastro, *see* Pyxous
Policoro, 24, 122, 134, 158, 202. *See also* Heraclea
    Lucaniae
Polieion, 24. *See also* Siris
political philosophy, 4 n7, 9, 218–235
Polyaenus, 169
Pomarico Vecchio, 174, 190
Poseidonia
    "barbarized", 172
    underground chamber in the agora, 84–86
postcolonial, 2–3, 5 n14, 6–7
Poteidaia, 18, 19, 23, 39
Prandi, Luisa
    on female agency in Heraclea Lucaniae, 72
Priene
    drainage, 67
    refoundation and settlement, 56–57
Prieto, Alberto
    on division lines at Metapontum, 130
    on Heraclea Tablets, 147

public granary, 191
public slaves, 222
Punic colonization, 3
Purcell, Nicholas
    on mountain regions, 166–167
Pyllos, 114, 164, 232
Pyrrhus, 192
Pythagoras, 132 n75, 136. *See also* Pythagorean
    philosophy
Pythagorean philosophy, Pythagoreans, 91,
    129 n63
Pyxous, 15–16, 33

Quilici, Lorenzo
    on settlement at Mt. Coppolo, 166, 179, 181–183

Rausch, Mario
    on ancenster cult, 85
red-figure pottery, *see* Apulian, Athenian, and
    Lucanian red-figure
rent (leasehold), 116, 151–154, 190–191
Rhegium, 195
    mother-city of Pyxous, 15–16, 34
Rhode, 30–31, 43
Rhodos, 219
Roccagloriosa, 16, 92, 190
roof tiles
    from burial areas, 93, 94, 95, 142
    from habitation sites, 49, 108, 142, 175, 179, 183,
        184
Rotondella, 181

Said, Edward, 1, 2, 218 n3
Samnite, Samnites, 168
    Samnite belt, 170–172, 181 n59
Samos, 18, 44
Santa Maria d'Anglona, *see* Anglona
Saprykin, Sergey
    on land distribution in Chersonesus
        Taurike, 126
schoinos, schoinoi, 148–151
Schwandner, Ernst-Ludwig
    on Classical settlements and type houses, 3–4, 10,
        13, 46, 53, 57
Scythia, Scythians
    fighting Greek colonies, 28, 165
    mixed settlement, 193
    slave trade, 32
    social structure, 225
seafaring, 165, 205
Seifert, Martina
    on childhood, 103
Selinus
    demography, 119
    early structures, 63
    tomb of the city-founder, 86
    Tritopatores, 85

Serra di Vaglio, 172–173, 174
Sestos, 44
Sevastopol, 124–125. *See also* Chersonesus
    Taurike
sewers, 64, 67–68, 73, 146
sheep, 138, 185, 187, 193. *See also* animal
    husbandry
Shepherd, Gillian
    on hybrid identities, 70
Sicily, 15–16, 28–30, 33, 70
Sigeion, 16
silver deposits/mines, 23, 214
Sinni (river), 108, 119, 181, 183, 196. *See also* Siris
Sinope, 23, 37
Siris
    Archaic settlement, 19, 24, 109,
        133–136, 168
    Classical settlement, 24, 26, 37, 60, 170, 197
    river, 166, 181. *See also* Sinni
Skione, 40
Skyros, 18, 35
Slapšak, Božidar
    on land division at Pharos, 127
slave trade, 32, 165–166
slaves, slavery, 4, 9, 47, 68, 70–71, 92 n50,
    95–96, 128, 137, 139, 145, 214, 216, 222,
    227, 229–235
Socrates, 9
Solon, 219–220, 224
Spain, 30–31, 161
Sparta
    intervention in Amphipolis, 23, 214
    imperialism and colonization, 13, 20, 26, 28, 29,
        33, 39, 88, 117, 221
    social order, 115, 204, 219, 222, 226, 233
Spivak, Gayatri, 2
    on voicelessness of the subaltern, 8
Stančič, Zoran
    on land division at Pharos, 127
stasis
    in Thurii, 25, 91, 115
statuettes, *see* figurines
stelae
    at Amhipolis, 94
    at Chersonesus Taurike, 70, 201
    at Issa, 202
steppe, 166
Strabo
    on Hippodamus, 219
    on Kabyle, 32
    on Lucanians and Brettioi, 168, 172
    on Massalia and Massaliote colonization,
        30–31, 91
    on Oreos, 19
    on Pyxous, 16
    on Tarentum and Heraclea, 170
Strymon (river), 23, 61, 214

Stymphalos, 65
Subaltern Studies Group, 8
subsistence, 194, 230, 231
surplus, 187, 210, 223
Sybaris
    female personal name, 19 n61
    place, 20, 24, 85, 117, 133, 168
synoikismos, synokismoi, 13, 54, 61, 75, 94
Syracuse
    imperialism and colonization, 15, 28–30, 34, 35,
        41, 43, 211, 213–214
Szidat, Joachim
    on Hippodamus, 220

Tanais, 32
Taras, *see* Tarentum
Tarentum
    foundation, 33
    mother-city of Heraclea Lucaniae, 24–26, 38, 51,
        57, 77–78, 87–88, 92, 99, 110–111, 119, 170, 206,
        208–210
    mother-city of Siris (Classical settlement),
        24, 37, 88
    red-figure pottery production, 198–199, 205
    stasis, 133
    wool production, 185–186
Tauric, Taurics, 70, 96. *See also* Chersonesus
    Taurike
Tauromenion, 44
tax, taxes, 131, 211
tenant, tenants, 123, 148, 151, 153–154
tents
    as dwellings in colonies, 62, 64, 69, 73
textiles, 185–187, 211–212. *See also* loom weights
Thasos, Thasians
    as colonists, 23, 43
    urbanism, 65–67
Theophrastus
    on rural population, 139, 155
Theopompus (historian)
    on criminals as colonists, 32
Thera, 33
Theron of Akragas, 15, 34
thetes, 17, 24
Third World, 6, 235
Thrace, Thracians, 16, 23, 32, 61, 72,
    165, 214, 225
Thucydides
    on Amphipolis, 61, 214–215
    on Athenian interest in the West, 25
    on cult sites in colonial areas, 17
    on Epidamnos, 13, 115, 116
    on Heraclea Trachis, 26
    on Kamarina, 213
    on Lesbos, 116
    on Poteidaia, 19
    on Thurii, 91

Thurii, 36
    economy and craft production, 197–199, 205
    foundation and relation with Athens, 19–22, 117,
        169, 210, 219
    interevention in Siris, 24–25, 37, 83, 88
    land division, 114–115
    necropolis, 89–92, 94–95, 99
    settlement, 60, 123, 162
Timmari, 92, 123, 172, 177
Timpa del Ponto, 181
Timpa della Bufaliera, 181–182
tomb clusters, 97–102
Tomb of the Policoro Painter, Policoro tomb, 76,
    78–88, 92, 94, 171, 198–199
Torelli, Mario
    on the Tomb of the Policoro Painter, 84
Torone, 40
Torre di Satriano, 167–168, 173, 176
tower, towers, 8 n23, 127, 160, 178,
    181–183
Trachis, *see* Heraclea Trachinia
trade, 32, 113–114, 138, 148, 161, 165–166, 185–189,
    194–195, 202–204, 212–215, 216, 226, 232,
    234–235
Tragurion, 30
transatlantic slave trade, 165
Trasydaeus, tyrant of Himera, 15
Trendall, Arthur D.
    on the Policoro Painter, 198
Tricarico, 173–176
Tritopatores, 85
Trogir, *see* Tragurion
tumulus, tumuli
    at Athens, 100–101
    at Poseidonia, 84
    at Thurii, 89–91, 95
Tursi
    land use in the 1950s, 122
Tyndaris, 28, 41, 60
type burials, 75, 88, 92, 94
type houses, 3, 47, 54, 61, 75, 117
tyrant, tyranny
    in ancient Greek political theory, 132
    at Athens, 16, 91
    in Sicily, 15–16, 28–29

ustrinum, 93

Valsinni, 181
van Dommelen, Peter
    on rural populations, 3
vase-painting, 8, 103. *See also* Apulian, Athenian,
    and Lucanian red-figure
Velia, *see* Elea
Vernant, Jean-Pierre
    on politics in Classical Greece, 230
vineyards, 123, 125, 151–153, 161, 190–192

Virginia Company, 62
Vis, *see* Issa
voicelessness, 7–10, 162, 217, 232

walking distance, 120–122, 134, 156, 159
Walter, Gérard
    on equality and division of labor, 220, 222
Weber, Max
    on Ackerbürger town, 118, 232
Williams, Bernard
    on conditions of subaltern workers, 235
wine, 85, 125, 154, 161, 189–190, 192, 194, 211–212.
        See also vineyards

Witcher, Robert
    on landscape archaeology, 2, 105 n1
wool, 91, 138, 185–189, 194

Xenokritos of Athens, 22, 91
Xenopohon
    on city foundations, 9, 33, 62

yoke, 149, 151

zeugitai, 17, 24

For EU product safety concerns, contact us at Calle de José Abascal, 56–1°,
28003 Madrid, Spain or eugpsr@cambridge.org.

www.ingramcontent.com/pod-product-compliance
Ingram Content Group UK Ltd.
Pitfield, Milton Keynes, MK11 3LW, UK
UKHW030855150625
459647UK00021B/2805